The Real
Benjamin
Franklin

"I am...a mortal enemy to arbitrary government and unlimited power. I am naturally very jealous for the rights and liberties of my country, and...I now take up a resolution to do...all that lies in my way for the service of my countrymen."

B Franklin

Volume 2 of the
AMERICAN CLASSIC SERIES

The Real
Benjamin
Franklin

Part I
Benjamin Franklin: Printer, Philosopher, Patriot
(A History of His Life)
By Andrew M. Allison

Part II
Timeless Treasures from Benjamin Franklin
(Selections from His Writings)
Prepared by W. Cleon Skousen
and M. Richard Maxfield

National Center for Constitutional Studies

Library of Congress Cataloging-in-Publication Data

The Real Benjamin Franklin.
    (Vol. 2 of the American Classic Series)
    Includes bibliographical references.
    Contents: Part 1. Benjamin Franklin, printer, philosopher, patriot (highlights of his life)/ by Andrew M. Allison. Part 2. Timeless Treasures from Benjamin Franklin (selections from his writings) / prepared by W. Cleon Skousen and M. Richard Maxfield.
    Includes index.
    1. Franklin, Benjamin, 1706-1790. 2. Statesman—United States—Biography. I. Allison, Andrew M., 1949– . II. Skousen, W. Cleon (Willard Cleon), 1913–2006 . III. Maxfield, M. Richard, 1934–. IV. Franklin, Benjamin, 1706–1790. V. Allison, Andrew M., 1949–. VI. Franklin, Benjamin, 1706–1790. Selections. 1982. VII. Series: American Classic Series (National Center for Constitutional Studies (U.S.)); v.2.
E302.6F8R28
973.3'092'4
[B]

82-70110
CIP

ISBN 10: 0-88080-001-1
ISBN 13: 978-0-88080-001-3

National Center for
Constitutional Studies
www.nccs.net

Contents

PART II: TIMELESS TREASURES
FROM BENJAMIN FRANKLIN............................ 307

A compilation of the most important passages from Franklin's writings, arranged alphabetically by subject matter. See pages 309-10 for a brief introduction and a note on sources.

Illustrations

Preface

There are many Benjamin Franklins. Or at least he has taken on many different forms in the history books and conversations of the last two centuries.

Some historians have shown us an aged statesman whose wise and steadying influence kept the Constitutional Convention together in 1787, while others have pictured a chuckling prankster who couldn't resist a funny story. Some remember Franklin for flying a kite in a thunderstorm; others think of him as a successful printer of the colonial era; still others know him only as an expounder of clever maxims ("A penny saved is a penny earned") or the author of a now famous autobiography.

More recently, a certain brand of biographers and journalists have conjured up sensational tales of a lecherous old diplomat in his seventies who enjoyed illicit affairs with adoring young French women. And a few years ago Franklin even reappeared as a British spy! Some of these myths are now being repeated and embellished in school textbooks and "educational" television programs.

There are many other versions of Franklin as well—some slanderous, some complimentary. New portrayals continue to come forward, multiplying and changing with each generation.

Which of all these Benjamin Franklins, if any, is real? This book is an attempt to answer that question. Or, more accurately, it is an attempt to let Franklin himself provide the answer. *The Real Benjamin Franklin* makes no effort to develop another "fresh interpretation" of the Sage of

Philadelphia. Instead, it seats us across the table from the one person who really knew Ben Franklin—that is, Franklin himself—and gives him an opportunity to explain his life and ideas in his own words.

No man's life can be truly understood apart from his ideas, nor can his ideas be fully appreciated apart from the experiences which shaped his life. For this reason *The Real Benjamin Franklin* includes both: the biography in Part I and the selected quotations in Part II are designed to complement each other. In both sections, Franklin's words are carefully documented from original sources.

This volume is part of a series being published by the National Center for Constitutional Studies, a nonprofit educational foundation dedicated to restoring Constitutional principles in the tradition of America's Founding Fathers. The AMERICAN CLASSIC SERIES is designed to revive an intelligent appreciation of the Founders and the remarkable system of free government which they gave us. The nation these men built is now in the throes of a political, economic, social, and spiritual crisis that has driven many to an almost frantic search for "modern solutions." The truth is that the solutions have been available for a long time—in fact, for nearly two hundred years—in the writings of our Founding Fathers. An honest examination of twentieth-century American history reveals that virtually every serious problem which has developed in our society can be traced to an ill-conceived departure from the sound principles taught by these great men. The citizen of today who turns back to the Founders' writings is often surprised by their timeless relevance—and perhaps equally dismayed that we have permitted ourselves to stray so far from such obvious truths.

It is our earnest hope that the AMERICAN CLASSIC SERIES will help the American people recapture the Founding Fathers' sense of direction and manifest destiny. If this generation will relearn and reapply their original success formula for freedom and prosperity, the United States of America may once again become a "beacon on the hill" to light the way of liberty for all mankind.

Andrew M. Allison, Editor
AMERICAN CLASSIC SERIES

Benjamin Franklin: Biographical Highlights

1706, January 17   Born in Boston, Massachusetts.

1714   Placed in the Boston Grammar School (age 8); completed only two years of formal schooling.

1718   Bound as an apprentice to his half-brother James, a printer (age 12); during his apprenticeship, published several newspaper pieces under the pseudonym "Silence Dogood."

1723, September   Ran away to Philadelphia, where he began working in the print shop of Samuel Keimer (age 17).

1724, November 5   Sailed to England (age 18); worked in London in the printing trade until his return to Philadelphia in July 1726.

1728   Set up a printing partnership with Hugh Meredith (age 22).

1729, October 2   Began publishing the *Pennsylvania Gazette* (age 23); bought out his partner the following summer.

1730, September 1   Married Deborah Read (age 24).

1732, December 19   Published the first issue of *Poor Richard's Almanack* (age 26).

1736, October 15   Appointed clerk of the Pennsylvania Assembly (age 30); his four-year-old son "Franky" died of smallpox the next month.

1737   Appointed postmaster of Philadelphia (age 31).

1739-40   Invented the "Franklin Stove" (age 33 or 34).

1743   Founded the American Philosophical Society (age 37).

1747, November   Organized a militia to defend Pennsylvania against the French (age 41).

1748, January 1   Formed a partnership with David Hall and retired from active business to pursue scientific interests (age 41).

1751, August   Elected a member of the Pennsylvania Assembly (age 45).

1752, June   Conducted his famous kite experiment outside Philadelphia to prove that lightning and electricity were identical (age 46).

1753, August 10	Appointed, jointly with William Hunter of Virginia, Deputy Postmaster General of North America (age 47).
1754, June	His plan for a union of the American colonies was approved by the Albany Congress (age 48); however, it was later rejected by the British government and by the colonial assemblies.
1756, January	As military commander of militia forces along the Pennsylvania frontier, supervised construction of three stockades for defense against the Indians (age 50).
1757, June 20	Sailed for England as an agent of the Pennsylvania Assembly (age 51); spent the next five years in London working to settle disputes between the Assembly and the colony's proprietors.
1762, August 24	Began his return voyage to Philadelphia (age 56); the following month his 31-year-old son William was appointed royal Governor of New Jersey.
1764, November 9	Traveled again to England as an Assembly agent (age 58); while there, he was also appointed an agent for Georgia, New Jersey, and Massachusetts.
1766, February 13	Examined before the House of Commons regarding the effects of the Stamp Act in America (age 60); his knowledgeable replies helped lead to the repeal of the unpopular law several days later.
1774, December 19	His wife, who had not accompanied him to England because of her fear of ocean travel, died in Philadelphia (age 68); Franklin learned of this in February.
1775, March 22	Sailed back to America, having failed in his repeated attempts to negotiate a peaceful settlement between Great Britain and the colonies (age 69).
1775, May 6	Chosen a delegate to the Second Continental Congress (age 69); served on many important committees and used his influence to help bring about American independence.

1776, September 26	Appointed by Congress to negotiate a treaty of alliance with France (age 70); arrived in Paris on December 21.
1778, February 6	Concluded treaties of alliance and of amity and commerce with the French government (age 72); presented to Louis XVI in March.
1783, September 3	Signed the definitive treaty of peace between Great Britain and the United States, for which he had been the principal American negotiator (age 77).
1785, September 14	Arrived back in Philadelphia, having served in Paris almost nine years (age 79).
1785, October 18	Elected President (Governor) of Pennsylvania (age 79); served in this post for three years.
1787, March	Appointed a delegate to the Constitutional Convention (age 81); despite his old age and failing health, he attended sessions daily and participated actively during the four-month convention.
1790, February 3	As president of the Pennsylvania Abolition Society, signed a memorial to Congress calling for an end to slavery (age 84).
1790, April 17	Died peacefully at his home in Philadelphia (age 84).

PART I

Benjamin Franklin:
Printer, Philosopher, Patriot

Andrew M. Allison

Chapter 1

An Unusual Boy in Boston

I n the early 1700s, the township of Boston in Massachusetts Bay was one of the largest and busiest seaports in colonial America. Despite endless daily chores and a strict Puritan ethic, plenty of fun was still available to Boston youngsters in those days. And one of these in particular—an unusually curious boy named Benjamin Franklin—always managed to provide an extra measure of entertainment and diversion for himself and his friends. A childhood incident reflects the kind of inventive genius which destined him to rise far above his humble beginnings:

> I amused myself one day with flying a paper kite; and approaching the bank of a pond, which was near a mile broad, I tied the string to a stake, and the kite ascended to a very considerable height above the pond while I was

swimming. In a little time, being desirous of amusing myself with my kite and enjoying at the same time the pleasure of swimming, I returned; and, loosing from the stake the string with the little stick which was fastened to it, went again into the water, where I found that, lying on my back and holding the stick in my hands, I was drawn along the surface of the water in a very agreeable manner.

Having then engaged another boy to carry my clothes around the pond, to a place which I pointed out to him on the other side, I began to cross the pond with my kite, which carried me quite over without the least fatigue and with the greatest pleasure imaginable.[1]

Interestingly enough, another experiment with a kite, almost forty years later, would help establish his growing international reputation as one of the foremost scientists of the Western world.

A Man of Many Roles

"Most people smile when they talk about Franklin," wrote one of his biographers.[2] This is because the image of Franklin which has come down to us is one of a plump, pleasant, bespectacled grandfather who loved to tell humorous stories and play practical jokes. And so he was; but he was also a man of much deeper substance.

Franklin always looked on himself as a printer, as it was the trade for which he was trained, and he was very serious about his work. Besides running his own printing

1. Letter to Barbeu Dubourg (1773), Albert Henry Smyth, ed., *The Writings of Benjamin Franklin*, 10 vols. (New York: The Macmillan Company, 1905-7), 5:545.

2. Claude-Anne Lopez and Eugenia W. Herbert, *The Private Franklin: The Man and His Family* (New York: W.W. Norton & Company, Inc., 1975), p. 28.

office in Philadelphia, where he published a newspaper, a yearly almanac, and scores of books and pamphlets, he formed a large number of partnerships with others to help set up printing shops all over the country.

We have already alluded to Franklin's fame as a natural philosopher, or scientist. In addition to his discoveries in the field of electricity, he contributed many useful inventions and scientific hypotheses which led scholars of the eighteenth century to consider him "the Newton of their age."[3]

And no one in that illustrious era was more public-spirited than Benjamin Franklin. After initiating a wide range of community projects to make life better for his fellow Philadelphians (a hospital, a library, a university, police and fire protection, etc.), he was repeatedly elected to governmental posts at the local and national levels. He eventually spent twenty-five years of his life overseas representing his country, and for his skillful negotiations with England and France he has sometimes been called "the only great diplomat that America ever produced."[4]

Franklin was the only person who helped prepare and who signed all four of the critical documents which marked the birth of the American nation: the Declaration of Independence, the treaty of alliance with France, the peace agreement with England, and the Constitution of the United States. As the oldest of the Founding Fathers, and in many respects the most advanced advocate of the American Revolution, he was referred to as "the father of

3. I. Bernard Cohen, *Benjamin Franklin: His Contribution to the American Tradition* (Indianapolis: The Bobbs-Merrill Company, Inc., 1953), p. xi.

4. Frank Donovan, ed., *The Benjamin Franklin Papers* (New York: Dodd, Mead & Company, 1962), p. 235.

Franklin's birthplace in Boston.

his country" before that term was applied to George Washington.[5]

"Father ... Was a Very Wise Man"

Josiah Franklin, Benjamin's father, was born in 1658, having descended from a long line of blacksmiths at Ecton, England. At the age of twenty-five he emigrated to America, seeking religious freedom (he was a dissenter from the Church of England), and by 1685 he had settled in Boston. After the death of his first wife he married Abiah Folger, who bore the last ten of his seventeen children.

Benjamin, the fifteenth child and the tenth and last boy—he described himself as "the youngest son of the youngest son for five generations back"[6]—came into this large family on January 17, 1706. Although Boston was iced over by the wintry cold, the newborn infant was wrapped in a blanket and carried that very day to the Old South Church (just across Milk Street from the Franklin home) for his baptism. As he began to grow up, he certainly did not lack for companionship; later in life he

5. Cohen, p. xii.

6. Leonard W. Labaree et al., eds., *The Autobiography of Benjamin Franklin* (New Haven: Yale University Press, 1964), p. 46; quoted from a portion of Franklin's memoirs written in 1771. This work will hereafter be cited as *Autobiography,* with the date of writing shown in parentheses.

could remember thirteen children sitting at one time at his parents' dinner table.

Young Ben greatly admired his father, whom he called "a very wise man."[7] Thirty years after Josiah's death, his famous son wrote this description of him:

> He had an excellent constitution of body, was of middle stature, but well set and very strong. He was ingenious, could draw prettily, was skilled a little in music, and had a clear, pleasing voice, so that when he played psalm tunes on his violin and sang withal, as he sometimes did in an evening after the business of the day was over, it was extremely agreeable to hear.

> He had a mechanical genius, too, and on occasion was very handy in the use of other tradesmen's tools. But his excellence lay in a sound understanding and solid judgment in prudential matters, both in private and public affairs. In the latter, indeed, he was never employed, the numerous family he had to educate and the straitness of his circumstances keeping him close to his trade; but I remember well his being frequently visited by the leading people, who consulted him for his opinion in affairs of the town or of the church he belonged to, and showed a good deal of respect for his judgment and advice. He was also much consulted by private persons about their affairs when any difficulty occurred, and frequently chosen an arbitrator between contending parties.

> At his table he liked to have, as often as he could, some sensible friend or neighbor to converse with, and always took care to start some ingenious or useful topic for

---

7. To Jane Mecom (17 July 1771), in Carl Van Doren, ed., *Benjamin Franklin's Autobiographical Writings* (New York: The Viking Press, 1945), p. 4.

discourse which might tend to improve the minds of his
children. By this means he turned our attention to what
was good, just, and prudent in the conduct of life. [8]

Swimming, Boating, and Poetry

Like most Boston boys, Benjamin enjoyed the water.
"Living near the water," he wrote, "I was much in and
about it, learned early to swim well, and to manage boats;
and when in a boat or canoe with other boys, I was
commonly allowed to govern, especially in any case of
difficulty." He also added a little note suggesting two of his
character traits: "Upon other occasions I was generally a
leader among the boys, and sometimes led them into
scrapes." [9]

But he displayed a more pensive side as well, even in his
youth. At the age of seven, Ben Franklin began his long
writing career by producing poetry to amuse his widowed
uncle in London. He continued the practice for several
years until his father discouraged it, "telling me verse-
makers were generally beggars. So I escaped being a poet,
most probably a very bad one." [10]

"I Do Not Remember When I Could Not Read"

"From a child I was fond of reading," Franklin later
wrote, "and all the little money that came into my hands
was ever laid out in books." He loved books of all kinds,
and was constantly buying or borrowing a new volume to
satisfy his "thirst for knowledge." [11] He must have begun

---

8. *Autobiography* (1771), pp. 54-55. Spelling, capitalization, and punctuation
have been modernized here and in other quotations in this biography.

9. Ibid., pp. 53-54.

10. Ibid., p. 60.

11. Ibid., pp. 57-58.

these studies at a very early age, as he said he could not remember a time when he was unable to read. "Often I sat up in my room reading the greatest part of the night."[12]

Impressed by Ben's bookishness, Josiah placed him in the Boston Grammar School at the age of eight, "intending to devote me, as the tithe of his sons, to the service of the church."[13] But the expense proved too great, so after the first year Ben was placed under the tutelage of a Mr. George Brownell to study writing and arithmetic. Following this second year of formal instruction, he was withdrawn from school altogether in order to assist his father in the family business—making candles and soap.

Ben worked with his father for two years, but he "disliked the trade, and had a strong inclination for the sea." Josiah was not eager for his youngest boy to become a sailor, however, having already lost his eldest son to the sea. "He therefore sometimes took me to walk with him," wrote Benjamin, "and see joiners, bricklayers, turners, braziers, etc., at their work, that he might observe my inclination and endeavor to fix it on some trade or other on land."[14]

Josiah's decision proved to be a fateful one. It not only fixed the direction of Ben's life, but it led to a chain of events which ultimately affected the course of American history.

---

12. Ibid., p. 59.
13. Ibid., p. 52.
14. Ibid., pp. 53, 57.

Chapter 2

The Youngest Printer in America

At length Josiah Franklin determined to place his twelve-year-old son in the printing trade. Young Ben was to be apprenticed to an older half-brother, James Franklin.

In 1717 my brother James returned from England with a press and letters to set up his business in Boston. I liked it much better than that of my father, but still had a hankering for the sea. To prevent the apprehended effect of such an inclination, my father was impatient to have me bound to my brother. I stood out some time, but at last was persuaded, and signed the indentures when I was yet but twelve years old. I was to serve as an apprentice till I was twenty-one years of age, only I was to be allowed journeyman's wages during the last year.

In a little time I made great proficiency in the business,
and became a useful hand to my brother. [1]

The terms of his apprenticeship, if typical of the times,
make it clear why he considered himself "bound" to his
half-brother: he was probably forbidden to buy or sell
anything without the approval of his master, and he was
not allowed to drink, gamble, or get married. But there
were also a few fringe benefits. His frequent contacts with
booksellers and other tradesmen greatly increased his
access to books, and he pursued his wide-ranging studies
more ardently than ever before. He even fixed his own
meals so that he could read at the shop while his fellow
workers took time out for lunch at their boardinghouse.

"Prose Writing Has Been of Great Use to Me"

Young Franklin also spent time polishing his writing
skills while serving his apprenticeship. Through constant
practice and by imitating the style of the *Spectator*, a satirical
London paper he had come across during his early teens,
he developed a power of expression which later made him
one of the most influential men in America. In old age he
reflected, "Prose writing has been of great use to me in the
course of my life, and was a principal means of my
advancement." [2]

James Franklin unwittingly provided an outlet for his
younger brother's pen by establishing in 1721 the *New
England Courant*, the fourth newspaper to be published in
the American colonies. Benjamin described how he
became a contributor at the age of sixteen:

---

1. *Autobiography* (1771), pp. 58-59.
2. Ibid., p. 60.

He [James] had some ingenious men among his friends who amused themselves by writing little pieces for this paper, which gained it credit and made it more in demand, and these gentlemen often visited us. Hearing their conversations, and their accounts of the approbation their papers were received with, I was excited to try my hand among them. But being still a boy, and suspecting that my brother would object to printing anything of mine in his paper if he knew it to be mine, I contrived to disguise my hand, and, writing an anonymous paper, I put it in at night under the door of the printing house. [3]

Thus was created "Silence Dogood," a fictional widow who shared with the editor of the *Courant* her humorous and sometimes profound observations on the fashions and foibles of colonial life. Ben secretly wrote these letters every two weeks for a period of seven months. When James and his "writing friends" occasionally gathered in the shop to try to guess Mrs. Dogood's true identity, the teenaged author was delighted to find that "none were named but men of some character among us for learning and ingenuity." [4]

"A Mortal Enemy to Arbitrary Government"

Some of the Dogood letters advocated timely social improvements, such as greater educational opportunities for women and an "office of insurance for widows." More commonly they expressed good-natured criticisms of various human vices which young Franklin had noticed among the Boston townspeople. "I have . . . a natural

---

3. Ibid., p. 67.
4. Ibid., pp. 67-68.

inclination to observe and reprove the faults of others, at which I have an excellent faculty," wrote Mrs. Dogood. "I speak this by way of warning to all such whose offenses shall come under my cognizance, for I never intend to wrap my talent in a napkin."[5]

The lively widow lashed out against drunkenness, hypocrisy, pride, "hoop petticoats" ("these monstrous topsy-turvy *mortar pieces* . . . look more like engines of war for bombarding the town than ornaments of the fair sex"),[6] and the shallow curriculum at Harvard ("they [the students] return . . . as great blockheads as ever, only more proud and self-conceited").[7] But also among the Dogood letters were more serious passages revealing Benjamin's early political convictions. One of these dealt with freedom of speech and the true source of governmental power:

> Without freedom of thought there can be no such thing as wisdom, and no such thing as public liberty without freedom of speech, which is the right of every man as far as by it he does not hurt or control the right of another; and this is the only check it ought to suffer, and the only bounds it ought to know.
>
> This sacred privilege is so essential to free governments that the security of property and the freedom of speech always go together; and in those wretched countries where a man cannot call his tongue his own, he can scarce call anything else his own.

5. *New England Courant* (16 Apr. 1722), Smyth 2:7.
6. Ibid. (11 June 1722), Smyth 2:20.
7. Ibid. (14 May 1722), Smyth 2:13.

Whoever would overthrow the liberty of a nation must begin by subduing the freeness of speech....

The administration of government is nothing else but the attendance of the *trustees of the people* upon the interest and affairs of the people; and as it is the part and business of the people, for whose sake alone all public matters are, or ought to be, transacted, to see whether they be well or ill transacted, so it is the interest and ought to be the ambition of all honest magistrates to have their deeds openly examined and publicly scanned. Only the wicked governors of men dread what is said of them. [8]

Here, as a sixteen-year-old boy, Franklin articulated certain fundamental principles of free government more than half a century before they were secured to the American people in the Declaration of Independence and the Bill of Rights. Elsewhere in the same series of letters, he revealed a deep commitment to individual rights and foreshadowed the long public career which would eventually make him one of the leading participants in the struggle for American independence.

I am...a mortal enemy to arbitrary government and unlimited power. I am naturally very jealous for the rights and liberties of my country, and the least appearance of an encroachment on those invaluable privileges is apt to make my blood boil exceedingly....

I now take up a resolution to do for the future all that lies in my way for the service of my countrymen. [9]

---

8. Ibid. (9 July 1722), Smyth 2:25-27.
9. Ibid. (16 and 30 Apr. 1722), Smyth 2:7, 8.

The printing press on which Franklin worked as a teenager, while apprenticed to his half-brother James in Boston.

Benjamin Franklin, Printer

Young Ben continued to write under his pseudonym "till my small fund of sense for such performances was pretty well exhausted," and then he let his half-brother in on the secret. James was not well pleased with the admiration his friends thereafter expressed for Benjamin's talents, "as he thought, probably with reason, that it tended to make me too vain. And perhaps this might be one occasion of the differences that we began to have about this time."[10]

Meanwhile, the older Franklin brother began to attract attention of a different kind. The Boston magistrates, taking offense at a political article which appeared in the *New England Courant* during the summer of 1722, arrested James and placed him in prison for one month. The paper continued under Ben's management. Several months later, on the heels of another offensive article, the Governor's council strictly forbade the publisher "to print or publish the *New England Courant* or any other pamphlet or paper of the like nature, except it be first supervised by

---

10. *Autobiography* (1771), p. 68.

the Secretary of the Province."[11] The paper's masthead was immediately changed to declare that it was "printed and sold by Benjamin Franklin." To avoid government censure, James cancelled Ben's old indentures and replaced them with new ones which were signed in secret and kept private.

Benjamin's first editorial preface, printed in February 1723, notified subscribers that the content of the *Courant* would be altered somewhat:

> The present undertaking . . . is designed purely for the diversion and merriment of the reader. Pieces of pleasancy and mirth have a secret charm in them to allay the heats and tumors of our spirits, and to make a man forget his restless resentments. They have a strange power to tune the harsh disorders of the soul and reduce us to a serene and placid state of mind.
>
> The main design of this weekly paper will be to entertain the town with the most comical and diverting incidents of humane life. [12]

Although the paper did become more moderate after its scrapes with the colonial authorities, the apprentice-turned-printer still took occasion to give his "diversion and merriment" a political twist. In one such article, appearing only a week after the *Courant* was first printed under Benjamin's name, he ridiculed the European titles of nobility and the clerical hierarchies which were becoming ever more objectionable to many Americans.

---

11. Quoted in Smyth 2:49n.
12. *New England Courant* (11 Feb. 1723), Smyth 2:50.

In old times it was no disrespect for men and women
to be called by their own names. Adam was never called
Master Adam; we never read of Noah Esquire, Lot
Knight and Baronet, nor the Right Honorable Abraham,
Viscount Mesopotamia, Baron of Canaan. No, no, they
were plain men, honest country graziers that took care
of their families and their flocks.

Moses was a great prophet and Aaron a priest of the
Lord; but we never read of the Reverend Moses nor the
Right Reverend Father in God, Aaron, by Divine
Providence Lord Archbishop of Israel. Thou never
sawest Madam Rebecca in the Bible, my Lady Rachel,
nor Mary, though a princess of the blood, after the death
of Joseph called the Princess Dowager of Nazareth. No,
plain Rebecca, Rachel, Mary, or the Widow Mary, or the
like. It was no incivility then to mention their naked
names as they were expressed. [13]

At the age of seventeen, Ben Franklin was the youngest
full-fledged printer in the American colonies—and already
one of the most articulate. He was clearly coming to enjoy
the trade his father had chosen for him.

---

13. Ibid. (18 Feb. 1723), in Carl Van Doren, *Benjamin Franklin* (New York:
The Viking Press, 1938), pp. 31-32.

Chapter 3

Ben Begins His World Travels

The *New England Courant* prospered admirably under Ben's management as it saw increases in both circulation and price. But James Franklin's jealousy toward his younger half-brother also increased. "My brother was passionate, and had often beaten me, which I took extremely amiss," wrote Ben. "And thinking my apprenticeship very tedious, I was continually wishing for some opportunity of shortening it."[1]

A New Home in Philadelphia

The opportunity came when a "fresh difference" arose between the two Franklins. Realizing he could take

---

1. *Autobiography* (1771), pp. 68-69. Franklin added in a marginal note, "I fancy his harsh and tyrannical treatment of me might [have been] a means of impressing me with that aversion to arbitrary power that has stuck to me through my whole life."

Having just run away from Boston, Franklin arrived in Philadelphia at the age of seventeen, his pockets stuffed with personal belongings and a loaf of bread under each arm. As he walked down Market Street, a young lady watching from one of the doorways (Miss Deborah Read) thought he made "a most awkward, ridiculous appearance." She later became his wife.

advantage of James's need to keep the new indentures secret, seventeen-year-old Ben decided to run away from Boston and strike out on his own. After selling some of his books to raise a little money, he boarded a ship headed southward along the Atlantic seacoast. Finding no work at the only printing establishment in New York, he sailed on to Philadelphia, where he arrived in October 1723. He later reflected on his "unlikely beginnings" in this city which was to become his new home:

I was in my working dress, my best clothes being to come round by sea. I was dirty from my journey; my pockets were stuffed out with shirts and stockings, and I knew no soul nor where to look for lodging. I was fatigued with travelling, rowing [he had helped man a rowboat on the last leg of his journey], and want of rest. I was very hungry, and my whole stock of cash consisted of a Dutch dollar and about a shilling in copper. [2]

---

2. Ibid., p. 75.

After purchasing three "great puffy rolls" of bread, he "walked off with a roll under each arm, and eating the other. Thus I went up Market Street." One of the homes he passed was that of a Miss Deborah Read, who someday—unbeknown to either of them—was to become Mrs. Benjamin Franklin. As the soiled, runaway apprentice walked by, his pockets bulging and bread under his arms, Deborah was standing in the doorway. "When she...saw me, [she] thought I made, as I certainly did, a most awkward, ridiculous appearance."[3]

Ben soon secured employment with Samuel Keimer, a Philadelphia printer. Keimer arranged lodging for his new journeyman at the home of John Read, who was Deborah's father. This new life of independence seemed to suit young Franklin quite well.

My chest and clothes being come by this time, I made rather a more respectable appearance in the eyes of Miss Read than I had done when she first happened to see me eating my roll in the street.

I began now to have some acquaintance among the young people of the town that were lovers of reading, with whom I spent my evenings very pleasantly; and gaining money by my industry and frugality, I lived very agreeably, forgetting Boston as much as I could and not desiring that any there should know where I resided.[4]

A Short Visit to Boston

But the secret was not to last long. Only a few months after Ben's arrival in Philadelphia, he became acquainted

---

3. Ibid., p. 76.
4. Ibid., p. 79.

with a man who convinced him to pay a visit to his father in Boston—and then to travel across the Atlantic Ocean. Sir William Keith, proprietary Governor of the Pennsylvania province, learned of the journeyman printer through a mutual friend and decided that he was "a young man of promising parts, and therefore should be encouraged." One day he appeared at the door of Keimer's shop and asked to see Benjamin Franklin. "I was not a little surprised," Ben wrote, "and Keimer stared like a pig poisoned." The Governor escorted the teenager to a nearby tavern and proposed that he set up in business for himself; if so, he would be given all the government printing contracts in the colony.

When Ben expressed doubts regarding his father's willingness to provide the necessary financial help, Governor Keith provided "an ample letter, saying many flattering things of me to my father and strongly recommending the project of my setting up at Philadelphia as a thing that must make my fortune." When a small vessel sailed for Boston in April 1724, Ben boarded it and returned home to discuss the proposal with his father.

Except for James, who felt insulted when Ben visited the old shop "having a genteel new suit from head to foot, a watch, and my pockets lined with near five pounds sterling in silver," his family members were very happy to see him again. But Josiah Franklin refused to offer a loan, believing it was unwise for his youngest son to venture into business when he was still three years away from adulthood. He consented to Ben's going back to Pennsylvania, however, and suggested that "by steady industry and a prudent parsimony I might save enough by the time I was one and twenty to set me up."[5]

Off to England

So Ben returned again to Philadelphia, disappointed but undaunted. This time Governor Keith offered to put up the money himself. He would send Ben to England with appropriate letters of credit and introduction, thus enabling him to personally select the press and types he needed and to establish ties with English booksellers and stationers. "I believed him one of the best men in the world," wrote Franklin. [6]

Although he eagerly made preparations for his departure, Ben found that there was one person to whom he was reluctant to bid farewell:

I had made some courtship during this time to Miss Read. I had a great respect and affection for her, and had some reason to believe she had the same for me. But as I was about to take a long voyage, and we were both very young, only a little above eighteen, it was thought most prudent by her mother to prevent our going too far at present, as a marriage, if it were to take place, would be more convenient after my return, when I should be, as I expected, set up in my business. Perhaps, too, she thought my expectations not so well founded as I imagined them to be.[7]

In the late fall of 1724, his boat was ready to sail. "Having taken leave of my friends," he said, "and interchanged some promises with Miss Read, I left

5. Ibid., pp. 80-83.
6. Ibid., p. 87.
7. Ibid., p. 89.

Sir William Keith, the proprietary Governor of Pennsylvania who sent eighteen-year-old Franklin to England under false pretenses.

Philadelphia in the ship."[8] One of Ben's associates, James Ralph, was traveling with him. They arrived in London the day before Christmas.

The Governor's Duplicity

Deborah's mother was right: the expectations of her future son-in-law were not nearly so well founded as he imagined them to be. Ben had wondered why Governor Keith's letters were not ready when he called for them just before embarking for England; he was assured that they would reach him safely as soon as he crossed the Atlantic. But the letters were never sent, and he was left to fend for himself in an unfamiliar place. He had this to say about the man who had hurled him into such a predicament:

> Had it been known that I depended on the Governor, probably some friend that knew him better would have advised me not to rely on him, as I afterwards heard it as his known character to be liberal of promises which he never meant to keep....
>
> What shall we think of a Governor's playing such pitiful tricks, and imposing so grossly on a poor, ignorant boy! It was a habit he had acquired. He wished

---

8. Ibid., p. 92.

to please everybody; and, having little to give, he gave expectations. [9]

But this philosophical perspective was developed much later, when Franklin was an old man. At the time, he must have felt a little perplexed. Resourceful as ever, however, he made the best of a bad situation and found work in a prosperous London printing shop named Palmer's.

Impressive Feats by the "Water American"

During his stay in London, Ben strengthened his mind by regularly borrowing new reading material from a nearby bookseller who kept "an immense collection of second-hand books.... This I esteemed a great advantage, and I made as much use of it as I could." And, despite his youth, he managed to become acquainted with several British authors and scientists. One of these "promised to give me an opportunity some time or other of seeing Sir Isaac Newton, of which I was extremely desirous; but this never happened." [10]

He also made a point of strengthening his body. After working as a compositor at Palmer's for nearly a year, he found "better work ... at Watts' near Lincoln's Inn Fields, a still greater printing house."

At my first admission into this printing house, I took to working at press, imagining I felt a want of the bodily exercise I had been used to in America, where presswork is mixed with composing. I drank only water; the other workmen, near fifty in number, were great guzzlers of beer. On occasion I carried up and down stairs a large form of types in each hand, when others carried but one

9. Ibid., pp. 86-87, 95.
10. Ibid., p. 97.

in both hands. They wondered to see from this and several instances that the Water American, as they called me, was *stronger* than themselves who drank *strong* beer. [11]

He may have been called the "Water American" for another reason as well. Having been an excellent swimmer from his early youth, he taught a couple of well-bred young men he had met at the printing shop how to swim. Later, when the three of them were in the company of "some gentlemen from the country," young Franklin was asked to demonstrate his unusual talents in the water. "At the request of the company," he later wrote, "I stripped and leaped into the river, and swam from near Chelsea to Blackfryars [a distance of about three-and-a-half miles], performing on the way many feats of activity both upon and under water that surprised and pleased those to whom they were novelties." [12]

Errata Committed in London

Although Benjamin was "pretty diligent" in his work and apparently earned a comfortable income, he admitted that he and his friend James Ralph (who had journeyed with him from Philadelphia) "spent . . . a good deal of my earnings in going to plays and other places of amusement. We had together consumed all my pistoles, and now just rubbed on from hand to mouth. . . . In fact, by our

---

11. Ibid., pp. 99-100.

12. Ibid., pp. 103-4. Just before he left England in 1726, Franklin was offered an opportunity to open a swimming school and thereby make "a good deal of money. And it struck me so strongly that, had the overture been sooner made me, probably I should not so soon have returned to America." Ibid., pp. 105-6.

expenses, I was constantly kept unable to pay my passage [back to America]."[13]

While engaged in all these new and exciting activities, he also began to "forget ... by degrees my engagements with Miss Read, to whom I never wrote more than one letter, and that was to let her know I was not likely soon to return. This was [one] of the great *errata* [printers' language for mistakes] of my life, which I should wish to correct if I were to live it over again."[14]

"Another *erratum*," according to Franklin, was the printing of a pamphlet he wrote while employed at Palmer's. It was entitled *A Dissertation on Liberty and Necessity, Pleasure and Pain.*

> The purport of it was to prove the doctrine of fate, from the supposed attributes of God, in some such manner as this: that in erecting and governing the world, as he was infinitely wise, he knew what would be best; infinitely good, he must be disposed, and infinitely powerful, he must be able to execute it; consequently all is right [that is, all the evil in the world as well as the good].
>
> There were only a hundred copies printed, of which I gave a few to friends, and afterwards disliking the piece, as conceiving it might have an ill tendency, I burned the rest except one copy.... I was not nineteen years of age when it was written. In 1730, I wrote a piece on the other side of the question.[15]

---

13. Ibid., p. 96.
14. Ibid.
15. To Benjamin Vaughn (9 Nov. 1779), Smyth 7:412.

Back to Philadelphia

Sometime in the summer of 1726, Ben was approached by Mr. Thomas Denham, a Quaker merchant whom he had met on the voyage from Philadelphia and had occasionally visited since their arrival in England.

> He now told me he was about to return to Philadelphia, and should carry over a great quantity of goods in order to open a store there. He proposed to take me over as his clerk to keep his books (in which he would instruct me), copy his letters, and attend the store.... The thing pleased me, for I was grown tired of London, remembered with pleasure the happy months I had spent in Pennsylvania, and wished again to see it. Therefore I immediately agreed....
>
> I now took leave of printing, as I thought, forever, and was daily employed in my new business, going about with Mr. Denham among the tradesmen to purchase various articles. [16]

All was ready by July 23, and Franklin, now twenty years old, embarked for his home in America. Reflecting on the year and a half he had spent in London, he wrote, "I had by no means improved my fortune, but I had picked up some very ingenious acquaintance whose conversation was of great advantage to me, and I had read considerably." [17] Although he thought he had abandoned the printing trade by this time, he still enjoyed writing very much. His daily "Journal of Occurrences in My Voyage to Philadelphia" (kept over a period of almost three months) not only records his keen observations of fish, birds, winds, eclipses, and other physical phenomena,

---

16. *Autobiography* (1771), p. 105.
17. Ibid., p. 106.

but it also provides an interesting account of the attitudes and activities of the twenty-one persons on board his sailing ship, the *Berkshire*. Here is one example:

> Our company is in general very unsuitably mixed to keep up the pleasure and spirit of conversation; and if there are one or two pairs of us that can sometimes entertain one another for half an hour agreeably, yet perhaps we are seldom in the humor for it together.
>
> I rise in the morning and read for an hour or two, perhaps, and then reading grows tiresome. Want of exercise occasions want of appetite, so that eating and drinking afford but little pleasure. I tire myself with playing at drafts, then I go to cards; nay, there is no play so trifling or childish but we fly to it for entertainment. A contrary wind, I know not how, puts us all out of good humor; we grow sullen, silent, and reserved, and fret at each other upon every little occasion. [18]

When the crew sighted another ship at sea on September 23, Franklin recorded the excitement. "My heart fluttered in my breast with joy when I saw so many human countenances, and I could scarce refrain from . . . laughter. . . . When we have been for a considerable time tossing on the vast waters, far from the sight of any land or ships, or any mortal creature but ourselves (except a few fish and sea-birds), the whole world, for aught we know, may be under a second deluge, and we, like Noah and his company in the ark, the only surviving remnant of the human race." [19]

---

18. "Journal of Occurrences in My Voyage to Philadelphia" (25 Aug. 1726), Smyth 2:70-71.

19. Ibid. (23 Sept. 1726), Smyth 2:76.

They finally came within view of land on October 9, but Ben "could not discern it so soon as the rest; my eyes were dimmed with the suffusion of two small drops of joy." Two days later he reached his lovely Philadelphia, and it seemed to him "the most joyful day I ever knew."[20]

---

20. Ibid. (9 and 11 Oct. 1726), Smyth 2:85, 86.

Chapter 4

Setting His Course in Philadelphia

Soon after his return to Philadelphia, Benjamin came across Sir William Keith, who in 1724 had sent him to England under false pretenses. Keith was no longer Governor of Pennsylvania. "I met him walking the streets as a common citizen. He seemed a little ashamed at seeing me, but passed without saying anything."[1] And Franklin himself felt some shame when he again saw Deborah Read, now Deborah Rogers. After receiving Ben's only letter from England, she had given in to her friends' urging and married John Rogers, a potter, in August 1725. She left him, however, when she learned that he had another wife. Rogers spent her dowry, fell into debt, and fled in 1727 to the West Indies, where he reportedly died.

---

1. *Autobiography* (1771), p. 106.

A Close Brush with Death

Young Franklin came close to death himself a few months after arriving in Philadelphia. He later described how the incident resulted in his return to the printing trade:

> Mr. Denham took a store in Water Street, where we opened our goods. I attended the business diligently, studied accounts, and grew in a little time expert at selling. We lodged and boarded together; he counseled me as a father, having a sincere regard for me; I respected and loved him. And we might have gone on together very happily, but in the beginning of February 1727, when I had just passed my twenty-first year, we both were taken ill.
>
> My distemper was a pleurisy, which very nearly carried me off. I suffered a good deal, gave up the point in my own mind, and was rather disappointed when I found myself recovering, regretting in some degree that I must now ... have all that disagreeable work to do over again.
>
> I forget what his distemper was. It held him a long time, and at length carried him off.... The store was taken into the care of his executors, and my employment under him ended.... [My former employer, Samuel] Keimer tempted me with an offer of large wages by the year to come and take the management of his printing house, that he might better attend his stationer's shop. I had heard a bad character of him in London ... and was not fond of having any more to do with him. I tried for further employment as a merchant's clerk; but not readily meeting with any, I closed again with Keimer.[2]

---

2. Ibid., pp. 107-8.

In Business for Himself

As manager of Keimer's printing shop, Franklin trained the apprentices and journeymen in their duties, cast his own types (using a mold he had contrived himself), and even manufactured his own ink. When Keimer obtained a contract to print paper money for the province of New Jersey, Franklin designed and prepared the first copperplate press in America.[3] As he became known for his diligence and for the quality of his work, his reputation in the community increased.

But his relationship with Keimer gradually deteriorated, and in early 1728 Franklin and Hugh Meredith, another of Keimer's employees, set up their own printing house with a loan from Meredith's father. It was certainly not an equal partnership, however, as "Meredith was no compositor, a poor pressman, and seldom sober."[4] So Franklin managed the shop by himself. By July 1730 he found new creditors and bought out Meredith's interest in the business. Now fully on his own, he continued to build his reputation for industry and good workmanship. "The industry of that Franklin," reported one respected Philadelphia merchant, "is superior to anything I ever saw of the kind. I see him still at work when I go home...and he is at work again before his neighbors are out of bed."[5]

> I began now gradually to pay off the debt I was under for the printing house. In order to secure my credit and character as a tradesman, I took care not only to be in

---

3. Van Doren, *Benjamin Franklin*, p. 72.

4. *Autobiography* (1771), p. 120.

5. Quoted in ibid., p. 119.

reality industrious and frugal, but to avoid all appearances of the contrary. I dressed plainly; I was seen at no places of idle diversion; I never went out fishing or shooting. A book, indeed, sometimes debauched me from my work, but that was seldom, snug, and gave no scandal. And to show that I was not above my business, I sometimes brought home the paper I purchased at the stores through the streets on a wheelbarrow.

Thus being esteemed an industrious, thriving young man, and paying duly for what I bought, the merchants who imported stationery solicited my custom, others proposed supplying me with books, and I went on swimmingly.[6]

The *Pennsylvania Gazette*

Even before dissolving his partnership with Hugh Meredith, Franklin became the publisher of Philadelphia's second newspaper, the *Pennsylvania Gazette*. (Samuel Keimer, who had initiated the paper in 1728, sold it to his former shop manager before going out of business altogether.) Franklin appealed for public support in the preface to his first issue of the *Gazette:* "There are many who have long desired to see a good newspaper in Pennsylvania, and we hope those gentlemen who are able will contribute towards the making this such.... We may assure the public that, as far as the encouragement we meet with will enable us, no care and pains will be omitted that may make the *Pennsylvania Gazette* as agreeable and useful an entertainment as the nature of the thing will allow."[7] Within a short time, his high hopes began to be realized.

---

6. Ibid., pp. 125-26.
7. Preface to the *Pennsylvania Gazette* (2 Oct. 1729), Smyth 2:155.

Our first papers made a quite different appearance from any before in the province, a better type and better printed. But some spirited remarks of my writing on the dispute then going on between Governor [William] Burnet and the Massachusetts Assembly struck the principal people, occasioned the paper and the manager of it to be much talked of, and in a few weeks brought them all to be our subscribers. Their example was followed by many, and our number went on growing continually.

This was one of the first good effects of my having learned a little to scribble. Another was that the leading men, seeing a newspaper now in the hands of one who could also handle a pen, thought it convenient to oblige and encourage me. [My competitor Andrew] Bradford still printed the votes and laws and other public business. He had printed an address of the [Pennsylvania] House to the Governor in a coarse, blundering manner. We reprinted it elegantly and correctly, and sent one to every member. They were sensible of the difference, it strengthened the hands of our friends in the House, and they voted us their printers for the year ensuing. [8]

At the age of twenty-three, Benjamin Franklin was truly on his way toward a successful business career.

Enlarging the Circle of Influence

While he was still working for Keimer in 1727, Franklin formed most of his "ingenious acquaintance into a club for mutual improvement, which we called the Junto. We met on Friday evenings."

---

8. *Autobiography* (1771), p. 121.

The rules I drew up required that every member in his turn should produce one or more queries on any point of morals, politics, or natural philosophy, to be discussed by the company, and once in three months produce and read an essay of his own writing on any subject he pleased. Our debates were to be under the direction of a president, and to be conducted in the sincere spirit of inquiry after truth, without fondness for dispute or desire of victory; and to prevent warmth, all expressions of positiveness in opinion, or of direct contradiction, were after some time made contraband and prohibited under small pecuniary penalties. [9]

As an old man, Franklin recalled that "the club continued almost [forty years] and was the best school of philosophy, morals, and politics that then existed in the province." [10] Many of the public projects which later improved the quality of life in Philadelphia originated in discussions of the Junto, and most of these were first advocated by the club's founder.

The Paper Money Controversy

Another opportunity for community involvement came in 1729. "About this time there was a cry among the people for more paper money, only £15,000 being extant in the province and that soon to be sunk. The wealthy inhabitants opposed any addition, being against all paper currency from an apprehension that it would depreciate,

---

9. Ibid., pp. 116-17. See Smyth 2:88-90 for a more complete indication of the rules which guided the Junto. See Van Doren, *Benjamin Franklin,* p. 77 for some examples of the questions which Franklin himself introduced for group discussion.

10. *Autobiography* (1771), p. 118.

as it had done in New England, to the prejudice of all creditors. We had discussed this point in our Junto, where I was on the side of an addition.... Our debates possessed me so fully of the subject that I wrote and printed an anonymous pamphlet on it."[11]

This pamphlet, entitled *A Modest Enquiry into the Nature and Necessity of a Paper Currency,* was published in April 1729. It argued, almost half a century before Adam Smith said the same thing in his *Wealth of Nations,* that the only reliable standard of value was the labor of the people. (Because of this and his other early expressions of basic economic principles, Franklin later came to be called "the first American economist.")[12]

> For many ages, those parts of the world which are engaged in commerce have fixed upon gold and silver as the chief and most proper materials for [a] medium [of exchange], they being in themselves valuable metals for their fineness, beauty, and scarcity. By these, particularly by silver, it has been usual to value all things else. But as silver itself is of no certain permanent value, being worth more or less according to its scarcity or plenty, therefore it seems requisite to fix upon something else more proper to be made a *measure of values,* and this I take to be *labor....*
>
> The riches of a country are to be valued by the quantity of labor its inhabitants are able to purchase, and not by the quantity of silver and gold they possess....

---

11. Ibid., p. 124.
12. Donovan, *The Benjamin Franklin Papers,* p. 30.

> Trade in general being nothing else but the exchange
> of labor for labor, the value of things is... most justly
> measured by labor. [13]

Having established this concept, the pamphlet went on to brilliantly urge a more plentiful supply of paper currency, which itself merely serves as a convenient exchange medium that *represents* the products of the people's labors.

> It was well received by the common people in general; but the rich men disliked it, for it increased and strengthened the clamor for more money. And they happening to have no writers among them that were able to answer it, their opposition slackened and the point was carried by a majority in the House. My friends there, who conceived I had been of some service, thought fit to reward me by employing me in printing the money, a very profitable job and a great help to me. This was another advantage gained by my being able to write. [14]

"This Dangerous Time of Youth"

Franklin's most meticulous biographer, Carl Van Doren, has provided this physical description of the young man who would someday receive international acclaim for his wisdom and accomplishments:

> Strongly built, rounded like a swimmer or a wrestler, not angular like a runner, he was five feet nine or ten

---

13. *A Modest Enquiry into the Nature and Necessity of a Paper Currency* (3 Apr. 1729), Smyth 2:144, 146. Using this same reasoning, many of today's economists believe that a nation's money supply should be closely tied to the gross national product (GNP) to prevent unnatural inflation of consumer prices.

14. *Autobiography* (1771), p. 124.

inches tall, with a large head and square, deft hands. His hair was blond or light brown, his eyes grey, full, and steady, his mouth wide and humorous with a pointed upper lip. His clothing was as clean as it was plain. Though he and others say he was hesitant in speech, he was prompt in action. [15]

But in those days he was not famous, and he certainly had not yet developed the wisdom and discipline that would come to him in later years. He was only twenty years of age when he returned to Philadelphia in 1726, and "this dangerous time of youth and the hazardous situations I was sometimes in among strangers, remote from the eye and advice of my father," [16] occasionally led him into "errata" which he afterwards regretted. He candidly acknowledged, for example, that "that hard-to-be-governed passion of youth had hurried me frequently into intrigues with low women that fell in my way." [17] At the same time, however, he expressed gratitude that "the kind hand of Providence, or some guardian angel, or accidental favorable circumstances and situations, or all together, preserved me... without any willful gross immorality or injustice that might have been expected from my want of religion." [18]

Early Moral and Religious Views

Franklin explained how this "want of religion" had come about in his early teens, while he still lived in Boston:

---

15. Van Doren, *Benjamin Franklin*, pp. 90-91.
16. *Autobiography* (1771), p. 115.
17. Ibid., p. 128.
18. Ibid., p. 115.

> My parents had early given me religious impressions
> and brought me through my childhood piously in the
> dissenting way [that is, they were dissenters from the
> Anglican church]. But I was scarce fifteen when, after
> doubting by turns of several points as I found them
> disputed in the different books I read, I began to doubt of
> revelation itself.
>
> Some books against deism fell into my hands.... It
> happened that they wrought an effect on me quite
> contrary to what was intended by them, for the
> arguments of the deists which were quoted to be refuted
> appeared to me much stronger than the refutations. In
> short, I soon became a thorough deist. [19]

Considering himself a "freethinker," Ben discussed his
ideas with others and used his argumentative skill to
persuade them that deism was right. In fact, one of the
reasons he gave for deciding to run away from Boston in
1723 was that his "indiscreet disputations about religion
began to make me pointed at with horror by good people
as an infidel or atheist." [20] As we noted earlier, Franklin's
unusual religious views also caused him to write and
publish a questionable pamphlet on "the doctrine of fate"
during his stay in London. But at least by 1728, he was
asking himself some hard questions about his system of
beliefs.

> My arguments perverted some others ... but each of
> them having afterwards wronged me greatly without

---

19. Ibid., pp. 113-14. Deism is a philosophy based on human reason rather
than revelation; most deists deny that the Creator intervenes in human
affairs.

20. Ibid., p. 71. In 1723, there was more religious toleration in
Philadelphia than among the Puritans in Boston.

the least compunction, and recollecting Keith's conduct towards me (who was another freethinker) and my own towards...Miss Read, which at times gave me great trouble, I began to suspect that this doctrine [of deism], though it might be true, was not very useful. My London pamphlet...appeared now not so clever a performance as I once thought it; and I doubted whether some error had not insinuated itself unperceived into my argument, so as to infect all that followed, as is common in metaphysical reasonings.

I grew convinced that *truth, sincerity, and integrity* in dealings between man and man were of the utmost importance to the felicity of life....Revelation had, indeed, no weight with me as such; but I entertained an opinion that, though certain actions might not be bad *because* they were forbidden by it, or good *because* it commanded them, yet probably those actions might be forbidden *because* they were bad for us, or commanded *because* they were beneficial to us, in their own natures. [21]

Franklin's Private Creed

As his own observations and experience led him to further consider these ideas, Franklin gradually developed more concrete beliefs about the proper relationship between God and man. In November 1728 he wrote his "Articles of Belief and Acts of Religion," which served as his personal creed and provided guidelines for his private worship through the remainder of his life. Included in the opening section, which he called "First Principles," were these words:

I conceive that he [God] has in himself some of those passions he has planted in us, and that, since he has

---

21. Ibid., pp. 114-15.

given us reason whereby we are capable of observing his wisdom in the creation, he is not above caring for us, being pleased with our praise, and offended when we slight him or neglect his glory.

I conceive for many reasons that he is a *good being;* and as I should be happy to have so wise, good, and powerful a being my friend, let me consider in what manner I shall make myself most acceptable to him.

Next to the praise resulting from and due to his wisdom, I believe he is pleased and delights in the happiness of those he has created; and since without virtue man can have no happiness in this world, I firmly believe he delights to see me virtuous, because he is pleased when he sees me happy....

I *love* him, therefore, for his goodness, and I *adore* him for his wisdom.

Let me, then, not fail to praise my God continually, for it is his due, and it is all I can return for his many favors and great goodness to me; and let me resolve to be virtuous, that I may be happy, that I may please him who is delighted to see me happy. Amen![22]

Then followed prayers of praise and thanksgiving to the Creator, and another prayer petitioning Him for divine help in "eschewing vice and embracing virtue." The beginning passages in this series of petitions reveal Franklin's sense of duty to his country as well as his feeling of obligation to God:

That I may be preserved from atheism and infidelity, impiety and profaneness, and in my addresses to thee

---

22. "Articles of Belief and Acts of Religion" (20 Nov. 1728), Smyth 2:93-94.

carefully avoid irreverence and ostentation, formality and odious hypocrisy—help me, O Father!

That I may be loyal to my prince and faithful to my country, careful for its good, valiant in its defense, and obedient to its laws, abhorring treason as much as tyranny—help me, O Father![23]

---

23. Ibid., p. 98.

Chapter 5

The Franklin Family

Sometime after the word reached Philadelphia that Deborah Read's first husband had died in the West Indies, Ben Franklin renewed the romance which had been interrupted by his voyage to England.

I pitied poor Miss Read's unfortunate situation, who was generally dejected, seldom cheerful, and avoided company. I considered my giddiness and inconstancy when in London as in a great degree the cause of her unhappiness, though the mother was good enough to think the fault more her own than mine, as she had prevented our marrying before I went thither and persuaded the other match in my absence.

Our mutual affection was revived, but there were now great objections to our union. That match [the marriage of Deborah and John Rogers] was indeed

looked upon as invalid, a preceding wife being said to be living in England; but this could not easily be proved because of the distance. And though there was a report of his death, it was not certain. Then, though it should be true, he had left many debts which his successor might be called on to pay.

"A Good and Faithful Helpmate"

We ventured, however, over all these difficulties, and I took her to wife September 1, 1730. None of the inconveniences happened that we had apprehended, she proved a good and faithful helpmate, assisted me much by attending the shop, we

Deborah Read Franklin, who proved "a good and faithful helpmate" to her husband for nearly fifty years. Fear of ocean travel kept her in Philadelphia while Franklin served his overseas missions, and he was away in England when she died in 1774.

throve together, and have ever mutually endeavored to make each other happy. Thus I corrected that great *erratum* as well as I could. [1]

---

1. *Autobiography* (1771), p. 129. Because Deborah would have been unable in these circumstances to get the previous ceremony legally annulled, this marriage was most likely "a simple common-law agreement under which [she] came to live in Franklin's house and started calling herself Mrs. Franklin, an arrangement considered perfectly adequate at the time." Lopez and Herbert, *The Private Franklin,* pp. 23-24.

Franklin's writings show that he was much more content with life after his marriage to Deborah. Thereafter, he frequently spoke of the married state as the happiest of all possible conditions. This passage, written to a friend in 1745, is typical of his expressions on the subject:

> Marriage is . . . the most natural state of man, and therefore the state in which you are most likely to find solid happiness. . . . It is the man and woman united that make the complete human being. Separate, she wants his force of body and strength of reason; he, her softness, sensibility, and acute discernment. Together they are more likely to succeed in the world. A single man has not nearly the value he would have in the state of union. He is an incomplete animal; he resembles the odd half of a pair of scissors. [2]

The Franklin Children

The first child to enter the Franklin family was William, apparently born in the spring of 1731. [3] He is commonly said to have been illegitimate—at least most historians think so, although "the only evidence that has been cited is that 'everybody knew it.'" [4] The identity of William's mother has long been debated by the scholars; many believe that Deborah conceived the child before she

---

2. "Advice on the Choice of a Mistress" (25 June 1745), Nathan G. Goodman, ed., *A Benjamin Franklin Reader* (New York: Thomas Y. Crowell Company, 1945), p. 683.

3. We have no record of William's birthdate, but Franklin wrote in April 1750 that he was "now nineteen years of age." Letter to Mrs. Abiah Franklin (12 Apr. 1750), Smyth 3:4.

4. Donovan, *The Benjamin Franklin Papers*, p. 237. The charge of William's illegitimacy was first made many years later, by Franklin's political enemies, during a bitter 1764 campaign for a seat in the Pennsylvania Assembly. Historians, forgetting that it was Franklin's habit to ignore public censure, have made much of the fact that he never tried to refute these attacks.

assumed the name of Mrs. Franklin, but that Benjamin took "all the blame" himself in order to "save Deborah's honor."[5] In any event, William was welcomed into the Franklin household and was reared and educated as a legitimate son. He later became the Governor of New Jersey.

Another son, Francis Folger Franklin, was born in October 1732. His father considered him "the delight of all that knew him,"[6] and both he and Deborah were crushed by grief when "Franky" died of smallpox at the age of four. Franklin, who had seen 10 percent of the population of Boston killed by a smallpox epidemic in the summer of 1721, "regretted bitterly" that he had not inoculated his

little boy before it was too late.[7] Thirty-six years later, he still had very tender feelings about "my son Franky...whom to this day I cannot think of without a sigh."[8]

Their third and last child, Sarah ("Sally"), was born in September 1743 (making her twelve years younger than her brother William).

Franklin's second son, Francis Folger, who tragically died of smallpox at the age of four.

5. Van Doren, *Benjamin Franklin,* pp. 91, 93; Lopez and Herbert, p. 22. Franklin and his wife spoke of Sarah Read (Deborah's mother) as William's grandmother. See Franklin's letter to Deborah (31 Jan. 1756), Smyth 3:328.

6. Inscription on the tombstone of Francis Folger Franklin (Nov. 1736), Van Doren, *Autobiographical Writings,* p. 38 (headnote).

7. Lopez and Herbert, p. 12; *Autobiography* (1788), p. 170.

8. To Mrs. Jane Mecom (13 Jan. 1772), Smyth 5:349.

She eventually gave her father seven grandchildren, and she finally became a nurse to him in his last days.

Franklin's "Fictitious Family"

Perhaps a word should be said here about the spurious accounts of additional Franklin children, as such claims have become increasingly popular in recent years. "Today," noted a 1975 magazine article, "Franklin folklore overflows with tales of womanizing, including a fictitious family of thirteen illegitimate children."[9] (Such stories have lately crept even into school textbooks!) Claude-Anne Lopez, a Franklin scholar at Yale University, has corrected these myths and provided some insight regarding their origins:

> Apart from the existence of William (who was treated as a legitimate son), there is hardly any explicit evidence to convict Franklin either of promiscuity or its opposite. But the rumors sprang up in his own lifetime and have gained ground ever since.
>
> The story of his "illegitimate daughter" is a case in point. In 1770, Franklin's close associate John Foxcroft married Judith Osgood in England. Franklin gave away the bride and referred to her thereafter as his "daughter" because he had acted as surrogate father at the wedding, by no means an unusual practice. Many were the women he would call wife or daughter throughout his life, in a teasing or affectionate manner without suspecting, of course, that anybody would take him literally, then or later.[10]

---

9. Alice J. Hall, "Benjamin Franklin: Philosopher of Dissent," *National Geographic,* July 1975, p. 118.

10. Lopez and Herbert, pp. 26-27. For a typical example of the "illegitimate daughter" story, see Sydney George Fisher, *The True Benjamin Franklin* (Philadelphia: J.B. Lippincott Company, 1899), pp. 104-5.

A Thriving Family Business

In addition to the immediate family, Deborah's widowed mother and an occasional apprentice or journeyman also lived with the Franklins—all on the second floor of the house, as the printing shop and a small general store occupied the ground level. Besides the salves and ointments concocted by Ben's mother-in-law (advertised as "sufficient to remove the most inveterate itch"),[11] the store offered a wide variety of foods and household items: coffee, tea, fish, cheeses, spices, quill pens, lead pencils, ink, stationery, maps, books, legal forms, broadcloth, stockings, lumber, stoves, sealing wax, spectacles, compasses, scales, and even a horse and carriage now and then.

Deborah was invaluable to her husband in maintaining a successful business. Over fifty years after their marriage, he would write to an acquaintance, "Frugality is an enriching virtue, a virtue I never could acquire in myself, but I was once lucky enough to find it in a wife, who thereby became a fortune to me."[12] He also appreciated her industry; she not only reared their children and ran the household, but also managed the store, kept the books, and later handled the postal accounts when Franklin was appointed postmaster. "She assisted me cheerfully in my business, folding and stitching pamphlets, tending shop, purchasing old linen rags for the paper makers, etc., etc. We kept no idle

---

11. Advertisement in the *Pennsylvania Gazette* (19 Aug. 1731), Leonard W. Labaree, William B. Willcox, et al., eds., *The Papers of Benjamin Franklin,* 21 vols. by 1978 (New Haven: Yale University Press, 1959-), 1:219.

12. To Miss Alexander (24 June 1782), Smyth 8:459.

servants, our table was plain and simple, our furniture of the cheapest." But Deborah did not let "frugality" prevent an occasional treat for her husband:

My breakfast was a long time bread and milk (no tea), and I ate it out of a twopenny earthen porringer with a pewter spoon. But mark how luxury will enter families and make a progress in spite of principle. Being called one morning to breakfast, I found it in a china bowl with a spoon of silver. They had been bought for me without my knowledge by my wife, and had cost her the enormous sum of three and twenty shillings, for which she had no other excuse or apology to make but that she thought *her* husband deserved a silver spoon and china bowl as well as any of his neighbors. [13]

---

13. *Autobiography* (1784), p. 145.

Chapter 6

Poor Richard and Other Projects

B y consistently applying the principles of "industry and frugality," the Franklins were able to pay off all their debts by 1732, only two years after they were married. Benjamin now owned his business free and clear, and he spared no pains to see that it continued to prosper. To increase the readership of his newspaper, the *Pennsylvania Gazette,* he often sparked humorous little controversies among the townspeople by printing "letters to the editor" which he had secretly written himself under such pseudonyms as "Anthony Afterwit," "Celia Single," and "Alice Addertongue." Sometimes he even argued *both* sides of a controversy, using two different names!

Franklin also attempted various innovations in the printing trade; some were more successful than others. In 1732 he started the first German-American newspaper, the *Philadelphische Zeitung*. Two years later he published *The Constitutions of the Free-Masons*, the first Masonic book printed in America (later that same year, Franklin became grand master of the local Masonic lodge). He published many other books as well, including the first American novel (Samuel Richardson's *Pamela*) in 1744. Franklin and those with whom he formed business ties—his numerous partners and apprentices, plus several relatives on both sides of the family—eventually established printing houses in Pennsylvania, Delaware, New Jersey, Maryland, South Carolina, New York, Rhode Island, Massachusetts, Connecticut, Georgia, North Carolina, Jamaica, and Dominica.[1]

Poor Richard's Almanack

"Franklin has been called the father of American humor," and *Poor Richard's Almanack* "the first jokebook."[2] The almanac also contained much that was serious, of course; but whatever its magic was, it became one of the most popular publications in colonial history almost overnight, selling a remarkable ten thousand copies annually for twenty-five years. *Poor Richard* (its actual title, taken from the pen name "Richard Saunders") was first published in December 1732. Like other almanacs of the time, it calculated tides, forecast the weather, and contained a mixture of astrology, recipes, jokes, poems, maxims, odd facts, and so forth. But this almanac was somehow different from the rest. Franklin explained his intent:

---

1. Van Doren, *Benjamin Franklin*, pp. 103, 117-23.
2. Donovan, *The Benjamin Franklin Papers*, p. 259.

I endeavored to make it both entertaining and useful, and it accordingly came to be in such demand that I reaped considerable profit from it.... And observing that it was generally read, scarce any neighborhood in the province being without it, I considered it as a proper vehicle for conveying instruction among the common people, who bought scarcely any other books.

I therefore filled all the little spaces that occurred... with proverbial sentences, chiefly such as inculcated industry and frugality, as the means of procuring wealth and thereby securing virtue, it being more difficult for a man in want to act always honestly, as (to use one of those proverbs) *it is hard for an empty sack to stand upright.* These proverbs... contained the wisdom of many ages and nations.[3]

Title page of the first issue of *Poor Richard's Almanack*. It sold about ten thousand copies annually for the next twenty-five years.

He was also aiming at the youth when deciding what to include in *Poor Richard:* "I have constantly interspersed

---

3. *Autobiography* (1788), pp. 163-64. In another place, Franklin noted that "not a tenth part of the wisdom [in the almanacs] was my own... but rather the gleanings I had made of the sense of all ages and nations." Preface to *Poor Richard Improved, 1758* (7 July 1757), Smyth 3:418.

moral sentences, prudent maxims, and wise sayings, many of them containing much good sense in very few words, and therefore apt to leave strong and lasting impressions on the memory of young persons, whereby they may receive benefit as long as they live, when both almanac and almanac-maker have been long thrown by and forgotten."[4] Many of these "prudent maxims" are still familiar to us today:

Early to bed and early to rise makes a man healthy, wealthy, and wise.

Men and melons are hard to know.

Would you live with ease, do what you ought and not what you please.

He's a fool that makes his doctor his heir.

Fish and visitors smell in three days.

Keep thy shop, and thy shop will keep thee.

A penny saved is a penny earned.

He that lieth down with dogs shall rise up with fleas.

Keep your eyes wide open before marriage, half shut afterwards.

Three may keep a secret if two of them are dead.

God helps them that help themselves.

Experience keeps a dear school, yet fools will learn in no other.

The used key is always bright.

Three removes are as bad as a fire.

A stitch in time saves nine.

He that falls in love with himself will have no rivals.

---

4. Preface to *Poor Richard, 1747* (Oct. 1746), Smyth 2:299.

"My First Project of a Public Nature"

In the midst of starting his family and establishing a successful business, Franklin maintained his habit of "improvement by constant study, for which I set apart an hour or two each day, and thus repaired in some degree the loss of the learned education my father once intended for me. Reading was the only amusement I allowed myself. I spent no time in taverns, games, or frolics of any kind. And my industry in my business continued as indefatigable as it was necessary."[5] He also encouraged his fellow members of the Junto to read as widely as they could:

> At the time I established myself in Pennsylvania, there was not a good bookseller's shop in any of the colonies to the southward of Boston.... Those who loved reading were obliged to send for their books from England. The members of the Junto had each a few.... I proposed that we should all of us bring our books to [the room we had rented for our meetings], where they would not only be ready to consult in our conferences, but become a common benefit, each of us being at liberty to borrow such as he wished to read at home.
>
> This was accordingly done, and for some time contented us. Finding the advantage of this little collection, I proposed to render the benefit from books more common by commencing a public subscription library.[6]

This was the beginning of the Library Company of Philadelphia, which Franklin called "my first project of a public nature." Years later he wrote with satisfaction that

---

5. *Autobiography* (1784), p. 143.

6. Ibid., pp. 141-42.

it was "the mother of all the North American subscription libraries now so numerous. It is become a great thing itself, and continually increasing. These libraries have improved the general conversation of the Americans, made the common tradesmen and farmers as intelligent as most gentlemen from other countries, and perhaps have contributed in some degree to the stand so generally made throughout the colonies in defense of their privileges."[7]

As a sidelight, we ought to note the practical lesson Franklin extracted from this endeavor (because of its impact on the many public enterprises he initiated thereafter).

> The objections and reluctances I met with in soliciting the subscriptions made me soon feel the impropriety of presenting oneself as the proposer of any useful project that might be supposed to raise one's reputation in the smallest degree above that of one's neighbors, when one has need of their assistance to accomplish that project. I therefore put myself as much as I could out of sight, and stated it as a scheme of a *number of friends* who had requested me to go about and propose it to such as they thought lovers of reading.

> In this way my affair went on more smoothly, and I ever after practiced it on such occasions; and from my frequent successes can heartily recommend it. The present little sacrifice of your vanity will afterwards be amply repaid.[8]

7. Ibid. (1771), pp. 130-31.
8. Ibid. (1784), p. 143.

A "Bold and Arduous Project"

During the course of his studies, Franklin taught himself several languages—French, Italian, Spanish, Latin, and German—chiefly to enable him to increase his knowledge by reading various important works that had not yet been translated into English. He also learned to play the harp, the violin, and the guitar (later he would add an unusal instrument of his own design, the "armonica"). And by 1733 he had entered upon a still more difficult and comprehensive exercise in self-improvement—"the bold and arduous project of arriving at moral perfection."

> I wished to live without committing any fault at any time; I would conquer all that either natural inclination, custom, or company might lead me into. As I knew, or thought I knew, what was right and wrong, I did not see why I might not *always* do the one and avoid the other. [9]

Seven years earlier, during his long voyage from London to Philadelphia, he had written a preliminary plan for his future conduct wherein he had resolved to be frugal, industrious, and truthful, and to "speak ill of no man whatever."[10] But this new undertaking was even more ambitious. It required faithful adherence to thirteen separate virtues: temperance, silence ("Speak not but what may benefit others or yourself. Avoid trifling conversation."), order, resolution ("Resolve to perform what you ought. Perform without fail what you resolve."), frugality, industry, sincerity, justice, moderation, cleanliness, tranquility ("Be not disturbed at trifles, or at

---

9. Ibid., p. 148.

10. Van Doren, *Autobiographical Writings*, pp. 25-26. Forty-five years after making these resolutions, Franklin observed that he had "pretty faithfully adhered to [them] quite through to old age." *Autobiography* (1771), p. 106.

accidents common or unavoidable."), chastity, and humility ("Imitate Jesus and Socrates.").[11]

As one might expect, he soon discovered that he had "undertaken a task of more difficulty than I had imagined. While my attention was taken up in guarding against one fault, I was often surprised by another."[12] So he settled on a method to help him succeed in his quest. He devised a little book and set it up in such a way that he could examine himself and mark his progress at the end of each day. He decided to focus on only one virtue at a time, "and when I should be master of that, then to proceed to another, and so on till I should have gone through the thirteen. . . . I determined to give a week's strict attention to each of the virtues successively. . . . Proceeding thus to the last, I could go through a course complete in thirteen weeks, and four courses in a year."[13] How did his project turn out? At the advanced age of seventy-eight he wrote:

> I entered upon the execution of this plan for self-examination and continued it, with occasional intermissions, for some time. I was surprised to find myself so much fuller of faults than I had imagined, but I had the satisfaction of seeing them diminish. . . . After a while I went through one course only in a year, and afterwards only one in several years, till at length I omitted them entirely, being employed in voyages and business abroad with a multiplicity of affairs that interfered; but I always carried my little book with me. . . .

11. *Autobiography* (1784), pp. 149-50.

12. Ibid., p. 148.

13. Ibid., pp. 150-52.

In truth, I found myself incorrigible with respect to *order;* and now I am grown old, and my memory bad, I feel very sensibly the want of it. But on the whole, though I never arrived at the perfection I had been so ambitious of obtaining, but fell far short of it, yet I was by the endeavor a better and happier man than I otherwise should have been. . . .

And it may be well my posterity should be informed that to this little artifice, with the blessing of God, their ancestor owed the constant felicity of his life down to his seventy-ninth year in which this is written. . . . I hope, therefore, that some of my descendants may follow the example and reap the benefits. [14]

Franklin and the Philadelphia Churches

Because of Franklin's recurring interest in morality and virtue, it might be thought that he felt very close to his church. He was indeed a profoundly religious man, but in fact he seldom attended church services after he left his father's home at the age of twelve.

I had been religiously educated as a Presbyterian; [15] and though some of the dogmas of that persuasion . . . appeared to me unintelligible, others doubtful, and I early absented myself from the public assemblies of the sect, Sunday being my studying day, I never was without

14. Ibid., pp. 155-57. He also complained of difficulty with the last virtue on his list: "There is perhaps no one of our natural passions so hard to subdue as *pride.* Disguise it, struggle with it, beat it down, stifle it, mortify it as much as one pleases, it is still alive and will every now and then peep out and show itself. . . . Even if I could conceive that I had completely overcome it, I should probably be proud of my humility." Ibid., p. 160.

15. Leonard W. Labaree added this clarification: "Strictly speaking, Franklin had been baptized and educated in what was coming to be called the Congregational Church, not the Presbyterian. Both had a common origin in the doctrines of John Calvin." Ibid., p. 145n.

some religious principles. I never doubted, for instance, the existence of the Deity, that he made the world and governed it by his providence; that the most acceptable service of God was the doing good to man; that our souls are immortal; and that all crime will be punished and virtue rewarded either here or hereafter.

These I esteemed to be the essentials of every religion; and being to be found in all the religions we had in our country, I respected them all, though with different degrees of respect, as I found them more or less mixed with other articles which, without any tendency to inspire, promote, or confirm morality, served principally to divide us and make us unfriendly to one another. [16]

The Presbyterian minister in Philadelphia occasionally visited Franklin and admonished him to attend Sunday worship services, "and I was now and then prevailed on to do so, once for five Sundays successively." But he found the minister's sermons "very dry, uninteresting, and unedifying, since not a single moral principle was inculcated or enforced, their aim seeming to be rather to make us Presbyterians than good citizens.... I ... was disgusted, and attended his preaching no more. I had some years before composed a little liturgy or form of prayer for my own private use ... entitled *Articles of Belief and Acts of Religion;* I returned to the use of this, and went no more to the public assemblies." [17]

---

16. Ibid., pp. 145-46.

17. Ibid., pp. 147-48. Franklin believed that "vital religion has always suffered when orthodoxy is more regarded than virtue; and the scriptures assure me that at the last day we shall not be examined [for] what we *thought* [i.e., our theological opinions], but what we *did.*" Letter to Josiah Franklin (13 Apr. 1738), Smyth 2:215; see also 3:145-46.

"I Emptied My Pocket . . . Gold and All"

He contributed annually to help support the Presbyterian minister, however, and he often helped provide funds for the erection of new church buildings in the area, "whatever might be the sect."[18] On one occasion he even served as a lottery manager to raise money for a steeple and bells to adorn the Episcopal church his wife attended. The only time he *almost* refused a requested donation was when the Reverend George Whitefield (an Anglican evangelist who visited America several times) sought contributions in 1739 to build an orphanage in Georgia.

> I did not disapprove of the design, but as Georgia was then destitute of materials and workmen and it was proposed to send them from Philadelphia at a great expense, I thought it would have been better to have built the house here and brought the children to it. This I advised, but he was resolute in his first project and rejected my counsel, and I thereupon refused to contribute.
>
> I happened soon after to attend one of his sermons, in the course of which I perceived he intended to finish with a collection, and I silently resolved he should get nothing from me. I had in my pocket a handful of copper money, three or four silver dollars, and five pistoles in gold. As he proceeded I began to soften, and concluded to give the coppers. Another stroke of his oratory made me ashamed of that, and determined me to give the

---

18. *Autobiography* (1784), p. 146. This included a large donation in 1788 toward building a Jewish synagogue in Philadelphia, despite a spurious legend (from our century) that Franklin was anti-Semitic and had delivered a speech against the Jews in the 1787 Constitutional Convention.

silver; and he finished so admirably that I emptied my
pocket wholly into the collector's dish, gold and all. [19]

Advancing on the Public Stage

While Franklin may not have been an ardent
churchgoer, he was certainly active in many other
organizations. In June 1734 he was appointed grand
master of the earliest known Masonic lodge in America,
St. John's of Philadelphia (eventually he was elected grand
master for the entire province). In October 1736 he was
appointed clerk of the Pennsylvania House of
Representatives, a position in which he served for fifteen
years until he became a member of that body. An
instructive incident occurred in 1737 when he was
nominated to be reappointed as clerk for a second annual
term. Although the vote was favorable for Franklin, he
was concerned that "a new member [had] made a long
speech against me in order to favor some other candidate."

> I...did not like the opposition of this new member,
> who was a gentleman of fortune and education, with
> talents that were likely to give him in time great
> influence in the House, which indeed afterwards
> happened. I did not, however, aim at gaining his favor by
> paying any servile respect to him, but after some time
> took [another] method.
>
> Having heard that he had in his library a certain very
> scarce and curious book, I wrote a note to him
> expressing my desire of perusing that book and
> requesting he would do me the favor of lending it to me
> for a few days. He sent it immediately; and I returned it
> in about a week, with another note expressing strongly
> my sense of the favor.

19. Ibid. (1788), p. 177.

When we next met in the House, he spoke to me (which he had never done before), and with great civility. And he ever afterwards manifested a readiness to serve me on all occasions, so that we became great friends, and our friendship continued to his death. [20]

In December 1736, after consultation with other Junto members and an anonymous promotional letter in the *Pennsylvania Gazette,* Franklin persuaded about thirty men to join him in forming the Union Fire Company. "Our articles of agreement obliged every member to keep always in good order and fit for use a certain number of leather buckets, with strong bags and baskets (for packing and transporting of goods) which were to be brought to every fire." Similar companies sprang up around the city and eventually "became so numerous as to include most of the inhabitants who were men of property." After fifty years, these companies were so well trained and equipped that Franklin was able to say, "I question whether there is a city in the world better provided with the means of putting a stop to beginning conflagrations."[21]

Also about this time, he proposed a tax-supported police force for Philadelphia. "Though the plan was not immediately carried into execution," he noted, "yet by preparing the minds of the people for the change, it paved the way for the law obtained a few years after."[22] And in 1737, he was appointed postmaster in Philadelphia. Now thirty-one years of age, Ben Franklin was steadily gaining more prominence in the public eye.

---

20. Ibid., pp. 171-72.
21. Ibid., pp. 174-75.
22. Ibid., pp. 173-74.

Chapter 7

Scientist and Militiaman

As a young man, Franklin had displayed a persistent interest in science (or "natural philosophy," as it was called in those days). As his business continued to prosper during the late 1730s, he devoted more and more time to various scientific pursuits. As early as 1737, he was writing in the *Pennsylvania Gazette* about the causes of earthquakes and to friends about the behavior of storms on the Atlantic coast. Also interested in botany, he introduced the yellow willow to America about this time.

By 1739 or 1740 he had invented the Pennsylvania Fireplace (known today as the "Franklin Stove"), a free-standing cast-iron unit which could efficiently heat an entire room with much less firewood than was commonly used. As the popularity of these stoves increased among the people, the colonial Governor offered to give the inventor "a patent for the sole vending of them for a term of years."

But I declined it from a principle which has ever weighed with me on such occasions, viz., that as we enjoy great advantages from the inventions of other, we should be glad of an opportunity to serve others by any invention of ours, and this we should do freely and generously.... The use of these fireplaces in very many houses, both of this and the neighboring colonies, has been and is a great saving of wood to the inhabitants. [1]

Creation of the American Philosophical Society

By 1743 Franklin had begun corresponding with other "ingenious men" throughout the colonies, and in May of that year he sent to these correspondents a circular letter proposing the formation of a society to promote the dissemination of "useful knowledge" in America.

The first drudgery of settling new colonies, which confines the attention of people to mere necessities, is now pretty well over; and there are many in every province in circumstances that set them at ease and afford leisure to cultivate the finer arts and improve the common stock of knowledge. To such of these who are men of speculation, many hints must from time to time arise, many observations occur, which if well examined, pursued, and improved might produce discoveries to the advantage of some or all of the British plantations, or to the benefit of mankind in general. [2]

---

1. *Autobiography* (1788), p. 192.

2. "A Proposal for Promoting Useful Knowledge Among the British Plantations in America" (14 May 1743), Smyth 2:228.

He proposed that the organization be called the American Philosophical Society and "that Philadelphia, being the city nearest the center of the continent colonies...and having the advantage of a good, growing library, be the center of the Society." The members, meeting and corresponding regularly, would consider improvements and discoveries in many fields of study: agriculture; mineralogy; mathematics; chemistry; "new mechanical inventions for saving labor"; "all new arts, trades, and manufactures"; geography; animal husbandry; "and all philosophical experiments that let light into the nature of things, tend to increase the power of man over matter, and multiply the conveniences or pleasures of life."[3]

Within a year the American Philosophical Society had been organized and had held several meetings. Thomas Hopkinson, a Philadelphia attorney and a member of the Junto, was the Society's first president; Franklin served as secretary (as he had offered to do in the initial proposal) until he was elected president in 1769.

First Electrical Experiments

Franklin's commitment to furthering scientific knowledge continued to increase. In 1745 he wrote to a fellow member of the American Philosophical Society: "I shall be very willing and ready, when you think proper to publish your piece on gravitation, to print it at my own expense and risk. If I can be the means of communicating anything valuable to the world, I do not always think of gaining, nor even of saving, by my business; but a piece of

---

3. Ibid., pp. 229-30.

that kind, as it must excite the curiosity of all the learned, can hardly fail of bearing its own expense."[4]

The events of the next several months would focus Franklin's attention on a field in which he would shortly rise to international preeminence. As early as 1743, during

a trip to Boston, he had witnessed a series of experiments in static electricity, conducted by a Dr. Archibald Spencer. "They were imperfectly performed," Franklin later noted, "as he was not very expert; but being on a subject quite new to me, they equally surprised and pleased me."[5] He apparently engaged in no experimentation himself, however, until the year 1746, when the Library Company of Philadelphia received an unusual gift from a London botanist named Peter Collinson—it was a glass tube designed for electrical experiments similar to those Franklin had seen three years earlier.

The machine Franklin used to conduct some of his most important electrical experiments, beginning in the year 1746.

4. To Cadwallader Colden (28 Nov. 1745), Smyth 2:290-91. The title of Colden's work was *Explication of the First Causes of Motion in Matter, and of the Cause of Gravitation.*

5. *Autobiography* (1788), p. 240.

"I eagerly seized the opportunity of repeating what I had seen at Boston," he wrote, "and by much practice acquired great readiness in performing those also which we had an account of from England, adding a number of new ones."[6] By March 1747 he was spending much of his time in these investigations, as he wrote Collinson:

> I never was before engaged in any study that so totally engrossed my attention and my time as this has lately done; for what with making experiments when I can be alone, and repeating them to my friends and acquaintance who, from the novelty of the thing, come continually in crowds to see them, I have during some months past had little leisure for anything else.[7]

With the discovery of the Leyden jar in Holland that year, Franklin's electrical experiments progressed more rapidly. He initiated the use of the terms *positive* and *negative*, discovered some principles of conductivity, and began to form several tentative hypotheses. Then, in the fall of 1747, his scientific studies were interrupted by urgent events which threatened the peace and safety of the American colonists.

Defending the Home Front

In July 1747, Spain and France (both nations had been at war with England for several years) sent privateers up the Delaware River near Philadelphia, where they attacked and plundered two farms and captured an American ship. Franklin immediately became concerned for the safety of

---

6. Ibid., p. 241.
7. To Peter Collinson (28 Mar. 1747), Smyth 2:302.

the province, but he knew it would be difficult to unite Pennsylvania's diverse religious and economic groups in any kind of military defense effort—especially in view of the Quakers' teaching that war was unlawful. Sitting as a clerk in the House of Representatives, he had often witnessed the futility of the Governor's attempts to secure legislation providing for a colonial militia. So Franklin decided on an approach of his own.

I determined to try what might be done by a voluntary association of the people. To promote this I first wrote and published a pamphlet entitled *Plain Truth,* in which I stated our defenseless situation in strong lights, with the necessity of union and discipline for our defense, and promised to propose in a few days an association to be generally signed for that purpose.

The pamphlet had a sudden and surprising effect. I was called upon for the instrument of association, and, having settled the draft of it with a few friends, I appointed a meeting of the citizens in [a] large building.... The house was pretty full. I had prepared a number of printed copies, and provided pens and ink dispersed all over the room. I harangued them a little on the subject, read the paper and explained it, and then distributed the copies, which were eagerly signed, not the least objection being made.

When the company separated and the papers were collected, we found above twelve hundred hands; and other copies being dispersed in the country, the subscribers amounted at length to upwards of ten thousand. These all furnished themselves as soon as they could with arms, formed themselves into companies and regiments, chose their officers, and met every week to be instructed in the manual exercise and other parts of military discipline.[8]

He then organized a lottery to raise funds for building a fort below the city and furnishing it with cannons. Some of these had to be purchased from England, so Franklin and three others journeyed to New York to borrow cannons from Governor George Clinton while they waited for their order to arrive. "He at first refused us peremptorily; but at dinner with his council, where there was great drinking of Madeira wine, as the custom of that place then was, he softened by degrees and said he would lend us six. After a few more bumpers he advanced to ten; and at length he very good-naturedly conceded eighteen."[9] (Governor Clinton seemed to be affected by the Madeira much as Franklin had been by George Whitefield's preaching in 1739!)

A Day of Fasting and Prayer

It was also Franklin who proposed, in January 1748, the first fast day in Pennsylvania. In connection with this proposal, he drew up a proclamation declaring that "it is the duty of mankind on all suitable occasions to acknowledge their dependence on the Divine Being" and expressing a prayer "that He would take this province under His protection, confound the designs and defeat the attempts of its enemies, and unite our hearts and strengthen our hands in every undertaking that may be

---

8. *Autobiography* (1788), pp. 182-83. The pamphlet was published in November 1747; reprinted in Smyth 2:336-53.

9. *Autobiography* (1788), p. 184.

for the public good, and for our defense and security in this time of danger."[10]

Franklin's popularity was greatly enhanced by his effectiveness in organizing a defensive military force in Pennsylvania. He later recalled that "the officers of the companies composing the Philadelphia Regiment, being met, chose me for their colonel; but conceiving myself unfit, I declined that station and recommended Mr. [Thomas] Lawrence, a fine person and man of influence, who was accordingly appointed." Franklin often appeared at the newly erected fort, "where the Associators kept a nightly guard while the war lasted; and among the rest I regularly took my turn of duty there as a common soldier."[11] He felt a great sense of relief when peace was concluded later that year; but his military experience would prove useful later on.

---

10. Quoted in Van Doren, *Benjamin Franklin*, p. 188.

11. *Autobiography* (1788), pp. 183, 184.

Chapter 8

"He Snatched the Lightning from the Heavens"

F ranklin recorded that during the 1740s his business was "continually augmenting, and my circumstances growing daily easier."[1] By 1748, his circumstances had in fact grown easy enough that he decided to withdraw from active involvement in the printing trade. In the summer of that year he formed a new partnership with David Hall, his shop foreman: Hall would run the shop, publish the *Pennsylvania Gazette* and *Poor Richard's Almanack*, and pay Franklin 50 percent of the profits; after eighteen years, Hall would become full owner of the business. A letter to a friend shows that the senior partner was pleased with this arrangement:

> I congratulate you on your return to your beloved retirement. I, too, am taking the proper measures for

---

1. *Autobiography* (1788), p. 180.

obtaining leisure to enjoy life and my friends, more than
heretofore, having put my printing house under the
care of my partner, David Hall, absolutely left off
bookselling, and removed to a more quiet part of the
town, where I . . . hope soon to be quite master of my
own time. . . .

Thus you see I am in a fair way of having no other
tasks than such as I shall like to give myself, and of
enjoying what I look upon as a great happiness: leisure
to read, study, make experiments, and converse at large
with such ingenious and worthy men as are pleased to
honor me with their friendship or acquaintance, on such
points as may produce something for the common
benefit of mankind, uninterrupted by the little cares and
fatigues of business.[2]

Upon his retirement, Franklin's annual income—from
his several business partnerships, his position as
postmaster, his real estate holdings, and the interest on
his savings—probably exceeded that of the Pennsylvania
Governor.[3] At the age of forty-two, he knew he was
entering a new phase of his life, and he wanted his
remaining years to be as serviceable to his fellowmen as
possible.

Further Achievements in Electricity

Now that Pennsylvania was no longer threatened by
hostile forces and Franklin was no longer bothered by the
"cares and fatigues of business," he turned his attention
once more to electrical experimentation. In addition to the
terms *positive* and *negative*, he coined several others that are

---

2. To Cadwallader Colden (29 Sept. 1748), Smyth 2:362-63.
3. Van Doren, *Benjamin Franklin*, pp. 123, 188-89; Lopez and Herbert, *The
Private Franklin*, p. 42.

used widely today: armature, battery, brush, charge, condense, conductor, electrical shock, and electrician are some examples. He also developed the first electrical battery and invented the lightning rod—for which he refused any patent or profit. He produced the first coherent theory of electricity, that of a "single fluid" in positive and negative states. He even experimented with shock treatments as a means of curing certain bodily disorders; by this process he apparently healed a young woman who had suffered cramps and violent convulsions for ten years. [4]

A Near Disaster

There were some dangers associated with Franklin's electrical experiments, of course. He told Peter Collinson about a frightening occurrence in December 1750:

> I found that a man can without great detriment bear a much greater electrical shock than I imagined. For I inadvertently took the stroke of two of those jars through my arms and body when they were very near full charged. It seemed a universal blow from head to foot throughout the body, and followed by a violent, quick trembling in the trunk which gradually went off in a few seconds.
>
> It was some minutes before I could collect my thoughts so as to know what was the matter; for I did not see the flash, though my eye was on the spot of the prime conductor from which it struck the back of my hand; nor did I hear the crack, though the bystanders say it was a loud one; nor did I particularly feel the stroke on

---

4. Lopez and Herbert, pp. 49-50.

my hand, though I afterwards found it had raised a swelling there....

My arms and [the] back of my neck felt somewhat numb the remainder of the evening, and my breastbone was sore for a week after, as if it had been bruised. What the consequences would be if such a shock were taken through the head I do not know. [5]

But his obsession to learn drove him on in spite of the danger. One of the episodes for which Franklin is best remembered is the daring experiment with his famous kite in the summer of 1752. Although he was not the first scientist to suggest that lightning and electricity were identical, he was the first to design an experiment that could prove it. He conceived a method for verifying the hypothesis in 1749, and in 1751 it was published (along with his other writings about electricity) in America, England, and France. [6] A French physicist named d'Alibard, after studying the proposal, successfully conducted the experiment on the outskirts of Paris in May 1752—actually a month before Franklin himself tried it in Philadelphia.

"He Snatched the Lightning from the Heavens"

Franklin believed that lightning could be attracted by a pointed metal rod, as could other electrical currents, and

---

5. To Peter Collinson (4 Feb. 1751), Van Doren, *Autobiographical Writings*, p. 72. See page 73 for another such incident; see also his letter to a friend in Boston [John Franklin] (25 Dec. 1750), Smyth 3:32-33.

6. See Franklin's letter to John Lining (18 Mar. 1755), Smyth 3:255.

Franklin performing his famous kite experiment outside Philadelphia in June 1752, assisted by his twenty-one-year-old son William.

he was waiting for a high tower or spire to be built in Philadelphia—one that was high enough to enable him to test his idea. Then it occurred to him that he could accomplish his end, perhaps even better, by means of a common kite. The following account of his memorable experiment is taken from Joseph Priestley's *History and Present State of Electricity,* written under Franklin's close direction and published in 1767.

> Preparing . . . a large silk handkerchief and two cross-sticks of proper length on which to extend it, he took the opportunity of the first approaching thunderstorm to take a walk in the fields, in which there was a shed convenient for his purpose. But, dreading the ridicule which too commonly attends unsuccessful attempts in science, he communicated his intended experiment to

nobody but his son, who assisted him in raising the kite [William was now twenty-one years old].

The kite being raised, a considerable time elapsed before there was any appearance of its being electrified. One very promising cloud had passed over it without any effect when, at length, just as he was beginning to despair of his contrivance, he observed some loose threads of the hempen string to stand erect and to avoid one another, just as if they had been suspended on a common conductor. Struck with this promising appearance, he immediately presented his knuckle to the key, and (let the reader judge of the exquisite pleasure he must have felt at that moment) the discovery was complete. He perceived a very evident electric spark.

Others succeeded, even before the string was wet, so as to put the matter past all dispute, and when the rain had wet the string he collected electric fire very copiously. This happened in June 1752, a month after the electricians in France had verified the same theory, but before he heard anything they had done.[7]

"A New Pair of Garters"

Following the 1751 publication of Franklin's scientific writings and d'Alibard's experiment in 1752, the German philosopher Immanuel Kant called Franklin "the Prometheus of modern times."[8] And many other honors and praises poured in from throughout America and Europe. He was awarded honorary graduate degrees by the College of William and Mary in Virginia and by several larger universities: Yale, Harvard, and eventually St. Andrews in Scotland and Oxford in England. "Thus,

7. Reprinted in Van Doren, *Autobiographical Writings,* p. 77.

8. Lopez and Herbert, p. 47. Prometheus was a legendary Greek character who stole fire from heaven as a gift for man.

without studying in any college," he said, "I came to partake of their honors."[9] (This is how he became known as "Doctor Franklin" despite only two years of formal schooling.)

In 1756 he was elected to the Royal Society in London and was presented their gold medal for distinguished accomplishment. Even the king of France sent his "thanks and compliments in an express manner to Mr. Franklin of Pennsylvania . . . for the useful discoveries in electricity." In describing his reaction to all this attention, Franklin compared himself to "a girl who was observed to grow suddenly proud, and none could guess the reason till it came to be known that she had got on a new pair of garters."[10]

Other Contributions to Science

Much of the recognition given to Franklin resulted from his work in electricity, but his studies, experiments, and writings actually contributed to—and sometimes pioneered in—many scientific fields. His broad range of inquiry included meteorology, physiology, medicine, chemistry, mathematics, botany, agriculture, geology, natural history, mechanics, and physics. In addition to those we have already noted, his inventions included bifocals, the flexible catheter, and daylight savings time. He experimented with the influence of color on heat absorption, and with the capacity of various mediums for conducting sound waves. His investigations in evaporative cooling anticipated the principle of electric

---

9. *Autobiography* (1788), p. 209.
10. To Jared Eliot (12 Apr. 1753), Smyth 3:124.

refrigeration. He helped organize the first American expedition to the Arctic under Captain Charles Swaine in 1753, and in his later years he developed a theory on the formation of the earth.

Although Franklin's increasing public responsibilities denied him the time to pursue his many scientific interests as systematically and thoroughly as he would have liked, he continued to study and experiment because he believed that "the quantity of human knowledge bears no proportion to the quantity of human ignorance,"[11] and that new discoveries could significantly improve the human condition. More than twenty years after Franklin's death, Thomas Jefferson wrote that his contributions to science were so highly esteemed throughout the Western world "because he always endeavored to direct [them] to something useful in private life."[12]

---

11. To William Shipley (27 Nov. 1755), Smyth 10:198.

12. Thomas Jefferson to Thomas Cooper (10 July 1812), Albert Ellery Bergh, ed., *The Writings of Thomas Jefferson,* 20 vols. (Washington: The Thomas Jefferson Memorial Association, 1907), 13:177. Jefferson also declared, "In physics ... no one of the present age has made more important discoveries [than Franklin]." *Notes on the State of Virginia* (1782), Bergh 2:94-95.

Chapter 9

Public Improvements and Political Offices

I n the midst of his various scientific pursuits, Franklin
continued to initiate public projects designed to improve the quality of life in Pennsylvania. One of these
was the creation of an academy for educating the young
people of the colony. Having unsuccessfully attempted
such a project six years earlier, he again turned his
attention to this enterprise in 1749.

Origins of the University of Pennsylvania

"The first step I took was to associate in the design a
number of active friends, of whom the Junto furnished a
good part. The next was to write and publish a pamphlet
entitled *Proposals Relating to the Education of Youth in
Pennsylvania*. This I distributed among the principal
inhabitants gratis [free]; and as soon as I could suppose

their minds a little prepared by the perusal of it, I set on foot a subscription for opening and supporting an academy."[1]

The pamphlet proposed that "some persons of leisure and public spirit" incorporate themselves by means of an appropriate charter, and that the members of the corporation "make it their pleasure, and in some degree their business," to

> visit the academy often, encourage and countenance the youth, countenance and assist the masters, and by all means in their power advance the usefulness and reputation of the design; that they look on the students as in some sort their children, treat them with familiarity and affection, and, when they have behaved well and gone through their studies and are to enter the world, zealously unite and make all the interest that can be made to establish them, whether in business, offices, marriages, or any other thing for their advantage.[2]

Then followed detailed recommendations for physical facilities, faculty members, and courses of study; reading, writing, drawing, mathematics, accounting, astronomy, geography, morality, religion, politics, oratory, debate, logic, languages, natural history, agriculture, commerce, and mechanics were some of the headings. The pamphlet's closing lines expressed the hope that this curriculum could help the students obtain "an *inclination* joined with an *ability* to serve mankind, [their] country, friends and family; which ability is (with the blessing of God) to be acquired or

---

1. *Autobiography* (1788), pp. 192-93.

2. *Proposals Relating to the Education of Youth in Pennsylvania* (1749), Smyth 2:389.

greatly increased by *true learning,* and should indeed be the great aim and end of all learning."[3]

These proposals had their intended effect, and Franklin's subsequent subscription efforts were successful. The academy, which eventually became the University of Pennsylvania, opened in January 1751; Franklin served as president for the first five years of its operation. Over thirty years later he wrote, "I have been continued one of its trustees from the beginning . . . and have had the very great pleasure of seeing a number of youth who have received their education in it distinguished by their improved abilities, serviceable in public stations, and ornaments to their country."[4]

Making Life Better in Philadelphia

Franklin's next public project was the Pennsylvania Hospital, which has since been called America's "first medical center."[5] The idea actually originated with Dr. Thomas Bond (one of the original members of the American Philosophical Society), but Franklin was its chief promoter. He remembered Dr. Bond's initial efforts:

> He was zealous and active in endeavoring to procure subscriptions for it; but the proposal being a novelty in America, and at first not well understood, he met with small success. At length he came to me, with the compliment that he found there was no such thing as carrying a public-spirited project through without my being concerned in it. "For," says he, "I am often asked

3. Ibid., p. 396.
4. *Autobiography* (1788), pp. 195-96.
5. Hall, "Benjamin Franklin: Philosopher of Dissent," p. 98.

by those to whom I propose subscribing, Have you consulted Franklin upon this business? And what does he think of it? And when I tell them that I have not (supposing it rather out of your line), they do not subscribe, but say they will consider of it."

I inquired into the nature and probable utility of his scheme, and receiving from him a very satisfactory explanation, I not only subscribed to it myself, but engaged heartily in the design of procuring subscriptions from others. Previously, however, to the solicitation, I endeavored to prepare the minds of the people by writing on the subject in the newspapers, which was my usual custom in such cases, but which he had omitted. [6]

When the hospital opened in 1755, Franklin was elected president of the board of managers.

There were other enterprises as well. In 1752 Franklin helped organize the first fire insurance company in America, the Philadelphia Contributorship for the Insurance of Houses from Loss by Fire. (He served as one of the twelve directors, his newspaper advertised for it, and the partnership of Franklin and Hall printed its insurance policies.) Shortly afterward he urged subscriptions to hire a street sweeper for the Philadelphia marketplace; and in 1757, after he had become a member of the Pennsylvania Assembly, he introduced a bill for paving the streets of the city. "Some may think these trifling matters not worth minding or relating," he wrote.

But when they consider that, though dust blown into the eyes of a single person or into a single shop on a

---

6. *Autobiography* (1788), pp. 199-200.

windy day is but of small importance, yet the great number of the instances in a populous city and its frequent repetitions give it weight and consequence, perhaps they will not censure very severely those who bestow some of attention to affairs of this seemingly low nature. Human felicity is produced not so much by great pieces of good fortune that seldom happen as by little advantages that occur every day. [7]

"The Public . . . Laid Hold of Me for Their Purposes"

Franklin had great plans for the use of his personal time when he retired from the printing trade in 1748. However, he was soon to find out that his life was to take a much different direction than he had envisioned.

> When I disengaged myself . . . from private business, I flattered myself that, by the sufficient though moderate fortune I had acquired, I had secured leisure during the rest of my life for philosophical studies and amusements. . . . But the public, now considering me as a man of leisure, laid hold of me for their purposes, every part of our civil government, and almost at the same time, imposing some duty upon me.

> The Governor put me into the commission of the peace; the corporation of the city chose me of the common council, and soon after an alderman; and the citizens at large chose me a burgess to represent them in the Assembly. This latter station was the more agreeable to me, as I was at length tired with sitting there to hear debates in which as clerk I could take no part . . . and I conceived my becoming a member would enlarge my power of doing good.

7. Ibid., p. 207.

I would not, however, insinuate that my ambition was not flattered by all these promotions. It certainly was. And they were still more pleasing as being so many spontaneous testimonies of the public's good opinion, and by me entirely unsolicited. [8]

He was first elected a member of the Assembly in 1751 (his son William took his place as clerk). "My election to this trust," he later wrote, "was repeated every year for ten years, without my ever asking any elector for his vote or signifying either directly or indirectly any desire of being chosen."[9] He seldom drew much attention to himself on the floor of the Assembly, preferring to use his influence behind the scenes. His astute method for bringing others to his point of view proved very effective in shaping the opinions of his fellow legislators:

I made it a rule to forbear all direct contradiction to the sentiments of others, and all positive assertion of my own. I even forbade myself, agreeable to the old laws of our Junto, the use of every word or expression in the language that imported a fixed opinion, such as *certainly, undoubtedly,* etc., and I adopted instead of them *I conceive, I apprehend,* or *I imagine* a thing to be so or so, or it so appears to me at present.

When another asserted something that I thought an error, I denied myself the pleasure of contradicting him abruptly, and of showing immediately some absurdity in his proposition; and in answering I began by observing that in certain cases or circumstances his opinion would be right, but that in the present case there *appeared* or *seemed* to me some difference, etc.

---

8. Ibid., pp. 196-97.
9. Ibid., p. 197.

I soon found the advantage of this.... The modest way in which I proposed my opinions procured them a readier reception and less contradiction; I had less mortification when I was found to be in the wrong, and I more easily prevailed with others to give up their mistakes and join with me when I happened to be in the right....

To this habit (after my character of integrity) I think it principally owing that I had early so much weight with my fellow citizens when I proposed new institutions, or alterations in the old, and so much influence in public councils when I became a member. For I was but a bad speaker, never eloquent, subject to much hesitation in my choice of words, hardly correct in language, and yet I generally carried my points. [10]

The Frustrations of Public Service

Serving in public office also brought its share of difficulties. According to Daniel Fisher, who once served as Franklin's personal clerk, Deborah Franklin complained in 1755 that "all the world claimed a privilege of troubling her Pappy (so she usually calls Mr. Franklin) with their calamities and distresses." [11] And Franklin himself complained to a friend in the same year:

I am heartily sick of our present situation; I like neither the Governor's conduct nor the Assembly's. And having some share in the confidence of both, I have endeavored to reconcile them, but in vain, and between them they make me very uneasy....

If my being able now and then to influence a good measure did not keep up my spirits, I should be ready to

---

10. Ibid. (1784), pp. 159-60.
11. Quoted in Van Doren, *Benjamin Franklin*, p. 231.

swear never to serve again as an Assemblyman, since both sides expect more from me than they ought, and blame me sometimes for not doing what I am not able to do, as well as for not preventing what was not in my power to prevent. [12]

But because he *was* "able now and then to influence a good measure," he *did* keep up his spirits. And he continued to serve.

_____

12. To Peter Collinson (26 June 1755), Smyth 3:265.

Chapter 10

Franklin's Early Efforts to Forge an American Union

I t was apparently in 1751, the year Franklin was first elected to the Pennsylvania Assembly, that he began to form in his mind the notion of a single American nation—as opposed to the traditional view of the British "plantations" as totally separate entities. The activities of the American Philosophical Society and Franklin's duties as postmaster at Philadelphia may have helped bring him to this new perspective, but it took a crisis to turn his thoughts toward a formal plan for uniting the colonies. That crisis was the Indian problem.

As the eighteenth century progressed, English immigrants to America pushed farther and farther west to claim more farmland and establish new settlements. Increasing numbers of Indian tribes were being displaced or threatened by this process, and their resentment and fear were sometimes vented in violent attacks on the frontier settlers. In early 1751, a member of the Governor's council in New York wrote a pamphlet regarding the importance of friendship with the Indians. Franklin's business partner in New York City, James Parker, was asked to publish the pamphlet; he sent a copy of the manuscript to Franklin for his consideration.

His First Plan for a Union of the Colonies

In his reply, Franklin agreed with the author of the pamphlet and observed that the "surest means" of maintaining the Indians' friendship were to convince them that they would benefit by trading with the English "and to unite the several governments so as to form a strength that the Indians may depend on for protection in case of a rupture with the French, or apprehend great danger from if they should break with us."

> A voluntary union entered into by the colonies themselves, I think, would be preferable to one imposed by Parliament; for it would be perhaps not much more difficult to procure, and more easy to alter and improve as circumstances should require and experience direct....
>
> Were there a general council formed by all the colonies, and a general Governor appointed by the Crown to preside in that council, or in some manner to concur with and confirm their acts and take care of the execution, everything relating to Indian affairs and the defense of the colonies might be properly put under their management. Each colony should be represented [on the basis of its payments] into the common treasury for the common expense....

> Perhaps if the council were to meet successively at the capitals of the several colonies, they might thereby become better acquainted with the circumstances, interests, strength or weakness, etc., of all, and thence be able to judge better of measures proposed from time to time. At least it might be more satisfactory to the colonies if this were proposed as a part of the scheme, for a preference might create jealousy and dislike. [1]

He further suggested that Parker urge the appointment of several influential New Yorkers to be sent "in the nature of ambassadors to the other colonies, where they might apply particularly to all the leading men, and by proper management get them to engage in promoting the scheme." If the endeavor were handled skillfully, said Franklin, "I imagine such a union might thereby be made and established." [2] As it turned out, nothing came of the proposal. But Franklin's thinking on this occasion had laid the groundwork for a more extensive undertaking three years later.

Rattlesnakes for Convicts

Having conceived a union of the American provinces, Franklin now began to look more critically at the relationship between the colonies and the mother country. For some time the English Parliament had been exporting convicted felons to America for "the improvement and well peopling of the colonies." Efforts of the colonial assemblies to prevent or limit this practice were repeatedly rebuffed by Parliament. So in May 1751,

---

1. To James Parker (20 Mar. 1751), Smyth 3:42-43.
2. Ibid., p. 41.

Franklin decided to take aim at the British government with his sharp pen. Writing under the name "Americanus" in the *Pennsylvania Gazette,* he satirically proposed a fitting response to the continuing importation of English criminals:

> Such a tender parental concern in our mother country for the welfare of her children calls aloud for the highest returns of gratitude and duty. . . .
>
> In some of the uninhabited parts of these provinces, there are numbers of these venomous reptiles we call *rattlesnakes*, felons-convict from the beginning of the world. . . . In the spring of the year, when they first creep out of their holes, they are feeble, heavy, slow, and easily taken; and if a small bounty were allowed per head, some thousands might be collected annually and *transported to Britain.*
>
> There I would propose to have them carefully distributed in St. James's Park, in the spring gardens, and other places of pleasure about London; in the gardens of all the nobility and gentry throughout the nation; but particularly in the gardens of the prime ministers, the lords of trade, and members of Parliament, for to them we are most particularly obliged. [3]

Also in 1751, Franklin wrote an impressive paper wherein he objected to an act recently passed by Parliament (at the urging of British ironmasters) to restrict the manufacture of iron in Pennsylvania. "Britain should not too much restrain manufactures in her colonies," he declared. "A wise and good mother will not

---

3. *Pennsylvania Gazette* (9 May 1751), Smyth 3:46-47.

do it. To distress is to weaken, and weakening the children weakens the whole family."[4] In the same paper he noted that the population growth rate in America was much more dynamic than that of England, due to the vast amounts of land available to colonial settlers and their children. He predicted that "our people must at least be doubled every twenty years," and that all of North America would eventually be inhabited.[5] Franklin could foresee the day when the mother country would have to listen more carefully to the economic and political demands of the American people.

Deputy Postmaster General

In August 1753, Franklin took on another responsiblity which further developed his emerging vision of a united America. He was appointed, with William Hunter of Virginia, as Deputy Postmaster General of the American colonies. Up to this time the postal operation had been characterized by debt and inefficiency, but Franklin and Hunter changed that. By demanding prompt and careful accounting from local postmasters and by investing their own money to redesign the system, they not only increased their own salaries but produced the first surplus income the American department had ever earned. In fact, they eventually "brought it to yield *three times* as much clear revenue to the Crown as the post office of Ireland."[6]

Because of Hunter's ill health, Franklin had to assume the principal responsibility for a successful operation, and

---

4. *Observations Concerning the Increase of Mankind, Peopling of Countries, etc.* (1751), Smyth 3:66.

5. Ibid., p. 65.

6. *Autobiography* (1788), p. 208.

he traveled widely throughout the colonies to inspect, audit, and improve the service of local post offices. Theretofore his public duties had kept him in Pennsylvania, but in the four-year period following his 1753 appointment he was away from home a total of fourteen months. The reforms he introduced in the postal system—including such innovations as local home delivery and a "dead letter" office—resulted in a substantial increase of correspondence among the American provinces. It has been said that "no one man before him had ever done so much to draw the scattered colonies together."[7]

"Join, or Die"

The French launched an official expedition in 1753 to build forts along the Ohio River. Recognizing the threat that a French collaboration with the Indian tribes would pose to English settlements, the British Board of Trade instructed several colonial governors in 1754 to appoint commissioners and send them to Albany, New York, for the purpose of treating officially with the chiefs of a confederation of tribes known as the "Six Nations." Franklin, who had already had some experience with the Indians (he had served on a commission in October 1753 to conclude a boundary agreement with the Six Nations), was among the delegates selected in Pennsylvania.

Even before his appointment, he had been deeply concerned about the growing prospects of war. In the May 9, 1754, issue of the *Pennsylvania Gazette* appeared America's first political cartoon, designed and probably drawn by

7. Van Doren, *Benjamin Franklin*, p. 213.

JOIN, or DIE.

America's first political cartoon, designed and probably drawn by Franklin for a 1754 issue of his *Pennsylvania Gazette*. As an effective device for urging the British colonies to unite in a common defense against the French and Indians, it was reprinted in many other newspapers throughout the provinces. The cartoon was used again at the outbreak of the American Revolution twenty years later.

Franklin. It pictured a snake cut into eight segments (labeled with initials representing New England, New York, New Jersey, Pennsylvania, Maryland, Virginia, North Carolina, and South Carolina) and was captioned "Join, or Die." This illustration was accompanied by a comment on the necessity of colonial union:

> The confidence of the French in this undertaking seems well grounded in the present disunited state of the British colonies, and the extreme difficulty of bringing so many different governments and assemblies to agree to any speedy and effectual measures for our

common defense and security, while our enemies have the great advantage of being under one direction, with one council and one purse.[8]

The cartoon was often reprinted in other colonial newspapers that year to urge the idea of American unity against the French. (It would be used again twenty years later, at the outbreak of the American Revolution, to urge unity against the British.)

Franklin worried, not only about disunity among the colonies themselves, but also about the ill feelings which were stirring between the Americans and the mother country as a result of certain acts of Parliament. On May 28 he confided his feelings to a friend in London:

> I am heartily concerned...at the dissensions so unseasonably kindling in the colony assemblies, when unanimity is become more than ever necessary to frustrate the designs of the French. May I presume to whisper my sentiments in a private letter?
>
> Britain and her colonies should be considered as one whole, and not as different states with separate interests. Instructions from the Crown to the colonies should have in view the commonweal of that whole, to which partial interests ought to give way; and they should never aim at extending the prerogative beyond its due bounds, nor abridging the just liberties of the people. In short, they should be plainly just and reasonable, and rather savor of fatherly tenderness and affection than of masterly harshness and severity.[9]

---

8. *Pennsylvania Gazette* (9 May 1754), Van Doren, *Autobiographical Writings,* p. 87 (headnote).

9. To Peter Collinson (28 May 1754), Labaree, Willcox, et al., *The Papers of Benjamin Franklin,* 5:332.

Several years later, after the struggle between the colonists and the British government became the central focus of Franklin's life, these ideas would echo through his correspondence again and again.

The Albany Congress of 1754

On his way to New York, Franklin wrote a paper which he called "Short Hints Towards a Scheme for Uniting the Northern Colonies."[10] It was similar to the proposal he had sent to James Parker in 1751, though some elaboration was now added. Upon reaching New York City, he showed the paper to "two gentlemen of great knowledge in public affairs; and being fortified by their approbation, I ventured to lay it before the congress." After the commissioners assembled in Albany and voted in favor of establishing a union of some kind, he learned that several other delegates (perhaps influenced by Franklin's cartoon) had also come with the same idea and had submitted plans of their own.

> A committee was then appointed, one member from each colony, to consider the several plans and report. Mine happened to be preferred, and with a few amendments was accordingly reported. By this plan, the general government was to be administered by a president-general appointed and supported by the Crown, and a grand council to be chosen by the representatives of the people of the several colonies met in their respective assemblies.
>
> The debates upon it in [the Albany] Congress went on daily, hand in hand with the Indian business. Many objections and difficulties were started, but at length

---

10. Reprinted in Smyth 3:197-99.

they were all overcome and the plan was unanimously agreed to, and copies ordered to be transmitted to the Board of Trade and to the assemblies of the several provinces. [11]

Unfortunately, the Albany Plan of Union was rejected by both sides. "Its fate was singular," wrote Franklin. "The assemblies did not adopt it as they all thought there was too much *prerogative* in it; and in England it was judged to have too much of the *democratic*." Even the Pennsylvania House of Representatives reacted unfavorably. They "took it up when I happened to be absent," he recalled, "which I thought not very fair, and reprobated it without paying any attention to it at all, to my no small mortification." [12] Nor was the Albany Congress any more successful in its primary object: although a general treaty was established renewing the Indians' earlier covenants with the English, no conclusive solution was actually reached.

Franklin's Famous Letters to Governor Shirley

There were many who favored a union of the colonies under some other arrangement. One of these was Governor William Shirley of Massachusetts, who proposed a smaller governing body composed of the royal governors and one or two members of each of their councils—in other words, all officers of the general government would be chosen by the Crown, and none by the American people. Funds for defense of the colonies would be raised through taxes imposed by Parliament.

-----

11. *Autobiography* (1788), p. 210.
12. Ibid., pp. 210, 212.

Franklin discussed this plan with Governor Shirley in December 1754 during a trip to Boston, and later in the month he sent three letters which carefully articulated his objections. These remarkable letters, which have since become valuable historical documents, contained the essential elements of the arguments used by American patriots twenty years later during their bitter struggle for independence. Several excerpts will give an indication of Franklin's deep insight into the fundamental problems besetting Anglo-American relations.

> Excluding the *people* of the colonies from all share in the choice of the grand council will give extreme dissatisfaction, as well as the taxing them by act of Parliament, where they have no representative. [13]

> The people ... will say, and perhaps with justice, that ... it is supposed an undoubted right of Englishmen not to be taxed but by their own consent, given through their representatives.

> That the colonies have no representatives in Parliament.

> That to propose taxing them by Parliament, and refuse them the liberty of choosing a representative council to meet in the colonies and consider and judge of the necessity of any general tax, and the quantum [amount], shows suspicion of their loyalty to the Crown, or of their regard for their country, or of their common sense and understanding, which they have not deserved.

> That compelling the colonies to pay money without their consent would be rather like raising contributions in an enemy's country than taxing of Englishmen for

---

13. To Governor William Shirley (17 Dec. 1754), Smyth 3:231.

their own public benefit.

That it would be treating them as a conquered people, and not as true British subjects. [14]

As we are not suffered to regulate our trade and restrain the importation and consumption of British superfluities... our whole wealth centers finally among the merchants and inhabitants of Britain, and if we make them richer and enable them better to pay taxes, it is nearly the same as being taxed ourselves, and equally beneficial to the Crown....

But to pay immediate heavy taxes, in the laying, appropriation, and disposition of which we have no part... must seem [a] hard measure to Englishmen, who cannot conceive that by hazarding their lives and fortunes in subduing and settling new countries, extending the dominion and increasing the commerce of the mother nation, they have forfeited the native rights of Britons. [15]

Uniting the colonies more intimately with Great Britain by allowing them representatives in Parliament... would be very acceptable to the colonies, provided they had a reasonable number of representatives allowed them, and that all the old acts of Parliament restraining the trade or cramping the manufactures of the colonies be at the same time repealed, and the British subjects on this side [of] the water put, in those respects, on the same footing with those in Great Britain....

Manufacture employs and enriches British subjects, but is it of any importance to the state whether the

---

14. To Governor Shirley (18 Dec. 1754), Smyth 3:232-34.
15. Ibid., pp. 236-37.

manufacturers live at Birmingham or Sheffield, or both, since they are still within its bounds, and their wealth and persons still at its command?

Could the Goodwin Sands be laid dry by banks, and land equal to a large country thereby gained to England and presently filled with English inhabitants, would it be right to deprive such inhabitants of the common privileges enjoyed by other Englishmen, the right of vending their produce in the same ports, or of making their own shoes, because a merchant or a shoemaker, living on the old land, might fancy it more for his advantage to trade or make shoes for them?

Would this be right, even if the land were gained at the expense of the state? And would it not seem less right if the charge and labor of gaining the additional territory to Britain had been borne by the settlers themselves? And would not the hardship appear yet greater if the people of the new country should be allowed no representatives in the Parliament enacting such impositions? [16]

As it turned out, no scheme for colonial union was actually implemented until many years after the Albany Congress. Franklin later reflected, "The different and contrary reasons of dislike to my plan make me suspect that it was really the true medium; and I am still of opinion it would have been happy for both sides [of] the water if it had been adopted."[17]

---

16. To Governor Shirley (22 Dec. 1754), Smyth 3:238, 239-40.

17. *Autobiography* (1788), p. 211.

Chapter 11

The Frontier "General"

While the Albany Congress of 1754 was still in session, a Virginia military force led by twenty-two-year-old Colonel George Washington was forced to surrender Fort Necessity to the French, who had already captured another English stronghold at the forks of the Ohio and had renamed it Fort Duquesne. The French and Indian War (known in Europe as the Seven Years' War) had now begun in earnest.

Quite a few weeks passed before news of the incident reached Benjamin Franklin, but he had known for some time that hostilities were imminent. It was primarily for this reason that he deeply regretted the rejection of his Albany Plan of Union. "The colonies, so united," he believed, "would have been sufficiently strong to have defended themselves; there would have been no need of troops from England."[1]

But troops *were* sent from England—plenty of them. In February 1755, two regiments of British regulars arrived under the command of General Edward Braddock; their assignment was to march over the mountains and recapture Fort Duquesne from the French.

Most of the burden of supplying and transporting Braddock's army fell on Virginia, Maryland, and Pennsylvania. Franklin, acting in his appointed role as "Deputy Postmaster and Manager of All His Majesty's Provinces and Dominions on the Continent of North America,"[2] met with Braddock to confer on the details of these arrangements. He found the general at Frederick, Maryland, "waiting impatiently for the return of those he had sent through the back parts of Maryland and Virginia to collect wagons. I stayed with him several days."

> When I was about to depart, the returns of wagons to be obtained were brought in, by which it appeared that they amounted only to twenty-five, and not all of these were in serviceable condition. The general and all the officers were surprised, declared the expedition was then at an end, being impossible, and exclaimed against the ministers for ignorantly landing them in a country destitute of the means of conveying their stores, baggage, etc., not less than 150 wagons being necessary.
>
> I happened to say I thought it was [a] pity they had not been landed rather in Pennsylvania, as in that country almost every farmer had his wagon. The general eagerly

---

1. *Autobiography* (1788), p. 211.
2. Van Doren, *Benjamin Franklin*, p. 211.

laid hold of my words and said, "Then you, sir, who are a man of interest there, can probably procure them for us; and I beg you will undertake it."[3]

Franklin accordingly circulated an "advertisement" among the Pennsylvania farmers and hired a sufficient number of teams and wagons to transport the troops' supplies overland. He advanced some of his own money to help make the initial rental payments which had been promised; and at the insistence of the farmers, who did not know Braddock, he gave his personal bond to guarantee reparations for any horses or wagons which might be lost in the campaign.

The Tragic Defeat of Braddock's Army

In conversation with General Braddock one day, Franklin cautioned him about a possible ambush by the Indians as the soldiers marched through heavily wooded areas en route to Fort Duquesne. "He smiled at my ignorance and replied, 'These savages may indeed be a formidable enemy to your raw American militia; but upon the King's regular and disciplined troops, sir, it is impossible they should make any impression.' I was conscious of an impropriety in my disputing with a military man in matters of his profession, and said no more."[4]

The general should have listened. During the overland march that summer he failed to provide adequate reconnaissance for his advance, and the British troops fell victims to a surprise attack on July 9, 1755, only nine miles

---

3. *Autobiography* (1788), p. 217.
4. Ibid., p. 224.

from their destination. Braddock was seriously hurt, 63 of his 86 officers were killed or wounded, and 714 of the regular of the total advance force of 1100 lost their lives. Several days later Braddock himself died after uttering the words, "Who'd have thought it?"[5] (The soldiers who were not gunned down fled in panic, leaving the wagons, provisions, artillery, and many of the horses to the enemy. Thus Franklin faced financial ruin because of the bond he had given; but Braddock's successor fortunately ordered reparation payments in October.)

"General" Franklin on the Pennsylvania Frontier

With no British defense force to protect them after Braddock's defeat, the Pennsylvanians were terrified. It was obvious that an armed militia was urgently needed, but there was still official resistance to the idea because of the Quakers' pacifism—the Quakers constituted a majority of the Assembly, though not of the population— and the continuing altercations between the Assembly and the Governor (now Robert Morris). Franklin, after making several preparatory moves to reduce resistance and conciliate differences, introduced a militia bill in the fall of 1755. It passed on November 25, allowing the men of the colony to voluntarily organize into military units and elect their own officers.

Franklin himself was appointed chairman of a seven-man committee to manage the defense funds appropriated by the Assembly. After printing in the *Pennsylvania Gazette* an article explaining the militia plan, he set out for the

---

5. Quoted in ibid., p. 226.

frontier communities with fifty cavalrymen to establish a line of defense against the Indians and the French. Although he carried no military rank at the time, the citizens along the frontier called him "General Franklin."

Following an Indian attack on one of the settlements in January 1756, Franklin was instructed to assume military rule in Northampton County. "I undertook this military business," he wrote, "though I did not conceive myself well qualified for it. [The Governor] gave me a commission with full powers and a parcel of blank commissions for officers, to be given to whom I thought fit. I had but little difficulty in raising men, having soon 560 under my command. My son . . . was my aide-de-camp, and of great use to me."[6]

Appointed by the proprietary Governor in 1756 to assume military command on the Pennsylvania frontier, Franklin supervised the construction of three stockades.

---

6. Ibid., pp. 230-31.

For the next several weeks, Franklin personally supervised 130 soldiers and a company of skilled axemen as they erected three stockades in Northampton County—one of which was named Fort Franklin by the volunteer troops. The "General" at least *pretended* to enjoy life on the frontier, despite his "hard lodging." He wrote his wife several letters thanking her for the "goodies" she occasionally sent to him and the other soldiers.

> We have enjoyed your roast beef, and this day began on the roast veal. All agree that they are both the best that ever were of the kind. Your citizens that have their dinners hot . . . know nothing of good eating. We find it in much greater perfection when the kitchen is fourscore miles from the dining room. [7]

An Embarrassing Incident

Word came in February 1756 that Governor Morris had called an early session of the Assembly and that Franklin was wanted back in Philadelphia. Satisfied with the completion of the three stockades, he turned his commission over to a Colonel Clapham ("a New England officer . . . experienced in Indian war") and returned to Philadelphia with his son William. Soon after their arrival, the officers of the Philadelphia Regiment met and elected Franklin their colonel. The Governor was not inclined to approve this commission, but members of the local militia demonstrated in front of his house and pressured him into it.

On March 17, an incident occurred which caused Colonel Franklin no small embarrassment. It was known that he was leaving for Virginia that morning on postal

---

7. To Deborah Franklin (25 Jan. 1756), Smyth 3:324.

business, and the officers of his regiment "took it into their heads that it would be proper for them to escort me out of town as far as the lower ferry."

> Just as I was getting on horseback they came to my door, between thirty and forty, mounted and all in their uniforms. I had not been previously acquainted with the project, or I should have prevented it ... and I was a good deal chagrined at their appearance, as I could not avoid their accompanying me. What made it worse was that, as soon as we began to move, they drew their swords and rode with them naked all the way.

> Somebody wrote an account of this to the proprietor [of the colony, Thomas Penn], and it gave him great offense. No such honor had been paid him when [he was] in the province, nor to any of his governors; and he said it was only proper to princes of the blood royal, which may be true for aught I know. [8]

Franklin afterward wrote of the incident: "I, who am totally ignorant of military ceremonies, and above all things averse to making show and parade or doing any useless thing that can serve only to excite envy or provoke malice, suffered at the time much more pain than I enjoyed pleasure, and have never since given an opportunity for anything of the sort." [9]

---

8. *Autobiography* (1788), pp. 238-39.
9. To Peter Collinson (5 Nov. 1756), Smyth 3:348.

Chapter 12

First Diplomatic Mission to England

Pennsylvania, being a proprietary rather than a royal colony, was owned by the descendants of its founder, William Penn. Unlike the earlier Penn, however, the current proprietors were not Quakers and did not look on the province as a "holy experiment." They were interested in the profits which came from leases, quit-rents, and land sales.

The Penns Versus the Pennsylvanians

A recurring cause of friction between the Pennsylvania Assembly (elected by the people) and the Governor (appointed by the proprietors) was the fact that the proprietors consistently instructed their governors to veto any appropriation bills which attempted to tax proprietary estates in the colony, as they felt their own

landholdings should be exempt from taxation. The people,
however, and their representatives in the Assembly,
considered this an unfair practice—especially during
periods when all other lands were taxed heavily for
defense spending, as in recent years.

Franklin, who was usually appointed to draft the
Assembly's pointed responses to the Governor's vetoes,
became one of the principal figures in these dissensions.
William Denny, who replaced Robert Morris as Governor
in 1756, sought out Franklin as soon as he arrived in
Philadelphia.

> He took me aside . . . and acquainted me that he had
> been advised by his friends in England to cultivate a
> friendship with me, as one who was capable of giving
> him the best advice and of contributing most effectually
> to the making his administration easy; that he therefore
> desired of all things to have a good understanding with
> me, and he begged me to be assured of his readiness on
> all occasions to render me every service that might be in
> his power.
>
> He said much to me also of the proprietor's good
> dispositions towards the province, and of the advantage
> it might be to us all, and to me in particular, if the
> opposition that had been so long continued to his
> measures were dropped, and harmony restored
> between him and the people, in effecting which it was
> thought no one could be more serviceable than myself,
> and I might depend on adequate acknowledgements and
> recompenses, etc., etc. . . .
>
> My answers were to this purpose, that my
> circumstances, thanks to God, were such as to make
> proprietary favors unnecessary to me, and that being a
> member of the Assembly I could not possibly accept of

any; that, however, I had no personal enmity to the proprietary, and that whenever the public measures he proposed should appear to be for the good of the people, no one should espouse and forward them more zealously than myself. [1]

"Ordered Home to England"

Unfortunately, when Governor Denny "came to do business with the Assembly," it was soon obvious that he was acting on the same unfortunate instructions which had been given to his predecessors, and Franklin "was as active as ever in the opposition." [2] Following several more months of wrangling between the Governor and the Assembly over the raising of defense funds—and after a number of dangerous victories by the Indians and the French—the Assembly resolved in early 1757 to send Franklin to England as a commissioner to argue their cause. "I am ...ordered home to England," he wrote (in those days he considered himself a thorough Briton, as did most of the colonists). [3] He also sent a note to his friend William Strahan, a London printer, to announce his expected arrival a few months later:

> Our Assembly talk of sending me to England speedily. Then look out sharp, and if a fat old fellow should come to your printing house and request a little smouting [part-time work], depend upon it 'tis your affectionate friend and humble servant. [4]

1. *Autobiography* (1788), pp. 246-47.
2. Ibid., p. 247.
3. To William Parsons (22 Feb. 1757), Smyth 3:377.
4. To William Strahan (31 Jan. 1757), Smyth 3:367.

On April 4, 1757, Franklin left Philadelphia with his son William, who had resigned his clerkship in the Assembly. After several idle weeks in New York while they waited for their ship to sail, they finally weighed anchor in mid-June.

During the voyage Franklin composed the preface to *Poor Richard* for 1758, wherein he assembled many of the short maxims inculcating "industry and frugality" which had appeared in earlier issues and "formed [them] into a connected discourse . . . as the harangue of a wise old man to the people attending an auction."[5] Later published separately as *The Way to Wealth*, this brief essay was eventually reprinted over a thousand times and translated into at least fifteen languages. (Ironically, it has branded Franklin with the reputation of a "penny pincher" in many circles today where people are unaware of his lifelong generosity to public and charitable causes.)

The Philosopher Meets the Proprietor

After a near shipwreck as they approached the English coast, the Franklins arrived in London on July 27. They spent the first night with Peter Collinson, the Quaker merchant and scientist with whom Franklin had corresponded for several years. William Strahan, another prominent correspondent who later became printer to the King, visited Collinson's home the next day to meet his distinguished guest; both of the Englishmen were "instantly captivated" by Franklin.[6]

---

5. *Autobiography* (1788), p. 164.
6. Van Doren, *Benjamin Franklin*, p. 272.

The pair from Pennsyl-
vania soon found lodging
in an apartment on Craven
Street, close to Parliament
and the ministerial offices.
William seemed to enjoy
his new surroundings, and
he made arrangements to
continue his study of law
(which he had begun in
Philadelphia under his
father's friend Joseph
Galloway). The elder
Franklin complained of the
polluted air in London:
"The whole town is one
great smoky house and
every street a chimney, the
air full of floating ... coal

No. 7 Craven Street in London,
where Franklin resided during the
many years he represented the American colonies in England.

soot, and you never get a sweet breath of what is pure
without riding some miles for it into the country."[7]

Working through intermediaries, Franklin at length
arranged a meeting with Thomas Penn, proprietor of
Pennsylvania. When the two came face to face to discuss
their differences, the uncomplimentary opinions they had
formed of each other at a distance seemed only to be
confirmed and strengthened. Part of their conversation,
as preserved in the surviving portion of a letter Franklin
wrote several months after the meeting, reveals the difficulty of his assignment in England.

---

7. Van Doren, *Benjamin Franklin,* p. 272.

Thomas Penn, son of William Penn and proprietor of Pennsylvania, with whom Franklin tried to negotiate in London.

"But," says I, "your father's charter expressly says that the Assembly of Pennsylvania shall have all the powers and privileges of an assembly according to the rights of free-born subjects of England, and as is usual in any of the British plantations in America."

"Yes," says he, "but if my father [William Penn] granted privileges he was not by royal charter empowered to grant, nothing can be claimed by such grant."

I said, "Then if your father had no right to grant the privileges he pretended to grant, and published all over Europe as granted, those who came to settle in the province on the faith of that grant, and in expectation of enjoying the privileges contained in it, were cheated, deceived, and betrayed."

He answered that they should have themselves looked to that; that the royal charter was no secret; they who came into the province on his father's offer of privileges, if they were deceived, it was their own fault. And that he said with a kind of triumphing, laughing insolence, such as a low jockey might do when a purchaser complained that he had cheated him on a horse. I was astonished to see him thus meanly give up his father's character, and conceived at that moment a more cordial and thorough contempt for him than I ever felt for any man living. [8]

8. To [Isaac Norris] (14 Jan. 1758), Labaree, Willcox, et al., *The Papers of Benjamin Franklin*, 7:361-62.

Homesickness

Franklin first expected to complete his business in London within a single summer, then a year, then two years. But he was absent from his home and family over five years before he returned to Philadelphia in 1762. During this period he wrote often to his wife, many times expressing how much he missed her. The salutation was always "My dear child" or "My dear Debby," and he usually closed with the words "your affectionate husband" or "your ever loving husband." In one of these letters he wrote:

> You may think, perhaps, that I can find many amusements here to pass the time agreeably. 'Tis true, the regard and friendship I meet with from persons of worth, and the conversation of ingenious men, give me no small pleasure; but at this time of life, domestic comforts afford the most solid satisfaction, and my uneasiness at being absent from my family, and longing desire to be with them, make me often sigh in the midst of cheerful company. [9]

On another occasion, in keeping with his habit of sending gifts from England to family members, he shipped Deborah a large jug for beer because its shape reminded him happily of her! "I have a thousand times wished you with me," he told her. [10] And he even persuaded his friend Strahan to write Mrs. Franklin a letter urging her to come to London. But she was terrified of the water, and

---

9. To Deborah Franklin (21 Jan. 1758), Smyth 3:430.
10. To Deborah Franklin (19 Feb. 1758), Smyth 3:435.

Franklin was sure she would never cross the ocean under any circumstances.

A Visit to Scotland

In February 1759, the University of St. Andrews in Scotland awarded Franklin an honorary Doctor of Laws degree; thereafter his friends called him "Doctor Franklin." In August of that year, he left with William for a tour of northern England and Scotland. Franklin thoroughly enjoyed himself there, meeting and dining with a number of Scottish intellectuals, including David Hume, Adam Smith, and Henry Home of Kames.

With Lord Kames in particular he established a warm and enduring friendship. After returning to London in October, Franklin wrote to this renowned judge and author that he considered the time he had spent in Scotland "six weeks of the *densest* happiness I have met with in any part of my life." In the same letter he shared his views regarding the recent favorable turns in the ongoing war between French and English forces in North America:

> No one can more sincerely rejoice than I do on the reduction of Canada; and this is not merely as I am a colonist, but as I am a Briton. I have long been of opinion that the *foundations of the future grandeur and stability of the British empire lie in America;* and though, like other foundations, they are low and little seen, they are nevertheless broad and strong enough to support the greatest political structure human wisdom ever yet erected.
>
> I am therefore by no means for restoring Canada. If we keep it, all the country from the St. Lawrence to the

Mississippi will in another century be filled with British people. Britain itself will become vastly more populous by the immense increase of its commerce; the Atlantic sea will be covered with your trading ships; and your naval power, thence continually increasing, will extend your influence round the whole globe and awe the world!

If the French remain in Canada, they will continually harass our colonies by the Indians and impede if not prevent their growth; your progress to greatness will at best be slow, and give room for many accidents that may forever prevent it. [11]

In much of his future correspondence, Franklin would repeat this call for private and public recognition of America's important place in the empire—until the year 1775, when it finally became clear that Englishmen across the Atlantic would have to seek another solution to their ill treatment from the Crown.

Triumph for the Pennsylvania Assembly

Meanwhile, Franklin continued to fight for his countrymen's right to tax the proprietary estates along with their own. It was not a simple task. "You may conjecture," he wrote the speaker of the Pennsylvania Assembly, "what reception a petition concerning

---

11. To Lord Kames (3 Jan. 1760), Smyth 4:4. Three months later Franklin published a pamphlet entitled *The Interest of Great Britain Considered with Regard to Her Colonies and the Acquisitions of Canada and Guadaloupe* (Smyth 4:32-82), which some have credited with an important influence on the British government's decision to retain Canada as part of the empire in the 1763 Treaty of Paris.

privileges from the colonies may meet with from those who think that even the people of England have too many."[12]

But he pushed ahead, often using the British press for the purpose of "removing the prejudices that art and accident have spread among the people of this country against us, and obtaining for us the good opinion of the bulk of mankind."[13] In 1759 he arranged and paid for the publication of a book entitled *An Historical Review of the Constitution and Government of Pennsylvania*. He wrote many letters for the British newspapers, almost always employing a fictitious name to hide his identity or arouse curiosity. (Including his second mission to England from 1764 to 1775, he used at least forty-two pseudonyms in ninety or more items placed in the English papers.)[14]

Because of these and other activities, Thomas Penn developed a great animosity toward the Pennsylvania agent. "When I meet him anywhere," wrote Franklin, "there appears in his wretched countenance a strange mixture of hatred, anger, fear, and vexation."[15] But Penn was not able to prevent the ultimate triumph of Franklin's cause. In August 1760, Franklin and his attorneys were summoned to a meeting of the Privy Council's Committee for Plantation Affairs. They were asked to defend a bill passed by the Pennsylvania Assembly the previous year

12. To Isaac Norris (19 Mar. 1759), in Van Doren, *Benjamin Franklin*, p. 283.

13. To the speaker and committee of the Pennsylvania Assembly (10 June 1758), Smyth 3:445.

14. Verner W. Crane, ed., *Benjamin Franklin's Letters to the Press, 1758-1775* (Chapel Hill: The University of North Carolina Press, 1950), p. xxix.

15. To Isaac Norris (9 June 1759), in Van Doren, *Benjamin Franklin*, p. 285.

which levied taxes on the proprietors' lands. (Many such bills had been passed before, but this was the first to escape Governor Denny's veto due to the pressing need for defense funds. All bills signed by the Governor were forwarded to England for royal assent.) Penn's attorneys were also called to the meeting to argue against the bill. Upon hearing both sides of the issue, and after accepting a minor amendment offered by Franklin on behalf of the Assembly, the committee voted to recommend the bill to the King for passage. Final approval was granted four days later, and the principle had been won.

Sightseeing and Science

Franklin remained in London for two more years at the request of the Pennsylvania Assembly. During these two years he continued his political activities in matters which concerned the province, but he also found more time for travel and for scientific pursuits. Soon after the meeting with the Privy Council committee, he and William visited Coventry, Cheshire, Wales, Bristol, and Bath. In 1761 they journeyed to Flanders and Holland, enjoying the beautiful sights and meeting with several men of science; they returned to London in time to attend the coronation ceremonies for King George III on September 22. [16]

For several months, Franklin was able to renew some of the experiments he had begun in Philadelphia after his retirement from business. He furthered his investigations into electricity, evaporation, and other areas of interest,

---

16. Franklin repeatedly expressed a high regard for the new English monarch during the early years of his reign. As late as 1768 he spoke of George III as "the best King any nation was ever blessed with." Letter to John Ross (14 May 1768), Smyth 5:133.

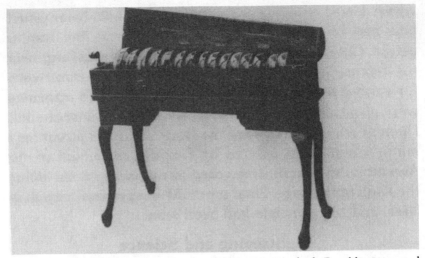

The "armonica," an unusual musical instrument which Franklin invented while in England. It was popular throughout Europe for nearly forty years, and both Mozart and Beethoven composed pieces for this instrument. In addition to the armonica, Franklin played the harp, the violin, and the guitar.

always comparing notes with his scientific correspondents. He developed ideas for another fireplace by experimenting in his London apartment.

Sometime during this period he also invented an unusual musical instrument which he called the "armonica." It was a long, wooden case containing a series of glass hemispheres which were mounted on an axle that could be turned with a foot pedal. These glass bowls were blown and ground to produce thirty-seven separate tones, which Franklin called "incomparably sweet beyond those of any other [instrument]."[17] A performer played the armonica by sitting in front of the open case and pressing his moistened fingers against the revolving edges of the glasses.

17. To Giambatista Beccaria (13 July 1762), Smyth 4:168.

Copies of the armonica were manufactured, sold, and later played at public recitals in Italy, Austria, Germany, and America. Both Mozart and Beethoven composed pieces for this novel instrument, which was quite popular throughout Europe for almost forty years. Franklin himself brought one home to Philadelphia, where he played duets with his daughter Sally as she performed on the harpsichord he had sent her from England.

In April 1762 Franklin was awarded another honorary degree by Oxford University. As his reputation increased, so did the admiration of other learned men of his time. Several weeks before he left England, the Scottish historian and philosopher David Hume wrote to him: "I am very sorry that you intend soon to leave our hemisphere. America has sent us many good things, gold, silver, sugar, tobacco, indigo, etc.; but you are the first philosopher, and indeed the first great man of letters for whom we are beholden to her."[18]

"I Must Go Home"

By July of 1762, Franklin could no longer bear being away from his wife and his home. "I feel here like a thing out of its place," he told his friend William Strahan, "and useless because it is out of its place. How then can I any longer be happy in England?...I must go home."[19] Deborah was just as eager for his return. After learning that he was soon to be on his way, she recorded in her household account book a purchase of "goodies for my Pappy, 2 jars."[20]

---

18. David Hume to BF (10 May 1762), in Smyth 4:154.
19. To William Strahan (20 July 1762), Smyth 4:172.
20. Account of expenses (1762), Labaree, Willcox, et al., 10:101.

But despite his longing for this joyous reunion, he still had mixed feelings about leaving England. The week before his departure he confided to Lord Kames:

> I ... cannot leave this happy island and my friends in it without extreme regret, though I am going to a country and a people that I love. I am going from the old world to the new; and I fancy I feel like those who are leaving this world for the next: grief at the parting; fear of the passage; hope of the future.[21]

Indeed, he secretly hoped he could eventually return to London with his wife and daughter. "Let me find you well and happy," he wrote Strahan, "when I come again to England, happy England! ... In two years at farthest I hope to settle all my affairs in such a manner as that I *may* then conveniently remove to England—provided we can persuade the good woman to cross the seas. That will be the great difficulty."[22] (It proved to be an even greater difficulty than Franklin anticipated. He did return to England two years later, but not with Deborah or Sally.)

William Stays Behind to Marry

When Franklin sailed in late August, his son was not with him. Upon completing his legal studies and being admitted to the English bar in 1758, William had written to his father: "I am extremely obliged to you for your care in supplying me with money, and shall ever have a grateful sense of that with the other numberless indulgencies I have received from your paternal affection. I shall be

---

21. To Lord Kames (17 Aug. 1762), Smyth 4:174.
22. To William Strahan (7 Dec. 1762), Smyth 4:182.

ready to return to America, or to go [to] any other part of the world, whenever you think it necessary."[23] But when the time came, he was not ready. On September 4, 1762, he married a young woman named Elizabeth Downes, and five days later he was commissioned royal Governor of New Jersey (friends of the elder Franklin had apparently helped secure this appointment). William and his bride would return to America early the next year so that he could assume his new post.

---

23. William Franklin to BF (3 Sept. 1758), in Labaree, Willcox, et al., 8:132.

Chapter 13

A Brief Philadelphia Interlude

I got home well the 1st of November," Franklin wrote a month after his return voyage from England, "and had the happiness to find my little family perfectly well."

My house has been full of a succession of [friends] from morning to night, ever since my arrival, congratulating me on my return with the utmost cordiality and affection. My fellow citizens, while I was on the sea, had at the annual election chosen me unanimously, as they had done every year while I was in England, to be their representative in Assembly, and would, they say, if I had not disappointed them by coming privately to town before they heard of my landing, have met me with five hundred horses.[1]

---

1. To William Strahan (2 Dec. 1762), Smyth 4:179.

This was the first Christmas season he had spent with his wife and daughter in six years, and he was delighted to be home again. Sally, he said, had "grown quite a woman, with many amiable accomplishments acquired in my absence."² He seldom left his family that winter except to attend sessions of the Assembly. Soon after the year 1763 opened, the Franklins began building a new three-story brick house on Market Street, just a few steps from the spot where Deborah first saw the runaway boy from Boston almost forty years earlier. (Construction progressed slowly, however, thanks to Franklin's many public responsibilities; Deborah and Sally were not able to move in until May 1765, several months after he left again for England.)

Following a perilous three-month voyage across the Atlantic, William and his wife reached Philadelphia in February. Elizabeth stayed with her mother-in-law to recover while the elder Franklin accompanied his son to New Jersey for the swearing-in ceremonies. Then the proud father remained a few weeks longer to journey with the new Governor through the province, where he "had the pleasure of seeing him [William] received everywhere with the utmost respect and even affection of all ranks of people."³

Postal Duties and the Paxton Boys

By April 1763, Franklin was away from his family again on public business. In his role as Deputy Postmaster General, he spent about six weeks inspecting post offices

---

2. To Lord Kames (2 June 1765), Smyth 4:374.
3. To William Strahan (28 Mar. 1763), Smyth 4:197.

in the southern colonies. Shortly after his return, he left again for a 1,780-mile postal inspection tour of New Jersey, New York, and New England; this time he was joined by Sally.

As Canada had recently been ceded to Great Britain by the Treaty of Paris, it now became Franklin's duty to extend postal services even farther northward by hiring mail carriers to ride day and night. He suffered two falls from his horse during this five-month journey through the northern provinces, on one occasion dislocating his shoulder in Rhode Island, so he was grateful to have Sally by his side to help nurse him back to health.

When he returned to Philadelphia in November, a crisis was brewing. Indian uprisings along the western frontier had inflamed many of the Pennsylvania farmers, and in December a mob calling themselves the "Paxton Boys" attacked and massacred a group of friendly Conestoga Indians living peaceably in Lancaster County. In January 1764 Franklin wrote and published a pamphlet denouncing this cruel and barbarous act and calling for justice, hoping thereby to restore reason to the province and turn public favor against the mob.[4] Soon thereafter he initiated the formation of another volunteer militia to defend Philadelphia against the Paxton Boys, who had vowed to attack a group of peaceful Indians being protected there.

Nearly a thousand inhabitants of Philadelphia had taken up arms by February 3. On that day the rioters reached

4. *A Narrative of the Late Massacres in Lancaster County* (Jan. 1764), Smyth 4:289-314.

Germantown, about eight miles out of the city, and Franklin reported that the "proprietary Governor did me the honor, in an alarm, to run to my house at midnight, with his counsellors at his heels, for advice, and made it his headquarters for some time."[5] After a few hours the Governor asked Franklin and three others to ride out to Germantown to meet the Paxton Boys. Their dangerous mission was successful: "The fighting face we put on and the reasonings we used with the insurgents...turned them back and restored quiet to the city."[6]

Writing to one of his correspondents in England, Franklin summed up the entire episode: "Within four and twenty hours, your old friend was a common soldier, a counsellor, a kind of dictator, and an ambassador to the country mob, and on his returning home, nobody again."[7]

Growing Opposition to the Proprietary Government

Although the Assembly was no longer prevented from taxing the proprietary estates in Pennsylvania, friction between them and the Governor continued to mount. The deplorable conduct of the current Governor—John Penn, the nephew of the proprietor himself—finally brought the issue to a head. His arbitrary vetoes and insulting messages to the Assembly threw "him and his government into sudden contempt," wrote Franklin. "All regard for him in the Assembly is lost. All hopes of happiness under a proprietary government are at an end."[8]

---

5. To John Fothergill, M.D. (14 Mar. 1764), Smyth 4:223.

6. To Lord Kames (2 June 1765), Smyth 4:376.

7. To John Fothergill, M.D. (14 Mar. 1764), Smyth 4:223.

8. Ibid., p. 224.

On March 24, 1764, the Assembly adjourned in order to consult with their constituents and learn how much popular support could be expected for a petition requesting King George III to end the proprietary government there and make Pennsylvania a royal colony. At about the same time Franklin wrote a pamphlet entitled *Cool Thoughts on the Present Situation of Our Public Affairs,* urging that the King assume the government of the province. It was published and distributed throughout Philadelphia on April 12. [9]

Ousted from Office, Then Sent Back to England

The legislators met again on May 26 and unanimously elected Franklin to succeed Isaac Norris as speaker of the Pennsylvania Assembly. His first act as speaker was to sign the controversial petition to George III. Arguments were heated on both sides of this issue (the opposition was led by a member named John Dickinson), and Franklin was vilely attacked in pamphlets and newspapers for his role in the matter. When he ran for his seat in the Assembly again that summer, the Proprietary party conducted a vehement campaign against him, printing charges that his son William was illegitimate and introducing other ugly accusations. In September he wrote to an English friend, "At present I am here as much the butt of party rage and malice, expressed in pamphlets and prints, and have as many pelted at my head in proportion, as if I had the misfortune of being your Prime Minister."[10]

9. Reprinted in Smyth 4:226-41.

10. To William Strahan (1 Sept. 1764), Labaree, Willcox, et al., *The Papers of Benjamin Franklin,* 11:332.

When the polls closed on October 1, Franklin had lost the election by twenty-five votes out of four thousand. But those who held his views still commanded a majority in the Assembly, and on October 26 they resolved to send him back to England to present their petition to the King. After quick preparations, he sailed on November 9. He was alone once more for the voyage, as Deborah refused to accompany him or to let Sally go either. Little did he know that he would be gone nearly eleven years this time, and that his dear wife would not live to see him come home again.

Chapter 14

In England Again: Fighting the Stamp Act

After a swift but stormy thirty-day passage, Franklin reached London on December 10, 1764. He set himself to work immediately on his assignment, maneuvering again through the press and through some of his contacts in the royal government. He had high hopes for success; just two months after his arrival he wrote to his wife, "A few months, I hope, will finish affairs here to my wish, and bring me to that retirement and repose with my little family so suitable to my years, and which I have so long set my heart upon."[1]

---

1. To Deborah Franklin (14 Feb. 1765), Smyth 4:360-61. Deborah did not receive any of her husband's correspondence from England until five months after his departure. When his first letter finally arrived in Philadelphia, she wrote back on April 7, "O my dear, how happy am I to hear that you are safe and well." Labaree, Willcox, et al., *The Papers of Benjamin Franklin*, 12:102.

But he was to be disappointed in these expectations, as George III's Privy Council were unwilling to act on the Pennsylvania Assembly's petition to dissolve the proprietary government in the colony. They took the position that it would be improper for the King to come between the proprietors and the people in their dispute. Even though Franklin continued to work toward his object for several more years, the matter was never actually resolved until the American colonies separated themselves from Great Britain altogether in 1776. In the meantime, an issue of even larger significance suddenly overshadowed Franklin's original mission.

Franklin's Efforts to Prevent the Stamp Act

British taxes had risen sharply as a result of the recent Seven Years' War. As early as March 1764, some of the King's ministers had devised a plan to raise revenue among the American colonists in order to alleviate this burden. They proposed that the Americans be required to purchase government-issued stamps to be placed on all legal documents, newspapers, pamphlets, almanacs, advertisements, and many other articles which were sold or distributed within the colonies. When Franklin learned of this plan, he knew his countrymen would object to it as a tax levied directly by Parliament, in which they had no representation. (Up to this time, the colonial assemblies had voted their own taxes to provide revenues specifically requested by the Crown.) He therefore decided to do whatever he could to prevent the implementation of this ill-fated scheme.

In February 1765 he met with the minister of finance, George Grenville, and tried to dissuade him from submitting the stamp proposal to Parliament. He recommended instead that revenue be raised from the colonies in the "usual constitutional way."[2] Failing in this effort, he collaborated with Thomas Pownall, former royal Governor of Massachusetts, in proposing an alternate plan. But Grenville would not be diverted. "I took every step in my power to prevent the passing of the Stamp Act," said Franklin. "But . . . we might as well have hindered the sun's setting."[3] The bill was brought before the House of Commons and passed on February 13.

False Charges and Dire Threats

American resistance to the Stamp Act was even greater than Franklin had expected. Besides forming the Stamp Act Congress in May 1765, the colonists had engaged in rioting, smuggling, and boycotts of some British goods. The stamps themselves were generally ignored, and many of the officers appointed to enforce the act resigned under threats on their lives. Franklin was amazed at "the rashness of the assembly in Virginia," which had approved Patrick Henry's inflammatory resolutions against British oppression. "I hope, however, that ours will keep within the bounds of prudence and moderation," he wrote to a friend in Pennsylvania, "for that is the only way to lighten or get clear of our burdens."

A firm loyalty to the Crown and faithful adherence to the government of this nation, which it is the safety as well as honor of the colonies to be connected with, will always be the wisest course for you and I to take,

---

2. Quoted in Van Doren, *Benjamin Franklin,* p. 320.
3. To Charles Thomson (11 July 1765), Smyth 4:390.

whatever may be the madness of the populace or their
blind leaders, who can only bring themselves and
country into trouble and draw on greater burdens by
acts of rebellious tendency. [4]

Because he spoke for moderation, Franklin was accused
by his political foes in Philadelphia of having urged the
passage of the Stamp Act, or at least having favored it, in
order to secure some profitable government post. Some
even charged that he had drafted the bill himself! During
the summer of 1765, a group of citizens who had been
influenced by this propaganda threatened to burn the
newly completed Franklin home on Market Street.
William, now in his third year as Governor of the
neighboring province, tried to bring his mother to New
Jersey for protection, but Deborah refused to budge. She
invited two of her male relatives to move in temporarily—
and to bring guns with them. "We made one room into a
magazine," she explained in a letter to her husband. "I
ordered some sort of defense upstairs, such as I could
manage myself."[5] The rioters soon lost their bravado and
decided it would be unwise to tangle with Mrs. Franklin.

After learning of this incident, Franklin wrote his wife
that he was proud of her spunk. "I honor much the spirit
and courage you showed, and the prudent preparations
you made in that time of danger," he told her. "The
woman deserves a good house that is determined to
defend it."[6] He also reacted characteristically to the

---

4. To John Hughes (9 Aug. 1765), Smyth 4:392.

5. Deborah Franklin to BF (22 Sept. 1765), in Labaree, Willcox, et al.,
12:271.

6. To Deborah Franklin (9 Nov. 1765), Labaree, Willcox, et al., 12:360.

unkind accusations of his political enemies, as shown in a letter to Joseph Galloway, a close associate in the Pennsylvania Assembly who had also been implicated:

> I received . . . a copy of that lying essay in which I am represented as the author of the Stamp Act, and you as concerned in it. . . . Your consolation, my friend, and mine, under these abuses must be that we do not deserve them. . . . Let us, as we ever have done, uniformly endeavor the service of our country according to the best of our judgment and abilities, and time will do us justice. Dirt thrown on a mud wall may stick and incorporate, but it will not long adhere to polished marble. [7]

"In a Continual Hurry from Morning to Night"

Rather than sulking over the lack of appreciation back home for his attempts to prevent the Stamp Act, Franklin redoubled his efforts and launched a battle to bring about its repeal. "Besides opposing the act before it was made, I never in my life labored any point more heartily than I did that of obtaining the repeal," he wrote. [8] He also recorded, "I was extremely busy attending members of both houses [of Parliament], informing, explaining, consulting, disputing, in a continual hurry from morning to night." [9]

The infamous act, which Franklin came to call the "mother of mischief," [10] had formally gone into operation on November 1, 1765, and it was immediately apparent

---

7. To Joseph Galloway (8 Nov. 1766), Van Doren, *Autobiographical Writings*, p. 157.

8. To Daniel Wister (27 Sept. 1766), Labaree, Willcox, et al., 13:429.

9. To Lord Kames (11 Apr. 1767), Smyth 5:16.

10. To Jonathan Williams (28 Apr. 1766), Smyth 4:454.

that the British government had made a mistake. The money lost in trade through American boycotts of English goods was far greater than the revenues that would have been gained had the colonists been willing to purchase the stamps. By December 4 a group of English merchants who had been trading with the Americans gathered in a London tavern and drew up petitions for the removal of the Stamp Act. They also sent a series of witnesses to testify to the House of Commons regarding the ill effects of this law. Parliament fiercely debated a motion for repeal throughout December and January.

Franklin returned to his use of the British newspapers in early 1766 to increase public awareness of the American position. Among the items he caused to be printed were his 1754 letters to Governor William Shirley, which demonstrated that the colonists' resistance to taxation without representation was deeply rooted.

Franklin's Famous Examination Before Parliament

As the debate over a repeal of the Stamp Act proceeded, the House of Commons ordered several persons who were considered experts on American affairs to appear and testify on the matter. It was inevitable that one of these witnesses would be Benjamin Franklin. The following excerpts are taken from his testimony, given on February 13 in response to questions put by various members of Parliament:

Q. Don't you know that the money arising from the stamps was all to be laid out in America?

A. I know it is appropriated by the act to the American service; but it will be spent in the conquered colonies, where the soldiers are, not in the colonies that pay it.

Q. Do you think it right that America should be protected by this country and pay no part of the expense?

A. That is not the case. The colonies raised, clothed, and paid during the last war near 25,000 men, and spent many millions.

Q. Do not you think the people of America would submit to pay the stamp duty if it were moderated?

A. No, never, unless compelled by force of arms.

Q. What was the temper of America towards Great Britain before the year 1763?

A. The best in the world. They submitted willingly to the government of the Crown and paid, in all their courts, obedience to acts of Parliament. Numerous as the people are in the several provinces, they cost you nothing in forts, citadels, garrisons, or armies to keep them in subjection. They were governed by this country at the expense of only a little pen, ink, and paper. They were led by a thread. They had not only a respect but an affection for Great Britain, for its laws, its customs and manners, and even a fondness for its fashions that greatly increased the commerce. Natives of Britain were always treated with particular regard; to be an Old England man was, of itself, a character of some respect and gave a kind of rank among us.

Q. And what is their temper now?

A. Oh, very much altered.

Q. Don't you think they would submit to the Stamp Act if it were modified, the obnoxious parts taken out and the duty reduced to some partuculars of small moment?

A. No; they will never submit to it.

Q. What is your opinion of a future tax imposed on the same principle with that of the Stamp Act? How would the Americans receive it?

A. Just as they do this. They would not pay it.

Q. Have you not heard of the resolutions of this house and of the House of Lords, asserting the right of Parliament relating to America, including a power to tax the people there?

A. Yes, I have heard of such resolutions.

Q. What will be the opinion of the Americans on those resolutions?

A. They will think them unconstitutional and unjust.

Q. Was it an opinion in America before 1763 that the Parliament had no right to lay taxes and duties there?

A. I never heard any objection to the right of laying duties to regulate commerce; but a right to lay internal taxes was never supposed to be in Parliament, as we are not represented there.

Q. But who is to judge of that, Britain or the colony?

A. Those that feel can best judge.

Q. You say the colonies have always submitted to external taxes, and object to the right of Parliament only in laying internal taxes; now can you show that there is any kind of difference between the two taxes to the colony on which they may be laid?

A. I think the difference is very great. An external tax is a duty laid on commodities imported; that duty is added to the first cost and other charges on the commodity and, when it is offered to sale, makes a part of the price. If the people do not like it at that price, they refuse it; they are not obliged to pay it. But an internal tax is forced from the people without consent if not laid by their own representatives. The Stamp Act says we shall have no commerce, make no exchange of property with each other, neither purchase, nor grant, nor recover debts; we shall neither marry nor make our wills, unless we pay such and such sums; and thus it is intended to extort our money from us, or ruin us by the consequences of refusing to pay it.

Q. Can anything less than a military force carry the Stamp Act into execution?

A. I do not see how a military force can be applied to that purpose.

Q. Why may it not?

A. Suppose a military force sent into America, they will find nobody in arms; what are they then to do? They cannot force a man to take stamps who chooses to do without them. They will not find a rebellion; they may indeed make one.

Q. If the act is not repealed, what do you think will be the consequences?

A. A total loss of the respect and affection the people of America bear to this country, and of all the commerce that depends on that respect and affection.

Q. How can the commerce be affected?

A. You will find that if the act is not repealed, they will take very little of your manufactures in a short time.

Q. Is it in their power to do without them?

A. I think they may very well do without them.

Q. Is it their interest not to take them?

A. The goods they take from Britain are either necessaries, mere conveniences, or superfluities. The first, as cloth, etc., with a little industry they can make at

Franklin being questioned before the British House of Commons in February 1766 regarding the effects of the Stamp Act in the colonies. The notorious law was repealed several days later, and when this examination was published it made Franklin a hero throughout America.

home; the second they can do without till they are able to provide them among themselves; and the last, which are much the greatest part, they will strike off immediately. They are mere articles of fashion, purchased and consumed because the fashion in a respected country, but will now be detested and rejected.

Q. Then no regulation with a tax would be submitted to?

A. Their opinion is that when aids to the Crown are wanted, they are to be asked of the several assemblies, according to the old established usage; who will, as they always have done, grant them freely. And that their money ought not to be given away without their consent by persons at a distance, unacquainted with their circumstances and abilities. The granting aids to the Crown is the only means they have of recommending themselves to their sovereign; and they think it extremely hard and unjust that a body of men in which they have no representatives should make a merit to itself of giving and granting what is not its own, but theirs, and deprive them of a right they esteem of the utmost value and importance, as it is the security of all their other rights.

Q. If the Stamp Act should be repealed, would not the Americans think they could oblige the Parliament to repeal every external tax law now in force?

A. It is hard to answer questions of what people at such a distance will think.

Q. But what do you imagine they will think were the motives of repealing the act?

A. I suppose they will think that it was repealed from a conviction of its inexpediency; and they will rely upon it that while the same inexpediency subsists, you will never attempt to make such another....

As to an internal tax, how small soever, laid by the legislature here on the people there while they have no representatives in this legislature, I think it will never be submitted to. They will oppose it to the last. They do not consider it as at all necessary for you to raise money on them by your taxes because they are, and always have been, ready to raise money by taxes among themselves and to grant large sums, equal to their abilities, upon requisition from the Crown. They have not only granted equal to their abilities, but during all the last war they granted far beyond their abilities, and beyond their proportion with this country (you yourselves being judges), to the amount of many hundred thousand pounds; and this they did freely and readily.

Q. But suppose Great Britain should be engaged in a war in Europe; would North America contribute to the support of it?

A. I do think they would as far as their circumstances would permit. They consider themselves as a part of the British empire, and as having one common interest with it; they may be looked on here as foreigners, but they do not consider themselves as such. They are zealous for the honor and prosperity of this nation and, while they are well used, will always be ready to support it as far as their little power goes.

Q. Would the repeal of the Stamp Act be any discouragement of your manufactures? Will the people that have begun to manufacture decline it?

A. Yes, I think they will.

Q. If the Stamp Act should be repealed, would it induce the assemblies of America to acknowledge the rights of Parliament to tax them, and would they erase their resolutions?

A. No, never.

Q. Are there no means of obliging them to erase those resolutions?

A. None that I know of; they will never do it unless compelled by force of arms.

Q. Is there a power on earth that can force them to erase them?

A. No power, how great soever, can force men to change their opinions.[11]

---

11. "The Examination of Doctor Benjamin Franklin in the British House of Commons Relative to the Repeal of the American Stamp Act" (13 Feb. 1766), Smyth 4:412-48. Before he was called into the witness chair, Franklin humorously suggested to one of the members of the House of Commons a modification of the Stamp Act which would quiet the Americans and yet

A Hero Among the Colonists

Franklin answered a great many more questions, surprising and deeply impressing the British lawmakers with his wealth of detailed knowledge about conditions in the American provinces. Eight days after his testimony, the House of Commons passed the motion to repeal the Stamp Act; within three more weeks the bill was carried through the House of Lords and received the assent of King George III.

Although much of the credit for this welcome reversal belongs to the Stamp Act Congress in New York, and to the pressures brought by the many English businessmen who had joined in support of the American opposition, there is no doubt that Franklin's testimony exerted a significant influence on Parliament's decision to rescind the hated law. The "Examination of Doctor Franklin" was published in London, Boston, New York City, Philadelphia, and Williamsburg, and was read widely throughout the provinces (it was also translated and published in German and French). Amid the many celebrations marking the repeal of the Stamp Act and the end of the colonial embargo, Franklin was lavishly honored as a great American hero.

---

permit it to be retained as a law, thus "saving the honor . . . of Parliament." He proposed an amendment changing its effective date from November 1, 1765, to November 1, *2765!* Smyth 10:231.

Chapter 15

Reflections and Travels in Europe

L ike other Americans, Franklin was relieved at the repeal of the Stamp Act in 1766. But the incident had caused him to reevaluate some of his earlier views on the relationship between the colonies and the royal government. Despite his long-standing enthusiasm for America's role in a growing British empire, he could see signs of a widening breach. He still favored "a union in Parliament between the two countries," but he now predicted that "it will never be done.... The Parliament here do at present think too highly of themselves to admit representatives from us, if we should ask it; and when they will be desirous of granting it, we shall think too highly of ourselves to accept of it."[1]

---

1. To Cadwallader Evans (9 May 1766), Smyth 4:456.

"A Total Separation...Will Be
the Final Consequence"

He was seriously concerned about the increasing abusiveness of the government toward the American provinces. To ease the humiliation of revoking the Stamp Act, Parliament had passed another law during the same session claiming the right to enact legislation binding the English colonies "in all cases whatsoever"—including taxation. So the principle was never given up. At about the same time, they passed another act requiring the colonists to bear the expenses of quartering a standing army of British regulars in America. "The New York Assembly has refused to do it," Franklin reported to a Scottish friend several months later, "and now all the talk here is of sending a force to compel them."

> The ministry that made the act, and all their adherents, call for vengeance. The present ministry are perplexed, and the measures they will finally take on the occasion are yet unknown. But sure I am that if *force* is used, great mischief will ensue; the affections of the people of America to this country will be alienated; your commerce will be diminished; and a total separation of interests [will] be the final consequence....

> I have lived so great a part of my life in Britain, and have formed so many friendships in it, that I love it and sincerely wish it prosperity; and therefore wish to see that union on which alone I think it can be secured and established. As to America, the advantages of such a union to her are not so apparent. She may suffer at present under the arbitrary power of this country; she may suffer for a while in a separation from it. But these are temporary evils that she will outgrow....

America, an immense territory favored by nature with all advantages of climate, soil, great navigable rivers and lakes, etc., must become a great country, populous and mighty, and will, in a less time than is generally conceived, be able to shake off any shackles that may be imposed on her, and perhaps place them on the imposers. In the meantime, every act of oppression will sour their tempers, lessen greatly if not annihilate the profits of your commerce with them, and hasten their final revolt; for the seeds of liberty are universally found there, and nothing can eradicate them.[2]

He believed that there yet remained among the colonists "so much respect, veneration, and affection for Britain that, if cultivated prudently with kind usage and tenderness for their privileges, they might be easily governed still for ages, without force or any considerable expense. But I do not see here a sufficient quantity of the wisdom that is necessary to produce such a conduct, and I lament the want of it."[3]

Longing for Home Again

In the summer of 1766, Franklin requested permission to return to Philadelphia, but the Pennsylvania Assembly reappointed him once more as their agent to the Crown. Apparently they had decided he was indispensable in the London post, for they renewed his appointment again the next year, and the one following—and for six more years thereafter.

He became more cautious about his finances after 1766, as that was the year his lucrative partnership with David

2. To Lord Kames (11 Apr. 1767), Smyth 5:18-22.
3. Ibid., p. 22.

Hall was dissolved. When Sally married a young merchant named Richard Bache in 1767, Franklin expressed regret to his wife that they could do no more than "fit her out handsomely in clothes and furniture, not exceeding in the whole five hundred pounds of value. For the rest, they must depend, as you and I did, on their own industry and care; as what remains in our hands will be barely sufficient for our support."[4]

The loss of income from the Philadelphia partnership was offset somewhat by the multiple appointments Franklin held during his remaining years in London. He was elected as agent to represent Georgia in 1768, New Jersey in 1769, and Massachusetts in 1770; each of these offices provided a modest salary. Nevertheless, he sorely missed his "dear Debby," whom he called "the most punctual of all my correspondents."[5] And Deborah missed him. She was greatly distressed by the repeated dashing of her hopes for his return, which she anticipated each spring and each fall. "I am in the dark," she once complained, "and my life of old age is one continued state of suspense."[6]

It was difficult for Deborah to provide love and comfort to her husband when they were an ocean apart, but she tried. After learning that Ben had suffered a series of physical ailments one spring, she responded: "I am very sorry to think that I should not have it in my power to attend on you. When will it be in your power to come home? How I long to see you, but I would not say a word

4. To Deborah Franklin (22 June 1767), Smyth 5:33.

5. To Deborah Franklin (10 June 1770), Smyth 5:264.

6. Deborah Franklin to BF (3 July 1767), in Labaree, Willcox, et al., *The Papers of Benjamin Franklin,* 14:207.

that would give you one moment's trouble.... If you are having the gout ... I wish I were near enough to rub it with a light hand."[7]

Among the Scholars of Europe

When his schedule permitted, Franklin did find some diversion from his arduous duties. In 1766 he traveled with Sir John Pringle, the Queen's physician, to Germany, where both were elected to the Royal Society of Sciences and enjoyed meeting with a number of European notables. The following year Franklin journeyed to France, again with Pringle. At Versailles they "had the honor of being presented to the King; he spoke to both of us very graciously and cheerfully."[8] The philosopher from America especially relished his discussions with the French scientists and economists. Following another trip to the Continent in 1769, he reported to a friend in Boston on the Europeans' attitude toward the Americans' struggle for political rights: "All Europe (except Britain) appears to be on our side [of] the question."[9]

Franklin was received warmly in Europe, especially in France. He opened correspondence with many French scientists and philosophers, who looked on him as one of the most highly esteemed scholars in Europe. He was particularly delighted when he received the rare honor of being chosen a foreign member of the Royal Academy in

---

7. Deborah Franklin to BF (16 Aug. 1770), in Labaree, Willcox, et al., 17:205.

8. To Miss Mary Stevenson (14 Sept. 1767), Smyth 5:51.

9. To Samuel Cooper (30 Sept. 1769), Smyth 5:231.

Paris, an organization which he said included "the most distinguished names of science."[10]

Although he was not so heartily celebrated in England, Franklin also associated with learned circles there. He met informally with several clubs in London for philosophical and political discussions, including one called the "Honest Whigs." The members of these groups appreciated their American friend's humor as much as his knowledge; the renowned author James Boswell, for example, described Franklin as "all jollity and pleasantry."[11] These associations with British scholars may have contributed to Franklin's election to the Society of the Arts while he was in England. Today that organization awards Franklin Medals to recognize outstanding achievements in the promotion of Anglo-American relations.

Scientist and Prankster

He also continued to pursue a broad range of scientific questions whenever he could. His correspondence during these years reveals an impressive array of investigations: mastodons, lead poisoning, astronomy, the effects of water depth on the movement of boats in canals, phonetics and spelling reform, the management of silkworms, the location and behavior of the Gulf Stream, sunspots, magnetism, the use of vegetation for purifying air, and the causes of the common cold were only a few of the areas in which he conducted experiments or formulated hypotheses. Several editions of his scientific writings were published in England, and a two-volume

---

10. To William Franklin (19 Aug. 1772), Smyth 5:415.
11. Quoted in Van Doren, *Benjamin Franklin,* p. 402.

French translation greatly enhanced his already glowing reputation on the Continent.

Franklin worked to further American interests in his scholarly activities as well as in his political ones. He sent various seeds from European nations to be planted in the colonies. He recommended a number of leading American thinkers to be elected to membership in European learned societies, or to be awarded honorary degrees by British universities. He procured scientific instruments for Harvard and purchased many books for the Library Company of Philadelphia. "I am amazed to see how books have grown upon me since my return to England," he wrote his son in 1772. "I brought none with me, and now have a roomful...consisting chiefly of such as contain knowledge that may hereafter be useful to America."[12]

In addition to conducting serious investigations, Franklin liked to amuse others with his scientific knowledge. On one spring day he was walking with some friends through a park in Buckinghamshire. As they approached a small brook being whipped by the wind, he told his companions that he had power to calm the waves. They were skeptical, but he immediately left them and proceeded two hundred paces upstream, instructing them to keep their eyes on the water. He then lifted his walking cane and made some magical gestures over the brook, and his friends stared in astonishment as its surface gradually became as smooth as a looking glass. Not until later did he disclose that he had been experimenting with the effects of oil on water, and that he happened to be carrying some oil at the time in the hollow joint of his cane!

---

12. To William Franklin (3 Nov. 1772), Smyth 5:445.

"Too Much an American ... Too Much an Englishman"

Franklin continued to advocate the rights of his countrymen by writing for the English newspapers and by "lobbying" members of Parliament. At times his work became discouraging. "As to my own sentiments," he confessed in 1768, "I am weary of suggesting them to so many different inattentive heads, though I must continue to do it while I stay among them."[13] On another occasion he said that "if it were not for the flattering expectation that by being fixed here I might more effectually serve my country, I should certainly determine for retirement without a moment's hesitation."[14] But he did believe that his being in England was good for his country, and because of this conviction he remained and carried on the fight.

During these years following the repeal of the Stamp Act, Franklin seemed to emerge as the unofficial spokesman for all of America rather than merely an agent for the Pennsylvania Assembly. Although it became increasingly evident that he could not succeed in his original mission to procure a change in his own province's form of government, his annual reappointment to the London post permitted him to "see what turn American affairs are likely to take.... A party is now growing in our favor, which I shall endeavor to increase and strengthen by every effort of tongue and pen."[15]

---

13. To William Franklin (13 Mar. 1768), Smyth 5:113.

14. To William Franklin (2 July 1768), Smyth 5:148.

15. To Joseph Galloway (20 Aug. 1768), Labaree, Willcox, et al., 15:189-90.

His task was made more difficult by the suspicions circulating against him on both sides of the Atlantic, due largely to the moderate positions he took while trying to mediate between the colonists and the leaders of the British government. "I do not find that I have gained any point in either country," he once observed, "except that of rendering myself suspected by my impartiality—in England, of being too much an American, and in America, of being too much an Englishman."[16] Arthur Lee, his associate in the Massachusetts agency after Franklin was appointed to represent that colony in 1770, hinted in letters to Boston that the senior agent was under the ministers' influence and was overly cautious because he hoped for an appointment to a higher Crown office. The ministers, on the other hand, made veiled threats about removing Franklin as Deputy Postmaster General because they were upset by some of the views he expressed in his letters to Philadelphia (Franklin's mail was sometimes opened and read by government officials before it left England).

But his conduct was affected very little by these charges and suspicions. "My rule," he told his sister, "in which I have always found satisfaction, is never to turn aside in public affairs through views of private interest, but to go straight forward in doing what appears to me right at the time, leaving the consequences with Providence."[17]

---

16. To an unknown correspondent (28 Nov. 1768), Smyth 5:182.

17. To Jane Mecom (30 Dec. 1770), Van Doren, *Autobiographical Writings*, p. 202.

Chapter 16

Franklin's Attitude Hardens

T he year 1767 marked a critical turn for the worse in Anglo-American relations. The New York Assembly was suspended as a result of the conflict over quartering British troops. Parliament passed the Townshend Act, imposing duties on various imports to the provinces. At the same time, America was virtually invaded by a host of English customs officials sent to collect the duties and enforce all regulations against smuggling. Among the colonists, these overzealous and often corrupt bureaucrats quickly became despicable symbols of British oppression.

Believing that these measures reflected a dangerous misjudgment of the American spirit, Franklin sat down and penned a comprehensive explanation of the colonists' resentment toward the abuses of the English government over the past several years. In January 1768 he had his friend William Strahan publish the lengthy article, entitled "Causes of the American Discontents Before 1768," in the popular *London Chronicle.*[1] Printed anonymously as though from an English merchant, it was intended to educate the public and to provide something of a caution to Parliament and the royal ministers. The article dealt forcefully with the problem of taxation without representation; the resentments created by unqualified governors and other Crown officers; the harmful effects of discouraging manufactures in America; and the confusion springing from the "new kind of loyalty" now required by Parliament, whereas the colonists up to that time had considered themselves bound only to the King.

"There Is a Malice Against Us..."

Franklin was upset when he found that an editor at the *Chronicle* had softened the language of his article. "He has drawn the teeth and pared the nails of my paper, so that it can neither scratch nor bite. It seems only to paw and mumble."[2] But his attitude toward the British government was gradually hardening, and his future expressions were to become still more forceful. He was especially irritated by the Townshend duties, and by March 1768 he had apparently abandoned his earlier distinction between "external" and "internal" taxes imposed by Parliament:

The more I have thought and read on the subject, the more I find myself confirmed in opinion that no middle

---

1. Reprinted in Smyth 5:78–89.
2. To William Franklin (9 Jan. 1768), Smyth 5:90.

doctrine can be well maintained.... Something might be made of either of the extremes, that Parliament has a power to make *all laws* for us or that it has a power to make *no laws* for us; and I think the arguments for the latter more numerous and weighty than those for the former. [3]

In the face of the Townshend Act, he urged his countrymen to remain firm; he believed that a united boycott of English goods would promote industry and frugality among the Americans, and might eventually bring a change in the laws without violence. But if the government were to persist in its abusive regulation of commerce, he predicted that "mutual provocations will...go on to complete the separation."[4]

After nearly three years of stiff American resistance, Parliament finally repealed most of the Townshend Act in April 1770. Unfortunately, however, they decided to retain the duty on tea; it was important to show the colonists that they still had the authority to impose taxes. Franklin considered this an unfortunate decision. "It is bad surgery," he said, "to leave splinters in a wound which must prevent its healing, or in time occasion it to open afresh."[5] But he was even more concerned about the attitude he observed in some of the ministers and some members of Parliament: "There is a malice against us in some powerful people that discovers itself in all their expressions when they speak of us; and incidents may yet arise on either side of the water that may give them

---

3. To William Franklin (13 Mar. 1768), Smyth 5:115.
4. To William Strahan (29 Nov. 1769), Smyth 5:245.
5. To Thomas Cushing (5 Feb. 1771), Smyth 5:296.

advantage and prevent those healing measures that all good men wish to take place."[6]

An Angry Interview with Lord Hillsborough

In October 1770 the Massachusetts House of Representatives voted to appoint Franklin as their agent in London. After receiving word of this, Franklin went in January 1771 to the home of the Secretary of State for American affairs, Lord Hillsborough, to notify him of the new appointment. He was at first turned away on the pretense that the Secretary was absent, then called back and shown into the reception room. As soon as Hillsborough heard the name Massachusetts (which was

viewed in England as the most obstinate of the colonies), he replied "with something between a smile and a sneer" that Franklin could not possibly serve as agent because the royal Governor had not approved the appointment. Franklin assured him that this was not an act requiring the Governor's assent, but was merely a resolution of the House. He then handed "the authentic copy of the vote" to Hillsborough, who took it with reluctance but

Lord Hillsborough, Secretary of State for American affairs, who angrily refused to receive Franklin's appointment as agent for the Massachusetts House of Representatives.

6. To Joseph Galloway (11 June 1770), Van Doren, *Autobiographical Writings*, p. 194.

refused to look at it. Their conversation became less cordial as it proceeded.

L.H. An information of this kind is not properly brought to me as Secretary of State. The Board of Trade is the proper place.

B.F. I will leave the paper, then, with Mr. Pownall [John Pownall, secretary to the Board of Trade] to be—

L.H. *(Hastily.)* To what end would you leave it with him?

B.F. To be entered on the minutes of that board, as usual.

L.H. *(Angrily.)* It shall not be entered there. No such paper shall be entered there while I have anything to do with the business of that board. The House of Representatives has no right to appoint an agent. We shall take no notice of any agents but such as are appointed by acts of assembly, to which the Governor gives his assent. We have had confusion enough already.... An agent appointed by act of assembly we can understand. No other will be attended to for the future, I can assure you.

B.F. I cannot conceive, my Lord, why the consent of the Governor should be thought necessary to the appointment of an agent for the people. It seems to me that—

L.H. *(With a mixed look of anger and contempt.)* I shall not enter into a dispute with YOU, sir, upon this subject.

B.F. I beg your Lordship's pardon; I do not presume to dispute with your Lordship. I would only say that it seems to me that every body of men who cannot appear in person, where business relating to them may be transacted, should have a right to appear by an agent. The concurrence of the Governor does not seem to me necessary. It is the business of the people that is to be done. He is not one of them; he is himself an agent....

L.H. No such appointment shall be entered. When I came into the administration of American affairs, I found them in great disorder. By *my firmness* they are now something mended; and while I have the honor to hold the seals, I shall continue the same conduct, the same *firmness.* I think my duty to the master I serve, and to the government of this nation, requires it of me. If that conduct is not approved, *they* may take my office from me when they please. I shall make a bow and thank them; I shall resign with pleasure.... But while I continue in it, I shall resolutely persevere in the same FIRMNESS. *(Spoken with great warmth, and turning pale in his discourse....)*

B.F. *(Reaching out his hand for the paper, which his Lordship returned to him.)* I beg your Lordship's pardon for taking up so much of your time. It is, I believe, of no great importance whether the appointment is acknowledged or not, for I have not the least conception that an agent can *at present* be of any use to any of the colonies. I shall therefore give your Lordship no further trouble. *(Withdrew.)*[7]

In a letter he sent several days later to the Reverend Samuel Cooper of Boston, Franklin noted that he had "since heard that his Lordship took great offense at some of my last words, which he calls extremely rude and abusive. He assured a friend of mine that they were equivalent to telling him to his face that the colonies could expect neither favor nor justice during his administration. I find he did not mistake me."[8]

---

7. Minutes of a conference with Lord Hillsborough (16 Jan. 1771), Smyth 5:302–4.

8. To Samuel Cooper (5 Feb. 1771), Smyth 5:299.

"The Seeds...of a Total Disunion"

What disturbed Franklin most was that the attitude displayed by Lord Hillsborough was typical of many officers of the British government. He nevertheless persevered in urging American leaders to stand firm in their cause. In February 1771 he wrote: "I hope the colony assemblies will show, by frequently repeated resolves, that they know their rights and do not lose sight of them. Our growing importance will ere long compel an acknowledgment of them, and establish and secure them to our posterity."[9] The following May, in a letter to the Massachusetts Committee of Correspondence (Thomas Cushing, James Otis, and Samuel Adams), he anticipated the sequence of events which might eventually lead to American independence:

> I think one may clearly see, in the system of customs to be exacted in America by act of Parliament, the seeds sown of a total disunion of the two countries, though as yet that event may be at a considerable distance.
>
> The course and natural progress seems to be, first, the appointment of needy men as officers, for others do not care to leave England; then, their necessities make them rapacious, their office makes them proud and insolent, their insolence and rapacity make them odious, and, being conscious that they are hated, they become malicious. Their malice urges them to a continual abuse of the inhabitants in their letters to administration, representing them as disaffected and rebellious, and (to encourage the use of severity) as weak, divided, timid, and cowardly. Government believes all; thinks it

---

9. To Thomas Cushing (5 Feb. 1771), Smyth 5:293-94.

necessary to support and countenance its officers; their quarreling with the people is deemed a mark and consequence of their fidelity; they are therefore more highly rewarded, and this makes their conduct still more insolent and provoking.

The resentment of the people will, at times and on particular incidents, burst into outrages and violence upon such officers, and this naturally draws down severity and acts of further oppression from hence. The more the people are dissatisfied, the more rigor will be thought necessary; severe punishments will be inflicted to terrify; rights and privileges will be abolished; greater force will then be required to secure execution and submission; the expense will become enormous; it will then be thought proper, by fresh exactions, to make the people defray it. Thence, the British nation and government will become odious, the subjection to it will be deemed no longer tolerable; war ensues, and the bloody struggle will end in absolute slavery to America or ruin to Britain by the loss of her colonies—the latter most probable, from America's growing strength and magnitude.

But as the whole empire must, in either case, be greatly weakened, I cannot but wish to see much patience and the utmost discretion in our general conduct, that the fatal period may be postponed, and that, whenever this catastrophe shall happen, it may appear to all mankind that the fault has not been ours.

"I do not pretend to the gift of prophecy," he concluded. "History shows that by these steps great empires have crumbled heretofore; and the late transactions we have so much cause to complain of show that we are in the same train, and that without a greater share of prudence and wisdom than we have seen both sides to be possessed of, we shall probably come to the same conclusion."[10]

---

10. To the Massachusetts Committee of Correspondence (15 May 1771), Smyth 5:317-19.

Chapter 17

Respite and Relaxation

D uring the summer of 1771, Franklin spent several weeks away from London. He stayed in Twyford with Jonathan Shipley, Bishop of St. Asaph and friend of the American cause. While there, he took his mind off political pressures and began to write his own life story in the form of a letter to his son. In less than two weeks he had written nearly half of the intriguing account which was later to become known as "the most famous autobiography in the world."[1] It was a candid and fascinating story of optimism which came forth, curiously enough, at a time of great distress in Franklin's life and that of his country. *The Autobiography of Benjamin Franklin*, as one scholar has noted, has been "translated and

1. Van Doren, *Autobiographical Writings*, p. 216 (headnote).

retranslated into a dozen languages, printed and reprinted in hundreds of editions, read and reread by millions of people, especially by young and impressionable Americans. The influence of these few hundred pages has been matched by that of no other American book."[2]

"Snug as a Bug in a Rug"

Before he left Twyford, Franklin had formed friendships with Shipley's young daughters. As a token of his affection, he presented them with the gift of a grey squirrel which Deborah had recently sent from Philadelphia. It soon became a family favorite and was named Mungo—although they sometimes called it Skugg, which was as common a nickname for squirrels in England as Puss was for cats.

Bishop Jonathan Shipley, an American sympathizer whose family became close friends to Franklin during his years in England. Franklin wrote the first portion of his famous *Autobiography* at the Shipley home in 1771.

Unfortunately, Mungo was killed by a dog about a year later. When Franklin received news of the small tragedy, he sent a letter of condolence to one of the Shipley girls. "I lament with you most sincerely the unfortunate end of poor Mungo," he wrote. "Few squirrels were better accomplished; for he had had a good education, had travelled far, and seen much of the world." He then composed a grand and lengthy epitaph for

---

2. Clinton Rossiter, *Seedtime of the Republic* (New York: Harcourt, Brace and Company, 1953), p. 303.

the lamented Mungo "in the monumental style and measure," which was followed by this afterthought:

> You see, my dear miss, how much more decent and proper this broken style is than if we were to say, by way of epitaph,

Here Skugg

Lies snug

As a bug

In a rug.

> and yet, perhaps, there are people in the world of so little feeling as to think that this would be a good enough epitaph for poor Mungo. [3]

Ireland and Scotland

In the fall of 1771, he took another journey away from London, chiefly for his health. He traveled to Ireland and visited the Irish Parliament, where he was invited to sit on the chamber floor as an honored guest. Also during this trip he happened to meet Lord Hillsborough, who was vacationing in Ireland at the same time. For reasons of his own, the Secretary of State showed the American agent "a thousand civilities" during the short time they spent together. [4] But Franklin concluded from his later conduct, after they both had returned to London, that "as Lord Hillsborough in fact got nothing out of me ... he threw me away as an orange that would yield no juice, and therefore [was] not worth more squeezing." [5]

Following a two-month stay in Ireland, during which Franklin made several friends for America, he went to

---

3. To Miss Georgiana Shipley (26 Sept. 1772), Smyth 5:438-39.
4. To William Franklin (30 Jan. 1772), Smyth 5:379.
5. To William Franklin (19 Aug. 1772), Smyth 5:413.

Scotland to enjoy the company of Lord Kames and David Hume. As he journeyed back toward London, he had the pleasant surprise of meeting for the first time his son-in-law, Richard Bache, who was then visiting relatives in England. To Franklin's dismay, however, Sally had not come along. This brief contact with the family must have turned his thoughts toward Philadelphia; two months after returning to London he confided in a letter to William: "I have of late great debates with myself whether or not I shall continue here any longer. I grow homesick, and being now in my sixty-seventh year, I begin to apprehend some infirmity of age may attack me and make my return impracticable."[6]

---

6. To William Franklin (30 Jan. 1772), Smyth 5:381.

Chapter 18

"I Will Make Your Master a Little King for This"

Despite his recurring thoughts of home, Franklin resumed his ceaseless efforts to defend American rights once he was back in London. "I shall ... continue to exert myself in behalf of my country," he wrote, "as long as I see a probability of my being able to do it any service."[1] He advised the colonial leaders to continue their petitions to the Crown, believing that "they will all have their weight in time."[2] Meanwhile, he counseled patience: "I hope that great care will be taken to keep our people quiet, since nothing is more wished for by our enemies than that by insurrections we should give a good pretense

---

1. To Samuel Cooper (13 Jan. 1772), Smyth 5:357.
2. To Thomas Cushing (5 Jan. 1773), Smyth 6:4.

King George III, whom Franklin sincerely admired after attending the coronation ceremonies in 1760. After the war broke out between America and Great Britain, the King looked on Franklin as the "evil genius behind the Revolution."

for increasing the military among us, and putting us under more severe restraints."[3]

He could also urge bolder actions. He strongly favored a proposal from the Virginia House of Burgesses that committees of correspondence be established in every colony, and he expressed his hope that a general congress would result. He further suggested that the colonies unitedly pass a resolution to refuse any more aids to the King for military purposes until their rights were recognized by the British government. "Such a step, I imagine, will bring the dispute to a crisis."[4]

By July 1773 Franklin had begun to believe, for the first time, that George III himself was behind some of the government abuses. That month he wrote to William: "Between you and I, the late measures have been, I suspect, very much the King's own, and he has in some cases a great share of what his friends call *firmness*. Yet, by some painstaking and proper management, the wrong impressions he has received may be removed, which is

---

3. To Thomas Cushing (9 Mar. 1773), Smyth 6:22.
4. To Thomas Cushing (7 July 1773), Smyth 6:77.

perhaps the only chance America has for obtaining *soon* the redress she aims at."[5]

"I Grew Tired of Meekness"

If anyone in England was able to effectively remove those "wrong impressions," it was Ben Franklin. Reverting to a strategy he had used throughout his diplomatic career, he prepared some hard-hitting material for the British press. In September 1773 the widely read *Public Advertiser* carried one of these articles, called "Rules by Which a Great Empire May Be Reduced to a Small One."[6] A satirical jab at the royal government, it listed twenty harsh measures which parodied—perhaps too precisely—the oppressive acts which had been imposed on the American colonies over the past decade. The ministers and legislators whose actions it described must have smarted under its bold tone; no doubt they could guess who the author was.

The next month, another of Franklin's compositions appeared in the *Gentleman's Magazine*. It was an unusual piece entitled "An Edict by the King of Prussia."

Dantzic, Sept. 5, 1773

FREDERIC, by the grace of God, King of Prussia, etc., etc....

Whereas it is well known to all the world, that the first German settlements made in the Island of Britain were by colonies of people subject to our renowned ducal ancestors, and drawn from their dominions...And

---

5. To William Franklin (14 July 1773), Smyth 6:98.
6. Reprinted in Smyth 6:127-37.

whereas it is just and expedient that a revenue should be raised from the said colonies in Britain ... and that those who are descendants of our ancient subjects, and thence still owe us due obedience, should contribute to the replenishing of our royal coffers ... We do therefore hereby ordain and command, that, from and after the date of these presents, there shall be levied and paid to our officers of the customs, on all goods, wares, and merchandises, and on all grain and other produce of the earth, exported from the said Island of Britain, and on all goods of whatever kind imported into the same, a duty of four and a half percent *ad valorem*, for the use of us and our successors....

The "edict" went on to describe various detailed regulations of British commerce which were to be imposed on pain of death. "We flatter ourselves," it concluded, "that these our royal regulations and commands will be thought just and reasonable by our much-favored colonists in England, the said regulations being copied from their statutes ... made by their Parliaments, or from instructions given by their Princes, or from resolutions of both Houses, entered into for the good government of their *own colonies in Ireland and America.*"[7]

Both of these articles were reprinted in newspapers throughout Great Britain, and they created a stir on both sides of the Atlantic. Franklin hoped that the result would be favorable for the American cause. In a letter to his sister in Boston, he explained his intent:

I had used all the smooth words I could muster, and I grew tired of meekness when I saw it without effect. Of

---

7. Reprinted in Smyth 6:118-24.

late, therefore, I have been saucy, and in two papers ... I have held up a looking glass in which some ministers may see their ugly faces, and the nation its injustice.

These papers have been much taken notice of; many are pleased with them, and a few very angry, who I am told will make me feel their resentment, which I must bear as well as I can, and shall bear the better if any public good is done, whatever the consequences to myself. In my own private concerns with mankind, I have observed that to kick a little when under imposition has a good effect. A little sturdiness when superiors are much in the wrong sometimes occasions consideration. And there is truth in the old saying that *if you make yourself a sheep, the wolves will eat you.* [8]

The Notorious Hutchinson Letters

Whatever the effects of Franklin's latest writings on English public opinion, they certainly did not improve his own standing with the royal ministers, who already resented him because of his boldness and perseverance in defending the colonists against government abuses. Hillsborough complained that Franklin was "a factious turbulent fellow, always in mischief ... enemy to the King's service,"[9] and Lord North considered him "the great fomenter of the opposition in America."[10] Some in the ministry even called him the "Judas in Craven Street."[11] After these most recent newspaper barbs,

---

8. To Jane Mecom (1 Nov. 1773), Van Doren, *Autobiographical Writings,* pp. 297-98.

9. In BF's letter to William Franklin (30 Jan. 1772), Smyth 5:378.

10. Quoted in Hall, "Benjamin Franklin: Philosopher of Dissent," p. 93.

11. Lopez and Herbert, *The Private Franklin,* p. 183.

which many Crown officers found personally insulting, they began to look for an opportunity to avenge themselves on this troublemaker. It was not long in coming.

In December 1772, Franklin had somehow acquired several letters written by Thomas Hutchinson, royal Governor of Massachusetts, in which the Governor urged his superiors to use a firm hand against the Boston rebels. He proposed the sending of more troops and several other measures which were later to become serious grievances in the Anglo-American struggle. Believing that the colonial leaders ought to know of these communications, and hoping that such knowledge would lessen resentment toward Parliament by showing that recent legislation was based on the Governor's misleading representations, Franklin secretly sent the Hutchinson letters to the Massachusetts Committee of Correspondence.

The committee ignored their agent's request that the matter be kept confidential. In fact, by June 1773 the letters had been published openly in the *Boston Gazette*. The fierce indignation which they kindled among the people virtually forced Governor Hutchinson out of the country, and he soon fled to England. Franklin wrote again to Boston, urging moderation and pacifism. But many Americans were outraged by the ugly revelations, and tensions rose in Massachusetts and elsewhere. Lord North later said of the Hutchinson letters, "These brought on the war."[12]

12. Quoted in Hall, p. 112.

Franklin Is Humiliated and Abused

The British ministers were furious about the "leaking" of the Hutchinson letters to the colonists, but they had no idea who was responsible. Then, in December 1773, Franklin learned that two innocent Englishmen were engaged in a public controversy over the matter. False charges had been made, and one of the two had been wounded in a duel; a second duel was likely to follow. To prevent tragedy, Franklin issued a statement in London's *Public Advertiser* on Christmas Day, acknowledging his own role in the Hutchinson affair.

The next month Franklin was summoned to appear before the Lords Committee of His Majesty's Privy Council for Plantation Affairs. He was told that the committee would conduct a hearing on the Massachusetts Assembly's earlier petition (which he, as agent, had submitted) for the formal removal of Governor Hutchinson. But even before the meeting began, it was obvious that something beyond a routine hearing was going to take place. "All the courtiers [court attendants] were invited," Franklin later reported, "as to an entertainment, and there never was such an appearance of privy councilors on any occasion, not less than thirty-five, besides an immense crowd of other auditors."[13]

Alexander Wedderburn, the solicitor-general representing the Governor, arose and stood at the table between the chairs of two councilors. After heatedly defending Hutchinson's conduct against that of the

13. To Thomas Cushing (15 Feb. 1774), Smyth 6:188–89.

Assembly, he turned toward Franklin and launched into a loud, sarcastic denunciation that lasted nearly an hour and was punctuated by frequent pounding on the table. The speech, described by one of Franklin's sympathizers as "beyond all bounds and decency,"[14] was so poisonous and vile that many of the spectators were deeply embarrassed. But the ministers themselves displayed no embarrassment.

> Not one of their Lordships checked and recalled the orator to the business before them, but on the contrary, a very few excepted, they seemed to enjoy highly the entertainment, and frequently burst out in loud applauses. This part of [Wedderburn's] speech was thought so good that they have since printed it in order to defame me everywhere, and particularly to destroy my reputation [in America]; but the grosser parts of the abuse are omitted, appearing, I suppose, in their own eyes, too foul to be seen on paper.[15]

"I Will Make Your Master a Little King for This"

Franklin stood silent and expressionless throughout Wedderburn's long and vicious attack. "I made no justification of myself from the charges brought against me," he wrote. "I made no return of the injury by abusing my adversaries, but held a cool, sullen silence."[16] Afterward, however, he reportedly whispered to the

---

14. Edmund Burke, quoted in Van Doren, *Benjamin Franklin,* p. 473.

15. To Thomas Cushing (15 Feb. 1774), Smyth 6:189-90.

16. "An Account of Negotiations in London for Effecting a Reconciliation Between Great Britain and the American Colonies," written to William Franklin (22 Mar. 1775), Smyth 6:319.

exultant solicitor-general, "I will make your master a little king for this."[17]

By the next morning, Franklin had decided that his sending the Hutchinson letters to Boston was "one of the best actions of his life, and...he should certainly do [it] again in the same circumstances."[18] He remained convinced that it was something which had to be done so that the colonial leaders in Massachusetts could appropriately respond to the Governor's inflammatory misrepre-

Alexander Wedderburn, Solicitor General in the ministry of Lord North, who publicly abused Franklin before a committee of the British Privy Council. Franklin, who stood silent during the long verbal attack, reportedly whispered to Wedderburn afterward, "I will make your master a little king for this."

sentations. But the royal ministers, as it turned out, were unwilling to hear both sides of the story. Whatever Franklin's personal feelings may have been while he was subjected to the ministers' abuse, he was even more distressed by what the incident symbolized for his countrymen:

> It may be supposed that I am very angry on this occasion.... But indeed, what I feel on my own account is half lost in what I feel for the public. When I see that all petitions and complaints of grievances are so odious to

---

17. Quoted in Hall, p. 112. This was a reference to George III's dominion. Despite Franklin's long efforts to prevent the alienation and revolt of the British colonies, which he believed would seriously weaken the empire, he soon became a leading figure in the cause of American independence.

18. Dr. Joseph Priestley (quoting Franklin), in Smyth 10:270.

The Real Benjamin Franklin

the government that even the mere pipe which conveys them becomes obnoxious, I am at a loss to know how peace and union are to be maintained or restored between the different parts of the empire.

Grievances cannot be redressed unless they are known; and they cannot be known but through complaints and petitions. If these are deemed affronts, and the messengers punished as offenders, who will henceforth send petitions? And who will deliver them?

It has been thought a dangerous thing in any state to stop up the vent of griefs. Wise governments have therefore generally received petitions with some indulgence, even when but slightly founded. Those who think themselves injured by their rulers are sometimes, by a mild and prudent answer, convinced of their error. But where complaining is a crime, hope becomes despair.[19]

On January 31, 1774, two days after Franklin appeared before the Privy Council committee, he was notified that he had been dismissed as Deputy Postmaster General for the colonies. Ironically, his political enemies in America were accusing him at about this time of making efforts to secure a higher post in the British government. "But they may expect it till doomsday," he observed. "For God knows my heart; I would not accept the best office the King has to bestow while such tyrannic measures are taking against my country.... They [the ministers] have done me honor by turning me out, and I will take care they shall not disgrace me by putting me in again."[20]

---

19. To Thomas Cushing (15 Feb. 1774), Smyth 6:190-91.

20. To Jane Mecom (28 July 1774), Van Doren, *Autobiographical Writings*, pp. 338-39.

Chapter 19

Tragedy Sends Franklin Home

Relations between Great Britain and the American provinces were rapidly worsening during this period, and no one regretted it more than Franklin. Zealous as he was for the rights of the colonists, he dreaded the possibility of a civil war that would tear the British empire apart. If only Lord North's ministry could be overturned by one more sympathetic to the American cause, he believed, then Parliament could be persuaded to repeal its oppressive laws and a thorough reconciliation could be effected. But in the meantime he was in "perpetual anxiety lest the mad measure of mixing soldiers among a people whose minds are in such a state of irritation may be attended with some sudden mischief; for an accidental quarrel, a personal insult, an imprudent order, an insolent execution of even a prudent one, or twenty other things may produce a tumult, unforeseen and therefore impossible to be prevented, in which such a carnage may ensue as to make a breach that can never afterwards be healed."[1]

Franklin Offers to Pay for the Boston Tea Party

And so when word reached England of the December 1773 Boston Tea Party, Franklin was upset. He considered it "an act of violent injustice" at the time, and he wrote to the Massachusetts Committee of Correspondence urging "a speedy reparation" for the tea that had been destroyed.[2] He even offered later on to pay for the tea out of his own pocket, "an engagement in which I must have risked my whole fortune,"[3] if Parliament would agree to withdraw the so-called Intolerable Acts which had followed the incident. But Parliament was in no mood to negotiate, and Franklin resented their oppression more than Boston's resistance, so he continued to urge firmness in his letters to the colonial leaders.

Fears of Arrest and Imprisonment

Hoping against hope, Franklin continued throughout the year 1774 to search for a way to head off the impending crisis. Although he no longer met with the royal ministers after the Wedderburn incident in late January, he was frequently approached in secret by prominent persons who shared his anxiety to save the

---

1. To Thomas Cushing (6 Oct. 1774), Smyth 6:250-51.

2. To Thomas Cushing and others (2 Feb. 1774), Smyth 6:179.

3. "An Account of Negotiations in London" (22 Mar. 1775), Smyth 6:394.

During secret negotiations with Admiral Lord Howe which were intended to prevent the impending war between England and her American colonies, Franklin occasionally played chess with the admiral's sister, Lady Howe.

empire from ruin. Among these were respected statesman and orator Edmund Burke, the former Prime Minister William Pitt (Lord Chatham), Lord Howe of the Admiralty, and other confidants of the North ministry.

By October, Franklin was being warned by some of his friends to flee England; he would undoubtedly be arrested and imprisoned, they said, if war were to break out in America. He was reluctant to leave just yet, however, because he knew that the colonists had formed a Continental Congress and were preparing a formal petition to the King for a redress of their grievances. "I have been frequently cautioned to secure my papers," he wrote, "and by some advised to withdraw. But I venture to stay, in compliance with the wish of others, till the result of the Congress arrives, since they suppose my being here might on that occasion be of use."[4]

4. To Joseph Galloway (12 Oct. 1774), Smyth 6:254.

"This Old Rotten State"

In his secret negotiations with Lord Howe and others, Franklin drew up a series of proposals for reconciliation between Great Britain and the colonies. These were presented to the ministry as a protest from English merchants, but they had no effect. Lord Chatham himself introduced a measure in Parliament which called for removing the British troops from Boston, but it "availed no more than the whistling of the winds."[5] And when the petition from the Continental Congress finally arrived, it met with the same fate:

> We flattered ourselves...that the King would have been pleased to recommend it to the consideration of Parliament by some message, but we were mistaken. It came down among a great heap of letters of intelligence from governors and officers in America, newspapers, pamphlets, handbills, etc., from that country—the last in the list—and was laid upon the table with them, undistinguished by any particular recommendation of it....
>
> To draw it into the attention of the House, we petitioned to be heard upon it, but were not permitted; and...from the constant refusal, neglect, or discouragement of American petitions these many years past, our country will at last be convinced that petitions are odious here, and that petitioning is far from being a probable means of obtaining redress.[6]

Having spent over ten years in this seemingly fruitless mission to England, Franklin was at last fed up. Perhaps

5. "An Account of Negotiations in London" (22 Mar. 1775), Smyth 6:362.

6. To Charles Thomson (5 Feb. 1775), Smyth 6:304.

independence was better for America than union with Great Britain after all. "When I consider the extreme corruption prevalent among all orders of men in this old rotten state," he declared in February 1775, "and the glorious public virtue so predominant in our rising country, I cannot but apprehend more mischief than benefit from a closer union."[7]

The Crushing News That Finally Sends Franklin Home

At the end of this same month, February 1775, Franklin received the tragic news which sealed his decision to return home. After more than forty-four years of marriage, his beloved "Debby" had suddenly died in Philadelphia. Their relationship had been a tender one, despite his long absences. "It seems but the other day," he had written her in 1773, "since you and I were ranked among the boys and girls, so swiftly does time fly. We have, however, great reason to be thankful that so much of our lives has passed so happily."[8] In April 1774 he sent word to his "dear love" that he hoped to be on the sea by summer, and to find her "well and hearty ... when I have the happiness once more of seeing you."[9]

But circumstances intervened, and he was not by her side when she succumbed to a stroke the following December. When the melancholy word reached him in England, he made arrangements to sail back to America and began packing his belongings. Almost two years later he would reflect, "I have lately lost my old and faithful

---

7. To Joseph Galloway (25 Feb. 1775), Smyth 6:311-12.

8. To Deborah Franklin (6 Jan. 1773), Smyth 6:4.

9. To Deborah Franklin (28 Apr. 1774), Smyth 6:230.

companion, and I every day become more sensible of the greatness of that loss which cannot now be repaired."[10]

March 20, 1775, was Franklin's last full day in London. Heavy-hearted, he spent the day with his friend Joseph Priestley. The two of them examined recent American newspapers and discussed the stormclouds gathering over the British empire. As the philosopher read, Priestley later recorded, "the tears trickled down his cheeks." He noted that Franklin "dreaded the war, and often said that if the difference should come to an open rupture, it would be a war of *ten years,* and he should not live to see the end of it.... That the issue would be favorable to America he never doubted."[11] Having done all he could to avert the disaster which he knew was coming, the aged patriot boarded his ship and headed home.

------

10. To Jan Ingenhousz (12 Feb. 1777), in Lopez and Herbert, *The Private Franklin,* p. 172.

11. John Towill Rutt, *Life and Correspondence of Joseph Priestley,* 2 vols. (London: R. Hunter, 1831-32), 1:210-12.

Chapter 20

The War Separates
Father and Son

The voyage across the Atlantic lasted six weeks this time, and Franklin landed in Philadelphia on May 5, 1775. The very next day he was unanimously chosen by the Pennsylvania Assembly to represent them as a delegate to the Second Continental Congress. Fighting had erupted at Lexington and Concord while he was on the ocean, and he arrived to find "the most perfect unanimity throughout the colonies."[1] Especially irritating to the colonists were the activities of General Thomas Gage and his troops in Boston. "All America is exasperated by his conduct, and more firmly united than ever. The

---

1. To David Hartley (6 May 1775), Van Doren, *Autobiographical Writings*, p. 403.

breach between the two countries is grown wider, and in danger of becoming irreparable."[2]

During this time of crisis, Franklin would prove invaluable to the soon-to-be-born United States of America. As the oldest and most experienced member of Congress—at the age of sixty-nine, he could have been the father of nearly half the other delegates—he provided the kind of wisdom and stability which was sorely needed in the early stages of the Revolutionary War. When Congress assembled in the Pennsylvania State House (later Independence Hall) on May 10, he played a fairly quiet role. But during the ensuing months he would become extremely active, serving on the most important committees and often taking the lead in shaping national policies.

Another Heartbreak

As Congress got under way, Franklin first turned his attention to an aspect of the Anglo-American struggle which was much closer to him than he would have wished: the growing disaffection of his own son. William had now served as Governor of New Jersey for over twelve years, much longer than any of his contemporaries in America. He had performed admirably in this station and had gained some popularity among the people. But while he attempted to respect the rights of colonial citizens, he also endeavored to maintain the favor of the British ministry. This had become increasingly difficult in recent years, and he now found himself walking a tightrope.

The philosophical differences between father and son first became apparent after the elder Franklin was

2. To Joseph Priestley (16 May 1775), Smyth 6:400.

appointed agent for Massachusetts, as this had pushed him to argue more aggressively against British abuses. William felt compelled to write to some of his political friends in London, assuring them that he did not necessarily share his father's opinions. These differences of opinion inevitably found their way into the correspondence between William and his father, as reflected in an October 1773 letter from Ben:

> You are a thorough government man, which I do not wonder at, nor do I aim at converting you. I only wish you to act uprightly and steadily, avoiding that duplicity which...adds contempt to indignation. If you can promote the prosperity of your people and leave them happier than you found them, whatever your political principles are, your memory will be honored. [3]

After Franklin was publicly humiliated by Wedderburn in January 1774, William wanted to be sure his political fortunes were not dimmed by his father's reputation; he pledged to Lord Dartmouth, then Secretary of State for American affairs, that "no attachments or connections shall ever make me swerve from the duty of my station."[4] Later that same year, some of William's private letters became known and were published (much like those of Governor Hutchinson), making him an object of suspicion in the colonies. The breach in the family widened.

Father and Son Become Enemies

Soon after returning to America in May 1775, Franklin met with his son near Philadelphia for several hours. He

3. To William Franklin (6 Oct. 1773), Smyth 6:144-45.
4. Quoted in Lopez and Herbert, *The Private Franklin*, p. 193.

Franklin's son William, who served more than twelve years as Governor of New Jersey. After the Revolution began, William remained loyal to the Crown and actively supported the British war effort, causing an irreparable breach between himself and his father. He later fled to England and died without land or money.

did his best to persuade William to resign his post and join the colonists in their struggle for independence. But the Governor would hear none of it. He had also hoped that his father would retire from public life, but when he realized that instead he would exert his energies to pull the provinces away from Great Britain, he concluded that the gap between them could not be healed. Unlike his father, he would remain loyal to the Crown.

By the following January, William was no longer functioning as Governor. The New Jersey militia placed him under house arrest until Congress could decide his fate. Five months later he was declared "an enemy of the liberties of this country,"[5] arrested by order of the New Jersey Assembly, and sentenced to two years of confinement in Connecticut. His wife, Elizabeth, died while he was serving this two-year term. When William was released in October 1778, he went straight to New York, then occupied by British troops. There he became president of the Board of Associated Loyalists, an organization which assisted the English army by

_____

5. Lopez and Herbert, p. 210.

providing intelligence reports and conducting raids on the rebel coasts. The two Franklins now found themselves on opposing sides in the war they had both hoped would never come.

Chapter 21

Dr. Franklin in Congress

Benjamin Franklin had good reason to feel bitter during the summer of 1775. He had lost his wife in death, he had lost his son to the enemy, and now his properties along the Atlantic seacoast were being destroyed by a war he had unsuccessfully tried to prevent. A famous letter he penned while sitting in Congress one day in July suggests what his temperament may have been that summer. It was addressed to his old friend William Strahan, the London printer who had been elected to the House of Commons.

> Mr. Strahan,
>
> You are a member of Parliament, and one of that majority which has doomed my country to destruction. You have begun to burn our towns and murder our people. Look upon your hands! They are stained with

the blood of your relations! You and I were long friends; you are now my enemy, and I am

Yours,

B. Franklin [1]

Whatever his personal losses and disappointments, however, Franklin always remained convinced that America would win the war. Settled in this confidence, he threw himself into public affairs as though he were a young man. "My time was never more fully employed," he observed. "In the morning at six, I am at the Committee of Safety, appointed by the [Pennsylvania] Assembly to put the province in a state of defense; which committee holds till near nine, when I am at the Congress, and that sits till after four in the afternoon." [2]

As chairman of the Pennsylvania Committee of Safety, he organized a militia force and provided for weapons, munitions, gunboats, a stockade, and other measures to defend the colony. In Congress, he served on numerous committees; some of these, for example, were assigned to draft proposals regarding an intercolonial postal system, the protection of colonial trade, Indian relations during the war, and logistical support for the American army.

Franklin's "Articles of Confederation"

On July 21, 1775, a remarkable proposal from Franklin's own pen was read before the delegates to Congress. Entitled "Articles of Confederation and Perpetual Union," it contained thirteen articles outlining a government for

---

1. To William Strahan (5 July 1775), Smyth 6:407. Franklin decided not to send this letter to Strahan, but he used it as a propaganda piece in American newspapers.

2. To Joseph Priestley (7 July 1775), Smyth 6:409.

the "United Colonies of North America."[3] (Many of its provisions were drawn from Franklin's 1754 Albany Plan of Union.) Thomas Jefferson, one of the youngest delegates, later recalled how the document was received.

Doctor Franklin put into my hands the draft of a plan of confederation, desiring me to read it and tell him what I thought of it. I approved it highly. He showed it to others. Some thought as I did; others were revolted at it. We found it could not be passed, and the proposing it to Congress as the subject for any vote whatever would startle many members so much that they would suspect we had lost sight of reconciliation with Great Britain, and that we should lose much more ground than we should gain by the proposition.

Yet, that the idea of a more firm bond of union than the undefined one under which we then acted might be suggested and permitted to grow, Doctor Franklin informed Congress that he had sketched the outlines of an instrument which might become necessary at a future day... and would ask leave for it to lay on the table of Congress, that the members might in the meantime be turning the subject in their minds and have something more perfect prepared by the time it should become necessary.

This was agreed to by the timid members, only on condition that no entry whatever should be made in the journals of Congress relative to this instrument. [The plan of union] was to continue in force only till a reconciliation with Great Britain. This was all that ever was done or proposed in Congress on the subject of a confederation before June 1776.[4]

---

3. Reprinted in Smyth 6:420-26.

4. Thomas Jefferson to M. Soules (13 Sept. 1786), Bergh, *The Writings of Thomas Jefferson*, 17:139-40.

Although he was the oldest member of Congress, Franklin wanted to move faster than did most of his colleagues. In this case he was almost an entire year ahead of the majority of delegates in his thinking. As Jefferson noted further, the Articles of Confederation which were later adopted differed "very considerably...from the sketch of Doctor Franklin," but this early proposal was a significant factor in turning the attention of Congress toward the establishment of a national government.

More Congressional Duties

In October 1775, Franklin and two other delegates traveled to Cambridge, Massachusetts, as a Congressional committee to confer with General George Washington regarding the support and reorganization of the Continental Army and other military matters. In November, Franklin was appointed with five others to form a Committee of Secret Correspondence for the purpose of maintaining contacts with persons in foreign nations who were friendly to the American cause. (Having already established many contacts in Europe, Franklin played an important role as chairman of this forerunner of the State Department.)

The following month a secret agent from France came to Philadelphia and met with this committee, indicating that the French foreign minister, the Comte de Vergennes, had authorized him to express the hope that the British colonies would declare their independence and begin trading with other European countries. Franklin moved in February 1776 that Congress open American ports to foreign trade. The motion failed, as many delegates were not yet ready for this tacit declaration of independence, but several days later they voted to send Silas Deane of Connecticut to represent Congress in France and search for political friends and sources of trade in Europe.

Franklin, who had had more diplomatic experience than any other colonist, drafted Deane's instructions; this document has since been called "a masterpiece of diplomatic counsel."[5] Later in the year, Franklin served on a committee assigned to draw up proposed treaties of alliance with foreign powers. This so-called Plan of 1776 formed the basis of the treaties which were eventually concluded with France.

A Brief Mission to Canada

In late March 1776, Congress sent Franklin and several others as commissioners to Montreal. Their object was to persuade the French Canadians to join the American colonies in the revolt against Great Britain. En route, Franklin was appalled when he saw the extensive damage which the English troops had done along the seacoast. When he got to New York City, he wrote a heated letter to one of the Crown officials he had known while in London (Anthony Todd, Secretary of the Post Office):

> How long will the *insanity* on your side [of] the water continue? Every day's plundering of our property and burning our habitations serves but to exasperate and unite us the more; the breach between you and us grows daily wider and more difficult to heal.

---

5. Van Doren, *Benjamin Franklin*, p. 541. Franklin's instructions to Deane are reprinted in Thomas Fleming, ed., *Benjamin Franklin: A Biography in His Own Words* (New York: Newsweek, Inc., 1972), pp. 268-71.

Britain without us can grow no stronger; without her
we shall become a tenfold greater and mightier people.
Do you choose to have so increasing a nation of
enemies? Do you think it prudent by your barbarities to
fix us in a rooted hatred of your nation, and make all our
innumerable posterity detest you? Yet this is the way in
which you are now proceeding. . . . And I now venture to
tell you that, though this war may be a long one (and I
think it will probably last beyond my time), we shall with
God's help get the better of you. [6]

He also observed to a friend in Boston that "every day
furnishes us with new causes of increasing enmity, and
new reasons for wishing an eternal separation, so that
there is a rapid increase of the formerly small party who
were for an independent government."[7] This firsthand
look at the war was making him more eager than ever for
the fateful step that was now only weeks away.

Not only did the mission to Montreal prove utterly
futile—the French Canadians had been alienated by some
earlier American actions—but Franklin, now seventy,
became dangerously ill when his party was iced in at
Saratoga. "I begin to apprehend that I have undertaken a
fatigue that, at my time of life, may prove too much for
me," he confided to Josiah Quincy, "so I sit down to write
to a few friends by way of farewell."[8] But the ice finally
thawed, and he made the difficult journey back to
Philadelphia.

---

6. To Anthony Todd (29 Mar. 1776), in Fleming, pp. 271-72.

7. To Josiah Quincy, Sr. (15 Apr. 1776), Smyth 6:446.

8. Ibid., p. 445.

The Declaration of Independence

Franklin was completely worn out when he returned from Canada. Although he was home by the end of May 1776, his health was still suffering nearly a month later. On June 21 he wrote to Washington, "I am just recovering from a severe fit of the gout, which has kept me from Congress and company ... so that I know little of what has passed there, except that a Declaration of Independence is preparing."[9]

Actually, his role in the issuing of the Declaration was more significant than this letter suggests. After the burning of Norfolk, Virginia, on New Year's Day, the sentiments of the American people had begun to move more rapidly toward independence. Thomas Paine, who had come from his native England to Philadelphia at Franklin's urging, now responded to another of Franklin's suggestions and published his *Common Sense* on January 10. This pamphlet, which argued compellingly for total separation from Great Britain, sold thousands of copies throughout the provinces almost overnight; it had a tremendous impact on the thinking of the colonists. After England declared a complete blockade against American seaports, the colonial assemblies, one by one, instructed their delegates in Congress to vote in favor of independence if such a motion were brought forward.

Richard Henry Lee of Virginia introduced the motion on June 7, 1776. The vote was delayed for nearly a month while some of the delegates requested instructions from home, and in the meantime Congress appointed a committee to draft a formal declaration of independence.

---

9. To George Washington (21 June 1776), Smyth 6:449-50.

Signing the Declaration of Independence in 1776 as a member of the Second Continental Congress. Franklin had served on the committee appointed to write the document.

The members of that committee were Benjamin Franklin, John Adams, Thomas Jefferson, Roger Sherman, and Robert Livingston. Jefferson was asked to prepare the draft. When he presented it to the committee for review, Franklin and Adams made a few alterations in the wording (for instance, Franklin revised Jefferson's "We hold these truths to be sacred and undeniable" to read "We hold these truths to be self-evident"); but they basically approved it in its original form to be submitted to Congress.

Lee's motion for independence was carried on July 2, and the final version of the Declaration was adopted two days later. When the engrossed copy was presented for the delegates' signatures on August 2, John Hancock (president of the Continental Congress) reportedly declared, "We must be unanimous; there must be no pulling different ways; we must all hang together." And Franklin is credited with this reply: "Yes, we must indeed all hang together, or most assuredly we shall all hang separately!"[10]

---

10. Quoted in Van Doren, *Benjamin Franklin*, p. 551.

Another Futile Attempt at Reconciliation

A week after the Declaration of Independence was adopted on July 4, 1776, Admiral Lord Howe arrived in command of the British fleet to join his brother, General William Howe, in putting down the American rebels. But he was also authorized to conclude a peace with the colonists if possible. Inasmuch as the British government did not recognize Congress, Lord Howe made his approach through Franklin, with whom he had negotiated earlier in London. Howe's letter spoke of "the King's paternal solicitude" and offered full pardon to all Americans who would submit to the Crown. After consulting with Congressional leaders, Franklin sent a tough response:

> Directing pardons to be offered to the colonies, who are the very parties injured, expresses indeed that opinion of our ignorance, baseness, and insensibility which your uninformed and proud nation has long been pleased to entertain of us; but it can have no other effect than that of increasing our resentments. It is impossible we should think of submission to a government that has, with the most wanton barbarity and cruelty, burnt our defenseless towns in the midst of winter, excited the savages to massacre our peaceful farmers, and our slaves to murder their masters, and is even now bringing foreign mercenaries to deluge our settlements with blood. These atrocious injuries have extinguished every remaining spark of affection for that parent country we once held so dear....
>
> Your Lordship mentions "the King's paternal solicitude for promoting the establishment of lasting peace and union with the colonies." If by peace is here meant a peace to be entered into between Britain and

America as distinct states now at war, and his Majesty has given your Lordship powers to treat with us of such a peace, I may venture to say, though without authority, that I think a treaty for that purpose not yet quite impracticable before we enter into foreign alliances. But I am persuaded you have no such powers.

Your nation, though, by punishing those American governors who have fomented the discord, rebuilding our burnt towns, and repairing as far as possible the mischiefs done us, might yet recover a great share of our regard and the greatest part of our growing commerce, with all the advantage of that additional strength to be derived from a friendship with us. But I know too well her abounding pride and deficient wisdom to believe she will ever take such salutary measures.

Franklin went on to say that he truly lamented the breaking up of "that fine and noble china vase, the British empire," but that he considered "this war against us . . . as both unjust and unwise; and I am persuaded that cool, dispassionate posterity will condemn to infamy those who advised it."[11]

Such a letter could not have been encouraging to Lord Howe. Nevertheless, he invited Congress to send representatives to meet with him privately to discuss a possible conciliation. Accordingly, Franklin, John Adams, and Edward Rutledge journeyed to Howe's headquarters at Staten Island in September. Their discussions were inconclusive, however; since Lord Howe was not authorized to treat formally with Congress, and since any British terms would have required a complete disavowal

---

11. To Lord Howe (30 July 1776), Smyth 6:459-61.

of American independence, it became clear that no diplomatic solution was possible.

A Demanding Summer

Franklin remained active in his public duties throughout the summer of 1776, with new tasks being added almost every week. Because of his previous experience, Congress appointed him Postmaster General of the new nation; by the end of the year his postal system handled the mails from Maine to Georgia. (He donated his annual salary of $1,000 for the relief of wounded American soldiers.)

He served on a committee with John Adams and Thomas Jefferson to draw up a proposal for the Great Seal of the United States, for which he suggested a motto that Jefferson later used on his own seal: "Rebellion to tyrants is obedience to God."[12] Although Congress later adopted a simpler design, a proposal developed by this committee was significant because of its recognition of important elements in the heritage of all Americans: one side of the seal depicted the Anglo-Saxon leaders Hengist and Horsa, while the other side portrayed the ancient Israelites being led through the wilderness by God's pillar of fire. (Jefferson, who prepared this original design, wanted to emphasize the historical influence of these two civilizations on his countrymen's personal liberties and on

---

12. Originally printed in the *Pennsylvania Evening Post* (14 Dec. 1775) as the last line of an imaginary epitaph for "John Bradshaw." Van Doren, *Autobiographical Writings,* pp. 412-13. See also Julian P. Boyd, ed., *The Papers of Thomas Jefferson,* 19 vols. by 1974 (Princeton, N.J.: Princeton University Press, 1950-   ), 1:677-79.

the political institutions of the United States; Franklin and Adams evidently concurred.)[13]

Franklin was also chosen to preside over the convention which framed the Pennsylvania state constitution that summer. Although his attendance at these sessions was somewhat limited by his other commitments in Congress, he did speak occasionally in the debates. When the convention approved a plan in September, he was happy to see that it included two of his favorite provisions: a plural executive council and a single legislative chamber. (To Franklin, the bicameral legislature seemed like a "snake with two heads and one body.")[14]

When the Congressional debates over a confederation of the American states opened in July, he took a more active role. Some of his motions were unsuccessful, such as the one on August 1 calling for representation in Congress on the basis of population (rather than an equal number of votes for each state). But as Jefferson later remembered, Franklin was able to bring his wit to bear when it was needed to ease tensions among his colleagues:

> The confederation of the states, while on the carpet before the old Congress, was strenuously opposed by the smaller states under apprehensions that they would be swallowed up by the larger ones. We were long engaged in the discussion; it produced great heats, much

---

13. See Gilbert Chinard, *Thomas Jefferson: The Apostle of Americanism*, 2nd ed. rev. (Ann Arbor: The University of Michigan Press, 1964), pp. 86-87; Richard S. Patterson and Richardson Dougall, *The Eagle and the Shield: A History of the Great Seal of the United States* (Washington: U.S. Department of State, 1976), pp. 16-18.

14. "Queries and Remarks Respecting Alterations in the Constitution of Pennsylvania" (Nov. 1789), Smyth 10:57.

ill humor, and intemperate declarations from some members.

Dr. Franklin at length brought the debate to a close with one of his little apologues. He observed that "at the time of the union of England and Scotland, the duke of Argyle was most violently opposed to that measure, and among other things predicted that, as the whale had swallowed Jonah, so Scotland would be swallowed by England. However," said the Doctor, "when Lord Bute came into the government, he soon brought into its administration so many of his countrymen that it was found in event that Jonah swallowed the whale." This little story produced a general laugh, and restored good humor, and the article of difficulty was passed. [15]

---

15. "Anecdotes of Benjamin Franklin," written by Thomas Jefferson to Robert Walsh (4 Dec. 1818), Bergh 18:167.

Chapter 22

Sent to France at
Age Seventy

On September 26, 1776, Congress appointed Benjamin Franklin, Thomas Jefferson, and Silas Deane as commissioners to negotiate a treaty of alliance with the French government. (Jefferson declined because of his wife's ill health, and Arthur Lee was later chosen in his place.) Franklin expressed his willingness, as usual: "I am old and good for nothing; but, as the storekeepers say of their remnants of cloth, 'I am but a fag end, and you may have me for what you please.'"[1]

Before departing, Franklin loaned all the money he could raise—between three and four thousand pounds—to Congress for the war effort. It was a time of crisis for the new nation; Washington's army had recently suffered

---

1. Quoted in Smyth 10:301.

serious defeats in New York, and Congress was still unable to agree on a form of national government. But the philosopher from Philadelphia never lost his faith in the eventual victory. The day before he sailed, he wrote these words: "I hope our people will keep up their courage. I have no doubt of their finally succeeding by the blessing of God, nor have I any doubt that so good a cause will fail of that blessing."[2] On October 26 he embarked for the hazardous voyage, leaving his fair city for what he may have thought was the last time.

Early Efforts for a Treaty

When Franklin sailed for France, he took with him two grandsons: William's sixteen-year-old son William Temple Franklin, commonly called Temple, and Sally's seven-year-old son Benjamin Franklin Bache. Temple would serve as his grandfather's personal secretary while "Benny" attended school in Europe. The vessel in which they crossed the Atlantic was the *Reprisal,* a warship owned by Congress. It must have been an anxious voyage, for in the event of a capture at sea Franklin would have been convicted of treason and hanged.

After a safe crossing, they dropped anchor on December 3, 1776, at Auray, France. Franklin, who already enjoyed quite a reputation among the French people, was warmly greeted on his arrival and was the guest of honor at many banquets and festivities during the overland journey to Paris. He finally reached the French capital on December 21, and immediately he went to work. Within two days he requested an audience with the foreign minister,

---

2. To an unknown correspondent (25 Oct. 1776), in Fleming, *Benjamin Franklin: A Biography in His Own Words,* p. 280.

Vergennes, and proposed "a treaty of amity and commerce between France and the United States."[3]

Unfortunately, this mission would not be simple. There was no hesitation on the part of French traders, who were already smuggling munitions to America (with the knowledge of Vergennes) by means of a fictitious commercial house called Roderigue Hortalez and

The Comte de Vergennes, foreign minister of France, with whom Franklin and his fellow commissioners negotiated the Franco-American alliance in early 1778.

Company. But the French government, not eager for another war with England and still unsure of the outcome of the American Revolution, was not yet willing to enter into a formal treaty. The objective of the American commissioners would require patience and careful diplomacy.

Idolized by the French People

Franklin apparently felt like quite an oddity as he compared himself to the elegant Frenchmen all around him. "Figure me in your mind," he wrote an old friend shortly after his arrival, "as jolly as formerly, and as strong and hearty, only a few years older; very plainly dressed, wearing my thin, gray, straight hair that peeps out under my only *coiffure*, a fine fur cap, which comes down my forehead almost to my spectacles. Think how this must appear among the powdered heads of Paris!"[4]

3. To the Comte de Vergennes (23 Dec. 1776), Smyth 6:477.
4. To Mrs. Thompson (8 Feb. 1777), Smyth 7:26.

But the citizens of France seemed to have no objections. As the news spread that Benjamin Franklin was in Paris, he was hailed everywhere as a national idol, the leader of the American Revolution, a great hero of the rights of man. John Adams, who later came to France to replace Silas Deane, attempted to characterize the impression Franklin made on the French people:

> His reputation was more universal than that of Leibnitz or Newton, Frederick or Voltaire, and his character more beloved and esteemed than any or all of them.... His name was familiar to government and people, to kings, courtiers, nobility, clergy, and philosophers, as well as plebeians, to such a degree that there was scarcely a peasant or a citizen, a *valet de chambre,* coachman, or footman, a lady's chambermaid or a scullion in a kitchen who was not familiar with it, and who did not consider him as a friend to humankind. When they spoke of him, they seemed to think he was to restore the golden age.... His plans and his example were to abolish monarchy, aristocracy, and hierarchy throughout the world. [5]

Franklin's name appeared constantly in the French newspapers, and he was frequently invited to dine with prominent persons. The statesman Turgot devised a now-famous Latin epigram for the American philosopher (one translation reads, "He snatched the lightning from the heavens and the scepter from tyrants"), and the renowned sculptor Houdon executed a marble bust of him in 1778. His picture was everywhere. As one newspaper put it, "It

---

5. Extract from the *Boston Patriot* (15 May 1811), Charles Francis Adams, ed., *The Works of John Adams,* 10 vols. (Boston: Little, Brown and Company, 1850-56), 1:660-63.

is the mode of today for everybody to have an engraving of M. Franklin over the mantelpiece."[6] Franklin himself wrote to his sister in 1779, "This popularity has occasioned so many paintings, busts, medals, and prints to be made of me, and distributed throughout the kingdom, that my face is now almost as well known as that of the moon."[7] By the next year he was complaining, "I have, at the request of friends, sat so much and so often to painters and statuaries that I am perfectly sick of it."[8]

"These Applications Are My Perpetual Torment"

He had no peace even at his private residence. "No one who did not witness it," recorded his grandson Temple Franklin, "can conceive how much his reputation as a philosopher, and his situation as American minister, subjected him to the applications of projectors, speculators, and adventurers of all descriptions."[9] Many of these persons were European military officers seeking written recommendations to serve in the American army under General Washington. "These applications are my perpetual torment," he lamented to a friend. "You can have no conception how I am harassed. All my friends are sought out and teased to tease me. Great officers of all ranks...worry me from morning to night."[10] He did finally recommend two such applicants: the Marquis de Lafayette, who later proved so helpful to the American

---

6. Quoted in Goodman, *A Benjamin Franklin Reader*, p. 22.

7. To Jane Mecom (25 Oct. 1779), Van Doren, *Autobiographical Writings*, p. 472.

8. To Thomas Digges (25 June 1780), Smyth 8:110.

9. Quoted in Van Doren, *Autobiographical Writings*, p. 460 (headnote).

10. To a friend (1777?), Smyth 7:81-82.

cause, and Frederick William Augustus von Steuben, who had served as an aide to Frederick the Great in the Prussian army (his extensive military background qualified him to drill Washington's troops at Valley Forge in early 1778).

British Spies in Paris

There was one group of people, however, who were very unhappy that Franklin was in Paris. The English ministers, who knew of his presence in France as soon as he had landed, greatly feared his influence with the French government; by now, George III warily looked on him as the "evil genius behind the Revolution."[11] As early as January 1777, the month after he arrived in Paris, a friend warned him that he was surrounded by British spies. But he replied in typically unruffled fashion:

> It is impossible . . . to prevent being watched by spies when interested people may think proper to place them for that purpose. I have long observed one rule which prevents any inconvenience from such practices. It is simply this, to be concerned in no affairs that I should blush to have made public, and to do nothing but what spies may see and welcome. When a man's actions are just and honorable, the more they are known, the more his reputation is increased and established. If I were sure, therefore, that my *valet de place* was a spy, as probably he is, I think I should not discharge him for that if in other respects I liked him.[12]

There *were* spies, as it turned out. One of these, though Franklin did not know it at the time, was Edward Bancroft,

---

11. Quoted in Hall, "Benjamin Franklin: Philosopher of Dissent," p. 93.
12. To Juliana Ritchie (19 Jan. 1777), Smyth 7:11.

his former friend in London (and a fellow member of the Royal Society) who now served on occasion as secretary to the American commissioners. Bancroft communicated with the English ambassador in Paris by means of secret messages (written in invisible ink!) which he sealed in a bottle and then deposited in the trunk of a hollow tree outside the city. Franklin did occasionally try to avoid British agents—he changed carriages en route to some of his meetings with Vergennes, for example—but he generally ignored them.

A notable instance of covert activity took place in the summer of 1778. One day near the middle of June, someone tossed through the gate of Franklin's courtyard a letter written in English over the pseudonym "Charles de Weissenstein." The lengthy communication, which was to be seen by no one but Franklin until he had read and thoroughly considered it, proposed a detailed "plan of reconciliation" and an outline for the future government of America. (This involved, among other things, "places, pensions, and peerages" for any Americans willing to cooperate.) Franklin was requested to draft a response and leave it with "a stranger...next Monday in the church of Notre Dame, to be known by a rose in his hat." He did prepare an answer, which he decided he could "convey in a less mysterious manner," but it was certainly not the kind of answer that would have pleased Weissenstein's superiors. It read in part:

> You conjure me in the name of the omniscient and just God before whom I must appear, and by my hopes of future fame, to consider if some expedient cannot be found to put a stop to the desolation of America and

prevent the miseries of a general war. As I am conscious of having taken every step in my power to prevent the breach, and no one to widen it, I can appear cheerfully before that God, fearing nothing from his justice in this particular, though I have much occasion for his mercy in many others.

As to my future fame, I am content to rest it on my past and present conduct, without seeking an addition to it in the crooked, dark paths you propose to me.... This your solemn address would therefore have been more properly made to your sovereign and his venal Parliament. He and they, who wickedly began and madly continue a war for the desolation of America, are alone accountable for the consequences. [13]

"A Most Amiable Nation to Live With"

After staying in Paris awhile, Franklin moved to a suburban village named Passy just outside the city. He described his new residence as "a fine house situated in a neat village on high ground, half a mile from Paris, with a large garden to walk in." Because of the large number of dinner invitations, he generally ate away from home—"six days in seven," he said. But "Sundays I reserve to dine at home with such Americans as pass this way; and I then have my grandson Ben, with some other American children from his school."[14] He was grateful to have his grandsons with him. He spoke of Temple as "my right hand,"[15] and he kept young Benny close to him at a

---

13. To Charles de Weissenstein (1 July 1778), Smyth 7:166-72.

14. To Mrs. Margaret Stevenson (25 Jan. 1779), Smyth 7:223.

15. To Richard and Sarah Bache (4 Oct. 1780), in Lopez and Herbert, *The Private Franklin*, p. 243.

boarding school in Passy (later he placed him in another school in Geneva).

He also enjoyed his neighbors, as he considered the French "a most amiable nation to live with."[16] Shortly after reaching Paris he took steps to strengthen the many private and scholarly friendships he had formed during earlier visits to France. In 1777 he was admitted as a member of the Masonic Lodge of the Nine Sisters; two years later he was chosen grand master. Some of the members of this lodge proved helpful to Franklin's diplomatic efforts because of their admiration for him and their interest in the American experiment in republican government. For example, one of them accepted Franklin's request to translate the American state constitutions into French so that copies could be provided to every foreign ambassador in Paris and eventually dispersed throughout Europe.

Franklin also made use of the press to influence public opinion and to encourage support of the Revolution among European governments. "By loans to America," he wrote in one piece, "they are opposing tyranny and aiding the cause of liberty, which is the cause of all mankind."[17] And he knew how to use his personal charm as well. Thomas Jefferson, who later joined Franklin in Paris, recalled an incident that illustrates Franklin's wit and subtle diplomacy in influential circles:

> When Dr. Franklin went to France on his revolutionary mission, his eminence as a philosopher,

---

16. To Josiah Quincy, Sr. (22 Apr. 1779), Smyth 7:290.

17. "Comparison of Great Britain and the United States in Regard to the Basis of Credit in the Two Countries" (1777), Smyth 7:8. This paper was translated into several languages and widely circulated throughout Europe.

his venerable appearance, and the cause on which he was sent rendered him extremely popular. For all ranks and conditions of men there entered warmly into the American interest. He was, therefore, feasted and invited into all the court parties. At these he sometimes met the old Duchess of Bourbon, who, being a chess player of about his force, they very generally played together. Happening once to put her king into prize, the Doctor took it. "Ah," said she, "we do not take kings so." "We do in America," said the Doctor. [18]

The more evidence Franklin found of widespread support for the American cause, the more sanguine became his hopes for victory in the war with Great Britain. "All Europe is on our side of the question," he said. "It is a common observation here that our cause is *the cause of all mankind,* and that we are fighting for their liberty in defending our own. It is a glorious task assigned us by Providence, which has, I trust, given us spirit and virtue equal to it, and will at last crown it with success." [19]

18. "Anecdotes of Benjamin Franklin," written by Jefferson to Robert Walsh (4 Dec. 1818), Bergh, *The Writings of Thomas Jefferson,* 18:167-68.

19. To Samuel Cooper (1 May 1777), Smyth 7:56.

Chapter 23

Negotiating the Historic French Alliance

Despite his confidence that America would ultimately triumph over Great Britain, Franklin remained bitterly resentful about the war itself. "Of all the wars in my time," he told a friend, "this on the part of England appears to me the wickedest, having no cause but malice against liberty and the jealousy of commerce."[1] His resentment increased when he learned that British troops had invaded Philadelphia and occupied his own home during the winter of 1777-78, forcing his daughter's family to flee and live with friends in the country for several months.

Franklin had maintained his correspondence with close friends in London since the outbreak of the war. After he

---

1. To Joseph Priestley (27 Jan. 1777), Smyth 7:18.

came to France, some of them indicated that they still hoped for reconciliation and a continuing union of the two countries. But Franklin now bristled at such an idea. "As to our submitting to the government of Great Britain," he replied to one of them, "it is vain to think of it. She has given us, by her numberless barbarities in the prosecution of the war ... so deep an impression of her depravity that we never again can trust her in the management of our affairs and interests.... You are unfit and unworthy to govern us."[2]

Protesting the Mistreatment of American Prisoners

The American commissioner was particularly upset over England's cruel treatment of his countrymen who had been captured in battle. He lodged several protests, including this one to Lord Stormont, the British ambassador to France:

> It has been said that among the civilized nations of Europe, the ancient horrors of [war] are much diminished. But the compelling men by chains, stripes, and famine to fight against their friends and relations is a new mode of barbarity which your nation alone has the honor of inventing. And the sending American prisoners of war to Africa and Asia, remote from all probability of exchange, and where they can scarce hope ever to hear from their families even if the unwholesomeness of the climate does not put a speedy end to their lives, is a manner of treating captives that

---

2. To David Hartley (14 Oct. 1777), Smyth 7:69-70.

you can justify by no precedent or custom except that of the black savages of Guinea. [3]

Stormont quickly returned the note with the curt reply, "The King's ambassador receives no letters from rebels but when they come to implore His Majesty's mercy." Franklin tried repeatedly, through several channels, to negotiate with England for the exchange of prisoners taken during the war. It was not until March 1779 that his efforts finally began to bear fruit.

The Franco-American Alliance

After the loss of Philadelphia to General Howe and the invasion from Canada by General Burgoyne's army of 8,000—both in 1777—the Americans were becoming desperate for foreign help in carrying on the war. Franklin and his fellow commissioners in Paris proposed a triple alliance between France, Spain, and the United States. France was enticed by the growing trade advantages of a treaty with the Americans; but she remained reluctant to enter the war without her Spanish allies, and Spain held back.

On October 17, 1777, Burgoyne's entire army surrendered at Saratoga. When news of this stunning victory reached Paris in early December, the American commissioners renewed their proposal for an alliance. Spain firmly decided against a treaty, so the French court now began debating the advisability of entering the war alone. England had also resumed its overtures for an early reconciliation with the United States, and several secret agents requested meetings with Franklin at his residence

---

3. To Lord Stormont (2 Apr. 1777), Smyth 7:37.

in Passy. He finally agreed to meet with Paul Wentworth, head of the British secret service in Paris, on January 6, 1778. (This was probably just a strategy designed to tantalize Vergennes, as Franklin knew the French government feared the possibility of a peaceful conclusion to the war before a trade agreement could be reached with the Americans.) The very next day, Louis XVI's royal council announced a favorable decision.

The formal treaty of alliance and another treaty of amity and commerce were signed by Franklin, Silas Deane, Arthur Lee, and the French plenipotentiary Conrad Alexandre Gerard on February 6 at the office of the foreign affairs ministry in Paris. In a letter written several days later, Franklin made some personal observations on the terms of the two treaties.

> The . . . King agrees to make a common cause with the United States if England attempts to obstruct the commerce of his subjects with them, and guarantees to the United States their liberties, sovereignty, and independence, absolute and unlimited, with the possessions they now have, or may have at the conclusion of the war; and the [United] States in return guarantees to him his possessions in the West Indies.
>
> The great principle in both treaties is a perfect equality and reciprocity, no advantages being demanded by France, or privileges in commerce, which the [United] States may not grant to any and every other nation. In short, the King has treated with us generously and magnanimously, taking no advantage of our present difficulties to exact terms which we would not willingly grant when established in prosperity and power. I may add that he has acted wisely in wishing the friendship

contracted by these treaties may be durable, which probably it might not be if a contrary conduct had been observed.[4]

"A Little Revenge"

At the signing ceremony, Dean noticed that Franklin wore an old, blue Manchester velvet suit which had long lain dormant. He asked why. "To give it a little revenge," replied Franklin. "I wore this coat on the day Wedderburn abused me at Whitehall."[5] When King George III learned of the Franco-American alliance and Franklin's role in it, he lashed out in anger at "that insidious man," charging that "hatred to this country is the constant object of his mind."[6]

Louis XVI reacted more graciously. In March 1778 he received Franklin and his associates in recognition of the new treaties. When the American philosopher entered the royal courtyard, something of a spectacle in his simple dress, he was wildly cheered by crowds of French citizens who seemingly forgot the etiquette

King Louis XVI receiving Franklin after the formal signing of the Franco-American treaty of alliance. This alliance was a major factor in determining the outcome of the Revolutionary War.

---

4. To Thomas Cushing (27 Feb. 1778), Smyth 7:110-11.

5. Quoted in Van Doren, *Benjamin Franklin*, p. 594.

6. Quoted in Donovan, *The Benjamin Franklin Papers*, pp. 190–91.

of the palace. The King spoke first, praising the conduct of the American envoys in Paris. "Firmly assure Congress," he then said, "of my friendship. I hope that this will be for the good of the two nations." Franklin responded, "Your Majesty may count on the gratitude of Congress and its faithful observance of the pledges it now takes."[7]

The treaties with France were ratified by Congress several weeks later, and the British ministry continued to express bitterness over the alliance. One of Franklin's friends from England, knowing the mood of his government, sent a brief note warning him to look out for his own safety. Franklin's answer was equally brief: "I thank you for your kind caution, but having nearly finished a long life, I set but little value on what remains of it.... Perhaps the best use such an old fellow can be put to is to make a martyr of him."[8]

Distempers and Accusations

It soon became apparent, however, that the only attacks Franklin had to fear were from his own colleagues and countrymen. John Adams arrived in Paris in April 1778 to replace Silas Deane, who had sailed back to America with the French ambassador appointed after the treaties were signed. The third commissioner, Arthur Lee, evidently wished that Franklin had also been sent back home. Lee, who had already charged Deane with financial misconduct, wrote to his brother in Congress that the "old doctor" was also "concerned in the plunder, and ... in time

---

7. Quoted in Van Doren, *Benjamin Franklin*, p. 595.
8. To David Hartley (Apr. 1778), Smyth 7:142-43.

we shall collect the proofs."[9] He further seemed to think that he was the only American in Paris with sufficient virtue and competence to properly manage the agency, so he deeply resented having to serve under the thumb of the senior commissioner. This resentment showed itself in the form of repeated dissensions and backbiting.

On one of the many occasions when Lee declared himself insulted over some trivial matter, Franklin decided he had had enough. His written response revealed an unusual degree of impatience if not outright indignation:

> It is true I have omitted answering some of your letters. I do not like to answer angry letters. I hate disputes. I am old, cannot have long to live, have much to do and no time for altercation. If I have often received and borne your magisterial snubbings and rebukes without reply, ascribe it to the right causes: my concern for the honor and success of our mission, which would be hurt by our quarreling; my love of peace; my respect for your good qualities; and my pity of your sick mind, which is forever tormenting itself with its jealousies, suspicions, and fancies that others mean you ill, wrong you, or fail in respect for you.
>
> If you do not cure yourself of this temper, it will end in insanity, of which it is the symptomatic forerunner, as I have seen in several instances. God preserve you from so terrible an evil; and for his sake, pray suffer me to live in quiet.[10]

---

9. Arthur Lee to Richard Henry Lee (12 Sept. 1778), in Lopez and Herbert, *The Private Franklin*, p. 235.

10. To Arthur Lee (3 Apr. 1778), Smyth 7:132. Franklin later said of Lee: "That genius must either find or make a quarrel wherever he is.... If some of the enemies he provokes do not kill him sooner, he will die in a madhouse." To Samuel Wharton (17 June 1780), Smyth 8:96.

Congress wisely revoked the joint commission in September 1778 and named Franklin sole minister to France. The following March he was presented to King Louis XVI in his new role and "went the rounds with the other foreign ministers in visiting all the royal family."[11] Ironically, the only delegation in Congress which had voted against Franklin's appointment was the one from Pennsylvania. Franklin was dismayed when he learned that their opposition was based on the fact that his personal secretary (his grandson Temple Franklin) happened to be the son of a loyalist.

> I am surprised to hear that my grandson . . . being with me should be an objection against me, and that there is a cabal for removing him. Methinks it is rather some merit that I have rescued a valuable young man from the danger of being a Tory, and fixed him in honest republican Whig principles. . . . It is enough that I have lost my *son;* would they add my *grandson?*[12]

As long as Franklin remained in France, petty jealousies and accusations continued to issue from his detractors in America. A common charge among them was that he harbored more loyalty for the French government than for his own. But Jefferson later observed that Franklin's political enemies were a product of his decisiveness and strength of expression rather than any malfeasance in public office. "As to the charge of subservience to France," he wrote, "it had not a shadow of foundation. He [Franklin] possessed the confidence of that government in the highest degree, insomuch that it may truly be said that

---

11. To John Adams (3 Apr. 1779), Smyth 7:278.
12. To Richard Bache (2 June 1779), Smyth 7:345.

they were more under his influence than he under theirs."[13]

More Duties, Greater Demands

As Franklin began in early 1779 to function as the sole American minister to France, he found that his duties were multiplying rapidly. "Besides his own office," noted one biographer, "he held also in effect that of United States consul-general, director of naval affairs, and judge of admiralty."[14] He met with many Europeans who had information that might be useful in the war effort, and many others who wanted to emigrate to the United States. He drafted instructions for John Paul Jones to use in a planned attack on the British coast. And he commissioned American privateers to raid British ships, then sat in judgment regarding the condemnation and sale of prizes taken in those raids.

He also spent a good deal of his time seeking loans from the French government—eighteen million livres' worth by 1782—and personally handled the payment of drafts received from Congress. In October 1780 he complained that the continual "storm of bills [from America] has terrified and vexed me to such a degree that I have been deprived of sleep."[15] He also confided to John Adams, who was at that time in Holland seeking additional loans, "I have long been humiliated with the idea of our running about from court to court begging for money."[16] At the

---

13. Thomas Jefferson to Robert Walsh (4 Dec. 1818), Bergh, *The Writings of Thomas Jefferson*, 15:176.

14. Van Doren, *Benjamin Franklin*, p. 616.

15. To John Jay (2 Oct. 1780), Smyth 8:142.

16. To John Adams (2 Oct. 1780), Smyth 8:146.

same time, he wrote to Congressional leaders and admonished them to exercise more restraint, self-reliance, and frugality in public expenditures. Franklin believed that the same virtues which had made him a successful businessman in earlier years could now help ensure the triumph of the American cause.

Chapter 24

Enjoying Life in Paris

I n the midst of his many diplomatic responsibilities, Franklin still found a little time for relaxation. He wrote to his sister in April 1779 that the vicinity in which he lived had "many good houses and families, with whom I live in friendship and pass a leisure hour, when I have one, with pleasure."[1]

"Let Us Avenge Ourselves!"

One of these neighbors was an elderly but handsome widow named Anne-Catherine de Ligniville Helvetius. Franklin formed a lively friendship with Madame Helvetius, and sometime in 1780 he apparently proposed marriage to her—"whether seriously or as part of a mock

1. To Jane Mecom (22 Apr. 1779), Goodman, *A Benjamin Franklin Reader,* p. 654.

Madame Helvetius, who rejected
Franklin's proposal of marriage in 1780.

romance with which they amused themselves is not clear," writes one historian.[2]

But she turned him down, professing a resolve to be faithful to the memory of her former husband. So her witty American friend promptly concocted a story to dissuade her from this "barbarous resolution." He described a dream wherein he had died and was "transported to the Elysian Fields," there to meet the late Helvetius. After they conversed awhile about conditions in France, Franklin asked why the man had not inquired about his dear wife, who was still very much in love with him.

"Ah," said he, "you make me recur to my past happiness, which ought to be forgotten in order to be happy here. For many years I could think of nothing but her, though at length I am consoled. I have taken another wife, the most like her that I could find; she is not indeed altogether so handsome, but she has a great fund of wit and good sense, and her whole study is to please me. She is at this moment gone to fetch the best nectar and ambrosia to regale me; stay awhile and you will see her."

2. Donovan, *The Benjamin Franklin Papers,* p. 255.

"I perceive," said I, "that your former friend is more faithful to you than you are to her; she has had several good offers, but has refused them all. I will confess to you that I loved her extremely; but she was cruel to me, and rejected me peremptorily for your sake."

[Shortly thereafter] the new Madame Helvetius entered with the nectar, and I recognized her immediately as my former American friend, Mrs. Franklin! I reclaimed her, but she answered me coldly: "I was a good wife to you for ... nearly half a century; let that content you. I have formed a new connection here, which will last to eternity."

As Franklin finished recounting this little fictional episode to Madame Helvetius, he reached his punch line: "I immediately resolved to quit those ungrateful shades, and return to this good world again to behold the sun and you. Here I am; let us *avenge ourselves!*" [3]

"Somebody ... Gave It Out That I Loved Ladies"

Among the friendships Franklin made during these years were several other women as well, including the younger Madame Brillon, who adopted him to take the place of her late father and called him "my Papa." [4] But the legend that he indulged in intimate affairs with the ladies of Paris is apparently just that—a legend. Part of a letter

3. To Madame Helvetius (1780?), Van Doren, *Autobiographical Writings,* pp. 458-59. This is a translation from the French original, and is one of several "bagatelles" which Franklin composed for his neighbors and printed on the private press he had set up at his residence in Passy.

4. Madame Brillon to BF (11 May 1779), in Smyth 10:412.

he wrote to his stepniece in Boston provides some insight
into the subject:

> You mention the kindness of the French ladies to me. I
> must explain that matter. This is the civilest nation upon
> earth. Your first acquaintances endeavor to find out
> what you like, and they tell others. If it is understood
> that you like mutton, dine where you will you find
> mutton. Somebody, it seems, gave it out that I loved
> ladies; and then everybody presented me their ladies (or
> the ladies presented themselves) to be *embraced,* that is, to
> have their necks kissed. For as to kissing of lips or
> cheeks, it is not the mode here; the first is reckoned
> rude, and the other may rub off the paint. [5]

Carl Van Doren, whose masterful biography of
Franklin was awarded the Pulitzer Prize, noted that "there
is no support for the tradition which insists that the
philosopher was a lively lecher in France."[6] Another
historian has asked, "Did he really have affairs with
French women? There is no shred of evidence. In that age
of diaries and memoirs not a single Parisienne ever
boasted that she had captured the famous *philosophe.*"[7] And
a third scholar places the whole matter in perspective:

> In any sophisticated social gathering at which the
> name of Benjamin Franklin comes up, somebody is
> almost sure to remark with a leer, "Say, that old boy was
> quite a man with the ladies," or "Wasn't he the old
> reprobate?" This concept of the worthy doctor seems to
> have started many years after his death and to have
> grown during recent years—there is no reference to it in

5. To Mrs. Elizabeth Partridge (11 Oct. 1779), Smyth 7:393-94.

6. Van Doren, *Benjamin Franklin,* p. 639.

7. Lopez and Herbert, *The Private Franklin,* p. 274.

early writings about him, except for scurrilous political slander regarding his son William's legitimacy.

There is not one iota of evidence in history to justify this image. True, Franklin liked women, and many women adored Franklin. He was closely associated with several, ranging from eleven-year-old Catherine Shipley in England to sixtyish Madame Helvetius in France. He spent much time in their company, and some of his most interesting writing is in correspondence with female friends. But there is nothing to indicate that his relations with any of them were other than gallant and intellectual. [8]

No wonder Jefferson wrote in later years: "I have seen, with extreme indignation, the blasphemies lately vended against the memory of the father of American philosophy. But his memory will be preserved and venerated as long as the thunder of heaven shall be heard or feared."[9]

Continuing Interest in Science

Although he was generally too busy to further his own scientific experiments while in France, Franklin maintained his lifelong interest in "natural philosophy" by visiting laboratories and by attending meetings of the Academy of Sciences and the Royal Society of Medicine, to which he was admitted in 1777. (He was also elected to membership in many other learned societies throughout Europe.) Various collections and translations of Franklin's scientific, philosophical, and political writings were published in France, England, Germany, and Italy, and his

---

8. Donovan, p. 235.

9. Thomas Jefferson to Jonathan Williams (3 July 1796), Bergh, *The Writings of Thomas Jefferson*, 9:348.

correspondence during these years continued to deal occasionally with geology, linguistics, and other scholarly topics.

In 1783 he witnessed, with about 50,000 other people, the first ascent of a hot-air balloon from Paris, and afterwards he wrote enthusiastically about the potential applications of such an achievement. (It is reported that when a skeptical bystander asked, "What good is it?" Franklin replied, "What good is a newborn baby?") [10] In 1784 he participated in a commission appointed by Louis XVI and the Academy of Sciences to investigate mesmerism—a scheme of healing ailments by "animal magnetism" which had been introduced by Friedrich Anton Mesmer, then in Paris. The expose published by this commission greatly boosted the international fame of Franklin, whose signature appeared first in the document.

It was also about this time that he invented bifocals. [11] But as usual, he sought no patent. "I have no private interest in the reception of my inventions by the world," he said, "having never made, nor proposed to make, the least profit by them." [12] The only apparent reasons for Franklin's interest in science were his natural curiosity and his sincere desire to improve the lot of his fellowmen. He believed that "true science" offered much to mankind in the future.

> The rapid progress *true* science now makes occasions my regretting sometimes that I was born so soon. It is impossible to imagine the height to which may be

---

10. Quoted in Donovan, p. 82.

11. See his letter to George Whatley (23 May 1785), Smyth 9:337-38.

12. To an unknown correspondent (4 Oct. 1777), Smyth 7:65.

carried, in a thousand years, the power of man over matter. We may perhaps learn to deprive large masses of their gravity and give them absolute levity for the sake of easy transport. Agriculture may diminish its labor and double its produce; all diseases may by sure means be prevented or cured, not excepting even that of old age, and our lives lengthened at pleasure even beyond the antediluvian standard. O that moral science were in as fair a way of improvement, that men would cease to be wolves to one another, and that human beings would at length learn what they now improperly call humanity! [13]

---

13. To Joseph Priestley (8 Feb. 1780), Smyth 8:10.

Chapter 25

The War Ends, The Diplomat Returns

Wanting to "spend the evening of life more agreeably in philosophic leisure,"[1] and fearing that his declining health would soon render him unable to meet the heavy demands of his office, Franklin wrote to the president of Congress in March 1781 and offered to resign as minister to France.

> I have passed my seventy-fifth year, and I find that the long and severe fit of the gout which I had the last winter has shaken me exceedingly, and I am yet far from having recovered the bodily strength I before enjoyed. I do not know that my mental faculties are impaired; perhaps I shall be the last to discover that. But I am sensible of great diminution in my activity, a quality I

---

1. To Jan Ingenhousz (2 Oct. 1781), Smyth 8:315.

think particularly necessary in your minister for this
court. I am afraid, therefore, that your affairs may
sometime or other suffer by my deficiency. . . .

I have been engaged in public affairs and enjoyed
public confidence, in some shape or other, during the
long term of fifty years, and honor sufficient to satisfy
any reasonable ambition; and I have no other left but
that of repose, which I hope the Congress will grant me
by sending some person to supply my place. [2]

But several months later he reported to an associate
that "the Congress have done me the honor to refuse
accepting my resignation, and insist on my continuing in
their service till the peace. I must therefore buckle again to
business, and thank God that my health and spirits are of
late improved."[3] Having learned on August 15 that he had
been appointed with John Adams, John Jay, and Henry
Laurens to negotiate peace with Great Britain, he shared
with Adams his personal reaction to this new
responsibility:

I have never known a peace made, even the most
advantageous, that was not censured as inadequate, and
the makers condemned as injudicious or corrupt.
"Blessed are the peacemakers" is, I suppose, to be
understood in the other world, for in this they are
frequently *cursed*. Being as yet rather too much attached
to this world, I had therefore no ambition to be
concerned in fabricating this peace, and know not how I
came to be put into the commission. I esteem it,
however, as an honor to be joined with you in so
important a business; and, if the execution of it shall

2. To Samuel Huntington (12 Mar. 1781), Smyth 8:220-21.
3. To William Carmichael (24 Aug. 1781), Smyth 8:294.

happen in my time, which I hardly expect, I shall endeavor to assist in discharging the duty according to the best of my judgment. [4]

Negotiating to End the War

When the news of Cornwallis's surrender at Yorktown reached Paris in November 1781, Franklin had more reason to believe that a peace treaty with England might be concluded in his lifetime. Parliament spent the next several months, however, debating whether the war should be continued, and it was not until March 1782 that the first negotiators arrived from London.

Franklin alone represented the American commissioners during the first three months of peace discussions. Adams was still in Holland seeking loans for the United States; Jay was in Spain for the same purpose; and Laurens was imprisoned in the Tower of London, having been captured at sea during his voyage to Europe. Among Franklin's early proposals was one calling for the cession of Canada to the United States, both to provide reparation for British aggression and to prevent future collisions.

John Jay finally came from Madrid in late June, but he was unable to participate in the negotiations until early August because of illness. Adams arrived at the end of October, and the three commissioners now turned their full attention to the task at hand. They met daily during the month of November to plan strategy and discuss detailed provisions. Their most serious differences with the English negotiators were over debts and reparations, fishing rights along the Atlantic seacoast, and the

---

4. To John Adams (12 Oct. 1781), Smyth 8:316.

An unfinished painting by Benjamin West depicting the American commissioners in Paris who negotiated the peace treaty with Great Britain in 1782. Left to right: John Jay; John Adams; Franklin; Henry Laurens (who arrived just before the negotiations were concluded, after a period of imprisonment in the Tower of London); and William Temple Franklin, who served as his grandfather's personal secretary during the years in France.

disposition of British loyalists who had fled their homes in America. In the end, Franklin's early demand for Canada was dropped, but the document on which the two sides settled generally followed the terms he had proposed at the outset of the discussions.

The provisions of this historic agreement were clearly advantageous to the United States, thus vindicating the long American struggle against foreign tyranny and enabling the new nation to advance on the world stage from a position of strength rather than weakness. The lasting significance of this diplomatic triumph is reflected in a recent observation made by two noted historians of the twentieth century: "The successful negotiation of the treaty of peace with Great Britain still stands as the greatest achievement in the history of American diplomacy. The United States obtained all its principal objectives—independence, adequate continental territory, access to international waterways, and fisheries. That solid achievement is a tribute to the perspicacity and stubbornness of the American peace negotiators—Benjamin Franklin, John Jay, and John Adams."[5]

The provisional treaty was signed on November 30, 1782, and sent back to the two respective governments for consideration. "At length we are in peace, God be praised," Franklin exclaimed to the daughter of his former landlady in London, "and long, very long, may it continue."[6] To Bishop Jonathan Shipley, another friend in England, he wrote:

> Let us now forgive and forget.... America will, with God's blessing, become a great and happy country; and England, if she has at length gained wisdom, will have gained something more valuable, and more essential to her prosperity, than all she has lost, and will still be a great and respectable nation.[7]

The final articles of peace were signed in Paris on September 3, 1783, and Franklin was exultant: "We are now friends with England and with all mankind. May we

---

5. Henry Steele Commager and Richard B. Morris, eds., *The Spirit of 'Seventy-Six: The Story of the American Revolution as Told by Participants* (New York: Harper & Row, Publishers, 1975), p. 1249.

6. To Mrs. Mary Hewson (27 Jan. 1783), Smyth 9:12.

7. To Jonathan Shipley (17 Mar. 1783), Smyth 9:23.

never see another war! For in my opinion there never was a good war, or a bad peace."[8]

"The Old Man's Wish"

After the peace negotiations were completed, Franklin was under less pressure than he had been for years. Thomas Barclay arrived from the United States to assume some of the duties of the ministry, and Thomas Jefferson came in 1784 to join Franklin and Adams in representing the United States to the European nations (Jefferson would replace Franklin as minister to France the next year). But the senior diplomat continued his efforts on behalf of his country. In March 1783 he concluded a treaty of amity and commerce with the Swedish government, and in 1785 he finalized a similar agreement with Prussia. He drew up plans to restore the postal service between England and America, and he wrote several informative papers which were translated and published throughout Europe (two of these were entitled *Remarks Concerning the Savages of North America* and *Information to Those Who Would Remove to America).* [9]

The greatest obstacle to Franklin's work habits was his physical condition. In 1780 he had been able to boast, "I do not find that I grow any older."[10] But his gout continued to worsen, he occasionally suffered from skin disorders, and during the peace talks in 1782 he was suddenly disabled by a bladder stone. "It is as yet very tolerable," he told John Jay in January 1784. "It gives me no pain but when in a carriage on the pavement, or when I make some

8. To Josiah Quincy, Sr. (11 Sept. 1783), Smyth 9:96.
9. These papers are reprinted in Smyth 8:603-14; 10:97-104.
10. To Thomas Bond (16 Mar. 1780), Smyth 8:37.

sudden, quick movement.... You may judge that my disease is not very grievous, since I am more afraid of the medicines than of the malady."[11]

In the days of his youth, one of Franklin's favorite songs had been "The Old Man's Wish." Each stanza ended with these lines:

> May I govern my passions with an absolute sway,
> Grow wiser and better as my strength wears away,
> Without gout or stone, by a gentle decay.

"But what signifies our wishing?" he lamented in 1785. "Things happen, after all, as they will happen. I have sung that wishing song a thousand times when I was young, and now find at fourscore that the three contraries have befallen me."[12]

Homeward Bound for the Last Time

Because of his ill health, Franklin feared in 1784 that, if he did not return to the United States soon, he would never be able to. "If I am kept here another winter," he wrote, "and as much weakened by it as by the last, I may as well resolve to spend the remainder of my days [in France]; for I shall be hardly able to bear the fatigues of the voyage in returning."[13] But he endured the winter a little better than he expected, and in May 1785 he finally received permission from Congress to sail to America. He still had some doubts about his ability to withstand such a journey, but he explained his plan to his daughter Sally and her husband: "The desire . . . of spending the little remainder

---

11. To John Jay (6 Jan. 1784), Smyth 9:150-51.
12. To George Whatley (23 May 1785), Smyth 9:333.
13. To Charles Thomson (13 May 1784), Smyth 9:213.

of life with my family is so strong as to determine me to try, at least, whether I can bear the motion of a ship. If not, I must get them to set me on shore somewhere in the channel, and content myself to die in Europe."[14]

As Franklin left his residence in Passy on July 12, he took with him a farewell gift from Louis XVI: a miniature portrait of the King set with 408 diamonds. He was also furnished with a royal litter, borne on Spanish mules, to carry him to the port at Havre in his delicate condition. Benny Bache, who followed behind in a carriage with his cousin Temple, recorded that his grandfather departed "in the midst of a very great concourse of the people of Passy; a mournful silence reigned around him, and was only interrupted by a few sobs."[15] Jefferson reflected afterward, "It seemed as if the village had lost its patriarch."[16]

"Nothing Has Ever Hurt Me So Much"

Reaching Havre on July 18, 1785, Franklin crossed the English Channel in a small packet ship and waited for his sailing vessel at Southampton. While there, he was visited by Bishop Jonathan Shipley and several friends from London. Another visitor, one whom he had not seen since 1775, was his son William. It was not a joyful reunion. As president of the Board of Associated Loyalists in New York several years before, William had ordered the hanging of a captured American soldier; in 1782 he fled to England, wanted for murder.

---

14. To Richard and Sarah Bache (10 May 1785), Smyth 9:327.

15. Quoted in Van Doren, *Benjamin Franklin*, p. 723.

16. Thomas Jefferson to an unknown correspondent (19 Feb. 1791), Bergh, *The Writings of Thomas Jefferson*, 8:129.

After the signing of the final peace treaty between England and the United States, William made an effort to end the silence which had stood between himself and his father for nine years. In a letter written in July 1784, he defended his conduct during the war but expressed his desire to "revive that affectionate intercourse and connection which, till the commencement of the late troubles, had been the pride and happiness of my life."[17] The elder Franklin replied that a resumption of correspondence would be "very agreeable" to him, but he candidly acknowledged that "nothing has ever hurt me so much and affected me with such keen sensations, as to find myself deserted in my old age by my only son; and not only deserted, but to find him taking up arms against me in a cause wherein my good fame, fortune, and life were all at stake."[18]

This final, brief meeting of the two Franklins in July 1785 apparently involved little more than the adjustment of certain "family affairs" (for example, William signed a deed to convey his land in New Jersey to his son Temple). They never saw each other again, and few if any letters passed between them thereafter. Seven months later, as Franklin reflected on the joys and sorrows of bringing up children in the world and following their conduct through life, he penned a short allegory describing his personal feelings:

> When we launch our little fleet of barks into the ocean, bound to different ports, we hope for each a

---

17. William Franklin to BF (22 July 1784), in Lopez and Herbert, *The Private Franklin*, p. 252.

18. To William Franklin (16 Aug. 1784), Smyth 9:252-53.

prosperous voyage. But contrary winds, hidden shoals, storms, and enemies come in for a share in the disposition of events; and though these occasion a mixture of disappointment, yet considering the risk where we can make no insurance, we should think ourselves happy if some return with success. [19]

---

19. To Jonathan Shipley (24 Feb. 1786), Smyth 9:490.

Chapter 26

Pennsylvania's New Governor

Cannons boomed in the harbor at Philadelphia to announce the arrival of Franklin's ship on September 14, 1785, and welcoming ceremonies honored him all over town for more than a week. He had eagerly looked forward to this return home, believing that he would no longer be subjected to the pressures of public duty. "I shall now be free of politics for the rest of my life," he wrote just before leaving Europe. "Welcome again, my dear philosophical amusements."[1]

But the citizens of Pennsylvania had other ideas. Only a few days after his vessel landed, three separate political parties in Philadelphia nominated Franklin for election to the state's Supreme Executive Council. "I had not

---

1. To Jan Ingenhousz (29 Apr. 1785), Smyth 9:318.

sufficient firmness to refuse their request," he admitted in a letter to Tom Paine, "though I apprehend they expect too much of me, and that . . . I shall find myself engaged again in business more troublesome than I have lately quitted." [2]

Franklin won the election on October 11, and he took his seat on the 17th. The very next day the Council chose him its president. Before the month was over, he had also been elected by the Assembly as President of Pennsylvania (the equivalent of Governor under their constitution)! He reluctantly accepted the appointment, taking his oath of office on October 31, but he complained privately to some friends in New York: "I find myself harnessed again in [my countrymen's] service for another year. They engrossed the prime of my life. They have eaten my flesh, and seem resolved now to pick my bones." [3]

Because of recurring health problems, Franklin missed many of his council meetings and had his vice-president, Charles Biddle, sign most of the official messages and proclamations. He was active in the legislative arena, however, using the weight of his reputation to urge and influence such measures as the reformation of the state penal code. The public was evidently happy with his performance; after one year in office he was reelected President without a single dissenting vote—except his own.

Domestic and Leisure Activities at Age Eighty

Franklin was glad to be back in his old circles again. By delegating many of his public responsibilities, he was able

---

2. To Thomas Paine (27 Sept. 1785), Smyth 9:467.

3. To Dr. and Mrs. John Bard (14 Nov. 1785), Smyth 9:476.

to find some time for leisure after all. Shortly after returning to Philadelphia he met with members of the Union Fire Company, promising to "have his bucket, etc., in good order by the next meeting."[4] He also resumed his chair as president of the American Philosophical Society, having been reelected annually since 1769.

After reaching his eightieth birthday on January 17, 1786, he devoted more attention to his lingering scholarly interests. Sometime that year he published a work entitled *Maritime Observations*, which contained the first scientific description of the Gulf Stream (based on data he had gathered during several transatlantic voyages, including the most recent one) and dealt with such varied topics as ships' riggings, icebergs, paddlewheels, sailors' diets, and lifeboats. He engaged in several agricultural experiments in his garden, and invented a number of household devices for his own convenience (his "long arm" for removing books from high shelves, a combination ladder-chair, and an overhead fan operated by a foot pedal are some examples). And he continued to read voraciously whenever he had an opportunity—even in the bathtub. One visitor to his home in 1787 said that he owned "the largest and by far the best private library in America."[5]

During his hours at home, Franklin occasionally indulged in some activities which were not quite so demanding. He described one of these to a friend in England:

---

4. Van Doren, *Benjamin Franklin*, p. 732.

5. Diary of Manasseh Cutler (13 July 1787), quoted in Smyth 9:480. Franklin's library contained more than four thousand books.

Cards we sometimes play here, in long winter evenings; but it is as they play at chess, not for money, but for honor, or the pleasure of beating one another.... I have indeed, now and then, a little compunction in reflecting that I spend time so idly; but another reflection comes to relieve me, whispering, "You know that the soul is immortal; why then should you be such a niggard of a little time, when you have a whole eternity before you?" So, being easily convinced, and, like other reasonable creatures, satisfied with a small reason when it is in favor of doing what I have a mind to, I shuffle the cards again and begin another game.[6]

Among his greatest pleasures was the fact that he was finally near his daughter's family, as they all lived together in the same residence. By the fall of 1786 he had "ordered an addition to the house I live in, it being too small for our growing family. There are a good many hands employed, and I hope to see it covered in before winter."[7] (During this construction project, it was discovered that the copper point of one of Franklin's old lightning rods "had been almost all melted and blown away . . . so that at length the invention has been of us some use to the inventor.")[8]

He had grown old, but the philosopher from Philadelphia was still as busy as ever. And although he had spent twenty-five of the past thirty years at the royal courts of Europe, his neighbors found that he was pretty

---

6. To Mrs. Mary Hewson (6 May 1786), Smyth 9:512.

7. To Jane Mecom (21 Sept. 1786), Smyth 9:540. This addition to Franklin's home included a dining hall large enough to seat twenty-four guests.

8. To Professor Landriani (14 Oct. 1787), Smyth 9:617.

much the same as they had remembered him. Amidst all of his public and private engagements, he managed to spend, as always, "many comfortable intervals . . . in conversation with friends, joking, laughing, and telling merry stories."[9]

---

9. To Mrs. Elizabeth Partridge (25 Nov. 1788), Smyth 9:683.

Chapter 27

Franklin at the
Constitutional Convention

By the fall of 1786 it was clear to many political observers in America that the Articles of Confederation, under which the new nation had functioned for several years, provided too little governing power at the federal level. "We discover... some errors in our... constitutions," Franklin wrote in November of that year, "which it is no wonder they should have, the time in which they were formed being considered. But these we shall mend."[1]

As a result of repeated efforts by George Washington, Alexander Hamilton, James Madison, and others, a federal convention was finally appointed by Congress to meet at Philadelphia in May 1787. Franklin was not among the

---

1. To Edward Bancroft (26 Nov. 1786), Smyth 9:551.

original delegates chosen to represent Pennsylvania at the
convention—he feared his bladder stone would prevent
his attendance—but he was added in late March after
becoming the first president of the Society for Political
Enquiries, an organization which met regularly to study
political science. On April 19 he expressed his hopes to his
successor in France, Thomas Jefferson:

> Our federal constitution is generally thought
> defective, and a convention ... is to assemble here next
> month to revise it and propose amendments. The
> delegates generally appointed, as far as I have heard of
> them, are men of character for prudence and ability, so
> that I hope good from their meeting. Indeed, if it does
> not do good it must do harm, as it will show that we have
> not wisdom enough among us to govern ourselves, and
> will strengthen the opinion of some political writers that
> popular governments cannot long support themselves. [2]

As the sessions got under way, he was highly pleased
with the group of men who had been chosen for the
important task of restructuring the national government;
indeed, he looked on the convention as "the most august
and respectable assembly he ever was in in his life." [3] He
attended consistently during the four months they met,
generally spending at least five hours each day with the
other delegates and often coming early to conduct state
business with the Executive Council (which also met in
the Pennsylvania State House). On occasion, when his
health permitted, he walked from his home to sessions of
the convention; but most of the time he was carried in a

---

2. To Thomas Jefferson (19 Apr. 1787), Smyth 9:574.
3. Benjamin Rush to Richard Price (2 June 1787), in Smyth 10:478.

sedan chair by inmates from the local prison. "I had sometimes wished I had brought with me from France a balloon sufficiently large to raise me from the ground," he mused. "In my malady it would have been the most easy carriage for me, being led by a string held by a man walking on the ground."[4]

Franklin's Role in the Convention

William Pierce, one of the delegates from Georgia, recorded his observations of Franklin in the Constitutional Convention:

> Dr. Franklin is well known to be the greatest philosopher of the present age.... But what claim he has to the politician, posterity must determine. It is certain that he does not shine much in public council; he is no speaker, nor does he seem to let politics engage his attention. He is, however, a most extraordinary man, and tells a story in a style more engaging than anything I ever heard.... He is eighty-two years old, and possesses an activity of mind equal to a youth of twenty-five years of age.[5]

---

4. To Jean-Baptiste le Roy (18 Apr. 1787), Smyth 9:572-73.

5. Quoted in Max Farrand, ed., *The Records of the Federal Convention of 1787*, 4 vols. (New Haven: Yale University Press, 1937), 3:91. Franklin was actually eighty-one at the time. Jefferson once observed that he had "served with General Washington in the legislature of Virginia before the Revolution, and, during it, with Dr. Franklin in Congress. I never heard either of them speak ten minutes at a time, nor to any but the main point which was to decide the question. They laid their shoulders to the great points, knowing that the little ones would follow of themselves." Autobiography (1821), Bergh, *The Writings of Thomas Jefferson*, 1:87.

Despite Pierce's assessment, other delegates to the Constitutional Convention were apparently more favorably impressed with Franklin's ability as a speaker. One of them, Jonathan Dayton of New Jersey, was later quoted as having said: "Happily for the United States, the Convention contained some individuals possessed of talents and virtues of the highest

Although Franklin himself acknowledged that he was "a bad speaker,"[6] he could not justly be accused of failing to carry his load during the convention proceedings. He said very little during the first few days, but as the sessions wore on he involved himself more and more deeply, introducing several motions and participating actively in debate. He urged, unsuccessfully, that members of the executive branch be given no salary; because of his distasteful experience with the British ministry, he feared that "our posts of honor" would become "places of profit."[7] He favored a limitation on the veto power of the executive, and argued also that the President should be limited to a single term of seven years: "In free governments the rulers are the servants, and the people their superiors and sovereigns. For the former, therefore, to return among the latter was not to *degrade* but to *promote* them."[8]

He spoke out for the right of Congress to impeach the President, believing that the other recourse was assassination, by which the incumbent would be "not only deprived of his life, but of the opportunity of vindicating his character."[9] He argued vigorously against a proposal

order, whose hearts were deeply interested in the establishment of a new and efficient form of government.... Among those personages, the most prominent was Dr. Franklin. He was esteemed the *mentor* of our body.... The words of the venerable Franklin fell upon our ears with a weight and authority even greater than we may suppose an oracle to have had in a Roman senate!" William Steele to Jonathan D. Steele (Sept. 1825), in Farrand 3:469-71.

6. *Autobiography* (1784), p. 160.

7. Speech on the subject of salaries (2 June 1787), Smyth 9:593.

8. Convention debate (26 July 1787), Farrand 2:120.

9. Convention debate (20 July 1787), Farrand 2:65.

to limit suffrage to freeholders, and he likewise opposed property qualifications and a fourteen-year residency requirement for holding public office. During a debate on the best mode of judicial appointments, he humorously related a Scottish method "in which the nomination proceeded from the lawyers, who always selected the ablest of the profession in order to get rid of him and share his practice among themselves."[10]

Franklin took positions on several other issues which he considered to be of real significance, but his most important role was a conciliatory one. As in 1776, he was the oldest of all the delegates, and the respect he commanded enabled him to wield a powerful influence in this regard. During June and July, a very delicate political question came before the convention—whether representation in Congress would be equal for each state, as under the Articles of Confederation, or according to population. As the debating grew more heated and unreasonable, Franklin became increasingly concerned. On June 11 he offered this observation to the assembly:

> It has given me great pleasure to observe that till this point, the proportion of representation, came before us, our debates were carried on with great coolness and temper. If anything of a contrary kind has on this occasion appeared, I hope it will not be repeated; for we are sent hither to *consult,* not to *contend,* with each other, and declarations of a fixed opinion, and of determined resolution never to change it, neither enlighten nor convince us. Positiveness and warmth on one side naturally beget their like on the other, and tend to create

10. Convention debate (5 June 1787), Farrand 1:120.

and augment discord and division in a great concern, wherein harmony and union are extremely necessary to give weight to our counsels and render them effectual in promoting and securing the common good. [11]

"God Governs in the Affairs of Men"

But the quarreling persisted, and Franklin concluded that more serious measures would be needed to prevent a break between the larger and smaller states. On June 28 he submitted his famous motion for daily prayers in the convention.

Mr. President,

The small progress we have made ... is, methinks, a melancholy proof of the imperfection of the human understanding.... In this situation of this assembly, groping, as it were, in the dark to find political truth, and scarce able to distinguish it when presented to us, how has it happened, Sir, that we have not hitherto once thought of humbly applying to the Father of Lights to illuminate our understandings? In the beginning of the contest with Britain, when we were sensible of danger, we had daily prayers in this room for the divine protection. Our prayers, Sir, were heard—and they were graciously answered....

I have lived, Sir, a long time; and the longer I live, the more convincing proofs I see of this truth, that *God governs in the affairs of men.* And if a sparrow cannot fall to the ground without his notice, is it probable that an empire can rise without his aid? We have been assured, Sir, in the sacred writings that "except the Lord build the house, they labor in vain that build it." I firmly believe

11. Speech on proportion of representatives (11 June 1787), Smyth 9:595-96; Farrand 1:197.

> this; and I also believe that, without his concurring aid,
> we shall succeed in this political building no better than
> the builders of Babel. . . .
>
> I therefore beg leave to move that, henceforth,
> prayers imploring the assistance of heaven and its
> blessings on our deliberations be held in this assembly
> every morning before we proceed to business, and that
> one or more of the clergy of this city be requested to
> officiate in that service. [12]

As it turned out, the motion was not carried because the
convention had no funds to hire a clergyman—and
because many of the delegates feared that introducing
such a change at that point, several weeks after the
proceedings had begun, would spark rumors of dissension
as the news spread throughout the states. But this
sobering proposal did manage to settle the atmosphere
considerably, and a new spirit of cooperation began to
emerge.

Two days after this incident, Franklin suggested that
the delegates consider some kind of compromise on the
representation issue. "When a broad table is to be made
and the edges of planks do not fit," he said, "the artist takes
a little from both and makes a good joint. In like manner
here, both sides must part with some of their demands in
order that they may join in some accommodating
proposition."[13] Charles Cotesworth Pinckney of South
Carolina moved on July 2 that a committee be formed for
this purpose. The committee was created with one

---

12. Motion for prayers in the convention (28 June 1787), Smyth 9:600-601.

13. Convention debate (30 June 1787), Farrand 1:488.

delegate from each state, and Franklin was appointed to represent Pennsylvania.

On Franklin's motion (which was based on an earlier proposal offered by Roger Sherman of Connecticut), the committee arrived at a compromise. The legislative branch would consist of two chambers: a House of Representatives, wherein representation would be based on population, and a Senate, wherein each state would have an equal number of votes.[14] Furthermore, all money bills would originate in the "first branch" (the House). This compromise motion was accepted by the committee and reported to the floor on July 5; six days later it was passed by the convention.

A looming crisis had been averted, and the assembly's deliberations proceeded more easily thereafter. By the end of the summer, this eminent gathering of American statesmen had hammered out a form of government which was unprecedented in the annals of history—one that was destined to produce the most powerful and prosperous nation on earth.

"A Republic, If You Can Keep It"

The final day of the Constitutional Convention was Monday, September 17, 1787. As the delegates gathered to place their signatures on the fateful document they had framed, Franklin knew that some of his colleagues were still not completely satisfied with the outcome of certain

---

14. See Farrand 1:523, 526n. It is ironic, in light of his long-held disapproval of bicameral legislatures, that Franklin was the committee member who introduced this motion. One writer referred to the incident as "Franklin's great victory in the convention." Van Doren, *Benjamin Franklin*, p. 749.

issues. So he made one last effort toward conciliation and harmony on this occasion:

I confess that I do not entirely approve of this Constitution at present. But, Sir, I am not sure I shall never approve it; for, having lived long, I have experienced many instances of being obliged, by better information or fuller consideration, to change my opinions even on important subjects, which I thought right but found to be otherwise. It is therefore that, the older I grow, the more apt I am to doubt my own judgment....

Thus I consent, Sir, to this Constitution, because I expect no better and because I am not sure that it is not the best. The opinions I have had of its errors I sacrifice to the public good. I have never whispered a syllable of them abroad. Within these walls they were born, and here they shall die. If every one of us, in returning to our constituents, were to report the objections he has had to it and endeavor to gain partisans in support of them, we might prevent its being generally received.... I hope, therefore, for our own sakes as a part of the people, and for the sake of our posterity, that we shall act heartily and unanimously in recommending this Constitution, wherever our influence may extend, and turn our future thoughts and endeavors to the means of having it well administered.

On the whole, Sir, I cannot help expressing a wish that every member of the convention who may still have objections to it would, with me, on this occasion doubt a little of his own infallibility and, to make manifest our unanimity, put his name to the instrument. [15]

---

15. Speech given at the final session (17 Sept. 1787), Smyth 9:607-9. As with his other speeches of more than a few words, Franklin wrote this one

After contemplating this design on the back of Washington's chair throughout the four months of the Constitutional Convention in 1787, Franklin finally declared at its successful conclusion, "It is a rising and not a setting sun." Despite his ill health at the age of eighty-one, he had worked vigorously during the convention to maintain harmony among the delegates and to help produce an effective form of government for the new American nation.

It was with this thought in mind that he then moved acceptance of Gouverneur Morris's somewhat ambiguous wording found in Article VII: "Done in convention by the unanimous consent of the states present."

James Madison recorded that as the delegates came forward to sign the document, "Dr. Franklin, looking towards the president's chair at the back of which a rising sun happened to be painted, observed to a few members

---

out in advance and had it read to the convention delegates by someone else (because his stone made standing very painful to him). Due to this practice, his important speeches during the convention have been preserved more accurately than those of most of the other participants.

near him that painters had found it difficult to distinguish in their art a rising from a setting sun. 'I have,' said he, 'often and often in the course of the session, and the vicissitudes of my hopes and fears as to its issue, looked at that behind the president without being able to tell whether it was rising or setting. But now at length I have the happiness to know that it is a rising and not a setting sun.'"[16] One historian tells us that when Franklin's turn came to add his signature to the Constitution, he "was helped forward from his place; afterward it was said the old man wept when he signed."[17]

Another member of the convention reported that after the delegates filed out of Independence Hall, an anxious woman approached Dr. Franklin and asked, "Well, Doctor, what have we got—a republic or a monarchy?"

"A republic," said Franklin, "if you can keep it."[18]

---

16. Quoted in Farrand 2:648.

17. Catherine Drinker Bowen, *Miracle at Philadelphia* (Boston: Little, Brown and Company, 1966), p. 263.

18. Papers of Dr. James McHenry on the Federal Convention of 1787, in Charles C. Tansill, comp., *Documents Illustrative of the Formation of the Union of the American States* (Washington: U.S. Government Printing Office, 1927), p. 952.

Chapter 28

"Life, Like a Dramatic Piece, Should...Finish Handsomely"

In the fall of 1787 Franklin was elected to serve a third term as President (Governor) of Pennsylvania—again "without a dissenting vote but my own," he noted. [1] He continued to carry out the duties of his office, although the Executive Council met at his home after he was injured by a fall in January 1788. He did not take an active role in the ratification fight for the new federal Constitution, believing that it would be improper for Pennsylvania's chief executive to participate in the state convention. However, his speech of September 17 was widely printed among the states during this period by the proponents of ratification.

---

1. To Jane Mecom (4 Nov. 1787), Smyth 9:621.

When it became clear that the Constitution would be ratified, Franklin began receiving inquiries from a number of persons who hoped he would fill a high station in the new government. To one of these he replied: "Your friend's ... age and infirmities render him unfit for the business, as the business would be for him. After the expiration of his presidentship, which will now be in a few months, he is *determined* to engage no more in public affairs.... General Washington is the man that all our eyes are fixed on for President, and what little influence I may have is devoted to him."[2] Indeed, support for Washington was almost universal. But it was "more doubtful who will be Vice President," wrote Thomas Jefferson. "The age of Dr. Franklin, and the doubt whether he would accept it, are the only circumstances that admit a question but that he would be the man."[3]

Franklin's Public Career Comes to an End

The end of Franklin's long public career finally came on October 14, 1788, when Thomas Mifflin succeeded him as President of Pennsylvania. "Having now finished my term," he recorded, "and promising myself to engage no more in public business, I hope to enjoy the small remains

2. To M. le Veillard (8 June 1788), Smyth 9:657-58.

3. Thomas Jefferson to William Carmichael (12 Aug. 1788), Bergh, *The Writings of Thomas Jefferson*, 7:125. Jefferson considered Washington and Franklin the "two characters of first magnitude" in the United States; the other political leaders of that day, he said, were "on the second line." Ibid. At about the same time, at least one American newspaper printed a "new federal song" whose five stanzas each concluded with these lines: "Great Washington shall rule the land/While Franklin's counsel aids his hand." *Pennsylvania Packet* (5 Aug. 1788), p. 2, quoted in Douglas Southall Freeman, *George Washington*, 7 vols. (New York: Charles Scribner's Sons, 1948-57), 6:147.

of life that are allowed me in the repose I have so long wished for."[4] He was now happy to sit peacefully and watch others carry on the affairs of state. When the new federal government came into being in the spring of 1789, he was "glad to see ... that our grand machine has at length begun to work. I pray God to bless and guide its operations."[5] And in September of that year he congratulated President Washington on "the growing strength of our new government under your administration. For my own personal ease, I should have died two years ago; but though those years have been spent in excruciating pain, I am pleased that I have lived them, since they have brought me to see our present situation."[6]

In Retirement

After retiring from the governorship in 1788, Franklin took advantage of the time he had left. In addition to his heavy correspondence, he wrote frequently on various scientific and political themes. He also continued to preside over the American Philosophical Society and the Society for Political Enquiries, both of which now held their meetings in his dining hall because of his inability to get around. "My friends indulge me with their frequent visits," he wrote in February 1789, "which I have now leisure to receive and enjoy."[7]

In spite of his physical pain, his mind was fortunately as strong as ever. One visitor to Franklin's home noted that

---

4. To the Duc de la Rochefoucauld (22 Oct. 1788), Smyth 9:665.
5. To Charles Carroll (25 May 1789), Smyth 10:7.
6. To President George Washington (16 Sept. 1789), Smyth 10:41.
7. To Alexander Small (17 Feb. 1789), Smyth 10:1.

"except for the stone ... [he] still retains his health, spirits, and memory beyond all conception, insomuch that there are few transactions, subjects, or publications, ancient or modern, that are of any note but what he retains, and when necessary in conversation will repeat and retain with wonderful facility."[8] And another visitor was "highly delighted with the extensive knowledge he appeared to have of every subject, the brightness of his memory, and clearness and vivacity of all his mental faculties, notwithstanding his age. His manners are perfectly easy, and everything about him seems to diffuse an unrestrained freedom and happiness. He has an incessant vein of humor, accompanied with an uncommon vivacity, which seemed as natural and involuntary as his breathing."[9]

Urged by many friends in America and overseas, Franklin resumed in 1788 his work on the memoirs he had begun to prepare seventeen years earlier in England. Sadly, however, by June 1789 he was "so interrupted by extreme pain, which obliges me to have recourse to opium, that between the effects of both I have but little time in which I can write anything."[10] He did progress a bit further on the autobiography by dictating portions of it to his grandson Benjamin Bache, but when he died the project remained unfinished.

Franklin the Abolitionist

At the age of fifty, Franklin had written that "life, like a dramatic piece, should ... finish handsomely.... I am very

---

8. Samuel Vaughan to Richard Price (4 Nov. 1786), in Smyth 10:477-78.
9. Diary of Manasseh Cutler (13 July 1787), quoted in Smyth 10:482.
10. To Benjamin Vaughan (3 June 1789), Smyth 10:32.

desirous of concluding with a bright point."[11] Now, as he neared the end, he apparently felt he had found his "bright point": the last months of his life were devoted to eradicating that "atrocious debasement of human nature," Negro slavery. [12]

He had not always felt that way. During earlier years, in fact, he himself had kept one or two slaves (as did many Philadelphians, including the humanitarian Quaker William Penn). But his views had changed since then, and in 1787 he became president of the Pennsylvania Abolition Society. Some of the most forceful writings to come from his pen resulted from his involvement in this cause.

Franklin seems to have first turned his attention to the plight of Negro slaves thirty years before this, when he traveled to England in 1757. Shortly after his arrival, the secretary of the Bray Associates, an Anglican organization dedicated to establishing schools for black children in the British colonies, approached him in London and asked for advice on opening such a school in Philadelphia. Impressed with the project, Franklin later served on the governing board of the Bray Associates for many years. When he returned to America and conducted postal inspection tours throughout the provinces, he visited the Negro schools which had been set up in several communities. "I was on the whole much pleased," he wrote to the other board members in London, "and from what I then saw have conceived a higher opinion of the natural capacities of the black race than I have ever before entertained. Their

---

11. To George Whitefield (2 July 1756), Smyth 3:339.
12. "An Address to the Public" (9 Nov. 1789), Smyth 10:67.

apprehension seems as quick, their memory as strong, and their docility in every respect equal to that of white children."[13]

During the early 1770s, while on his second diplomatic mission to England, he wrote several pieces criticizing the role of the British government in the American slave trade (the Board of Trade, for example, had refused colonial attempts to limit or end the importation of slaves). He also began corresponding at that time with Anthony Benezet, one of the leading abolitionists in America. Franklin's views on slavery during this period were reflected in a 1773 letter he sent to Dr. Benjamin Rush, a correspondent in Philadelphia: "I hope that in time the endeavors of the friends to liberty and humanity will get the better of a practice that has so long disgraced our nation and religion."[14] Some of his writings began to call for an end to the slave trade altogether, and eventual liberty for those who were currently in bondage—or at least for their children.

A Final Appeal to the Public

And now, in his last years, he was giving much of his remaining energy to the cause of abolition. As noted earlier, he began serving in 1787 as president of the Pennsylvania Abolition Society (the actual name was much longer: the Pennsylvania Society for Promoting the

---

13. To John Waring (17 Dec. 1763), Labaree, Willcox, et al., *The Papers of Benjamin Franklin,* 10:396. Franklin wrote elsewhere that "the Negroes who are free live among the white people, but are generally improvident and poor. I think they are not deficient in natural understanding, but they have not the advantage of education. They make good musicians." To the Marquis de Condorcet (20 Mar. 1774), Smyth 6:222.

14. To Benjamin Rush (14 July 1773), Smyth 6:100.

Abolition of Slavery and the Relief of Free Negroes Unlawfully Held in Bondage). Partly due to his influence, Pennsylvania became the first state to pass legislation providing for the gradual emancipation of slaves. In the fall of 1789, Franklin drew up a plan to advise and educate free blacks and prepare them for gainful employment; on November 9 he announced it in "An Address to the Public" from the Abolition Society:

> To instruct, to advise, to qualify those who have been restored to freedom for the exercise and enjoyment of civil liberty, to promote in them habits of industry, to furnish them with employments suited to their age, sex, talents, and other circumstances, and to procure their children an education calculated for their future situation in life; these are the great outlines of the ... plan which we have adopted, and which we conceive will essentially promote the public good and the happiness of these our hitherto too-much-neglected fellow creatures.
>
> A plan so extensive cannot be carried into execution without considerable pecuniary resources, beyond the present ordinary funds of the Society. We hope much from the generosity of enlightened and benevolent freemen, and will gratefully receive any donations or subscriptions for this purpose. [15]

Finally, in February 1790—just two months before his death—Franklin issued his last public appeal, calling for an end to human slavery. It was actually a memorial to Congress, which he signed as president of the Abolition Society, but it was eventually reprinted in many American

---

15. "An Address to the Public" (9 Nov. 1789), Smyth 10:67-68.

newspapers. The memorial declared that "mankind are all formed by the same Almighty Being, alike objects of his care, and equally designed for the enjoyment of happiness." It went on to observe that "many important and salutary powers" had been vested in Congress for "promoting the welfare and securing the blessings of liberty to the people of the United States," and then insisted that "these blessings ought rightfully to be administered, without distinction of color, to all descriptions of people." The document concluded with these stirring words:

> From a persuasion that equal liberty was originally the portion, and is still the birthright, of all men, and influenced by the strong ties of humanity and the principles of their institution, your memorialists conceive themselves bound to loosen the bands of slavery, and promote a general enjoyment of the blessings of freedom. Under these impressions, they earnestly entreat your serious attention to the subject of slavery; that you will be pleased to countenance the restoration of liberty to those unhappy men who alone in this land of freedom are degraded to perpetual bondage, and who, amidst the general joy of surrounding freemen, are groaning in servile subjection; that you will devise means for removing this inconsistency from the character of the American people; that you will promote mercy and justice toward this distressed race; and that you will step to the very verge of the power vested in you for discouraging every species of traffic in the persons of our fellowmen. [16]

16. Memorial to Congress (3 Feb. 1790), quoted in Matthew T. Mellon, *Early American Views on Negro Slavery* (New York: Bergman Publishers, 1969), pp. 20-22.

Coming from Franklin himself, it created quite a stir in Congress and was followed by warm debates on emancipation of the slaves. But because of the serious breach threatened by the slave states, and because the Constitution prohibited federal interference with slavery before the year 1808, this and similar petitions were eventually placed on the shelf. The issue would have to be reckoned with at a later time, decades after Franklin was gone.

The Death of Doctor Franklin

Franklin approached everything with a scientific inquisitiveness—even death. "Having seen during a long life a good deal of this world," he wrote, "I feel a growing curiosity to be acquainted with some other." [17] Although he still tried to maintain his physical strength ("I live temperately, drink no wine, and use daily the exercise of the dumbbell"), [18] and although he still enjoyed greatly the companionship of Sally and her family ("I have seven grandchildren by my daughter, who play with and amuse me, and she is a kind, attentive nurse to me when I am at any time indisposed"), [19] his thoughts seemed to turn more and more toward his approaching end. "I am grown so old as to have buried most of the friends of my youth, and . . . I seem to have intruded myself into the company of

---

17. To Jonathan Shipley (24 Feb. 1786), Smyth 9:491.

18. To M. le Veillard (15 Apr. 1787), Smyth 9:560. He also abstained from tobacco. According to Dr. Benjamin Rush, Franklin declared in his eighty-first year that "he had never snuffed, chewed, or smoked." Quoted in Van Doren, *Benjamin Franklin*, p. 770.

19. To Alexander Small (17 Feb. 1789), Smyth 10:1-2.

Franklin's daughter, Sarah ("Sally") Bache, who bore him seven grandchildren and served as his nurse during his last years.

posterity, when I ought to have been abed and a-sleep."[20]

He apparently had no fear of death, for in his mind it marked a passage into another existence. Years earlier he had observed:

It is the will of God and nature that these mortal bodies be laid aside when the soul is to enter into real life. This is rather an embryo state, a preparation for living. A man is not completely born until he be dead. Why, then, should we grieve that a new child is born among the immortals, a new member added to their happy society?

We are spirits. That bodies should be lent us, while they can afford us pleasure, assist us in acquiring knowledge, or in doing good to our fellow creatures, is a kind and benevolent act of God. When they become unfit for these purposes, and afford us pain instead of pleasure, instead of an aid become an encumbrance, and answer none of the intentions for which they were given, it is equally kind and benevolent that a way is

20. To George Whatley (18 May 1787), Smyth 9:588-89.

provided by which we may get rid of them. Death is that way.[21]

Certainly his own body had "become an encumbrance" during the final months. In September 1789 he wrote to a friend, "I have a long time been afflicted with almost constant and grievous pain, to combat which I have been obliged to have recourse to opium, which indeed has afforded me some ease from time to time; but then it has taken away my appetite and so impeded my digestion that I am become totally emaciated, and little remains of me but a skeleton covered with skin."[22] Two months later he recorded that he had grown "thinner and weaker, so that I cannot expect to hold out much longer."[23] The following April 17, at the age of eighty-four years and three months, he died peacefully in his bed.

"The Work Shall Not Be Lost"

Over twenty thousand mourners—"the largest crowd yet assembled in America"—gathered in Philadelphia to pay their last respects to the old philosopher who had done so much for their country.[24] The House of Representatives voted to wear mourning for a month, and the French National Assembly later did so for three days. Thomas Jefferson summarized the feelings of most Americans: "His death was an affliction which was to happen to us at some time or other. We have reason to be thankful he was so long spared; that the most useful life

---

21. To Miss Elizabeth Hubbard (23 Feb. 1756), Smyth 3:329.

22. To M. le Veillard (5 Sept. 1789), Smyth 10:35.

23. To Jean-Baptiste le Roy (13 Nov. 1789), Smyth 10:69.

24. Hall, "Benjamin Franklin: Philosopher of Dissent," p. 122. The funeral cortege was said to be half a mile long.

should be the longest also; that it was protracted so far beyond the ordinary span allotted to man as to avail us of his wisdom in the establishment of our . . . freedom."[25]

As a young man, Franklin had prepared an epitaph for himself:

The body of
B. Franklin, printer
(Like the cover of an old book,
Its contents torn out
And stripped of its lettering and gilding),
Lies here, food for worms.
But the work shall not be lost;
For it will (as he believed) appear once more
In a new and more elegant edition,
Revised and corrected
By the Author.[26]

The epitaph was never used (it was replaced by a much simpler inscription on his gravestone in the Christ Church cemetery, where he had asked to be "buried by the side of my wife"),[27] but it reflected both the wit and the faith of this remarkable man.

Franklin once penned these lines to a friend he had known since his youth: "Let us sit till the evening of life is spent; the last hours are always the most joyous. When we

25. Thomas Jefferson to an unknown correspondent (19 Feb. 1791), Bergh 8:130.

26. Epitaph (written in 1728), Van Doren, *Autobiographical Writings*, p. 29. Franklin's belief in a physical resurrection is revealed here and in some of his later expressions.

27. Codicil to last will and testament (23 June 1789), Smyth 10:507.

can stay no longer, 'tis time enough then to bid each other good night, separate, and go quietly to bed."[28] Yet the thought that he is lying quietly in bed is somehow an unconvincing one. For many of us it is tempting to believe that, somewhere in that other world to which he looked forward, Ben Franklin can still be found "joking, laughing, and telling merry stories" to those around him—and continuing his lifelong quest for knowledge, self-improvement, and the liberty of his fellowmen.

The graves of Benjamin and Deborah Franklin, located in the Christ Church cemetery at Philadelphia.

---

28. To Hugh Roberts (7 July 1765), Smyth 4:387.

Bibliography

Becker, Carl L. "Benjamin Franklin." *Dictionary of American Biography,* 6:585–98. Edited by Allen Johnson and Dumas Malone. 20 vols. Published under the auspices of the American Council of Learned Societies. New York: Charles Scribner's Sons, 1928–36.

Crane, Verner W., ed. *Benjamin Franklin's Letters to the Press, 1758–1775.* Chapel Hill: The University of North Carolina Press, 1950.

Donovan, Frank, ed. *The Benjamin Franklin Papers.* New York: Dodd, Mead & Company, 1962.

Farrand, Max, ed. *The Records of the Federal Convention of 1787.* 4 vols. New Haven: Yale University Press, 1937.

Fleming, Thomas, ed. *Benjamin Franklin: A Biography in His Own Words.* New York: Newsweek, Inc., 1972.

Franklin, Benjamin. *The Autobiography of Benjamin Franklin.* Edited by Leonard W. Labaree et al. New Haven: Yale University Press, 1964.

——————. *A Benjamin Franklin Reader.* Edited by Nathan G. Goodman. New York: Thomas Y. Crowell Company, 1945.

——————. *Benjamin Franklin's Autobiographical Writings.* Edited by Carl Van Doren. New York: The Viking Press, 1945.

——————. *The Papers of Benjamin Franklin.* Edited by Leonard W. Labaree, William B. Willcox, et al. 21 vols. by 1978. New Haven: Yale University Press, 1959–.

——————. *The Writings of Benjamin Franklin.* Edited by Albert Henry Smyth. 10 vols. New York: The Macmillan Company, 1905–7.

Hall, Alice J. "Benjamin Franklin: Philosopher of Dissent." *National Geographic,* July 1975, pp. 93–122.

Jefferson, Thomas. *The Writings of Thomas Jefferson.* Edited by Albert Ellery Bergh. 20 vols. Washington: The Thomas Jefferson Memorial Association, 1907.

Lopez, Claude-Anne, and Herbert, Eugenia W. *The Private Franklin: The Man and His Family.* New York: W.W. Norton & Company, Inc., 1975.

Van Doren, Carl. *Benjamin Franklin.* New York: The Viking Press, 1938.

Zall, P. M., ed. *Ben Franklin Laughing: Anecdotes from Original Sources by and about Benjamin Franklin.* Berkeley: University of California Press, 1980.

Index

A

Abolition, BF's efforts for, of Negro slavery, 269–73

Academy of Sciences (Paris), BF attends meetings of, 233

Adams, John, serves on committee assigned to prepare Declaration of Independence, 202; confers with Admiral Lord Howe on Staten Island in futile attempt at Anglo-American reconciliation, 204–5; serves on committee to propose national seal, 205–6; describes attitude of French people toward BF, 212; replaces Silas Deane as commissioner to France, 224; seeks loans in Holland for American war effort, 227, 239; appointed to help negotiate peace with England, 238; participates in peace discussions, 239–40

Adams, Samuel, serves on Massachusetts Committee of Correspondence, 165

"An Address to the Public," written by BF, 271

Albany Congress of 1754, BF appointed a commissioner to, 96; approves BF's plan of colonial union, 99–100; fails to improve relations with Indians, 100; French and Indian War erupts during, 105

Albany Plan of Union, by BF, accepted by Albany Congress, 99–100; rejected by British

government and by colonial assemblies, 100; BF on, 100, 103, 105

America, BF on, as foundation of British empire's "future grandeur and stability," 120–21; BF on growing power and influence of, in 1767, 151; BF on universal "seeds of liberty" in, 151; BF on "public virtue" in, 187. See also Colonies; Revolutionary War; United States

American Philosophical Society, founded by BF, 68–69; BF serves as president of, 69, 249, 267

"Americanus" (BF pseudonym), satirical proposal by, in *Pennsylvania Gazette,* 94

Anglo-Saxons, leaders of, depicted on original design proposed for United States seal, 205–6

Anti-Semitism, false legend about BF's, 63n

Arctic, BF helps organize first American expedition to the, 82

Armonica, musical instrument invented by BF, 124; popularity of, in Europe and America, 125

"Articles of Belief and Acts of Religion," written by BF, 41–43, 62

Articles of Confederation, BF proposes original version in 1775, 196–98; Congressional debates on, 206–7; weaknesses of, result in Constitutional Convention, 253

growth rate in America, 95; on Albany Plan of Union, 100, 103, 105; on taxing power of Parliament, 101-2, 142, 144, 145; on colonial representation in Parliament, 102, 149; on British retention of Canada after French and Indian War, 120-21 and n; on America as foundation of British empire's "future grandeur and stability," 120-21; on King George III, 123n, 174-75; on need for moderation among colonists in wake of Stamp Act, 137-38; on criticism from political enemies, 139; on external versus internal taxes, 142-43, 160; on manufactures in American colonies, 143-44; on growing power and influence of America in 1767, 151; on Europeans' attitude toward American cause, 153, 218; his rule of conduct in public duties, 157; on extent of Parliament's authority to legislate for American colonies, 160-61; on a government's responsibility to hear citizens' grievances, 182; on Boston Tea Party, 184; on futility of Anglo-American reconciliation, 186-87; on England during Revolutionary War, 199-200, 203-4, 216, 219, 220; on Revolutionary War, 210, 219; on spies, 214; on mistreatment of American prisoners, 220-21; on treaties with France, 222-23; on French ladies, 232; on patents, 234; on peace negotiations, 238-39; on Treaty of Paris (1783), 240-41; on joys and sorrows of rearing children, 245;

on importance and composition of Constitutional Convention, 254; on need for impeachment provision in Constitution, 256; on need for daily prayers in Constitutional Convention, 258-59; on need for unanimity among delegates at signing of Constitution, 260-62; on natural abilities of Negroes, 269-70 and n; on need for education among free Negroes, 271; on emancipation of Negro slaves, 272; on death, 274-75

Writings: "Silence Dogood" letters, 12-16; his pseudonyms, 13, 94, 122; *A Dissertation on Liberty and Necessity, Pleasure and Pain,* 27, 40; *A Modest Enquiry into the Nature and Necessity of a Paper Currency,* 37-38; "Articles of Belief and Acts of Religion," 41-43, 62; *Poor Richard's Almanack,* 54-56; *Plain Truth,* 72; *Proposals Relating to the Education of Youth in Pennsylvania,* 83-84; "Short Hints Towards a Scheme for Uniting the Northern Colonies" (Albany Plan of Union), 99-100; letters to Governor William Shirley, 101-3, 140; *The Way to Wealth,* 116; *The Interest of Great Britain Considered with Regard to Her Colonies and the Acquisitions of Canada and Guadaloupe,* 121n; *Cool Thoughts on the Present Situation of Our Public Affairs,* 133; his writings translated and published throughout Europe, 154-55, 217n, 233, 241-42; "Causes of the American Discontents Before 1768," 160; *The Autobiography of Benjamin Franklin,* 169-70, 268;

M

N

O

S

PART II

Timeless Treasures from Benjamin Franklin

Prepared by

W. Cleon Skousen

and

M. Richard Maxfield

During his lifetime, Benjamin Franklin received wide acclaim as a "natural philosopher," or what we would call a scientist. But he was also a philosopher in a much broader sense. His witty maxims from *Poor Richard's Almanack* have been repeated and reprinted throughout the Western world for more than two centuries, and yet most people today are quite unfamiliar with his extensive writings in such fields as economics, religion, education, journalism, political science, medicine, and meteorology. The range of subject areas treated in his public and private papers is incredibly broad; he is just as comfortable when discussing a complex theory of continental drift as he is when giving practical advice on human relations.

Some of the quotations in this section are included chiefly for their historical interest, as Franklin had much to say about himself, his contemporaries, and the important events of his day. But these pages will also reveal that, like the other Founding Fathers, he penned many observations which are of great value to our own generation because of their remarkable relevance to the political, economic, and social challenges we face today.

Whatever his topic, Franklin's readers quickly develop a personal affection for the man himself as they discover the warmth and the humor which characterize his expressions. Sprinkled among the many jewels of keen insight and mature wisdom are lots of whimsical little passages which demonstrate that Ben Franklin never stopped enjoying the lighter side of life.

These representative selections are arranged alphabetically by subject matter for the convenience of the user. Most of the material is excerpted from Albert Henry Smyth, ed., *The Writings of Benjamin Franklin*, 10 vols. (New York: The Macmillan Company, 1905–7). Several quotations are taken from Leonard W. Labaree, William B. Willcox, et al., eds., *The Papers of Benjamin*

Franklin, 21 vols. by 1978 (New Haven: Yale University Press, 1959–; cited as Labaree & Willcox), and a few are from other sources which are cited fully where they appear in the text. Spelling, capitalization, and punctuation have been modernized in most cases for the sake of clarity and readability.

Timeless Treasures
from
Benjamin Franklin

Prepared by

W. Cleon Skousen
and
M. Richard Maxfield

A

ADAMS (John), Policy Differs from Franklin's.—The king [of France, Louis XVI], a young and virtuous prince, has, I am persuaded, a pleasure in reflecting on the generous benevolence of the action in assisting an oppressed people, and proposes it as a part of the glory of his reign. I think it right to increase this pleasure by our thankful acknowledgments, and that such an expression of gratitude is not only our duty, but our interest. A different conduct seems to me what is not only improper and unbecoming, but what may be hurtful to us. Mr. Adams, on the other hand, who at the same time means our welfare and interest as much as I or any man can do, seems to think a little apparent stoutness, and greater air of independence and boldness in our demands, will procure us more ample assistance. It is for Congress to judge and regulate their affairs accordingly.—Smyth 8:127. (1780.)

ADAMS (John), Very Suspicious of French.—I ought not, however, to conceal from you that one of my colleagues is of a very different opinion from me in these matters. He thinks the French minister one of the greatest enemies of our country, that he would have straightened our boundaries, to prevent the growth of our people; contracted our fishery, to obstruct the increase of our seamen; and retained the Royalists among us, to keep us divided; that he privately opposes all our negotiations with foreign courts, and afforded us, during the war, the assistance we received, only to keep it alive, that we might be so much the more weakened by it; that to think of gratitude to France is the greatest of follies, and that to be influenced by it would ruin us. He makes no secret of his having these opinions, expresses them publicly, sometimes in presence of the English ministers, and speaks of hundreds of instances which he could produce in proof of them. None of which, however, have yet appeared to me.—Smyth 9:61. (1783.)

ADAMS (John), Franklin's Estimation of.—I am persuaded ... that he means well for his country, is always an honest man, often a wise one, but sometimes, and in some things, absolutely out of his senses.—Smyth 9:62. (1783.)

ADAMS (John), His Defense of the American (State) Constitutions Received at the Constitutional Convention.—I received by Dr. White the letter you did me the honor of writing to me the 27th of January, together with two copies of your Defence of the American Constitutions, one for myself for which I beg you would accept my thanks, the other for the Philosophical Society whose secretary will of course officially acknowledge the obligation. That work is in such request here, that it is already put to press, and a numerous edition will speedily be abroad.—Smyth 9:585. (1787.)

ADVICE TO AMERICANS, In View of All God Had Done for Them.—*Be quiet and thankful.*—Smyth 10:122.

ADVICE TO HIS DAUGHTER, As Franklin Departs to England.—My dear child: The natural prudence and goodness of heart God has blessed you with make it less necessary for me to be particular in giving you advice. I shall therefore only say, that the more attentively dutiful and tender you are towards your good mama, the more you will recommend yourself to me. But why should I mention *me*, when you have so much higher a promise in the commandments, that such conduct will recommend you to the favor of God. You know I have many enemies, all indeed on the public account (for I cannot recollect that I have in a private capacity given just cause of offense to anyone whatever), yet they are enemies, and very bitter ones; and you must expect their enmity will extend in some degree to you, so that your slightest indiscretions will be magnified into crimes, in order the more sensibly to wound and afflict me. It is therefore the more necessary for you to be extremely circumspect in all your behavior, that no advantage may be given to their malevolence.

Go constantly to church, whoever preaches. The act of devotion in the common prayer book is your principal business there, and if properly attended to, will do more towards amending the heart than sermons generally can do. For they were composed by men of much greater piety and wisdom, than our common composers of sermons can pretend to be; and therefore I wish you would never miss the prayer days; yet I do not mean you should despise sermons, even of the preachers you dislike, for the discourse is often much better than the man, as sweet and clear waters come through very dirty earth. I am the more particular on this head, as you seemed to express a little before I came away, some inclination to leave our church, which I would not have you do.

For the rest, I would only recommend to you in my absence, to acquire those useful accomplishments, arithmetic and bookkeeping. This you might do with ease, if you would resolve not to see company on the hours you set apart for those studies.

We expect to be at sea tomorrow, if this wind holds; after which I shall have no opportunity of writing you, till I arrive (if it please God I do arrive) in England. I pray that his blessing may attend you, which is worth more than a thousand of mine, though they are never wanting. Give my love to your brother and sister, as I cannot write to them, and remember me affectionately to the young ladies your friends, and to our good neighbors. I am, my dear child, your affectionate father.—Smyth 4:286. (1764.)

ADVICE TO MRS. FRANKLIN, Go More Often to Church.—You spent your Sunday very well, but I think you should go oftener to church. I approve of your opening all my English letters, as it must give you pleasure to see that people who knew me there so long and so intimately, retain so sincere a regard for me.—Smyth 4:202. (1763.)

ADVICE TO A YOUNG WOMAN.—I hear you are now in Boston, gay and lovely as usual. Let me give you some fatherly advice. Kill no more pigeons than you can eat. Be a good girl and don't forget your catechism. Go constantly to meeting—or church—till you get a good husband, then stay at home and nurse the children, and live like a Christian. Spend your spare hours, in sober whisk, prayers, or learning to cypher. You must practice *addition* to your husband's estate, by industry and frugality; *subtraction* of all unnecessary expenses; *multiplication* (I would gladly have taught you that myself, but you thought it time enough, and wouldn't learn) he will soon make you a mistress of it. As to *division*, I say with brother Paul, *Let there be no division among ye.* But as your good sister Hubbard (my love to her) is well acquainted with *the Rule of Two,* I hope you will become an expert in the *Rule of Three;* that when I have again the pleasure of seeing you, I may find you like my grape vine, surrounded with clusters, plump, juicy, blushing, pretty little rogues, like their Mama.—Smyth 3:288. (1755.)

AERONAUTICS, Balloons Just the Beginning.—This experiment is by no means a trifling one. It may be attended with important consequences that no one can foresee. We should not suffer pride to prevent our progress in science.

Beings...far superior to ours have not disdained to amuse themselves with making and launching balloons, otherwise we should never have enjoyed the light of those glorious objects that rule our day and night, nor have had the pleasure of riding round the sun ourselves upon the balloon we now inhabit.—Smyth 9:118. (1783.)

AERONAUTICS, Importance Emphasized.—It appears as you observe to be a discovery of great importance, and what may possibly give a new turn to human affairs. Convincing sovereigns of the folly of wars may perhaps be one effect of it; since it will be impracticable for the most potent of them to guard his dominions. Five thousand balloons, capable of raising two men each, could not cost more than five ships of the line; and where is the prince who can afford so to cover his country with troops for its defense, as that ten thousand men descending from the clouds might not in many places do an infinite deal of mischief before a force could be brought together to repel them?—Smyth 1:80. (1786.)

AGRICULTURE, True Source of Wealth.—For the true source of riches is husbandry. Agriculture is truly *productive of new wealth;* manufacturers only change forms, and, whatever value they give to the materials they work upon, they in the mean time consume an equal value in provisions, etc. So that riches are not *increased* by manufacturing; the only advantage is, that provisions in the shape of manufactures are more easily carried for sale to foreign markets.—Smyth 5:102. (1768.)

AGRICULTURE, Most Honorable Employment.—I think agriculture the most honorable of all employ-

ments, being the most independent. The farmer has no need of popular favor, nor the favor of the great, the success of his crops depending only on the blessing of God upon his honest industry.—Smyth 10:3. (1789.)

AGRICULTURE. See also FARMERS; WEALTH.

ALBANY PLAN OF UNION, Essential.—One principal encouragement to the French, in invading and insulting the British American dominions, was their knowledge of our disunited state, and of our weakness arising from such want of union; and that from hence different colonies were, at different times, extremely harassed, and put to great expense both of blood and treasure, who would have remained in peace, if the enemy had had cause to fear the drawing on themselves the resentment and power of the whole; the said commissioners, considering also the present encroachments of the French, and the mischievous consequences that may be expected from them, if not opposed with our force, came to a unanimous resolution, *that a union of the colonies is absolutely necessary for their preservation.*—Smyth 3:203. (1754.)

ALBANY PLAN OF UNION, Franklin's First Attempt to Unite the Colonies.—I projected and drew a plan for the union of all the colonies under one government, so far as might be necessary for defense, and other important general purposes. As we passed through New York, I had there shown my project to Mr. James Alexander and Mr. Kennedy, two gentlemen of great knowledge in public affairs, and, being fortified by their approbation, I ventured to lay it before the Congress. It then appeared that several of the commissioners had formed plans of the same kind. A previous question was first taken, whether a union should be established, which passed in the affirmative unanimously. A committee was then appointed, one member from each colony, to consider the several plans and report. Mine happened to be preferred, and, with a few amendments, was accordingly reported.—Autobiography. Smyth 1:387. (1788.)

ALBANY PLAN OF UNION, Rejected.—The debates upon it in [the Albany] Congress went on daily, hand in hand with the Indian business. Many objections and difficulties were started, but at length they were all overcome, and the plan was unanimously agreed to, and copies ordered to be transmitted to the Board of Trade and to the assemblies of the several provinces. Its fate was singular: the assemblies did not adopt it, as they all thought there was too much *prerogative* in it, and in England it was judged to have too much of the *democratic.*—Autobiography. Smyth 1:388. (1788.)

ALBANY PLAN OF UNION, 1754.—(For full text, see Smyth 3:207-26.)

ALMANACK, Designed to Impress the Youth.—For besides the astronomical calculations, and other things usually contained in almanacks, which have their daily use indeed while the year continues, but then become of no value, I have constantly interspersed *moral* sentences, *prudent* maxims, and *wise* sayings, many of them containing *much good sense* in *very few* words, and therefore apt to leave *strong* and *lasting* impressions on the memory of young persons, whereby they may receive benefit as long as they live, when both almanack and almanack-maker have been long thrown by and forgotten.—Smyth 2:299. (1746.)

ALMANACK, Franklin's "Wisdom" Gleaned from All Ages.—I was conscious that not a tenth part of the wisdom was my own, which he ascribed to me, but rather the *gleanings* I had made of the sense of all ages and nations.—Smyth 3:418. (1757.)

ALMANACK, Poor Richard's, Origin of.—In 1732 I first published my almanack, under the name of *Richard Saunders;* it was continued by me about twenty-five years, commonly called *Poor Richard's Almanack.* I endeavored to make it both entertaining and useful, and it accordingly came to be in such demand, that I reaped considerable profit from it, vending annually near ten thousand. And observing that it was generally read, scarce any neighborhood in the province being without it, I considered it as a proper vehicle for conveying instruction among the common people, who bought scarcely any other books.—Autobiography. Smyth 1:342. (1788.)

AMERICA, Settled by Well-Educated Men.—Many of the first settlers of these provinces were men who had received a good education in *Europe*, and to their wisdom and good management we owe much of our present prosperity.—Smyth 2:388. (1749.)

AMERICA, The Hope of the World.—Our affairs in general stand in a fair light throughout Europe. Our cause is universally approved. Our constitutions of government have been translated and printed in most languages, and are so much admired for the spirit of liberty that reigns in them, that it is generally agreed we shall have a vast accession of people of property after the war, from every part of this continent, as well as from the British Islands. We have only to persevere to be great and happy.—Smyth 7:294. (1779.)

AMERICA, Liberty in, Inspires All Mankind.—Establishing the liberties of America will not only make that people happy, but will have some effect in diminishing the misery of those who in other parts of the world groan under despotism, by rendering it more circumspect and inducing it to govern with a lighter hand.—Smyth 8:416. (1782.)

AMERICA, Land of Opportunity.—Persons of moderate fortunes and capitals who, having a number of children to provide for, are desirous of bringing them up to industry, and to secure estates for their posterity, have opportunities of doing it in America which Europe does not afford.—Smyth 8:608. (1782.)

AMERICA, Room for Many Artisans.—Artisans generally live better and more easily in America

than in Europe; and such as are good economists make a comfortable provision for age, and for their children. Such may, therefore, remove with advantage to America.—Smyth 8:612. (1782).

AMERICA, Described by Franklin in 1783.—Guard ... against mistaken notions of the American people. You have deceived yourselves too long with vain expectations of reaping advantage from our little discontents. We are more thoroughly an enlightened people, with respect to our political interests, than perhaps any other under heaven. Every man among us reads, and is so easy in his circumstances as to have leisure for conversations of improvement, and for acquiring information. Our domestic misunderstandings, when we have them, are of small extent, though monstrously magnified by your microscopic newspapers. He who judges from them, that we are falling into anarchy, or returning to the obedience of Britain, is like one who, being shown some spots in the sun, should fancy that the whole disk would soon be overspread by them, and that there should be an end of daylight. The great body of intelligence among our people surrounds and overpowers our petty dissensions, as the sun's great mass of fire diminishes and destroys his spots. Do not therefore any longer delay the evacuation of New York, in the vain hopes of a new revolution in your favor, if such a hope has indeed had any effect in causing that delay. It is now nine months since the evacuations were promised.—Smyth 9:87. (1783.)

AMERICA, Prophetic Warning by Franklin That Went Unheeded.—A few years of peace will improve, will restore and increase our strength; but our future safety will depend on our union and our virtue. Britain will be long watching for advantages, to recover what she has lost. If we do not convince the world that we are a nation to be depended on for fidelity in treaties; if we appear negligent in paying our debts, and ungrateful to those who have served and befriended us; our reputation, and all the strength it is capable of procuring, will be lost, and fresh attacks upon us will be encouraged and promoted by better prospects of success. Let us therefore beware of being lulled into a dangerous security; and of being both enervated and impoverished by luxury; of being weakened by internal contentions and divisions; of being shamefully extravagant in contracting private debts, while we are backward in discharging honorably those of the public; of neglect in military exercises and discipline, and in providing stores of arms and munitions of war, to be ready on occasion; for all these are circumstances that give confidence to enemies, and diffidence to friends; and the expenses required to prevent a war are much lighter than those that will, if not prevented, be absolutely necessary to maintain it.—Smyth 9:213. (1784.)

AMERICA, Post-Revolutionary Disunity Disbelieved by Franklin.—Your [English] papers are full of our divisions and distresses, which have no existence but in the imagination and wishes of English newswriters and their employers.—Smyth 9:286. (1785.)

AMERICA, Cause of Depression Following Revolutionary War.—Some traders, indeed, complain that trade is dead; but this pretended evil is not an effect of inability in the people to buy, pay for, and consume the usual articles of commerce, as far as they have occasion for them; it is owing merely to there being too many traders, who have crowded hither from all parts of Europe with more goods than the natural demand of the country requires. And what in Europe is called the debt of America, is chiefly the debt of these adventurers and super-cargoes to their principals, with which the settled inhabitants of America, who never paid better for what they want and buy, have nothing to do. As to the content-ment of the inhabitants with the change of government, methinks a stronger proof cannot be desired, than what they have given in my reception. You know the part I had in that change, and you see in the papers the addresses from all ranks with which your friend was welcomed home, and the sentiments they contain confirmed yesterday in the choice of him for President by the Council and new Assembly, which was unanimous, a single voice in seventy-seven excepted.—Smyth 9:472. (1785.)

AMERICA, Disorders After the Revolution.—These states in general enjoy peace and plenty.

There have been some disorders in the Massachusetts and Rhode Island governments; those in the former are quelled for the present; those of the latter, being contentions for and against paper money, will probably continue some time. Maryland too is divided on the same subject, the Assembly being for it and the Senate against it. Each is now employed in endeavoring to gain the people to its party against the next elections, and it is probable the Assembly may prevail. Paper money in moderate quantities has been found beneficial; when more than the occasions of commerce require, it depreciated and was mischievous; and the populace are apt to demand more than is necessary. In this state we have some, and it is useful, and I do not hear any clamor for more.— Smyth 9:564. (1787.)

AMERICA, Prosperity in, Following Revolutionary War.—Such has been the goodness of Divine Providence to these regions, and so favorable the climate, that since the three or four years of hardship in the first settlement of our fathers here, a famine or scarcity has never been heard of among us; on the contrary, though some years may have been more and others less plentiful, there has always been provision enough for ourselves, and a quantity to spare for exportation. And although the crops of last year were generally good, never was the farmer better paid for the part he can spare commerce, as the published price currents abundantly testify. The lands he possesses are also continually rising in value with the increase of population; and on the whole he is enabled to give such good wages to those who work for him that all who are acquainted with the old world must agree that in no part of it are the laboring poor so well fed, well clothed, well lodged, and well paid as in the United States of America.

If we enter the cities, we find that since the Revolution the owners of houses and lots of ground have had their interest vastly augmented in value. Rents have risen to an astonishing height, and thence encouragement to increase building, which gives employment to an abundance of workmen, as does also the increased luxury and splendor of living of the inhabitants, thus made richer. These workmen all demand and obtain much higher wages than any other part of the world would afford them, and are paid in ready money. This rank of people therefore do not, or ought not, to complain of hard times; and they make a very considerable part of the city inhabitants.—Smyth 10:118.

AMERICA. See also COLONIES; MANIFEST DESTINY.

AMERICAN PHILOSOPHICAL SOCIETY, Founded by Franklin.— Proposed, that one society be formed of *virtuosi* or ingenious men, residing in the several colonies, to be called *The American Philosophical Society*, who are to maintain a constant correspondence.

That Philadelphia, being the city nearest the center of the continent colonies, communicating with all of them northward and southward by post, and with all the islands by sea, and having the advantage of a good growing library, be the center of the Society.

That at Philadelphia there be always at least seven members, viz. a physician, a botanist, a mathematician, a chemist, a mechanician, a geographer, and a general natural philosopher, besides a president, treasurer, and secretary.

That these members meet once a month, or oftener, at their own expense, to communicate to each other their observations and experiments, to receive, read, and consider such letters, communications, or queries as shall be sent from distant members; to direct the dispersing of copies of such communications as are valuable to other distant members, in order to procure their sentiments thereupon.—Smyth 2:229. (1743.)

ANGLO-SAXON SETTLEMENTS IN BRITAIN.—It is well known to all the world that the first German settlements made in the Island of Britain were by colonies of people...under the conduct of Hengist, Horsa, Hella, Uff, Cerdicus, Ida, and others.—Smyth 6:119. (1773.)

ARNOLD (Benedict), Infamy of.— You ask for news from America, and particularly what effects attended the defection of Arnold, and what were his motives. He tried to draw others after him, but in vain; not a man followed him. We discovered his motive by an intercepted letter, a copy of which I enclose, which shows it was a bribe of five thousand pounds sterling. This he received in bills of exchange on London, where

the money was put into the funds on his account. He lives covered with infamy, and despised even by those who expected to be served by his treachery.—Smyth 8:311. (1781.)

ARNOLD (Benedict). See also LAFAYETTE (Marquis de), and Benedict Arnold.

ARTICLES OF CONFEDERATION, First Draft by Franklin in 1775.—(For full text, see Smyth 6:420-26.)

ARTICLES OF CONFEDERATION, Admired in Europe.—The disputes about the Constitution seem to have subsided. It is much admired here, and all over Europe, and will draw over many families of fortune to settle under it, as soon as there is a peace. The defects, that may on seven years' trial be found in it, can be amended, when the time comes for considering them.— Smyth 8:44. (1780.)

ASTRONOMY, Views of Franklin.—When I stretch my imagination through and beyond our system of planets, beyond the visible fixed stars themselves, into that space that is every way infinite, and conceive it filled with suns like ours, each with a chorus of worlds forever moving round him, then this little ball on which we move seems, even in my narrow imagination, to be almost nothing, and myself less than nothing, and of no sort of consequence.—Smyth 2:92. (1728.)

AUTOBIOGRAPHY, Pressure of Business Prevents Writing.—My three years of service will expire in October, when a new president must be chosen; and I had the project of retiring then to my grandson's estate in New Jersey, where I might be free from the interruption of visits, in order to complete that work for your satisfaction; for in this city my time is so cut to pieces by friends and strangers, that I have sometimes envied the prisoners in Bastille.—Smyth 9:645. (1788.)

AUTOBIOGRAPHY, Franklin's Purpose in Writing.—I am recovering from a long-continued gout, and am diligently employed in writing the history of my life. . . . I am now in the year 1756, just before I was sent to England. To shorten the work, as well as for other reasons, I omit all facts and transactions that may not have a tendency to benefit the young reader, by showing him from my example, and my success in emerging from poverty, and acquiring some degree of wealth, power, and reputation, the advantages of certain modes of conduct which I observed, and of avoiding the errors which were prejudicial to me. If a writer can judge properly of his own work, I fancy, on reading over what is already done, that the book will be found entertaining, interesting, and useful, more so than I expected when I began it. If my present state of health continues, I hope to finish it this winter.—Smyth 9:675. (1788.)

B

BACHELORS, Should Pay Fines (from the Fictional "Speech of Miss Polly Baker").—But take into your wise consideration the great and growing number of bachelors in the country, many of whom, from the mean fear of the expenses of a family, have never sincerely and honorably courted a woman in their lives; and by their manner of living leave unproduced (which is little better than murder) hundreds of their posterity to the thousandth generation. Is not this a greater offense against the public good than mine? Compel them, then, by law, either to marriage, or to pay double the fine of fornication every year. What must poor young women do, whom customs and nature forbid to solicit the men, and who cannot force themselves upon husbands, when the laws take no care to provide them any, and yet severely punish them if they do their duty without them; the duty of the first and great command of nature and nature's God, *increase and multiply;* a duty, from the steady performance of which nothing has been able to deter me, but for its sake I have hazarded the loss of the public esteem, and have frequently endured public disgrace and punishment; and therefore ought, in my humble opinion, instead of a whipping, to have a statue erected to my memory.—Smyth 2:467. (1747.)

BACHELORS, In England.—I love to hear of everything that tends to increase the number of good people. You cannot conceive how shamefully the mode here is a single life. One can scarce be in the company of a dozen men of circumstance and fortune, but what it is odds that you find on inquiry eleven of them are single. The great complaint is the excessive expensiveness of English wives.—Smyth 4:24. (1760.)

BACHELORS, Poll Tax on.—Q. How much is the poll tax in your province laid on unmarried men? A. It is, I think, fifteen shillings, to be paid by every single freeman, upwards of twenty-one years old.—Smyth 4:432. (1766.)

BACHELORS, Franklin's Philosophy Concerning.—The account you give me of your family is pleasing, except that your eldest son continues so long unmarried. I hope he does not intend to live and die in celibacy. The wheel of life, that has rolled down to him from Adam without interruption, should not stop with him. I would not have one dead, unbearing branch in the genealogical tree of the Sargents. The married state is, after all our jokes, the happiest, being conformable to our natures. Man and woman have each of them qualities and tempers, in which the other is deficient, and which in union contribute to the common felicity. Single and separate, they are not the complete human being; they are like the odd halves of scissors; they cannot answer the end of their formation.—Smyth 9:14. (1783.)

BACHELORS. See also FAMILY; MARRIAGE.

BIBLE, Important Lessons Applicable to Any Age.—As the Scriptures are given for our reproof, instruction and warning, may we make a due use of this example, before it be too late!—Smyth 2:340. (1747.)

BIFOCAL GLASSES, Franklin's Invention.—I . . . had formerly two pairs of spectacles, which I shifted

Franklin around 1738-46 (age 32 to 40). Portrait by Robert Feke.

occasionally, as in traveling I sometimes read, and often wanted to regard the prospects. Finding this change troublesome, and not always sufficiently ready, I had the glasses cut, and half of each kind associated in the same circle. . . . By this means, as I wear my spectacles constantly, I have only to move my eyes up or down, as I want to see distinctly far or near, the proper glasses being always ready. This I find more particularly convenient since my being in France, the glasses that serve me best at table to see what I eat, not being the best to see the faces of those on the other side of the table who speak to me.—Smyth 9:338. (1785.)

BOOKS, Collected for America.—I am amazed to see how books have grown upon me since my return to England. I brought none with me, and have now a roomful; many collected in Germany, Holland and France; and consisting chiefly of such as contain knowledge that may hereafter be useful to America.— Smyth 5:445. (1772.)

BOOKS, Wasteful Layout Used to Increase Prices.—And one can scarce see a new book, without observing the excessive artifices made use of to puff up a paper of verses into a pamphlet, a pamphlet into an octavo, and an octavo into a quarto, with scabboardings, white-lines, sparse titles of chapters, and exorbitant margins, to such a degree, that the selling of paper seems now the object, and printing on it only the pretense. I enclose the copy of a page in a late comedy. Between every two lines there is a white space equal to another line. You have a law, I think, against butchers' blowing of veal to make it look fatter; why not one against booksellers' blowing of books to make them look bigger.—Smyth 9:305. (1785.)

BORROWING, Much Money Used for Non-necessities.—Upon inquiry of those who present these bills to me for acceptance, what the money is to be laid out in, I find that most of it is for superfluities, and more than half of it for tea. How unhappily in this instance the folly of our people, and the avidity of our merchants, concur to weaken and impoverish our country. I formerly computed, that we consumed before the war, in that single article, the value of 500,000 pounds sterling annually. Much of this was saved by stopping the use of it. I honored the virtuous resolution of our women in foregoing that little gratification, and I lament that such virtue should be of so short duration. Five hundred thousand pounds sterling, annually laid out in defending ourselves, or annoying our enemies, would have great effects. With what face can we ask aids and subsidies from our friends, while we are wasting our own wealth in such prodigality?—Smyth 7:290. (1779.)

BORROWING, Embarrassing.— Our credit and weight in Europe depend more on what we do than on what we say; and I have long been humilated with the idea of our running about from court to court begging for money and friendship, which are the more withheld the more eagerly they are solicited, and would perhaps have been offered if they had not been asked. The supposed necessity is our only excuse. The proverb says, *God helps them that help themselves.* And the world too in this sense is very godly.— Smyth 8:146. (1780.)

It seems to me that we have, in most instances, hurt our credit and importance by sending all over Europe, begging alliances, and soliciting declarations of our independence. The nations perhaps from thence seem to think that our independence is something they have to sell, and that we don't offer enough for it.—Smyth 8:501. (1782.)

BOSTON, Occupation by General Gage.—General Gage, being with his army (before the declaration of open war) in peaceable possession of Boston, shut its gates, and placed guards all around to prevent its communication with the country. The inhabitants were on the point of starving. The General, though they were evidently at his mercy, fearing that, while they had any arms in their hands, frantic desperation might possibly do him some mischief, proposed to them a capitulation, in which he stipulated, that if they would deliver up their arms, they might leave the town with their families and *goods*. In faith of this agreement, they delivered their arms. But when they began to pack up for their departure, they were informed that by the word *goods*, the General understood only household goods, that is, their beds, chairs, and tables, not *merchant goods*, those he was informed they were indebted for to the merchants of England, and he must secure them for the creditors. They were accordingly all seized, to an immense value, *what had been paid for not excepted*.—Smyth 10:109. (1786?)

BOSTON, Franklin Fears He Will Never See It Again.—It would certainly, as you observe, be a very great pleasure to me, if I could once again visit my native town, and walk over the grounds I used to frequent when a boy, and where I enjoyed many of the innocent pleasures of youth, which would be so brought to my remembrance, and where I might find some of my old acquaintance to converse with. But when I consider how well I am situated here, with everything about me that I can call either necessary or convenient; the fatigues and bad accommodations to be met with and suffered in a land journey, and the unpleasantness of sea voyages to one who, although he has crossed the Atlantic eight times, and made many smaller trips, does not recollect his having ever been at sea without taking a firm resolution never to go to sea again; and that, if I were arrived in Boston, I should see but little of it, as I could neither bear walking nor riding in a carriage over its pebbled streets; and, above all, that I should find very few indeed of my old friends living, it being now sixty-five years since I left it to settle here;—all this considered, I say, it seems probable, though not certain, that I shall hardly again visit that beloved place.—Smyth 9:650. (1788.)

BOSTON TEA PARTY, Speedy Reparation Recommended by Franklin.—A speedy reparation will immediately set us right in the opinion of all Europe. And though the mischief was the act of persons unknown, yet as probably they cannot be found or brought to answer for it, there seems to be some reasonable claim on the society at large in which it happened. Making voluntarily such reparation can be no dishonor to us or prejudice to our claim of rights, since Parliament here has frequently considered in the same light similar cases; and only a few years since, when a valuable saw mill which had been erected at a great expense was violently destroyed by a number of persons supposed to be sawyers, but unknown, a grant was made out of the public treasury of two thousand pounds to the owner as a compensation.—Smyth 6:179. (1774.)

BOSTON TEA PARTY, England United in Taking Reprisal.—The violent destruction of the tea seems to have united all parties here [England] against our province, so that the bill now brought into Parliament for shutting up Boston as a port till satisfaction is made, meets with no opposition.—Smyth 6:223. (1774.)

BOSTON TEA PARTY, Offenders May Be Carried to England for Trial.—By the inquiries that I hear are made, I suspect there may be a design to seize some persons who are supposed to be the ringleaders, and bring them here [England] for trial.—Smyth 6:223. (1774.)

BOSTON TEA PARTY, Parliament Responds with the "Intolerable Acts."—A bill is brought in [to Parliament] to alter the charter appointing the council by the crown, giving power to the governors to nominate and commission magistrates without consent of council, and forbidding any town meeting to be held in the province (except the annual one for choosing town officers) without the permission of the governor, and for that business only for which such permission shall be requested. The manner of appointing jurors is likewise to be

altered. And another bill is to provide for the security of persons who may be concerned in executing or enforcing acts of Parliament there, by directing their trials for anything done by them to be in some neighboring province or in Great Britain at the discretion of the governor.—Smyth 6:228. (1774.)

BRADDOCK (General Edward), Franklin's Reaction to Ambush.—I have been employed almost all this summer in the service of an unfortunate army, and other public affairs, that have brought me greatly in arrears with my correspondents. I have lost the pleasure of conversing with them, and I have lost my labor. I wish these were the only losses of the year; but we have lost a number of brave men, and all our credit with the Indians. I fear these losses may soon be productive of more and greater.—Smyth 3:279. (1755.)

BRADDOCK (General Edward), Sent as a Substitute for a Militia of the United Colonies.—The British government, not choosing to permit the union of the colonies as proposed at Albany, and to trust that union with their defense, lest they should thereby grow too military, and feel their own strength, suspicions and jealousies at this time being entertained of them, sent over General Braddock [in 1755] with two regiments of regular English troops for that purpose.—Autobiography. Smyth 1:393. (1788.)

BRADDOCK (General Edward), Ambush Described.—The General, being wounded, was brought off with difficulty; his secretary, Mr. Shirley, was killed by his side; and out of eighty-six officers, sixty-three were killed or wounded, and seven hundred and fourteen men killed out of eleven hundred. These eleven hundred had been picked men from the whole army; the rest had been left behind with Colonel Dunbar, who was to follow with the heavier part of the stores, provisions, and baggage. The flyers, not being pursued, arrived at Dunbar's camp, and the panic they brought with them instantly seized him and all his people; and though he had now above one thousand men, and the enemy who had beaten Braddock did not at most exceed four hundred Indians and French together, instead of proceeding, and endeavoring to recover some of the lost honor, he ordered all the stores, ammunition, etc., to be destroyed, that he might have more horses to assist his flight towards the settlements, and less lumber to remove. He was there met with requests from the governors of Virginia, Maryland, and Pennsylvania, that he would post his troops on the frontier, so as to afford some protection to the inhabitants; but he continued his hasty march through all the country, not thinking himself safe till he arrived at Philadelphia, where the inhabitants could protect him. This whole transaction gave us Americans the first suspicion that our exalted ideas of the prowess of British regulars had not been well founded.—Autobiography. Smyth 1:402. (1788.)

BRIBERY, Attempt to Bribe Franklin.—This demonstrates that you [the Englishmen] do not yet know us, and that you fancy we do not know you; but it is not merely this flimsy faith, that we are to act upon; you offer us *hope*, the hope of *places, pensions, and peerages*. These, judging from yourselves, you think are motives irresistible. This offer to corrupt us, Sir, is with me your credential, and convinces me that you are not a private volunteer in your application. It bears the stamp of British court character. It is even the signature of your king. But think for a moment in what light it must be viewed in America.—Smyth 7:172. (1778.)

BUSINESS, Attending to Details in.—Not to oversee workmen, is to leave them your purse open. Trusting too much to others' care is the ruin of many; for, as the Almanack says, *In the affairs of this world, men are saved, not by faith, but by the want of it;* but a man's own care is profitable; for, saith *Poor Dick, Learning is to the studious, and riches to the careful,* as well as *Power to the bold, and Heaven to the virtuous.* And farther, *If you would have a faithful servant, and one that you like, serve yourself.* And again, he adviseth to circumspection and care, even in the smallest matters, because sometimes *A little neglect may breed great mischief;* adding, *for want of a nail the shoe was lost; for want of a shoe the horse was lost; and for want of a horse the rider was lost, being overtaken and slain by the enemy; all for want of care about a horse-shoe nail.*—Smyth 3:412. (1757.)

C

CANADA, Better British Than French.—No one can more sincerely rejoice than I do on the reduction of Canada; and this is not merely as I am a colonist, but as I am a Briton. I have long been of opinion that the *foundations of the future grandeur and stability of the British empire lie in America;* and though, like other foundations, they are low and little seen, they are, nevertheless, broad and strong enough to support the greatest political structure human wisdom ever yet erected. I am therefore by no means for restoring Canada. If we keep it, all the country from the St. Lawrence to the Mississippi will in another century be filled with British people. Britain itself will become vastly more populous, by the immense increase of its commerce; the Atlantic sea will be covered with your [British] trading ships; and your naval power, thence continually increasing, will extend your influence round the whole globe, and awe the world! If the French remain in Canada, they will continually harass our colonies by the Indians, and impede if not prevent their growth; your progress to greatness will at best be slow, and give room for many accidents that may forever prevent it.—Smyth 4:4. (1760.)

CANADA, Colonists Demand Rights for.—We cannot endure despotism over any of our fellow subjects. We must all be free, or none.—Smyth 6:383. (1775.)

CANADA, Proposal to Purchase.—To prevent those occasions of misunderstanding which are apt to arise where the territories of different powers border on each other, through the bad conduct of frontier inhabitants on both sides, Britain shall cede to the United States the provinces or colonies of Quebec, St. John's, Nova Scotia, Bermuda, East and West Florida, and the Bahama Islands, with all their adjoining and intermediate territories now claimed by her.

In return for this cession, the United States shall pay to Great Britain the sum of [to be determined] sterling.—Smyth 6:452. (1776.)

CANADA, Some Englishmen Intended to Surrender.—I am glad to learn that . . . there is a disposition in England to give us up Canada and Nova Scotia.—Smyth 8:478. (1782.)

CANADA, Could Have Been Purchased for Much Less Than the Cost of the French and Indian War.—I am confident that Canada might have been purchased from France for a tenth part of the money England spent in the conquest of it. And if, instead of fighting with us for the power of taxing us, she had kept us in good humor by allowing us to dispose of our own money, and now and then giving us a little of hers, by way of donation to colleges, or hospitals, or for cutting canals, or fortifying ports, she might have easily drawn from us much more by our occasional voluntary grants and contributions, than ever she could by taxes. Sensible people will give a bucket or two of water to a dry pump, that they may afterwards get from it all they have occasion for.

Her ministry were deficient in that little point of common sense. And so they spent one hundred millions of her money, and after all lost what they contended for.—Smyth 9:613. (1787.)

CANCER, Use of Poke-Weed to Cure.—I am heartily glad to hear more instances of the success of the poke-weed in the cure of that horrible evil to the human body, a cancer.—Smyth 3:86. (1752.)

CANCER, Of the Breast.—I know a cancer in the breast is often thought incurable; yet we have here in town a kind of shell made of some wood, cut at a proper time, by some man of great skill (as they say), which has done wonders in that disease among us, being worn for some time on the breast. I am not apt to be superstitiously fond of believing such things, but the instances are so well attested, as sufficiently to convince the most incredulous.— Smyth 2:181. (1731.)

CANNON, Borrowed from New York by Franklin.—Meanwhile, Colonel Lawrence, William Allen, Abram Taylor, Esq., and myself were sent to New York [in 1747] by the associators, commissioned to borrow some cannon of Governor Clinton. He at first refused us peremptorily; but at dinner with his council, where there was great drinking of Madeira wine, as the custom of that place then was, he softened by degrees, and said he would lend us six. After a few more bumpers he advanced to ten; and at length he very good-naturedly conceded eighteen.—Autobiography. Smyth 1:363. (1788.)

CAPITAL PUNISHMENT, Reserved for First-Degree Murder.—If I think it right that the crime of murder should be punished with death, not only as an equal punishment of the crime, but to prevent other murders, does it follow that I must approve of inflicting the same punishment for a little invasion on my *property* by theft? If I am not myself so barbarous, so bloody-minded and revengeful, as to kill a fellow-creature for stealing from me 14/3, how can I approve of a law that does it? Montesquieu, who was himself a judge, endeavors to impress other maxims. He must have known what humane judges feel on such occasions, and what the effect of those feelings.—Smyth 9:295. (1785.)

CARD PLAYING, To Pass Away the Time.—Cards we sometimes play here, in long winter evenings; but it is as they play at chess, not for money, but for honor, or the pleasure of beating one another. This will not be quite a novelty to you, as you may remember we played together in that manner during the winter at Passy. I have indeed now and then a little compunction in reflecting that I spend time so idly; but another reflection comes to relieve me, whispering, *"You know that the soul is immortal; why then should you be such a niggard of a little time, when you have a whole eternity before you?"* So, being easily convinced, and, like other reasonable creatures, satisfied with a small reason when it is in favor of doing what I have a mind to, I shuffle the cards again and begin another game.—Smyth 9:512. (1786.)

CATHOLIC CHURCH, U.S. Bishop Should Be an American.—I understand that the bishop or spiritual person who superintends or governs the Roman Catholic clergy in the United States of America resides in London, and is supposed to be under obligations to that court, and subject to be influenced by its ministers. This gives me some uneasiness, and I cannot but wish that one should be appointed to that office who is of this nation and who may reside there among our friends.—Smyth 9:125. (1783.)

CHARITY, Mankind All of One Family.—Some time or other you may have an opportunity of assisting with an equal sum a stranger who has equal need of it. Do so. By that means you will discharge any obligation you may suppose yourself under to me. Enjoin him to do the same on occasion. By pursuing such a practice, much good may be done with little money. Let kind offices go round. Mankind are all of a family.—Smyth 8:299. (1781.)

CHARITY, Reluctance to Help the Indolent.—People fear assisting the negligent, the indolent, and the careless, lest the aids they afford should be lost.—Smyth 8:391. (1782.)

CHARITY. See also POOR.

CHARLESTON, Fire Destroys 600 Houses.—I condole with you sincerely on the great loss sustained in Charleston by the fire in January last, said to have destroyed 600

houses, valued with the goods at a million sterling.—Smyth 7:123. (1778.)

CHESS, History of.—Playing at chess is the most ancient and most universal game known among men; for its original is beyond the memory of history, and it has, for numberless ages, been the amusement of all the civilized nations of Asia, the Persians, the Indians, and the Chinese. Europe has had it above a thousand years; the Spaniards have spread it over their part of America; and it has lately begun to make its appearance in the United States. It is so interesting in itself, as not to need the view of gain to induce engaging in it; and thence it is seldom played for money.—Smyth 7:357. (1779.)

CHESS, As a Mode of Mental Training.—The game of chess is not merely an idle amusement. Several very valuable qualities of the mind, useful in the course of human life, are to be acquired or strengthened by it, so as to become habits, ready on all occasions. For life is a kind of chess, in which we often have points to gain, and competitors or adversaries to contend with, and in which there is a vast variety of good and ill events, that are in some degree the effects of prudence or the want of it. By playing at chess, then, we may learn,

I. *Foresight*, which looks a little into futurity, and considers the consequences that may attend an action; for it is continually occurring to the player, "If I move this piece, what will be the advantages or disadvantages of my new situation?..."

II. *Circumspection,* which surveys the whole chessboard, or scene of action; the relations of the several pieces and situations, the dangers they are respectively exposed to....

III. *Caution,* not to make our moves too hastily....

And *lastly,* we learn by chess the habit of not being discouraged by present appearances in the state of our affairs, the habit of hoping for a favorable change, and that of persevering in the search of resources.—Smyth 7:358. (1779.)

CHILDREN, Value of.—Four daughters! How rich! I have but one, and she necessarily detained from me at 1000 leagues distance. I feel the want of that tender care of me, which might be expected from a daughter, and would give the world for one.—Smyth 8:455. (1782.)

CHILDREN, Importance of Home Training.—You cannot be more pleased in talking about your children, your methods of instructing them, and the progress they make, than I am in hearing it, and in finding that, instead of following the idle amusements which both your fortune and the custom of the age might have led you into, your delight and your duty go together by employing your time in the education of your offspring. This is following nature and reason, instead of fashion; than which nothing is more becoming the character of a woman of sense and virtue.—Smyth 8:455. (1782.)

CHILDREN, In France, Need More Attention from Parents.—I wish success to the new project of assisting the poor to keep their children at home, because I think there is no nurse like a mother (or not many), and that if parents did not immediately send their infants out of their sight, they would in a few days begin to love them, and thence be spurred to greater industry for their maintenance.—Smyth 9:335. (1785.)

CHILDREN, Joys and Sorrows of Rearing.—When we launch our little fleet of barks into the ocean, bound to different ports, we hope for each a prosperous voyage; but contrary winds, hidden shoals, storms, and enemies come in for a share in the disposition of events; and though these occasion a mixture of disappointment, yet, considering the risk where we can make no insurance, we should think ourselves happy if some return with success.—Smyth 9:490. (1786.)

CHILDREN. See also FAMILY.

CHRISTIANITY, Rational.—Sir John has asked me if I knew where he could go to hear a preacher of *rational* Christianity. I told him I knew several of them, but did not know where their churches were in town; out of town, I mentioned yours at Newington, and offered to go with him. He agreed to it, but said we should first let you know our intention. I suppose, if nothing in his profession prevents, we may come, if you please, next Sunday; but if you sometimes preach in town, that will be most convenient to him, and I request you would by a line let me know when and where. If there are dissenting preachers of that sort at this end of the town, I wish you would recommend one to me, naming the place of his meeting. And if you please, give me a list of several, in different parts of the town; perhaps he may incline to take a round among them.—Smyth 5:440. (1772.)

CHURCH BUILDINGS, Cold and Uncomfortable.—Many pious and devout persons, whose age or infirmities will not suffer them to remain for hours in a cold church, especially in the winter season, are obliged to forego the comfort and edification they would receive by their attendance at divine service.— Smyth 6:166. (1774.)

CHURCH OF ENGLAND, Services Too Long.—The morning and evening services, as practiced in England and elsewhere, are so long, and filled with so many repetitions, that the continued attention suitable to so serious a duty becomes impracticable, the mind wanders and the fervency of devotion is slackened.—Smyth 6:166. (1774.)

CHURCHES, Establishing New Congregations Is Multiplying, Not Dividing.—Your tenderness of the church's peace is truly laudable; but, methinks, to build a new church in a growing place is not properly *dividing* but *multiplying*; and will really be the means of increasing the number of those who worship God in that way. Many who cannot now be accommodated in the church go to other places, or stay at home; and if we had another church, many who go to other places or stay at home, would go to church.—Smyth 3:18. (1750.)

CHURCHES, Have Persecuted One Another in the Past.—If we look back into history for the character of the present sects in Christianity we shall find few that have not in their turns been persecutors, and complainers of persecution. The primitive Christians thought persecution extremely wrong in the pagans, but practiced it on one another. The first Protestants of the church of England blamed persecution in the Romish church, but practiced it against the Puritans. These found it wrong in the bishops, but fell into the same practice themselves, both here and in New England. To account for this we should remember, that the doctrine of *toleration* was not then known, or had not prevailed in the world. Persecution was, therefore, not so much the fault of the sect as of the times. It was not in those days deemed wrong *in itself*. The general opinion was only, that those *who are in error* ought not to persecute *the truth;* but *possessors of truth* were in the right to persecute *error* in order to destroy it. Thus every sect, believing itself possessed of *all truth*, and that every tenet differing from theirs was *error*, conceived that, when the power was in their hands, persecution was a duty required of them by that God whom they supposed to be offended with heresy. By degrees more moderate *and more modest* sentiments have taken place in the Christian world; and among Protestants, particularly, all disclaim persecution, none vindicate it, and but few practice it. We should then cease to reproach each other with what was done by our ancestors, but judge of the present character of sects or churches by their *present conduct* only.—Smyth 5:400. (1772.)

CHURCHES, England Compared to Colonies.—In New England, where the legislative bodies are almost to a man dissenters from the church of England,

1. There is no test to prevent churchmen from holding offices.

2. The sons of churchmen have the full benefit of the universities.

3. The taxes for support of public worship, when paid by churchmen, are given to the Episcopal minister.

In Old England,

1. Dissenters are excluded from all offices of profit and honor.

2. The benefits of education in the universities are appropriated to the sons of churchmen.

3. The clergy of the dissenters receive none of the tithes paid by their people, who must be at the additional charge of maintaining their own separate worship.— Smyth 5:403. (1772.)

CHURCHES, Clergy Fought for English Liberty.—This kingdom is a good deal indebted for its liberties to the public spirit of its ancient clergy, who joined with the barons in obtaining Magna Charta, and joined heartily in forming the curses of excommunication against the infringers of it.—Smyth 6:87. (1773.)

CLOTHING INDUSTRY, In Colonies.—I have lately been among the clothing towns in Yorkshire, and by conversing with the manufacturers there, am more and more convinced of the natural impossibility there is that, considering our

Franklin in 1759 (age 53). Portrait by Benjamin Wilson.

increase in America, England should be able much longer to supply us with clothing. Necessity, therefore, as well as prudence, will soon induce us to seek resources in our own industry, which becoming general among the people, encouraged by resolutions of your court, such as I have the pleasure of seeing in your late votes, will do wonders. Family manufactures will alone amount to a vast saving in the year; and a steady determination and custom of buying only of your own artificers wherever they can supply you, will soon make them more expert in working, so as to dispatch more business, while constant employment enables them to afford their work still cheaper.—Smyth 5:327. (1771.)

COLONIAL GOVERNORS, Often Miscreants.—Governors often come to the colonies merely to make fortunes, with which they intend to return to Britain; are not always men of the best abilities or integrity; have many of them no estates here, nor any natural connections with us, that should make them heartily concerned for our welfare; and might possibly be fond of raising and keeping up more forces than necessary, from the profits accruing to themselves, and to make provision for their friends and dependants.—Smyth 3:233. (1754.)

COLONIAL GOVERNORS, Those Appointed by the Crown Seldom Qualified.—They are generally strangers to the provinces they are sent to govern, [and] have no estate, natural connection, or relation there to give them an affection for the country; . . . they come only to make money as fast as they can; [they] are sometimes men of vicious characters and broken fortunes, sent by a minister merely to get them out of the way; . . . [and] as they intend staying in the country no longer than their government continues, and purpose to leave no family behind them, they are apt to be regardless of the good will of the people, and care not what is said or thought of them after they are gone.—Smyth 5:83. (1768.)

COLONIES, Original Charters Establish Unworkable Boundaries for Some.—The grants to most of the colonies are of long, narrow slips of land, extending west from the Atlantic to the South Sea. They are much too long for their breadth; the extremes at too great a distance; and therefore unfit to be continued under their present dimensions.—Smyth 3:361. (1756.)

COLONIES, Sovereignty in King, Not Parliament.—In this view, they seem so many separate little states, subject to the same prince. The *sovereignty of the king* is therefore easily understood. But nothing is more common here than to talk of the *sovereignty of Parliament*, and the *sovereignty of this nation* over the colonies; a kind of sovereignty , the idea of which is not so clear, nor does it clearly appear on what foundation it is established.—Smyth 5:20. (1767.)

COLONIES, Separation from England Inevitable.—Upon the whole, I have lived so great a part of my life in Britain, and have formed so many friendships in it, that I love it, and sincerely wish it prosperity; and therefore wish to see that union, on which alone I think it can be secured and established. As to America, the advantages of such a union to her are not so apparent. She may suffer at present under the arbitrary power of this country; she may suffer for a while in a separation from it; but these are temporary evils that she will outgrow. Scotland and Ireland are differently circumstanced. Confined by the sea, they can scarcely increase in numbers, wealth and strength, so as to over-balance England. But America, an immense territory, favored by nature with all advantages of climate, soil, great navigable rivers, and lakes, etc. must become a great country, populous and mighty; and will, in a less time than is generally conceived, be able to shake off any shackles that may be imposed on her, and perhaps place them on the imposers. In the meantime, every act of oppression will sour their tempers, lessen greatly if not annihilate the profits of your commerce with them, and hasten their final revolt; for the seeds of liberty are univerally found there, and nothing can eradicate them. And yet, there remains among that people so much respect, veneration and affection for Britain that, if cultivated prudently, with kind usage, and tenderness for thieir privileges, they might be easily governed still for ages, without force, or any considerable expense. But I do not see here a sufficient quantity of the wisdom that is necessary to produce such a conduct, and I lament the want of it.—Smyth 5:21. (1767.)

COLONIES, British Attitude.— The plan of our adversaries is to render assemblies in America useless; and to have a revenue independent of their grants, for all the purposes of their defense, and supporting governments among them. It is our interest to prevent this.—Smyth 5:43. (1767.)

COLONIES, Generous in Aiding Britain.—From the time that the colonies were first considered as capable of granting aids to the crown, down to the end of the last war, it is said that the constant mode of obtaining those aids was by *requisition* made from the crown through its governors to the several assemblies, in circular letters from the Secretary of State in his Majesty's name, setting forth the occasion, requiring them to take the matter into consideration; and expressing a reliance on their prudence, duty and affection to his Majesty's government, that they would grant such sums, or raise such numbers of men, as were suitable to their respective circumstances.

The colonies, being accustomed to this method, have from time to time granted money to the crown, or raised troops for its service, in proportion to their abilities; and during all the last war beyond their abilities, so that considerable sums were returned them yearly by Parliament, as they had exceeded their proportion.—Smyth 5:78. (1768.)

COLONIES, Manufacturing Discouraged in.—There cannot be a stronger natural right than that of a man's making the best profit he can of the natural produce of his lands, provided he does not thereby hurt the state in general. Iron is to be found everywhere in America, and beaver furs are the natural produce of that country; hats, and nails, and steel are wanted there as well as here [England]. It is of no importance to the common welfare of the empire whether a subject of the King's gets his living by making hats on this or that side of the water. Yet the hatters of England have prevailed to obtain an act in their own favor, restraining that manufacture in America, in order to oblige the Americans to send their beaver to England to be manufactured, and purchase back the hats, loaded with the charges of a double transportation. In the same manner have a few nail-makers, and a still smaller body of steel-makers (perhaps there are not half a dozen of these in England) prevailed totally to forbid by an act of Parliament the erecting of slitting mills or steel furnaces in America, that the Americans may be obliged to take all the nails for their buildings, and steel for their tools, from these artificers, under the same disadvantages.—Smyth 5:86. (1768.)

COLONIES, Misjudged by Parliament.—Whenever there is any news of discontent in America, the cry is, "Send over an army or a fleet, and reduce the dogs to *reason.*"

It is said of choleric people, that with them there is *but a word and a blow.*

I hope *Britain* is not so choleric, and will never be so angry with her *colonies* as to *strike* them. But that if she should ever think it may be necessary, she will at least let the *word* go before the *blow,* and reason with them.—Smyth 5:128. (1768.)

COLONIES, Cannot Be Subdued Easily.—I believe our [British] officers and soldiers as brave as any in the world; and from that very opinion of their bravery I conjecture they would not generally relish the being ordered on this murdering service against their countrymen; to shed English blood, to stifle the British spirit of liberty now rising in the colonies; that *liberty* which we should rather wish to see nourished and preserved there, as on a loss of it here (which from our vices is perhaps not far distant) we or our posterity may have occasion to resort to and participate of; and possibly some of the ablest officers may choose, with Sir *Jeffery Amherst,* rather to resign their commissions. But whatever may be the bravery and military powers of our troops, and whatever the zeal with which they would proceed in such a war, there are reasons that make me suspect that it will not be so soon terminated as some folks would have us believe.

My reasons are drawn chiefly from a computation founded on *facts.* It is well known that America is a country full of forests, mountains, etc., [and] that in such a country a small irregular force can give abundance of trouble to a regular one that is much greater.—Smyth 5:163. (1768.)

COLONIES, Union with Britain Not Desired.—Upon the whole, as we are not presumptuous enough to ask a *union* with Britain, such as England contracted with Scotland, we have no "proposition" to make, but that she would leave us the enjoyment of our native and dear-bought privileges, and not attempt to alter or innovate our constitutions, in the exercise of which everything went prosperously for both countries, till the idea of taxing us by the power of Parliament unfortunately entered the heads of your ministers, which had occasioned a public discussion of questions that had better never been started, and thrown all into confusion.—Smyth 5:168. (1768.)

COLONIES, Dumping Ground for Criminals.—We call Britain the mother country; but what good mother would introduce thieves and criminals into the company of her children to corrupt and disgrace them? And how cruel is it to force, by the high hand of power, a particular country of your subjects, who have not deserved such usage, to receive your outcasts, repealing all the laws they make to prevent their admission, and then reproach them with the detested mixture you have made! "Their emptying their jails into our settlements," says a writer of that country, "is an insult and contempt, the cruellest perhaps that ever one people offered to another."—Smyth 5:216. (1769.)

COLONIES, Must Secure Rights for Posterity.—You are in my opinion perfectly right in your supposition, that "the redress of American grievances likely to be proposed by the ministry will at first only be partial; and that it is intended to retain some of the revenue duties, in order to establish a right of Parliament to tax the colonies." But I hope that, by persisting steadily in the measure you have so laudably entered into, you will, if backed by the general honest resolution of the people to buy British goods of no others, but to manufacture for themselves, or use colony manufactures only, be the means, under God, of recovering and establishing the freedom of our country entire, and of handing it down complete to posterity.—Smyth 5:220. (1769.)

COLONIES, Will Gradually Be Enriched Through Industry and Frugality.—And in the mean time the country will be enriched by its industry and frugality. These virtues will become habitual. Farms will be more improved, better stocked, and rendered more productive by the money that used to be spent in superfluities. Our artificers of every kind will be enabled to carry on their business to more advantage; gold and silver will become more plenty among us, and trade will revive, after things shall be well settled, and become better and safer than it has lately been; for an industrious, frugal people are best able to buy, and pay best for what they purchase.—Smyth 5:220. (1769.)

COLONIES, Treatment by England.—They [the colonies] have been rebuked in angry letters. Their petitions have been refused or rejected by Parliament. They have been threatened with the punishment of treason by resolves of both houses. Their assemblies have been dissolved, and troops have been sent among them; but all these ways have only exasperated their minds and widened the breach. Their agreements to use no more British manufactures have been strengthened; and these measures, instead of composing differences and promoting a good correspondence, have almost annihilated your commerce with those countries, and greatly endangered the national peace and general welfare.—Smyth 5:240. (1769.)

COLONIES, Independence Not Their Goal in 1769.—The notion that prevails here of their being desirous to set up a kingdom or commonwealth of their own is, to my certain knowledge, entirely groundless.

I therefore think that, on a total repeal of all duties, laid expressly for the purpose of raising a revenue on the people of America without their consent, the present uneasiness would subside.—Smyth 5:242. (1769.)

COLONIES, Supported in England by Dissenters.—We have for sincere friends and well-wishers the body of dissenters generally throughout England, with many others, not to mention Ireland and all the rest of Europe, who, from various motives, join in applauding the spirit of liberty with which we have claimed and insisted on our privileges, and wish us success, but whose suffrage cannot have much weight in our affairs.—Smyth 5:253. (1770.)

COLONIES, Originally Considered Themselves Distinct States.—That the colonies originally were constituted distinct states, and intended to be continued such, is clear to me from a thorough consideration of their original charters, and the whole conduct of the crown and nation towards them until the restoration. Since that period, the Parliament here has usurped an authority of making laws for them which before it had not. We have for some time submitted to that usurpation, partly through ignorance and inattention, and partly from our weakness and

inability to contend. I hope, when our rights are better understood here, we shall, by prudent and proper conduct, be able to obtain from the equity of this nation a restoration of them.—Smyth 5:260. (1770.)

COLONIES, Contrasted with Ireland and Scotland.—I have lately made a tour through Ireland and Scotland. In those countries a small part of the society are landlords, great noblemen, and gentlemen, extremely opulent, living in the highest affluence and magnificence. The bulk of the people [are] tenants, extremely poor, living in the most sordid wretchedness, in dirty hovels of mud and straw, and clothed only in rags.

I thought often of the happiness of New England, where every man is a freeholder, has a vote in public affairs, lives in a tidy, warm house, has plenty of good food and fuel, with whole clothes from head to foot, the manufacture perhaps of his own family. Long may they continue in this situation!—Smyth 5:362. (1772.)

COLONIES, Reaction in England Toward America.—I think I see some alarm at the discontents in New England, and some appearance of softening in the disposition of government, on the idea that matters have been carried too far there. But all depends upon circumstances and events. We govern from hand to mouth. There seems to be no wise regular plan.— Smyth 6:31. (1773.)

COLONIES, Always Responded to Necessary Requisitions of the

Crown.—Another villainous falsehood advanced against the Americans is that, though we [English] have been at such expense in protecting them, they refuse to contribute their part to the public general expense of the empire. The fact is, that *they never did refuse a requisition of that kind.*—Smyth 6:216. (1774.)

COLONIES, Firmness Disappointing to Parliament.—The coolness, temper and firmness of the American proceedings; the unanimity of all the colonies, in the same sentiments of their rights, and of the injustice offered to Boston; and the patience with which those injuries are at present borne, without the least appearance of submission; have a good deal surprised and disappointed our enemies, and the tone of public conversation, which has been violently against us, begins evidently to turn; so that I make no doubt that before the meeting of Parliament it will be as general in our favor.—Smyth 6:238. (1774.)

COLONIES, Unity a Surprise to England.—I rejoice to find that the whole continent have so justly, wisely and unanimously taken up our cause as their own. This is an unexpected blow to the ministry, who relied on our being neglected by every other colony; this they depended on as another circumstance that must force our immediate submission, of which they were likewise perfectly sure. They are now a little disconcerted, but I hear yet from that quarter no talk of retreating or changing of measures. The language of those

about the court rather is that the King must now go on, whatever be the consequence. On the other hand, our friends are increasing and endeavoring to *unite.* I have been taking pains among them, to show the mischief that must arise to the whole from a dismembering of the empire, which all the measures of the present mad administration have a tendency to accomplish, and which can only be prevented by such a union of the friends of liberty in both houses as will compel a change of that administration and those measures.—Smyth 6:244. (1774.)

COLONIES, Relationship with British Government.—From a thorough inquiry (on occasion of the Stamp Act) into the nature of the connection between Britain and the colonies, I became convinced that the bond of their union is not the Parliament, but the King. That in removing to America, a country out of the realm, they did not carry with them the statutes then existing; for, if they did, the Puritans must have been subject *there* to the same grievous acts of conformity, tithes, spiritual courts, etc., which they meant to be free from by going thither; and in vain would they have left their native country, and all the conveniences and comforts of its improved state, to combat the hardships of a new settlement in a distant wilderness, if they had taken with them what they meant to fly from, or if they had left a power behind them capable of sending the same chains after them, to bind them in America. They took with them, however, by compact, their allegiance to the King, and a legislative power for the making a new body of laws with his assent, by which they were to be governed. Hence they became distinct states, under the same prince, as Scotland and England were before the union, as Ireland is, as Jersey, Guernsey and Hanover are, governed each by its own laws, and by the same sovereign; having each the power of granting their own money to that sovereign. And the privilege of not being taxed but by their own representatives.

At the same time, I considered the King's supreme authority over all the colonies as of the greatest importance to them, affording a *dernier resort* for settling all their disputes, a means of preserving peace among them with each other, and a center in which their common force might be united against a common enemy. This authority I therefore thought, when acting within its due limits, should be ever as carefully supported by the colonists as by the inhabitants of Britain.—Smyth 6:260. (1774.)

COLONIES, Franklin's Efforts to Mediate Between British Government and.—To keep up, as much as in me lay, a reverence for the King and respect for the British nation on that side [of] the water, and on this some regard for the colonies (both tending to promote . . . harmony), I industriously, on all occasions in my letters to America, represented the measures that were grievous to them as being neither *royal* nor *national* measures, but the schemes of an administration which wished

to recommend itself for its ingenuity in finance, or to avail itself of new revenues in creating, by places and pensions, new dependencies; for that the King was a good and gracious prince, and the people of Britain their real friends. And on this side the water, I represented the people of America as fond of Britain, concerned for its interests and its glory, and without the least desire of a separation from it. In both cases I thought, and still think, I did not exceed the bounds of truth, and I have the heartfelt satisfaction attending good intentions, even when they are not successful.— Smyth 6:261. (1774.)

COLONIES, Unanimity and Resolution.—The unanimity and resolution of the colonies astonishes their enemies here [in England], being totally unexpected. By its continuance, you will undoubtedly carry all your points; by giving way you will lose everything. Strong chains will be forged for you, and you will be made to pay for both the iron and the workmanship. I rejoice to see the zeal with which your cause is taken up by the other colonies. But were they all to desert New England, she ought, in my opinion, to hold the same determination of defending her rights, even if all Europe were to league with Britain in attempting to enslave her. And I think she would finally succeed; for it is inconceivable what a small, virtuous, determined people may effect, with the blessing of God, in defense of their liberty against millions of adversaries.—Labaree & Willcox

21:323. (1774.)

COLONIES, Eyes of World on Them.—The eyes of all Christendom are now upon us, and our honor as a people is become a matter of the utmost consequence to be taken care of. If we tamely give up our rights in this contest, a century to come will not restore us in the opinion of the world; we shall be stamped with the character of dastards, poltrons, and fools; and be despised and trampled upon, not by this haughty, insolent nation only, but by all mankind. Present inconveniences are, therefore, to be borne with fortitude, and better times expected.—Smyth 6:310. (1775.)

COLONIES. See also AMERICA; ENGLAND.

COMMERCE, When Unfair Because of Ignorance.—Where the labor and expense of producing [exchanged] commodities are known to both parties, bargains will generally be fair and equal. Where they are known to one party only, bargains will often be unequal, knowledge taking its advantage of ignorance.—Smyth 5:201. (1769.)

COMMERCE, Should Be Mutually Beneficial.—Commerce among nations, as well as between private persons, should be fair and equitable, by equivalent exchanges and mutual supplies. The taking unfair advantages of a neighbor's necessities, though attended with temporary success, always breeds bad blood. To lay duties on a commodity exported, which our neighbors want, is a knavish attempt to get something for nothing.—Smyth 7:176. (1778.)

COMMERCE. See also FREE TRADE.

COMMISSIONERS, Too Many in Paris.—Speaking of commissioners in the plural puts me in mind of inquiring if it can be the intention of Congress to keep *three* commissioners at this court; we have indeed four with the gentleman intended for Tuscany, who continues here, and is very angry that he was not consulted in making the treaty, which he could have mended in several particulars; and perhaps he is angry with some reason, if the instructions to him do, as he says they do, require us to consult him. We shall soon have the fifth; for the envoy to Vienna, not being received there, is, I hear, returning hither. The necessary expense of maintaining us all is, I assure you, enormously great. I wish that the utility may equal it ... but, as to our number, whatever advantage there might be in the joint counsels of three for framing and adjusting the articles of the treaty, there can be none in managing the common business of a resident here. On the contrary, all the advantages in negotiation that result from secrecy of sentiment, and uniformity in expressing it, and in common business from dispatch, are lost. In a court, too, where every word is watched and weighed, if a number of commissioners do not every one hold the same language, in giving their opinion on any public transaction, this lessens their weight.—Smyth 7:178. (1778.)

COMPOSITION, Training in.—Writing one's own language well is the next necessary accomplishment after good speaking. It is the writing master's business to take care that the boys make fair characters, and place them straight and even in the lines. But to *form their style,* and even to take care that the stops and capitals are properly disposed, is the part of the *English* master. The boys should be put on writing letters to each other on any common occurrences, and on various subject.—Smyth 3:26. (1750.)

CONGRESS, An Arena for the Reconciling of Contesting Forces.— We must not expect that a new government may be formed, as a game of chess may be played, by a skillful hand, without a fault. The players of our game are so many, their ideas so different, their prejudices so strong and so various, and their particular interests, independent of the general, seeming so opposite, that not a move can be made that is not contested; the numerous objections confound the understanding; the wisest must agree to some unreasonable things, that reasonable ones of more consequence may be obtained.— Smyth 9:659. (1788.)

CONGRESS, Franklin Preferred Unicameral.— It is very possible, as you suppose, that all the articles of the proposed new government will not remain unchanged after the first meeting of the Congress. I am of opinion with you, that the *two* chambers were not necessary, and I disliked some other articles that are in, and wished for some that are not in, the proposed plan. I nevertheless

hope it may be adopted.—Smyth 9:645. (1788.)

CONGRESS. See also CONTI-NENTAL CONGRESS.

CONSCIENTIOUS OBJECTORS, Quakers Protected under Pennsylvania Statute.— This province was first settled by (and a majority of the assemblies have ever since been of) the people called Quakers, who, though they do not, as the world is now circumstanced, condemn the use of arms in others, yet are principled against bearing arms themselves; and to make any law to compel them thereto, against their consciences, would not be only to violate a fundamental in our constitution, and be a direct breach of our charter of privileges, but would also in effect be to commence persecution against all that part of the inhabitants of the province.— Smyth 3:296. (1755.)

CONSTITUTION, Importance of a Written.— I wish most sincerely... that a constitution [were] formed and settled for America, that we might know what we are and what we have, what our rights and what our duties in the judgment of this country as well as in our own. Till such a constitution is settled, different sentiments will ever occasion misunderstandings.— Smyth 6:196. (1774.)

CONSTITUTION (U.S.), Franklin Urges Convention Delegates to Approve It.— I confess that I do not entirely approve of this Constitution at present; but, Sir, I am not sure I shall never approve it; for, having lived long, I have experienced many instances of being obliged, by better information or fuller consideration, to change my opinions even on important subjects, which I once thought right but found to be otherwise. It is therefore that, the older I grow, the more apt I am to doubt my own judgment....

In these sentiments, Sir, I agree to this Constitution, with all its faults, if they are such; because I think a general government necessary for us, and there is no *form* of government but what may be a blessing to the people, if well administered; and I believe, farther, that this is likely to be well administered for a course of years, and can only end in despotism, as other forms have done before it, when the people shall become so corrupted as to need despotic government, being incapable of any other. I doubt, too, whether any other convention we can obtain may be able to make a better constitution; for, when you assemble a number of men, to have the advantage of their joint wisdom, you inevitably assemble with those men all their prejudices, their passion, their errors of opinion, their local interests, and their selfish views. From such an assembly can a *perfect* production be expected? It therefore astonishes me, Sir, to find this system approaching so near to perfection as it does; and I think it will astonish our enemies, who are waiting with confidence to hear that our councils are confounded like those of the builders of Babel, and that our states are on the point of separation, only to meet hereafter for the purpose of cutting one another's throats.

Thus I consent, Sir, to this Constitution, because I expect no better, and because I am not sure that it is not the best. The opinions I have had of its *errors* I sacrifice to the public good. I have never whispered a syllable of them abroad. Within these walls they were born, and here they shall die. If every one of us, in returning to our constituents, were to report the objections he has had to it, and endeavor to gain partisans in support of them, we might prevent its being generally received, and thereby lose all the salutary effects and great advantages resulting naturally in our favor among foreign nations, as well as among ourselves, from our real or apparent unanimity. Much of the strength and efficiency of any government, in procuring and securing happiness to the people, depends on *opinion,* on the general opinion of the goodness of that government, as well as of the wisdom and integrity of its governors.

I hope, therefore, for our own sakes, as a part of the people, and for the sake of our posterity, that we shall act heartily and unanimously in recommending this Constitution, wherever our influence may extend, and turn our future thoughts and endeavors to the means of having it *well administered.*

On the whole, Sir, I cannot help expressing a wish that every member of the convention who may still have objections to it, would with me on this occasion doubt a little of his own infallibility, and, to make *manifest* our *unanimity*, put his name to this instrument.—Smyth 9:607. (1787.)

CONSTITUTION (U.S.), To Be Modified and Strengthened as Time Goes By.—The first Congress will probably mend the principal [weaknesses], and future Congresses the rest. That which you mention did not pass unnoticed in the convention. Many, if I remember right, were for making the President incapable of being chosen after the first four years; but a majority were for leaving the [electorate] free to choose whom they pleased; and it was alleged that such incapability might tend to make the President less attentive to the duties of the office, and to the interests of the people, than he would be if a second choice depended on their good opinion of them. We are making experiments in politics; what knowledge we shall gain by them will be more certain, though perhaps we may hazard too much in that mode of acquiring it.—Smyth 9:666. (1788.)

CONSTITUTION (U.S.), Extensively Discussed Before Ratification.—Our affairs mend daily and are getting into good order very fast. Never was any measure so thoroughly discussed as our proposed new Constitution. Many objections were made to it in the public papers, and answers to these objections. Much party heat there was, and some violent personal abuse. I kept out of the dispute, and wrote only one little paper on the occasion which I enclose. You seem to me to be so apprehensive about our President's being perpetual. Neither he nor we have any such intention. What danger there may be of such an event we are all aware of, and shall take care effectually to prevent it. The choice is from four years to four years; the appointments will be small; thus we may change our President if we don't like his conduct, and he will have less inducement to struggle for a new election. As to the two chambers, I am of your opinion that one alone would be better; but, my dear friend, nothing in human affairs and schemes is perfect; and perhaps that is the case of our opinions.—Smyth 9:673. (1788.)

CONSTITUTION (U.S.), Coming In as Franklin Is Going Out.—Our new Constitution is now established, and has an appearance that promises permanency; but in this world nothing can be said to be certain, except death and taxes.

My health continues much as it has been for some time, except that I grow thinner and weaker, so that I cannot expect to hold out much longer.—Smyth 10:69. (1789.)

CONSTITUTION OF PENNSYLVANIA, Franklin Warns Against Abandoning Fundamental Principles.—I hope that our representatives in the convention will not hastily go into these innovations [new political theories], but take the advice of the prophet, *"Stand in the old ways, view the ancient paths, consider them well, and be not among those that are given to change."*—Smyth 10:60. (1789.)

CONSTITUTION OF PENNSYL-

VANIA, Franklin's Comments on Proposed Changes.—(For full text, see Smyth 10:54–60. [1789.])

CONSTITUTIONAL CONVENTION OF 1787, To Revise Articles of Confederation.—There seems to be but little thought at present in the particular states of mending their particular constitutions; but the grand federal constitution is generally blamed as not having given sufficient powers to Congress, the federal head. A convention is therefore appointed to revise the constitution, and propose a better. You will see by the enclosed paper that your friend is to be one in that business, though he doubts his malady [will] permit his giving constant attendance.—Smyth 9:564. (1787.)

CONSTITUTIONAL CONVENTION OF 1787, Need to Consult, Not Contend.—It has given me great pleasure to observe that till this point, *the proportion of representation,* came before us, our debates were carried on with great coolness and temper. If anything of a contrary kind has, on this occasion, appeared, I hope it will not be repeated; for we are sent hither to *consult,* not to *contend,* with each other; and declarations of a fixed opinion, and of determined resolution never to change it, neither enlighten nor convince us. Positiveness and warmth on one side naturally beget their like on the other and tend to create and augment discord and division in a great concern, wherein harmony and union are extremely necessary to give weight to our counsels, and

render them effectual in promoting and securing the common good.— Smyth 9:595. (1787.)

CONSTITUTIONAL CONVENTION OF 1787, Divine Influence on.—I have so much faith in the general government of the world by Providence that I can hardly conceive a transaction of such momentous importance to the welfare of millions now existing, and to exist in the posterity of a great nation, should be suffered to pass without being in some degree influenced, guided, and governed by that omnipotent, omnipresent, and beneficent Ruler in whom all inferior spirits live and move and have their being.—Smyth 9:702. (1788.)

CONSTITUTIONAL CONVENTION OF 1787. See also PRAYER.

CONSTITUTIONAL RIGHTS, Usurped by England.—After some questions respecting the present state of affairs in America and discourse thereupon, he [Lord Grenville] said to me [in 1757]: "You Americans have wrong ideas of the nature of your constitution; you contend that the king's instructions to his governors are not laws, and think yourselves at liberty to regard or disregard them at your own discretion. But those instructions are not like the pocket instructions given to a minister going abroad, for regulating his conduct in some trifling point of ceremony. They are first drawn up by judges learned in the laws; they are then considered, debated, and perhaps amended in council, after which they are signed by the king. They are then, so far as they relate to you, the *law of the land,* for the King is the LEGISLATOR OF THE COLONIES." I told his lordship this was new doctrine to me. I had always understood from our charters that our laws were to be made by our assemblies, to be presented indeed to the king for his royal assent, but that being once given the king could not repeal or alter them. And as the assemblies could not make permanent laws without his assent, so neither could he make a law for them without theirs. He assured me I was totally mistaken. I did not think so, however, and his lordship's conversation having a little alarmed me as to what might be the sentiments of the court concerning us, I wrote it down as soon as I returned to my lodgings. I recollected that about 20 years before, a clause in a bill brought into Parliament by the ministry had proposed to make the king's instructions laws in the colonies, but the clause was thrown out by the Commons, for which we adored them as our friends and friends of liberty, till by their conduct towards us in 1765 it seemed that they had refused that point of sovereignty to the king only that they might reserve it for themselves.— Autobiography. Smyth 1:434. (1789.)

CONSTITUTIONS, Provide Orderly Government.—*History* will also give occasion to expatiate on the advantage of civil orders and constitutions; how men and their properties are protected by joining in societies and establishing government; their industry encouraged and rewarded, arts invented, and life made more comfortable; the advantages of *liberty,* mischiefs of *licentiousness,* benefits arising from good laws and a due execution of justice, etc. Thus may the first principles of sound *politics* be fixed in the minds of youth.—Smyth 2:393. (1749.)

CONSTITUTIONS OF STATES, Studied in Europe.—That it may be better known everywhere what sort of people, and what kind of government, they will have to treat with, I prevailed with a friend, the Duc de Rochefoucauld, to translate our book of constitutions into French, and I presented copies to all the foreign ministers.... They are much admired by the politicians here, and it is thought will induce considerable emigrations of substantial people from different parts of Europe to America. It is particularly a matter of wonder that, in the midst of a cruel war raging in the bowels of our country, our sages should have the firmness of mind to sit down calmly and form such complete plans of government. They add considerably to the reputation of the United States.— Smyth 9:71. (1783.)

CONSTITUTIONS OF STATES, Admired Abroad.—It has been well taken, and has afforded matter of surprise to many, who had conceived mean ideas of the state of civilization in America, and could not have expected so much political knowledge and sagacity had existed in our wildernesses. And from all parts I have the satisfaction to hear that our constitutions in general are much admired. I am persuaded that this step will not only tend to promote the emigration to our country of substantial people from all parts of Europe, by the numerous copies I shall disperse, but will facilitate our future treaties with foreign courts, who could not before know what kind of government and people they had to treat with.—Smyth 9:132. (1783.)

CONTENTION, Reprehensible.—It is a bad temper of mind that takes a delight in opposition.—Smyth 6:205. (1774.)

CONTENTION, Destroys Good Will.—In the course of my observation, these disputing, contradicting, and confuting people are generally unfortunate in their affairs. They get victory sometimes, but they never get good will, which would be of more use to them.—Autobiography. Smyth 1:390.(1788.)

CONTINENTAL CONGRESS, Franklin's Admiration for.—When I consider that Congress, as consisting of men, the free, unbiased, unsolicited choice of the freeholders of a great country, selected from no other motives than the general opinion of their wisdom and integrity, to transact affairs of the greatest importance to their constituents, and indeed of as great consequence as any that have come under consideration in any great council for ages past; and that they have gone through them with so much coolness, though under great provocations to resentment; so much firmness, under cause to apprehend danger; and so much

unanimity, under every endeavor to divide and sow dissensions among them; I cannot but look upon them with great veneration.—Labaree & Willcox 21:443. (1775.)

CONTINENTAL DRIFT THEORY, By Franklin.—I only remarked that at the lowest part of that rocky mountain which was in sight, there were oyster shells mixed in the stone; and part of the high county of Derby being probably as much above the level of the sea, as the coal mines of Whitehaven were below it, seemed a proof that there had been a great *bouleversement* in the surface of that island, some part of it having been depressed under the sea, and other parts which had been under it being raised above it. Such changes in the superficial parts of the globe seemed to me unlikely to happen if the earth were solid to the center. I therefore imagined that the internal parts might be a fluid more dense, and of greater specific gravity than any of the solids we are acquainted with; which therefore might swim in or upon that fluid. Thus the surface of the globe would be a shell, capable of being broken and disordered by the violent movements of the fluid on which it rested.—Smyth 8:597. (1782.)

COOK (Captain James), Protected by Both Sides.—This is, therefore, most earnestly to recommend to every one of you that, in case the said ship, which is not expected to be soon in the European seas on her return, should happen to fall into your hands, you would not consider her as an enemy, nor suffer any plunder to be made of the effects contained in her, nor obstruct her immediate return to England, by detaining her or sending her into any other part of Europe or to America, but that you would treat the said Captain Cook and his people with all civility and kindness, affording them, as common friends to mankind, all the assistance in your power, which they may happen to stand in need of.—Smyth 7:242. (1779.)

CRAMP, How Swimmer Can Cure.—When he is seized with the cramp in the leg, the method of driving it away is, to give to the parts affected a sudden, vigorous, and violent shock; which he may do in the air as he swims on his back.—Smyth 5:543. (1772.)

CREDIT, Is Money.—Remember that *credit* is money. If a man lets his money lie in my hands after it is due, he gives me the interest, or so much as I can make of it during that time. This amounts to a considerable sum where a man has good and large credit, and makes good use of it.—Smyth 2:370. (1748.)

CREDIT, Same for Government and Individuals.—The same circumstances that give a private man credit ought to have, and will have, their weight with lenders of money to *public bodies* or to nations.—Smyth 7:2. (1777.)

CREDIT BUYING, No Bargain.—He that sells upon credit asks a price for what he sells equivalent to the principal and interest of his money for the time he is likely to be kept out it; therefore he that buys upon credit pays interest for what he buys. And he that pays ready money

might let that money out to use; so that he that possesses anything he has bought pays interest for the use of it.—Smyth 2:212. (1737.)

CRIMINALS, Parliament Sends Them to Colonies.—Thus inconveniences have been objected to that *good* and *wise* act of Parliament, by virtue of which all the *Newgates* and *dungeons* in *Britain* are emptied into the colonies. It has been said that these theives and villains introduced among us spoil the morals of youth in the neighborhoods that entertain them, and perpetrate many horrid crimes. But let not *private interests* obstruct *public* utility. Our *Mother* knows what is best for us. What is a little *housebreaking, shoplifting,* or *highway robbing;* what is a son now and then *corrupted* and *hanged,* a daughter *debauched* and *poxed,* a wife *stabbed,* a husband's *throat cut,* or a child's *brains beat out* with an axe, compared with this 'improvement and well peopling of the colonies!'—Smyth 3:47. (1751.)

CRIMINALS, English, Continue Their Depredations in America.—The Petition of B.F., Agent for the Province of Pennsylvania, most humbly showeth that the transporting of felons from England to the plantations in America is, and has long been, a great grievance to the said plantations in general. That the said felons, being landed in America, not only continue their evil practices to the annoyance of his Majesty's good subjects there, but contribute greatly to corrupt the morals of the servants and poorer people among whom they are mixed. That many of the said felons escape from the servitude to which they were destined into other colonies, where their condition is not known; and, wandering at large from one populous town to another, commit many burglaries, robberies, and murders, to the great terror of the people; and occasioning heavy charges for apprehending and securing such felons, and bringing them to justice.—Smyth 9:620. (1787.)

CRIMINALS, Immigrants from Prisons of England Should Be Shipped Back.—The felons she [England] planted among us have produced such an amazing increase that we are not enabled to make ample remittance in the same commodity. And since the wheelbarrow law is not found effectually to reform them, and many of our vessels are idle through her restraints on our trade, why should we not employ those vessels in transporting the felons to Britain?—Smyth 9:628. (1787.)

CRITICISM, "Rubs Off When Dry."—Having been from youth more or less engaged in public affairs, it has often happened to me in the course of my life to be censured sharply for the part I took in them. Such censures I have generally passed over in silence, conceiving, when they were just, that I ought rather to amend than defend; and when they were undeserved, that a little time would justify me. Splashes of dirt thrown upon my character, I suffered while fresh to remain; I did not choose to spread by endeavoring to remove them, but relied on the vulgar adage

that they would all rub off when they were dry.—Smyth 6:258. (1774.)

CRITICISM, Advice About.—Hereafter, if you should observe on occasion to give your officers and friends a little more praise than is their due, and confess more fault than you can justly be charged with, you will only become the sooner for it a great captain. Criticizing and censuring almost everyone you have to do with will diminish friends, increase enemies, and thereby hurt your affairs.—Smyth 8:116. (1780.)

CRITICISM, Often Best Ignored.—You know that when my papers were first published, the Abbe Nollet, then high in reputation, attacked them in a book of letters. An answer was expected from me, but I made none to that book, nor to any other. They are now all neglected, and the truth seems to be established. You can always employ your time better than in polemics.—Smyth 8:314. (1782.)

CRITICISM. See also ENEMIES; MALICE.

CURRENCY. See MONEY; PAPER MONEY.

D

DAMPER, Franklin Refers to His Invention of.—I have executed here an easy, simple contrivance, that I have long since had in speculation, for keeping rooms warmer in cold weather than they generally are, and with less fire.—Smyth 3:461. (1758.)

DARTMOUTH (Lord), Friend to Franklin.—I find myself upon very good terms with our new minister,

Franklin in 1762 (age 56). Engraving by Edward Fisher, after a painting by Mason Chamberlin.

Lord Dartmouth, who we have reason to think means well to the colonies. I believe all are now sensible that nothing is to be got by contesting with or oppressing us.— Smyth 5:459. (1772.)

DEANE (Silas), Recalled by Congress.—I have no doubt that he will be able clearly to justify himself; but, having lived intimately with him now fifteen months, the greatest part of the time in the same house, and been a constant witness of his public conduct, I cannot omit giving this testimony, though unasked, in his behalf, that I esteem him a faithful, active, and able minister.—Smyth 7:128. (1778.)

DEBT, Debilitating to Integrity.— But what madness must it be to *run in debt* for these superfluities! We are offered, by the terms of this vendue, *six months' credit*; and that perhaps has induced some of us to attend it, because we cannot spare the ready money, and hope now to be fine without it. But, ah, think what you do when you run in debt; *you give to another power over your liberty*. If you cannot pay at the time, you will be ashamed to see your creditor; you will be in fear when you speak to him; you will make poor, pitiful, sneaking excuses, and by degrees come to lose your veracity, and sink into base, downright lying; for, as *Poor Richard* says, *the second vice is lying, the first is running in debt*. And again, to the same purpose, *lying rides upon debt's back*. Whereas a free-born *Englishman* ought not to be ashamed or afraid to see or speak to any man living. But poverty often deprives a man of all spirit and virtue: *'Tis hard for an empty bag to stand upright*, as *Poor Richard* truly says.—Smyth 3:416. (1757.)

DEBT, Avoid Debt and Be Secure.— Being out of debt myself, my credit could not be shaken by any run upon me; out of debt, as the proverb says, was being out of danger.—Smyth 5:442. (1772.)

DEBTS, American Colonists Pay War Debts Faster Than England.— America borrowed ten millions sterling during the last war, for the maintenance of her army of 25,000 men and other charges, [and] had faithfully *discharged and paid* that debt, and all her other debts, in 1772. Whereas Britain, during those ten years of peace and profitable commerce, had made little or no reduction of her debt.—Smyth 7:2. (1777.)

DECISIONS, Franklin's Method of Making.—My way is, to divide half a sheet of paper by a line into two columns; writing over the one *Pro*, and over the other *Con*. Then during three or four days' consideration, I put down under the different heads short hints of the different motives, that at different times occur to me, *for* or *against* the measure. When I have thus got them all together in one view, I endeavor to estimate their respective weights; and where I find two, one on each side, that seem equal, I strike them both out. If I find a reason *pro* equal to some *two* reasons *con*, I strike out the three. If I judge some two reasons *con* equal to some three reasons *pro*, I stike out the five; and thus proceeding I find at length where the balance lies; and if after a day or two of farther consideration, nothing new that is of importance occurs on either side, I come to a determination accordingly. And, though the weight of reasons cannot be taken with the precision of algebraic quantities, yet, when each is thus considered, separately and comparatively, and the whole lies before me, I think I can judge better, and am less liable to make a rash step; and in fact I have found great advantage from this kind of equation, in what may be called *moral* or *prudential algebra.*—Smyth 5:437. (1772.)

DEFENSE, Need for the Vigilant to Warn of Public Danger.—But the more insensible we generally are of public danger, and indifferent when warned of it, so much the more freely, openly, and earnestly ought such as apprehend it to speak their sentiments; that if possible, those who seem to sleep may be awakened, to think of some means of avoiding or preventing the mischief before it be too late.—Smyth 2:337. (1747.)

DEFENSE, A Duty of Government.—*Protection* is as truly due from the government to the people, as *obedience* from the people to the government.—Smyth 2:347. (1747.)

DEFENSE, Strong Defenses Discourage War.—The very fame of our strength and readiness would be a means of discouraging our enemies; for 'tis a wise and true saying, that *One sword often keeps another in the scabbard.* The way to secure peace is to be prepared for war. They that are on their guard, and appear ready to receive their adversaries, are in much less danger of being attacked than the supine, secure and negligent.—Smyth 2:352. (1747.)

DEFENSE, Advantage of Citizens Who Have the Foresight to Prepare Themselves.—It is proposed to breed gunners by forming an artillery club, to go down weekly to the battery and exercise the great guns. The best engineers against Cape Breton were of such a club, tradesmen and shopkeepers of Boston. I was with them at the castle at their exercise in 1743.—Smyth 2:356. (1747.)

DEFENSE, Importance of Military Strength.—Our great security lies, I think, in our growing strength, both in numbers and wealth; that creates an increasing ability of assisting this nation in its wars, which will make us more respectable, our friendship more valued, and our enmity feared; thence it will soon be thought proper to treat us not with justice only, but with kindness, and thence we may expect in a few years a total change of measures with regard to us; unless, by a neglect of military discipline, we should lose all martial spirit, and our western people become as tame as those in the eastern dominions of Britain, when we may expect the same oppressions; for there is much truth in the Italian saying, *Make yourselves sheep, and the wolves will eat you.*—Smyth 6:3. (1773.)

DEFENSE, People Must Pay for.— Our people certainly ought to do more for themselves. It is absurd, the pretending to be lovers of liberty while they grudge paying for the defense of it. It is said here that an impost of five per cent on all goods imported, though a most reasonable proposition, had not been agreed to by all the states, and was therefore frustrated; and that your newspapers acquaint the world with this, with the non-payment of interest to the creditors of the public. The knowledge of these things has hurt our credit.—Smyth 8:645. (1782.)

DENMARK, Esteem of King for Franklin.—The King of Denmark, traveling in England under an assumed name, sent me a card expressing in strong terms his esteem for me, and inviting me to dinner with him at St. James's.— Smyth 8:503. (1782.)

DICTIONARY, Should Be Used While Reading.—As many of the terms of science are such as you cannot have met with in your common reading and may therefore be unacquainted with, I think it would be well for you to have a good dictionary at hand, to consult immediately when you meet with a word you do not comprehend the precise meaning of. This may at first seem troublesome and interrupting; but it is a trouble that will daily diminish, as you will daily find less and less occasion for your dictionary, as you become more acquainted with the terms; and in the meantime you will read with more satisfaction, because with more understanding.—Smyth 4:19. (1760.)

DISPUTES, Franklin Declines to Debate His Philosophical Opinions. —I have never entered into any controversy in defense of my philosophical opinions; I leave them to take their chance in the world. If they are *right*, truth and experience will support them; if *wrong*, they ought to be refuted and rejected.— Smyth 7:65. (1777.)

DISPUTES, Settle Without War.—I wish to see . . . the discovery of a plan that would induce and oblige nations to settle their disputes without first cutting one another's throats. When will human reason be sufficiently improved to see the advantage of this! When will men be convinced that even successful wars at length become misfortunes to those who unjustly commenced them, and who triumphed blindly in their success, not seeing all its consequences.— Smyth 8:9. (1780.)

DRUNKENNESS AND IMMO-RALITY, Forbidden to Pennsylvania Militia.—You are to keep good order among your men, and prevent drunkenness and other immoralities, as much as may be, and not suffer them to do any injury to the inhabitants whom they come to protect.—Smyth 3:322. (1756.)

E

EAGLE, Franklin Preferred the Turkey as the National Bird.—For my own part, I wish the bald eagle had not been chosen as the representative of our country. He is a bird of bad moral character; he does not get his living honestly. You may have seen him perched on some dead tree near the river where, too lazy to fish for himself, he watches the labor of the fishing hawk; and, when that diligent bird has at length taken a fish, and is bearing it to his nest for the support of his mate and young ones, the bald eagle pursues him, and takes it from him. With all this injustice he is never in good case; but, like those among men who live by sharping and robbing, he is generally poor, and often very lousy. Besides, he is a rank coward. The little *kingbird*, not bigger than a sparrow, attacks him boldly and drives him out of the district.... The turkey is in comparison a much more respectable bird, and withal a true original native of America.— Smyth 9:166. (1784.)

EAGLE. See also TURKEY.

EARTH, Subjected to Catastrophic Changes to Make It More Useful.— Had the different strata of clay, gravel, marble, coals, limestone, sand, minerals, etc., continued to lie level, one under the other, as they

may be supposed to have done before those convulsions, we should have had the use only of a few of the uppermost of the strata, the others lying too deep and too difficult to be come at; but the shell of the earth being broken, and the fragments thrown into this oblique position, the disjointed ends of a great number of strata of different kinds are brought up today, and a great variety of useful materials put into our power, which would otherwise have remained eternally concealed from us. So that what has been usually looked upon as a *ruin* suffered by this part of the universe was, in reality, only a preparation, or means of rendering the earth more fit for use, more capable of being to mankind a convenient and comfortable habitation.—Smyth 3:427. (1758.)

EARTH, A Great Magnet.—It has long been a supposition of mine that the iron contained in the substance of this globe has made it capable of becoming, as it is, a great magnet. That the fluid of magnetism exists perhaps in all space; so that there is a magnetical north and south of the universe as well as of this globe, and that if it were possible for a man to fly from star to star, he might govern his course by the compass. That it was by the power of this general magnetism this globe became a particular magnet.— Smyth 8:599. (1782.)

EDUCATION, Important Function of Government.—The good education of youth has been esteemed by wise men in all ages as the surest foundation of the happiness both of private families and of common-wealths. Almost all governments have therefore made it a principal object of their attention, to establish and endow with proper revenues, such seminaries of learning as might supply the succeeding age with men qualified to serve the public with honor to themselves, and to their country.—Smyth 2:388. (1749.)

EDUCATION, The Aim and End of Learning.—The idea of what is *true merit* should also be often presented to youth, explained and impressed on their minds, as consisting in an *inclination* joined with an *ability* to serve mankind, one's country, friends and family; which *ability* is (with the blessing of God) to be acquired or greatly increased by *true learning;* and should indeed be the great *aim* and *end* of all learning.—Smyth 2:396. (1749.)

EDUCATION, Should Improve Virtue of People.—I think also that general virtue is more probably to be expected and obtained from the *education* of youth than from the *exhortation* of adult persons; bad habits and vices of the mind being, like diseases of the body, more easily prevented than cured.—Smyth 3:17. (1750.)

EDUCATION, Need for a Charity School in Philadelphia.—By our opening a charity school, in which one hundred poor children are taught reading, writing, and arithmetic, with the rudiments of religion, we have gained the general good will of all sorts of people, from whence donations and bequests may be reasonably expected to accrue

from time to time.—Smyth 3:92. (1752.)

EDUCATION, Adapted to Different Cultures.—The little value *Indians* set on what we prize so highly, under the name of learning, appears from a pleasant passage that happened some years since, at a treaty between some colonies and the Six Nations. When everything had been settled to the satisfaction of both sides, and nothing remained but a mutual exchange of civilities, the English commissioners told the Indians that they had in their country a college for the instruction of youth, who were there taught various languages, arts, and sciences; that there was a particular foundation in favor of the Indians to defray the expense of the education of any of their sons who should desire to take the benefit of it; and said, if the Indians would accept the offer, the English would take half a dozen of their brightest lads, and bring them up in the best manner. The Indians, after consulting on the proposals, replied that it was remembered that some of their youths had formerly been educated at that college, but that it had been observed that for a long time after they returned to their friends, *they were absolutely good for nothing;* being neither acquainted with the true methods of killing deer, catching beavers, or surprising an enemy. The proposition they look on, however, as a mark of kindness and good will of the English to the Indian nations, which merited a grateful return; and therefore, if the English gentlemen would send a dozen or two of their children to Opondago, the Great Council would take care of their education, bring them up in what was really the best manner, and make men of them.—Smyth 3:138. (1753.)

ELDERLY, Neglect of.—Nothing is more apt to sour the temper of aged people than the apprehension that they are neglected; and they are extremely apt to entertain such suspicions.—Smyth 5:180. (1768.)

ELECTRIC SHOCK, Franklin's First Experience.—The flash was very great, and the crack as loud as a pistol; yet, my senses being instantly gone, I neither saw the one nor heard the other; nor did I feel the stroke on my hand, though I afterwards found it raised a round swelling where the fire entered, as big as half a pistol-bullet.... That part of my hand and fingers which held the chain was left white, as though the blood had been driven out, and remained so eight or ten minutes after, feeling like dead flesh; and I had a numbness in my arms and the back of my neck which continued till the next morning, but wore off. Nothing remains now of this shock, but a soreness in my breast-bone, which feels as if it had been bruised. I did not fall, but suppose I should have been knocked down if I had received the stroke in my head. The whole was over in less than a minute.—Smyth 3:32. (1750.)

ELECTRIC SHOCK, Knocks Down Six Men.—The knocking down of the six men was performed with two of my large jars not fully charged. I laid one end of my discharging rod upon the head of the first; he laid his hand on the head of the second; the second his hand on the head of the third, and so to the last, who held, in his hand, the chain that was connected with the outside of the jars. When they were thus placed, I applied the other end of my rod to the prime conductor, and they all dropped together. When they got up, they all declared they had not felt any stroke, and wondered how they came to fall; nor did any of them either hear the crack, or see the light of it.—Smyth 3:257. (1755.)

ELECTRICITY, Operation of.—This matter of lightning, or of electricity, is an extremely subtile fluid, penetrating other bodies, and subsisting in them, equally diffused.

When by any operation of art or nature, there happens to be a greater proportion of this fluid in one body than in another, the body which has most will communicate to that which has least, till the proportion becomes equal; provided the distance between them be not too great; or, if it is too great, till there be proper conductors to convey it from one to the other.

If the communication be through the air without any conductor, a bright light is seen between the bodies, and a sound is heard. In our small experiments we call this light and sound the electric spark and snap; but in the great operations of nature, the light is what we call *lightning,* and the sound (produced at the same time, though generally arriving later to our ears than the light does to our eyes) is, with its echoes, called *thunder.*—Smyth 5:55. (1767.)

ELECTRICITY, Franklin's Theory Adopted in Europe.—I concluded [about 1753] to let my papers shift for themselves, believing it was better to spend what time I could spare from public business in making new experiments, than in disputing about those already made. I therefore never answered M. Nollet, and the event gave me no cause to repent my silence; for my friend M. le Roy, of the Royal Academy of Sciences, took up my cause and refuted him; my book was translated into the Italian, German, and Latin languages; and the doctrine it contained was by degrees universally adopted by the philosophers of Europe, in preference to that of the abbe; so that he lived to see himself the last of his sect, except Monsieur B—— of Paris, his *eleve* and immediate disciple.—Autobiography. Smyth 1:419. (1788.)

ELOCUTION, Type of Material to Be Memorized.—Let all their bad habits of speaking, all offenses against good grammar, all corrupt or foreign accents, and all improper phrases, be pointed out to them. Short speeches from the *Roman*, or other history, or from our *Parliamentary debates*, might be got by heart, and delivered with the proper action, etc. Speeches and scenes in our best tragedies and comedies, avoiding everything that could injure the morals of youth, might likewise be got by rote, and the boys exercised in delivering or acting them; great care being taken to form their manner after the truest models.—Smyth 3:25. (1750.)

EMIGRATION, Advantages of Living in America.—With regard to the future establishment of your children, which you say you want to consult me about, I am still of opinion that America will afford you more chances of doing it well than England. All the means of good education are plenty there, the general manners are simple and pure, temptations to vice and folly fewer, the profits of industry in business as great and sure as in England; and there is one advantage more, which your command of money will give you there, I mean the laying out a part of your fortune in a new land, now to be had extremely cheap; but which must be increased immensely in value, before your children come of age, by the rapid population of the country.—Smyth 9:90. (1783.)

EMIGRATION RESTRICTIONS, Violate Historic English Freedoms.—During a century and a half that Englishmen have been at liberty to remove if they pleased to America, we have heard of no law to restrain that liberty and confine them as prisoners in this island.—Smyth 6:292. (1774.)

EMIGRATION RESTRICTIONS, New English Law Unjust.—God commands to increase and replenish the earth; the proposed law would forbid increasing, and confine Britons to their present number, keeping half that number too in wretchedness. The common people of Britain and of Ireland contributed by the taxes they paid, and by the blood they lost, to the success of that war which brought into our hands the vast unpeopled territories of North America; a country favored by Heaven with all the advantages of climate and soil. Germans are now pouring into it, to take possession of it, and fill it with their posterity; and shall Britons and Irelanders, who have a much better right to it, be forbidden to share of it, and instead of enjoying there the plenty and happiness that might reward their industry, be compelled to remain here in poverty and misery?— Smyth 6:298. (1774.)

EMIGRATION TO AMERICA, Inducements to Foreigners.—All who are established there have come at their own charge. The country affords to strangers a good climate, fine wholesome air, plenty of provisions, good laws, just and *cheap* government, with all the liberties, civil and religious, that reasonable men can wish for. These inducements are so great, and the number of people in all nations of Europe who wish to partake of them is so considerable, that if the States were to undertake transporting people at the expense of the public, no revenues that they have would be sufficient.—Smyth 8:355. (1782.)

The only encouragements we hold out to strangers are a good climate, fertile soil, wholesome air and water, plenty of provisions and fuel, good pay for labor, kind neighbors, good laws, liberty, and a hearty welcome; the rest depends on a man's own industry and virtue. Lands are cheap, but they must be bought. All settlements are undertaken at private expense; the public contributes nothing but

defense and justice.—Smyth 9:21. (1783.)

EMIGRATION TO AMERICA, Expected.—I think there will be great emigrations from England, Ireland, and Germany. There is a great contest among the ports, which of them shall be of those to be declared *free* for the *American trade.*— Smyth 9:34. (1783.)

ENEMIES, Franklin Comments on Personal.—I thank you much for your friendly hints of the operations of my enemies, and of the means I might use to defeat them. Having in view at present no other point to gain but that of rest, I do not take their malice so much amiss, as it may further my project, and perhaps be some advantage to you. Lee and Izard are open and, so far, honorable enemies; the Adamses, if enemies, are more covered. I never did any of them the least injury, and can conceive no other source of their malice but envy. To be sure, the excessive respect shown me here by all ranks of people, and the little notice taken of them, was a mortifying circumstance; but it was what I could neither prevent nor remedy.—Smyth 8:236. (1781.)

ENEMIES, Advantage of Personal.—As to the friends and enemies you just mention, I have hitherto, thanks to God, had plenty of the former kind; they have been my treasure; and it has perhaps been of no disadvantage to me that I have had a few of the latter. They serve to put us upon correcting the faults we have, and avoiding those we are in danger of having. They counteract the mischief flattery might do us, and their malicious attacks make our friends more zealous in serving us and promoting our interest. At present, I do not know of more than two such enemies that I enjoy, viz. Lee and Izard. I deserved the enmity of the latter, because I might have avoided it by paying him a compliment, which I neglected.—Smyth 8:306. (1781.)

ENEMIES, Difference Between Political and Personal.—I have, as you observe, some enemies in England, but they are my enemies as an *American;* I have also two or three in America, who are my enemies as a *minister;* but I thank God there are not in the whole world any who are my enemies as a *man;* for by his grace, through a long life, I have been enabled so to conduct myself that there does not exist a human being who can justly say, "Ben. Franklin has wronged me." This, my friend, is in old age a comfortable reflection. You too have, or may have, your enemies; but let not that render you unhappy. If you make a right use of them, they will do you more good than harm. They point out to us our faults; they put us upon our guard, and help us to live more correctly.—Smyth 9:151. (1784.)

ENEMIES. See also CRITICISM; MALICE.

ENGLAND, Its Culture Worth Preserving.—I pray God to preserve long to Great Britain the English laws, manners, liberties, and religion. Notwithstanding the complaints so frequent in your public papers, of the prevailing corruption and degeneracy of the people, I know you have a great deal of virtue still subsisting among you; and I hope the [English] constitution is not so near a dissolution as some seem to apprehend.—Smyth 3:141. (1753.)

ENGLAND, American Union with, Contemplated.—I have something further considered that matter, and am of opinion that such a union would be very acceptable to the colonies, provided they had a reasonable number of representatives allowed them; and that all the old acts of Parliament restraining the trade or cramping the manufactures of the colonies be at the same time repealed, and the British subjects *on this side the water* put, in those respects, on the same footing with those in Great Britain, till the new Parliament, representing the whole, shall think it for the interest of the whole to reenact some or all of them.—Smyth 3:238. (1754.)

ENGLAND, Hostile Toward Her Own People.—Besides your rudeness to foreigners, you are far from being civil even to your own family. The Welch you have always despised for submitting to your government. But why despise your own English, who conquered and settled Ireland for you; who conquered and settled America for you? Yet these you now think you may treat as you please, because forsooth, they are a *conquered* people. Why despise the Scotch, who fight and die for you all over the world? Remember you courted Scotland for one hundred years, and would fain have had your wicked will of her. She virtuously resisted all your importunities, but at length kindly consented to become your lawful wife. You then solemnly promised to love, cherish, and honor her, as long as you both should live; and yet you have ever since treated her with the utmost contumely which you now extend to your common children.—Smyth 4:398. (1766.)

ENGLAND, Farmers Operate at a Disadvantage.—I am one of that class of people that feeds you all, and at present is abused by you all; in short, I am a *farmer.*

By your newspapers we are told that God had sent a very short harvest to some other countries of Europe. I thought this might be in favor of Old England; and that now we should get a good price for our grain, which would bring millions among us, and make us flow in money; that, to be sure, is scarce enough. But the wisdom of government forbade the exportation. "Well," says I, "then we must be content with the market price at home."

"No," say my lords the mob, "you sha'nt have that. Bring your corn to market if you dare; we'll sell it for you for less money, or take it for nothing." Being thus attacked by both ends *of the constitution,* the head and tail *of government,* what am I to do? Must I keep my corn in the barn, to feed and increase the breed of rats? Be it so; they cannot be less thankful than those I have been used to feed. Are we farmers the only people to be grudged the profits of our honest labor? And why?—Smyth 5:535. (1766.)

ENGLAND, Manufacturers Should Be Requested to Accept What They Advocate for Farmers.—Now, if it be a good principle that the exportation of a commodity is to be restrained, that so our people at home may have it the cheaper, stick to that principle and go through-stitch with it. Prohibit the exportation of your cloth, your leather, and shoes, your ironware and your manufactures of all sorts, to make them all cheaper at home. And cheap enough they will be, I will warrant you, till people leave off making them.—Smyth 5:536. (1766.)

ENGLAND, Franklin's Attitude Toward.—I hate neither *England* nor *Englishmen,* driven though my ancestors were, by mistaken oppression of former times, out of this happy country, to suffer all the hardships of an *American* wilderness. I retain no resentment on that account. I wish prosperity to the nation; I honor, esteem, and love its people. I only hate calumniators and boutefeus on either side the water, who would for the little dirty purposes of faction set brother against brother, turn friends into mortal enemies, and ruin an empire by dividing it.—Smyth 5:110. (1768.)

ENGLAND, People Not Hostile to Colonies.—Let it be known that there is much good will towards *America* in the generality of this nation; and that however government may sometimes happen to be mistaken or misled, with relation to *American* interests, there is no general intention to oppress us; and that, therefore, we may rely upon having every real grievance removed on proper representations.—Smyth 5:111. (1768.)

ENGLAND, Severe Winter of 1771.—We have had a severe and tedious winter here. There is not yet the smallest appearance of spring. Not a bud has pushed out, nor a blade of grass. The turnips that used to feed the cattle have been destroyed by the frost. The hay in most parts of the country is gone, and the cattle perishing for want, the lambs dying by thousands, through cold and scanty nourishment. Tuesday last I went to dine at our friend Sir Matthew Featherstone's through a heavy storm of snow. His windows you know look into the park. Towards evening I observed the snow still lying over all the park, for the ground was before too cold to thaw it, being itself frozen and ice in the canal. You cannot imagine a more winterlike prospect!—Smyth 5:313. (1771.)

ENGLAND, Politics and Business.—The interest of a few merchants here has more weight with government than that of thousands at a distance.—Smyth 6:39. (1773.)

ENGLAND, Many Favor Colonists.—With regard to the sentiments of people in general here concerning America, I must say that we have among them many friends and wellwishers. The dissenters are all for us, and many of the merchants and manufacturers.—Smyth 6:78. (1773.)

ENGLAND, Attitude Toward Colonies.—The great defect here is, in all sorts of people, a want of

attention to what passes in such remote countries as America; an unwillingness even to read anything about them if it appears a little lengthy, and a disposition to postpone the consideration even of the things they know they must at last consider, that so they may have time for what more immediately concerns them, and withal enjoy their amusements, and be undisturbed in the universal dissipation. In other respects, though some of the great regard us with a jealous eye, and some are angry with us, the majority of the nation rather wish us well, and have no desire to infringe our liberties. And many console themselves under the apprehensions of declining liberty here, that they or their posterity shall be able to find her safe and vigorous in America.—Smyth 6:93. (1773.)

ENGLAND, Union with Her Would Only Corrupt America.—When I consider the extreme corruption prevalent among all orders of men in this old rotten state, and the glorious public virtue so predominant in our rising country, I cannot but apprehend more mischief than benefit from a closer union. I fear they will drag us after them in all the plundering wars which their desperate circumstances, injustice, and rapacity may prompt them to undertake; and their wide-wasting prodigality and profusion is a gulf that will swallow up every aid we may distress ourselves to afford them.

Here numberless and needless places, enormous salaries, pensions, perquisites, bribes, groundless quarrels, foolish expeditions, false accounts or no accounts, contracts and jobs, devour all revenue and produce continual necessity in the midst of natural plenty. I apprehend, therefore, that to unite us intimately will only be to corrupt and poison us also.—Smyth 6:311. (1775.)

ENGLAND, Incapacity to Subdue America.—Tell our dear good friend, Dr. Price, who sometimes has his doubts and despondencies about our firmness, that America is determined and unanimous; a very few Tories and placemen excepted, who will probably soon export themselves. Britain, at the expense of three millions, has killed one hundred and fifty Yankees this campaign, which is twenty thousand pounds a head; and at Bunker Hill she gained a mile of ground, half of which she lost again by our taking post on Ploughed Hill. During the same time sixty thousand children have been born in America. From these *data* his mathematical head will easily calculate the time and expense necessary to kill us all, and conquer our whole territory.—Smyth 6:429. (1775.)

ENGLAND, Unworthy to Govern. —As to our submitting to the government of Great Britain, it is vain to think of it. She has given us, by her numberless barbarities in the prosecution of the war and in the treatment of prisoners, by her malice in bribing slaves to murder their masters, and savages to massacre the families of farmers, with her baseness in rewarding the unfaithfulness of servants, and debauching the virtue of honest seamen entrusted with our property, so deep an impression of her depravity that we never again can trust her in the management of our affairs and interests. It is now impossible to persuade our people, as I long endeavored, that the war was merely ministerial, and that the nation bore still a good will to us. The infinite number of addresses printed in your gazettes, all approving this conduct of your government towards us, and encouraging our destruction by every possible means, the great majority in Parliament constantly manifesting the same sentiments, and the popular public rejoicings on occasion of any news of the slaughter of an innocent and virtuous people, fighting only in defense of their just rights; these, together with the recommendations of the same measures by even your celebrated moralists and divines, in their writings and sermons that are cited, approved, and applauded in your great national assemblies; all join in convincing us that you are no longer the magnanimous and enlightened nation we once esteemed you, and that you are unfit and unworthy to govern us, as not being able to govern your own passions.—Smyth 7:69. (1777.)

ENGLAND, Too Eager for War, Too Demanding in Peace.—Britain, having injured us heavily by making this unjust war upon us, might think herself well off if *on reparation of those injuries* we admitted her to *equal* advantages with other nations in commerce; but certainly she had no reason to expect *superior.* . . . Her known fondness for war, and the many instances of her readiness to engage in wars on frivolous occasions, were probably sufficient to cause an immediate rejection of every proposition for an *offensive* alliance with her. And . . . if she made war against France on our account, a peace with us, at the same time, was impossible; for . . . having met with friendship from that generous nation, when we were cruelly oppressed by England, we were under ties stronger than treaties could form, to make common cause; which we should certainly do to the utmost of our power.—Smyth 7:144. (1778.)

ENGLAND, Distrust Toward.— Your Parliament never had a right to govern us, and your king has forfeited it by his bloody tyranny. But I thank you for letting me know a little of your mind, that, even if the Parliament should acknowledge our independence, the act would not be binding to posterity, and that your nation would resume and prosecute the claim as soon as they found it convenient from the influence of your passions, and your present malice against us. We suspected before that you would not be actually bound by your conciliatory acts, longer than till they had served their purpose of inducing us to disband our forces; but we were not certain that you were knaves by principle, and that we ought not to have the least confidence in your offers, promises, or treaties, though

confirmed by Parliament.—Smyth 7:169. (1778.)

ENGLAND, Despised by All Europe.—In truth, that country appears to have no friends on this side the water; no other nation wishes it success in its present war, but rather desires to see it effectually humbled; no one, not even their old friends the Dutch, will afford them any assistance. Such is the mischievous effect of pride, insolence, and injustice on the affairs of nations, as well as on those of private persons!—Smyth 8:77. (1780.)

ENGLAND, Mobs Pillage Parts of London.—London has been in the utmost confusion for seven or eight days. The beginning of this month, a mob of fanatics, joined by a mob of rogues, burnt and destroyed property to the amount, it is said, of a million sterling. Chapels of foreign ambassadors, houses of members of Parliament that had promoted the act for favoring Catholics, and the houses of many private persons of that religion, were pillaged and consumed, or pulled down, to the number of fifty; among the rest, Lord Mansfield's is burnt, with all his furniture, pictures, books, and papers. Thus he, who approved the burning of American houses, has had fire brought home to him. He himself was horribly scared, and Governor Hutchinson, it is said, died outright of the fright. The mob, tired with roaring and rioting seven days and nights, were at length suppressed, and quiet restored on the 9th, in the evening. Next day

Lord George Gordon was committed to the tower.—Smyth 8:99. (1780.)

ENGLAND, Conciliation with.—If proper means are used to produce, not only a peace, but what is much more interesting, a thorough reconciliation, a few years may heal the wounds that have been made in our happiness, and produce a degree of prosperity of which at present we can hardly form a conception.—Smyth 8:593. (1782.)

ENGLAND, Franklin's Analysis of Her Internal Problems.—America will, with God's blessing, become a great and happy country; and England, if she has at length gained wisdom, will have gained something more valuable, and more essential to prosperity, than all she has lost; and will still be a great and respectable nation. Her great disease at present is the number and enormous salaries and emoluments of office. Avarice and ambition are strong passions, and, separately, act with great force on the human mind; but when both are united, and may be gratified in the same object, their violence is almost irresistible, and they hurry men headlong into factions and contentions, destructive of all good government. As long, therefore, as these great emoluments subsist, your Parliament will be a stormy sea, and your public councils confounded by private interests. But it requires much public spirit and virtue to abolish them; more perhaps than can now be found in a nation so long corrupted.—Smyth 9:23. (1783.)

ENGLAND, Suffering from a "Crazy Constitution."—When you wrote the letter I am now answering, your nation was involved in the confusion of your new election. When I think of your present crazy constitution and its diseases, I imagine the enormous emoluments of place to be among the greatest; and, while they exist, I doubt whether even the reform of your representation will cure the evils constantly arising from your perpetual factions. As it seems to be a settled point at present that the minister must govern the Parliament, who are to do everything he would have done; and he is to bribe them to do this, and the people are to furnish the money to pay these bribes; the Parliament appears to me a very expensive machine for government, and I apprehend the people will find out in time that they may as well be governed, and that it will be much cheaper to be governed, by the minister alone; no Parliament being preferable to the present.—Smyth 9:255. (1784.)

ENGLAND, Arrogance of Leaders Before the Revolutionary War.—The word *general* puts me in mind of a general, your General Clarke, who had the folly to say in my hearing at Sir John Pringle's that, with a thousand British grenadiers, he would undertake to go from one end of America to the other and geld all the males, partly by force and partly by coaxing. It is plain he took us for a species of animals very little superior to brutes. The Parliament too believed the stories of another foolish general, I forget his name, that the Yankees never *felt bold*. Yankee was understood to be a sort of yahoo, and the Parliament did not think the petitions of such creatures were fit to be received and read in so wise an assembly. What was the consequence of this monstrous pride and insolence? You first sent small armies to subdue us, believing them more than sufficient, but soon found yourselves obliged to send greater; these, whenever they ventured to penetrate our country beyond the protection of their ships, were either repulsed and obliged to scamper out, or were surrounded, beaten, and taken prisoners.— Smyth 9:261. (1784.)

ENGLAND, Misrepresenting Conditions in Post-Revolutionary America.—Your newspapers are filled with accounts of distresses and miseries that these States are plunged into since their separation from Britain. You may believe me when I tell you that there is no truth in those accounts. I find all property of lands and houses augmented vastly in value; that of houses in towns at least fourfold. The crops have been plentiful and yet the produce sells high, to the great profit of the farmers. At the same time, all imported goods sell at low rates, some cheaper than the first cost. Working people have plenty of employ and high pay for their labor.—Smyth 9:472. (1785.)

The English papers not only sent me gratis, as you observe, to Algiers, but they are sending all the United States to destruction. By their accounts you would think we were in the utmost distress, in want of everything, all in confusion, no government, and wishing again for that of England. Be assured, my friend, that these are all fictions, mere English wishes, not American realities. There are some few faults in our constitutions, which is no wonder, considering the stormy season in which they were made, but those will soon be corrected. And for the rest, I never saw greater and more indubitable marks of public prosperity in any country. The produce of our agriculture bears a good price, and is all paid for in ready hard money, all the laboring people have high wages, everybody is well clothed and well lodged, the poor provided for or assisted, and all estates in town and country much increased in value. As to wishing for the English government, we should as soon wish for that of Morocco.— Smyth 9:493. (1786.)

ENGLAND. See also COLONIES.

ENTAILED ESTATES, A Curse to Any Nation.—If, to keep up the dignity of the family, estates are entailed entire on the eldest male heir, another pest to industry and improvement of the country is introduced, which will be followed by all the odious mixture of pride and beggary, and idleness, that have half depopulated and *decultivated* Spain; occasioning continual extinction of families by the discouragements of marriage and neglect in the improvement of estates.—Smyth 9:163. (1784.)

EQUAL PROTECTION OF RIGHTS.—An *equal* dispensation of protection, rights, privileges, and advantages is what every part is entitled to, and ought to enjoy; it being a matter of no moment to the state whether a subject grows rich and flourishing on the Thames or the Ohio, in Edinburgh or Dublin. These measures never fail to create great and violent jealousies and animosities between the people favored and the people oppressed; whence a total separation of affections, interests, political obligations, and all manner of connections necessarily ensue, by which the whole state is weakened, and perhaps ruined forever!—Smyth 6:291. (1774.)

EQUALITY, Felt by All Freemen.—The King of Denmark, traveling England under an assumed name, sent me a card expressing in strong terms his esteem for me, and inviting me to dinner with him at St. James's.... Such compliments might probably make me a little proud, if we Americans were not naturally as much so already as the porter, who, being told he had with his burden jostled the great Czar Peter (then in London, walking the street): "Poh!" says he, "we are all Czars here."—Smyth 8:503. (1782.)

EUROPE, Working Conditions for Artisans.—In the long-settled countries of Europe, all arts, trades, professions, farms, etc., are so full that it is difficult for a poor man, who has children, to place them where they may gain, or learn to gain, a decent livelihood. The artisans, who fear creating future rivals in business, refuse to take apprentices but upon conditions of money, maintenance, or the like, which the parents are unable to comply with. Hence the youth are dragged up in ignorance of every

gainful art, and obliged to become soldiers, or servants, or thieves, for a subsistence.—Smyth 8:612. (1782.)

EUROPE, United States of Europe Urged by Franklin.—I send you enclosed the proposed new federal Constitution for these states. I was engaged four months of the last summer in the convention that formed it. It is now sent by Congress to the several states for their confirmation. If it succeeds, I do not see why you might not in Europe carry the project of good Henry the 4th into execution, by forming a federal union and one grand republic of all its different states and kingdoms, by means of a like convention, for we had many interests to reconcile.—Smyth 9:619. (1787.)

EXERCISE, Franklin's Theory of.—I have been ready to say (using round numbers without regard to exactness, but merely to mark a great difference) that there is more exercise in *one* mile's riding on horseback, than in *five* in a coach; and more in *one* mile's walking on foot, than in *five* on horseback; to which I may add, that there is more in walking *one* mile up and down stairs, than in *five* on a level floor.—Smyth 5:412. (1772.)

EXERCISE, Franklin Talks to Himself About.—But let us examine your course of life. While the mornings are long, and you have leisure to go abroad, what do you do? Why, instead of gaining an appetite for breakfast by salutary exercise, you amuse yourself with books, pamphlets, or newspapers, which commonly are not worth the reading. Yet you eat an inordinate breakfast, four dishes of tea, with cream, and one or two buttered toasts, with slices of hung beef, which I fancy are not things the most easily digested. Immediately afterward you sit down to write at your desk, or converse with persons who apply to you on business. Thus the time passes till one, without any kind of bodily exercise. But all this I could pardon, in regard, as you say, to your sedentary condition. But what is your practice after dinner? Walking in the beautiful gardens of those friends with whom you have dined would be the choice of men of sense; yours is to be fixed down to chess, where you are found engaged for two or three hours! This is your perpetual recreation, which is the least eligible of any for a sedentary man because, instead of accelerating the motion of the fluids, the rigid attention it requires helps to retard the circulation and obstruct internal secretions. Wrapped in the speculations of this wretched game, you destroy your constitution.—Smyth 8:155. (1780.)

EXPERIENCE, A Painful Teacher. —*Experience keeps a dear school, but fools will learn in no other, and scarce in that;* for it is true, *we may give advice, but we cannot give conduct,* as *Poor Richard* says. However, remember this, *They that won't be counselled, can't be helped,* as *Poor Richard* says; and farther, that, *if you will not hear reason, she'll surely rap your knuckles.*—Smyth 3:418. (1757.)

EYEGLASSES, Advice.—You take notice of the failing of your eyesight. Perhaps you have not spectacles that

suit you, and it is not easy there to provide one's self. People, too, when they go to a shop for glasses, seldom give themselves time to choose with care; and, if their eyes are not rightly suited, they are injured. Therefore I send you a complete set, from number one to thirteen, that you may try them at your ease; and having pitched on such as suit you best at present, reserve those of higher numbers for future use, as your eyes grow still older; and with the lower numbers, which are for younger people, you may oblige some other friends.—Smyth 5:335. (1771.)

EYES OF OTHERS, Ruin Us.— Almost all the parts of our bodies require some expense. The feet demand shoes; the legs, stockings; the rest of the body, clothing; and the belly, a good deal of victuals. *Our* eyes, though exceedingly useful, ask, when reasonable, only the cheap assistance of spectacles, which could not much impair our finances. But *the eyes of other people* are the eyes that ruin us. If all but myself were blind, I should want neither fine clothes, fine houses, nor fine furniture.—Smyth 9:248. (1784.)

F

FAITH, Reflected Best in Good Works.—The faith you mention has doubtless its use in the world. I do not desire to see it diminished, nor would I endeavor to lessen it in any man. But I wish it were more productive of good works than I have generally seen it; I mean real good works, works of kindness, charity, mercy, and public spirit; not holiday-keeping, sermon-reading or hearing; performing church ceremonies, or making long prayers, filled with flatteries and compliments, despised even by wise men, and much less capable of pleasing the Deity. The worship of God is a duty; the hearing and reading of sermons may be useful; but, if men rest in hearing and praying, as too many do, it is as if a tree should value itself on being watered and putting forth leaves, though it never produced any fruit.

Your great Master thought much less of these outward appearances and professions than many of his modern disciples. He prefered the *doers* of the word to mere *hearers;* the son that seemingly refused to obey his father, and yet performed his commands, to him that professed his readiness but neglected the work; the heretical but charitable Samaritan to the uncharitable though orthodox priest and sanctified Levite; and those who gave food to the hungry, drink to the thristy, raiment to the naked, entertainment to the stranger, and relief to the sick, though they never heard of his name, he declares shall in the last day be accepted, when those who cry Lord! Lord! who value themselves on their faith, though great enough to perform miracles, but have neglected good works, shall be rejected.—Smyth 3:145. (1753.)

FAMILY, Foundation of Governments.—Marriage, or a union of the sexes, though it be in itself one of the smallest societies, is the original fountain from whence the greatest

and most extensive governments have derived their beings.—Nathan G. Goodman, ed., *A Benjamin Franklin Reader* (New York: Thomas Y. Crowell Company, 1945), p. 715. (1746.)

FAMILY, Quarrels Denounced by Franklin.—Above all things I dislike family quarrels, and, when they happen among my relations, nothing gives me more pain. If I were to set myself up as a judge of those subsisting between you and brother's widow and children, how unqualified must I be, at this distance, to determine rightly, especially having heard but one side. They always treated me with friendly and affectionate regard; you have done the same. What can I say between you, but that I wish you were reconciled, and that I will love that side best that is most ready to forgive and oblige the other?—Smyth 3:404. (1757.)

FAMILY, How to Afford.—*What maintains one vice, would bring up two children.* You may think perhaps that a *little* tea, or a *little* punch now and then, diet a *little* more costly, clothes a *little* finer, and a *little* entertainment now and then, can be no *great* matter; but remember what *Poor Richard* says, *many a little makes a mickle;* and farther, beware of little *expenses; a small leak will sink a great ship;* and again, *who dainties love, shall beggars prove;* and moreover, *fools make feasts, and wise men eat them.*—Smyth 3:413. (1757.)

FAMILY, Should Be Kept Busy.—In families also, where the children and servants of families have some spare time, it is well to employ it in making something, and in spinning or knitting, etc., *to gather up the fragments* (of time) that nothing may be lost, for those fragments, though small in themselves, amount to something great in the year, and the family must eat, whether they work or are idle.—Smyth 5:102. (1768.)

FAMILY. See also BACHELORS; CHILDREN; MARRIAGE.

FARMERS, Stubbornly Resist Improved Methods.—I have perused your two essays on field husbandry, and think the public may be much benefited by them; but, if the farmers in your neighborhood are as unwilling to leave the beaten road of their ancestors as they are near me, it will be difficult to persuade them to attempt any improvement.—Smyth 2:383. (1749.)

FARMERS, Discriminated Against. —You say poor laborers cannot afford to buy bread at a high price unless they had higher wages. Possibly. But how shall we farmers be able to afford our laborers higher wages if you will not allow us to get, when we might have it, a higher price for our corn?

By all that I can learn, we should at least have had a guinea a quarter more, if the exportation had been allowed. And this money England would have got from foreigners. But, it seems, we farmers must take so much less, that the poor may have it so much cheaper.

This operates, then, as a tax for the maintenance of the poor. A very good thing, you will say. But I ask, why a partial tax? Why laid on us farmers only? If it be a good thing,

pray, messieurs the public, take your share of it by indemnifying us a little out of your public treasury. In doing a good thing, there is both honor and pleasure; you are welcome to your share of both.

For my own part, I am not so well satisfied of the goodness of this thing. I am for doing good to the poor, but I differ in opinion about the means. I think the best way of doing good to the poor is not making them easy *in* poverty, but leading or driving them *out* of it.—Smyth 5:537. (1772.)

FARMERS. See also AGRICULTURE; WEALTH.

FASHIONS, More Important Than Salvation.—The mode has a wonderful influence on mankind; and there are numbers who, perhaps, fear less the being in hell than out of the fashion.—Smyth 2:378. (1749.)

FASHIONS, Too Many Wartime Frivolities.—The war indeed may in some degree raise the prices of goods, and the high taxes which are necessary to support the war may make our frugality necessary; and, as I am always preaching that doctrine, I cannot in conscience or in decency encourage the contrary, by my example, in furnishing my children with foolish modes and luxuries. I therefore send all the articles you desire that are useful and necessary, and omit the rest; for, as you say you should "have great pride in wearing anything I send, and showing it as your father's taste," I must avoid giving you an opportunity of doing that with either lace or feathers. If you wear your cambric ruffles as I do, and take care not to mend the holes, they will come in time to be lace; and feathers, my dear girl, may be had in America from every cock's tail.—Smyth 7:349. (1779.)

FASTING, Suggested in Pennsylvania by Franklin.—Calling in the aid of religion, I proposed to them [in 1748] the proclaiming a fast, to promote reformation and implore the blessing of Heaven on our undertaking. They embraced the motion; but, as it was the first fast ever thought of in the province, the secretary had no precedent from which to draw the proclamation. My education in New England, where a fast is proclaimed every year, was here of some advantage; I drew it in the accustomed style, it was translated into German, printed in both languages, and divulged through the province.—Autobiography. Smyth 1:363. (1788.)

FIRE, Security in Paris from.—It appears to me of great importance to build our dwelling houses, if we can, in a manner more secure from danger by fire. We scarce ever hear of a fire in Paris. When I was there, I took particular notice of the construction of their houses; and I did not see how one of them could well be burnt. The roofs are slate or tile; the walls are stone; the rooms generally lined with stucco or plaster instead of wainscot; the floors of stucco, or of sixsquare tiles painted brown; or of flagstone, or marble; if any floor were of wood, it was oak wood, which is not so inflammable as pine. Carpets prevent the coldness of stone or

Franklin in 1766 (age 60). Portrait by David Martin.

brick floor offending the feet in winter, and the noise of treading on such floor overhead is less inconvenient than on boards.

The stairs too, at Paris, are either stone or brick with only a wooden edge or corner for the step; so that on the whole, though the Parisians commonly burn wood in their chimneys, a more dangerous kind of fuel than that used here, yet their houses escape extremely well, as there is little in a room that can be consumed by fire, except the furniture. Whereas in London, perhaps scarce a year passes in which half a million of property and many lives are not lost by this destructive element.—Smyth 5:266. (1770.)

FIRE FIGHTING, Organized in Philadelphia by Franklin.—About this time [1736] I wrote a paper (first to be read in [the] Junto, but it was afterward published) on the different accidents and carelessnesses by which houses were set on fire, with cautions against them and means proposed of avoiding them. This was much spoken of as a useful piece, and gave rise to a project, which soon followed it, of forming a company for the more ready extinguishing of fires, and mutual assistance in removing and securing of goods when in danger. Associates in this scheme were presently found, amounting to thirty. Our articles of agreement obliged every member to keep always in good order, and fit for use, a certain number of leather buckets, with strong bags and baskets (for packing and transporting of goods), which were to be brought to every fire; and we agreed to meet once a month and spend a social evening together, in discoursing and communicating such ideas as occurred to us upon the subject of fires, as might be useful in our conduct on such occasions.—Autobiography. Smyth 1:353. (1788.)

FLATTERY, Reaction of Elderly Franklin.—The time has been when such flattering language as from great men might have made me vainer, and had more effect on my conduct, than it can at present, when I find myself so near the end of life as to esteem lightly all personal interests and concerns, except that of maintaining to the last, and leaving behind me the tolerably good character I have hitherto supported.—Smyth 8:518. (1782.)

FOREIGN LANGUAGES, Franklin Studied French, Italian, Spanish, and Latin.—I had begun in 1733 to study languages; I soon made myself so much a master of the French as to be able to read the books with ease. I then undertook the Italian.... I afterwards with a little painstaking, acquired as much of the Spanish as to read their books also.... When I had attained an acquaintance with the French, Italian, and Spanish, I was surprised to find, on looking over a Latin Testament, that I understood so much more of that language than I had imagined, which encouraged me to apply myself again to the study of it, and I met with more success, as those preceding languages had greatly smoothed my way.—Autobiography. Smyth 1:347. (1788.)

FOREIGN OFFICERS, Over-recommended.—Frequently, if a man has no useful talents, is good for nothing and burdensome to his relations, or is indiscreet, profligate, and extravagant, they are glad to get rid of him by sending him to the other end of the world; and for that purpose scruple not to recommend him to those they wish should recommend him to others.—Smyth 7:80. (1777.)

FOREIGN OFFICERS, Recruiting of, Discouraged.—I know that officers going to America for employment will probably be disappointed; that our armies are full; that there are a number of expectants unemployed, and starving for want of subsistence; that my recommendation will not make vacancies, nor can it fill them, to the prejudice of those who have a better claim; that some of those officers I have been prevailed on to recommend have, by their conduct, given no favorable impression of my judgment in military merit; and then the voyage is long, the passage very expensive, the hazard of being taken and imprisoned by the English very considerable. If, after all, no place can be found affording a livelihood for the gentleman in question, he will perhaps be distressed in a strange country, and ready to blaspheme his friends, who, by their solicitations, procured for him so unhappy a situation.—Smyth 7:80. (1777.)

FOREIGN OFFICERS, Their Applications a Perpetual Torment. —These applications are my perpetual torment. People will believe, notwithstanding my continually repeated declarations to the contrary, that I am sent hither to engage officers.... You can have no conception how I am harassed. All my friends are sought out and teased to tease me. Great officers of all ranks, in all departments; ladies, great and small, besides professed solicitors, worry me from morning to night. The noise of every coach now that enters my court terrifies me. I am afraid to accept an invitation to dine abroad, being almost sure of meeting with some officer or officer's friend, who, as soon as I am put in good humor by a glass or two of champagne, begins his attack upon me.—Smyth 7:81. (1777.)

FORTS, Constructed in Pennsylvania Wilderness Under Franklin's Leadership.—We all continue well, thanks be to God. We have been hindered with bad weather, yet our fort is in a good defensible condition, and we have every day more convenient living. Two more are to be built, one on each side of this, at about fifteen miles distance. I hope both will be done in a week or ten days, and then I purpose to bend my course homewards.—Smyth 3:324. (1756.)

I hope in a week or ten days, weather favoring, that those two forts may be finished, the line of forts completed and garrisoned, the rangers in motion, and the intermediate guards and watches disbanded, unless they are permitted and encouraged to go after the enemy to the Susquehanna.— Smyth 3:326. (1756.)

FORTS, Method of Building, on the Frontier in 1756.—Each pine made three palisades of eighteen feet long, pointed at one end. While these were preparing, our other men dug a trench all round, of three feet deep, in which the palisades were to be planted; and [from] our wagons, the bodies being taken off, and the fore and hind wheels separated by taking out the pin which united the two parts of the perch, we had ten carriages, with two horses each, to bring the palisades from the woods to the spot. When they were set up, our carpenters built a stage of boards all round within, about six feet high, for the men to stand on when to fire through the loopholes. We had one swivel gun, which we mounted on one of the angles, and fired it as soon as fixed, to let the

Indians know, if any were within hearing, that we had such pieces; and thus our fort, if such a magnificent name may be given to so miserable a stockade, was finished in a week, though it rained so hard every other day that the men could not work.—Autobiography. Smyth 1:410. (1788.)

FRANCE, Use of Cosmetics in.— Here are some fair women at Paris, who I think are not whitened by art. As to rouge, they don't pretend to imitate nature in laying it on. There is no gradual diminution of the color, from the full bloom in the middle of the cheek to the faint tint near the sides, nor does it show itself differently in different faces. I have not had the honor of being at any lady's toilette to see how it is laid on, but I fancy I can tell you how it is or may be done. Cut a hole of three inches diameter in a piece of paper; place it on the side of your face in such a manner as that the top of the hole may be just under your eye; then with a brush dipped in the color, paint face and paper together; so when the paper is taken off there will remain a round patch of red exactly the form of the hole.— Smyth 5:50. (1767.)

FRANCE, Politeness of the People in.—The civilities we everywhere receive give us the strongest impressions of the French politeness. It seems to be a point settled here universally, that strangers are to be treated with respect; and one has just the same deference shown one here by being a stranger, as in England by being a lady. The customhouse officers at Port St.

Denis, as we entered Paris, were about to seize two dozen of excellent Bordeaux wine given us at Boulogne, and which we brought with us; but as soon as they found we were strangers, it was immediately remitted on that account. At the church of Notre Dame, where we went to see a magnificent illumination, with figures, etc., for the deceased Dauphiness, we found an immense crowd who were kept out by guards; but the officer being told that we were strangers from England, he immediately admitted us, accompanied and showed us everything. Why don't we practice this urbanity to Frenchmen? Why should they be allowed to outdo us in anything?—Smyth 5:53. (1767.)

FRANCE, Franklin's Description of the Ladies in.—You mention the kindness of the French ladies to me. I must explain that matter. This is the civilist nation upon earth. Your first acquaintances endeavor to find out what you like, and they tell others. If it is understood that you like mutton, dine where you will you find mutton. Somebody, it seems, gave it out that I loved ladies; and then everybody presented me their ladies (or the ladies presented themselves) to be *embraced*, that is to have their necks kissed. For as to kissing of lips or cheeks, it is not the mode here; the first is reckoned rude, and the other may rub off the paint. The French ladies have, however, 1000 other ways of rendering themselves agreeable; by their various attentions and civilities, and their sensible conversation. 'Tis a delightful people to live with.—Smyth 7:393. (1779.)

FRANCE, Generosity in Financing American Revolution.—We have been assisted with near 20 millions since the beginning of last year, besides a fleet and army; and yet I am obliged to worry them with my solicitations for more, which makes us appear insatiable.—Smyth 8:365. (1782.)

FRANCE, American Gratitude to.—Mr. Grenville conceived that it was carrying gratitude very far to apply this doctrine [of a "debt of kindness"] to our situation in respect to France, who was really the party served and obliged by our separation from England, as it lessened the power of her rival and relatively increased her own.

I told him I was so strongly impressed with the kind assistance afforded us by France in our distress, and the generous and noble manner in which it was granted, without exacting or stipulating for a single privilege or particular advantage to herself in our commerce or otherwise, that I could never suffer myself to think of such reasonings for lessening the obligation; and I hoped, and indeed did not doubt, [that] my countrymen were all of the same sentiments.—Smyth 8:498. (1782.)

FRANKLIN (Benjamin), Profit Not Important When Publishing for the Good of Mankind.—I shall be very willing and ready, when you think proper to publish your piece on gravitation, to print it at my own expense and risk. If I can be the means of communicating anything valuable to the world, I do not always think of gaining, nor even of saving, by my business; but a piece of that kind, as it must excite the curiosity of all the learned, can hardly fail of bearing its own expense.—Smyth 2:290. (1745.)

FRANKLIN (Benjamin), Wistful Hope of Retiring from Public Life and Business.—I have refused engaging further in public affairs. The share I had in the late association, etc., having given me a little present run of popularity, there was a pretty general intention of choosing me a representative of the city at the next election of Assembly men; but I have desired all my friends who spoke to me about it to discourage it, declaring that I should not serve if chosen. Thus you see I am in a fair way of having no other tasks than such as I shall like to give myself, and of enjoying what I look upon as a great happiness, leisure to read, study, make experiments, and converse at large with such ingenious and worthy men as are pleased to honor me with their friendship or acquaintance, on such points as may produce something for the common benefit of mankind, uninterrupted by the little cares and fatigues of business.—Smyth 2:362. (1748.)

FRANKLIN (Benjamin), Prefers Utility to Wealth.—So the years roll round, and the last will come; when I would rather have it said *He lived usefully,* than *He died rich.*—Smyth 3:5. (1750.)

FRANKLIN (Benjamin), Educated as a "Tradesman."—The trustees have put it on me, as I first moved the English education here, to sketch out the idea of the English school; for which I am indeed very unfit, having neither been educated myself (except as a tradesman) nor ever concerned in educating others. However, I have done something towards it, which I now enclose to you; and beg you would either amend it, or (which perhaps will be easier to do) give us a complete scheme of your own.—Smyth 3:20. (1750.)

FRANKLIN (Benjamin), His Mother's Death.—I received yours with the affecting news of our dear good mother's death. I thank you for your long continued care of her in her old age and sickness. Our distance made it impracticable for us to attend her, but you have supplied all. She has lived a good life, as well as a long one, and is happy.—Smyth 3:89. (1752.)

FRANKLIN (Benjamin), Expression of Humility.—By Heaven we understand a state of happiness, infinite in degree, and eternal in duration; I can do nothing to deserve such rewards; he that for giving a draught of water to a thirsty person should expect to be paid with a good plantation, would be modest in his demands compared with those who think they deserve Heaven for the little good they do on earth. Even the mixed, imperfect pleasures we enjoy in this world are rather from God's goodness than our merit; how much more such happiness of Heaven. For my own part I have not the vanity to think I deserve it, the folly to expect it, nor the ambition to desire it; but content myself in submitting to the

will and disposal of that God who made me, who has hitherto preserved and blessed me, and in whose Fatherly goodness I may well confide, that he will never make me miserable, and that even the afflicitions I may at any time suffer shall tend to my benefit.—Smyth 3:144. (1753.)

FRANKLIN (Benjamin), Receives Honorary Degrees from Harvard and Yale.—The business of the post office occasioned my taking a journey this year [1753] to New England, where the college of Cambridge, of their own motion, presented me with the degree of Master of Arts. Yale College, in Connecticut, had before made me a similar compliment.*—Autobiography. Smyth 1:386. (1788.)

*"In July [1853] he received the honorary degree of A.M. from Harvard College, Cambridge, and September commencement of the same year he received the diploma of the same degree from us at Yale College, which he calls his first academic honours, because we from 1749 and onward adopted with avidity and before all the rest of the learned world his electrical and philosophical discoveries."— *The Literary Diary of Ezra Stiles* (1901), 3:391.

FRANKLIN (Benjamin), Attachment to Family.—I began to think of and wish for home; and, as I drew nearer, I found the attraction stronger and stronger. My diligence and speed increased with my impatience. I drove on violently, and made such long stretches that a very few days brought me to my own house, and to the arms of my good old wife and children, where I remain, thanks to God, at present well and happy.—Smyth 3:246. (1755.)

'Tis true, the regard and friendship I meet with from persons of worth, and the conversation of ingenious men, give me no small pleasure; but at this time of life, domestic comforts afford the most solid satisfaction, and my uneasiness at being absent from my family, and longing desire to be with them, make me often sigh in the midst of cheerful company.—Smyth 3:430. (1758.)

FRANKLIN (Benjamin), Frustrations in Pennsylvania Assembly.—I was chosen last year in my absence and was not at the winter sitting when the House sent home that address to the King, which I am afraid was both ill-judged and ill-timed. If my being able now and then to influence a good measure did not keep up my spirits, I should be ready to swear never to serve again as an Assembly man, since both sides expect more from me than they ought, and blame me sometimes for not doing what I am not able to do, as well as for not preventing what was not in my power to prevent.—Smyth 3:265. (1755.)

FRANKLIN (Benjamin), Castigated by Former Admirers.—A number of falsehoods are now privately propagated to blast my character; of which I shall take no notice till they grow bold enough to show their faces in public. Those who caressed me a few months since are now endeavoring to defame me everywhere by every base act.—Smyth

3:278. (1755.)

FRANKLIN (Benjamin), Comments on His Public Acclaim.—You ask in your last how I do, and what I am doing, and whether everybody loves me yet, and why I make them do so. In regard to the first, I can say, thanks to God, that I do not remember I was ever better. I still relish all the pleasures of life that a temperate man can in reason desire, and through favor I have them all in my power. This happy situation shall continue as long as God pleases, who knows what is best for his creatures, and I hope will enable me to bear with patience and dutiful submission any change he may think fit to make that is less agreeable. As to the second question, I must confess (but don't you be jealous) that many more people love me now than ever did before; for since I saw you I have been enabled to do some general services to the country, and to the army, for which both have thanked and praised me, and say they love me. They say so, as you used to do; and if I were to ask any favors of them, they would perhaps as readily refuse me; so that I find little real advantage in being beloved, but it pleases my humor.—Smyth 3:282. (1755.)

FRANKLIN (Benjamin), Letter to a Young Admirer.—Mrs. Franklin was very proud that a young lady should have so much regard for her old husband as to send him such a present. We talk of you every time it comes to table. She is sure you are a sensible girl, and a notable housewife, and talks of bequeathing me to you as a legacy; but I ought to wish you a better, and hope she will live these hundred years; for we are grown old together, and if she has any faults, I am so used to them that I don't perceive them.—Smyth 3:284. (1755.)

FRANKLIN (Benjamin), Commander of Militia Defending Frontier.—While the several companies in the city and country were forming, and learning their exercise, the Governor prevailed with me to take charge of our northwestern frontier, which was infested by the enemy, and provide for the defense of the inhabitants by raising troops and building a line of forts. I undertook this military business [in 1756], though I did not conceive myself well qualified for it. He gave me a commission with full powers, and a parcel of blank commissions for officers, to be given to whom I thought fit. I had but little difficulty in raising men, having soon five hundred and sixty under my command. My son, who had in the preceding war been an officer in the army raised against Canada, was my aide-de-camp, and of great use to me.—Autobiography. Smyth 1:407. (1788.)

FRANKLIN (Benjamin), Pressure of Public Service.—I am just returned from my military expedition, and now my time is taken up in the Assembly. Providence seems to require various duties of me. I know not what will be next; but I find the more I seek for leisure and retirement from business, the more I am engaged in it.—Smyth 3:328. (1756.)

FRANKLIN (Benjamin), Sent to England as Agent of Pennsylvania.—The Assembly finally finding the proprietary obstinately persisted in manacling their deputies with instructions inconsistent, not only with the privileges of the people, but with the service of the crown, resolved to petition the king against them, and appointed me [in 1757] their agent to go over to England, to present and support the petition.—Autobiography. Smyth 1:423. (1788.)

I am to take leave of you, being ordered home to England by the Assembly, to obtain some final settlement of the points that have occasioned so many unhappy disputes. I assure you I go with the sincerest desire of procuring peace, and therein I know I shall have your prayers for my success. God bless you, and grant that at my return I may find you well and happy.—Smyth 3:377. (1757.)

FRANKLIN (Benjamin), Nearly Shipwrecked During 1757 Trip to England.—It was midnight, and our captain fast asleep; but Captain Kennedy, jumping upon deck, and seeing the danger, ordered the ship to wear round, all sails standing; an operation dangerous to the masts, but it carried us clear, and we escaped shipwreck, for we were running right upon the rocks on which the light-house was erected. This deliverance impressed me strongly with the utility of lighthouses, and made me resolve to encourage the building more of them in America, if I should live to return there.—Autobiography. Smyth 1:433. (1788.)

FRANKLIN (Benjamin), Sick for Two Months in England.—During my illness, which continued near eight weeks, I wrote you several little letters, as I was able. The last was by the packet which sailed from Falmouth above a week since. In that I informed you that my intermitting fever, which had continued to harass me by frequent relapses, was gone off, and I have ever since been gathering strength and flesh.— Smyth 3:419. (1757.)

FRANKLIN (Benjamin), Worries over Wife's Health.—It gives me concern to receive such frequent accounts of your being indisposed; but we both of us grow in years, and must expect our constitutions, though tolerably good in themselves, will by degrees give way to the infirmities of age.—Smyth 3:438. (1758.)

FRANKLIN (Benjamin), Visits Home of His Ancestors.—From Wellingborough we went to Ecton, about three or four miles, being the village where my father was born, and where his father, grandfather, and great-grandfather had lived, and how many of the family before them we know not. We went first to see the old house and grounds; they came to Mr. Fisher with his wife, and, after letting them for some years, finding his rent something ill paid, he sold them. The land is now added to another farm, and a school kept in the house. It is a decayed old stone building, but still known by the name of Franklin House.— Smyth 3:452. (1758.)

FRANKLIN (Benjamin), Contem-plates Permanent Move to England. —Mr. [William] Strahan...was very urgent with me to stay in England and prevail with you [Mrs. Deborah Franklin] to remove hither with Sally.... I gave him, however, two reasons why I could not think of removing hither. One, my affection to Pennsylvania, and long established friendships and other connections there. The other, your invincible aversion to crossing the seas. And without removing hither, I could not think of parting with my daughter to such a distance. I thanked him for the regard shown us in the proposal; but gave him no expectation that I should forward the letters. So you are at liberty to answer or not, as you think proper. Let me, however, know your sentiments.—Smyth 4:9. (1760.)

I cannot, I assure you, quit even this disagreeable place without regret, as it carries me still farther from those I love, and from the opportunities of hearing of their welfare. The attraction of reason is at present for the other side of the water, but that of inclination will be for this side. You know which usually prevails. I shall probably make but this one vibration and settle here forever. Nothing will prevent it if I can, as I hope I can, prevail with Mrs. F. to accompany me, especially if we have a peace.— Smyth 4:176. (1762.)

In two years at farthest I hope to settle all my affairs in such a manner as that I *may* then conveniently remove to England—provided we can persuade the good woman to cross the seas. That will be the great difficulty; but you can help me a little in removing it.—Smyth 4:182. (1762.)

No friend can wish me more in England than I do myself. But before I go, everything I am concerned in must be so settled here as to make another return to America unnecessary.—Smyth 4:207. (1763.)

FRANKLIN (Benjamin), Commitment to a Life Worthy of His Family.—I am concerned that so much trouble should be given you by idle reports concerning me. Be satisfied, my dear, that while I have my senses, and God vouchsafes me his protection, I shall do nothing unworthy the character of an honest man, and one that loves his family.—Smyth 4:22. (1760.)

FRANKLIN (Benjamin), Treatment of His Mother-In-Law.—I condole with you most sincerely on the death of our good mother, being extremely sensible of the distress and affliction it must have thrown you into. Your comfort will be that no care was wanting on your part towards her, and that she had lived as long as this life could afford her any rational enjoyment. 'Tis, I am sure, a satisfaction to me that I cannot charge myself with having ever failed in one instance of duty and respect to her during the many years that she called me Son. The circumstances attending her death were indeed unhappy in some respects; but something must bring us all to our end, and few of us shall see her length of days.—Smyth 4:150. (1762.)

FRANKLIN (Benjamin), Feels Useless in England, Longs to Return to America.—I feel here like a thing out of its place, and useless because it is out of its place. How then can I any longer be happy in England? You have great power of persuasion, and might easily prevail on me to do anything; but not any longer to do nothing. I must go home.—Smyth 4:172. (1762.)

FRANKLIN (Benjamin), Reelected to Pennsylvania Assembly While Returning to America.—My house has been full of a succession of [friends] from morning to night ever since my arrival, congratulating me on my return with the utmost cordiality and affection. My fellow citizens, while I was on the sea, had, at the annual election, chosen me unanimously, as they had done every year while I was in England, to be their representative in Assembly, and would, they say, if I had not disappointed them by coming privately to town before they heard of my landing, have met me with 500 horse. Excuse my vanity in writing this to you who know what has provoked me to it.—Smyth 4:179. (1762.)

FRANKLIN (Benjamin), Ten Weeks Crossing the Atlantic.—We had a long passage near ten weeks from Portsmouth to this place, but it was a pleasant one; for we had ten sail in company and a man-of-war to protect us; we had pleasant weather and fair winds, and frequently visited and dined from ship to ship; we called too at the delightful Island of Madeira, by way of half-way house, where we replenished our stores and took in many refreshments. It was the time of their vintage, and we hung the ceiling of the cabin with bunches of fine grapes, which served as a dessert at dinner for some weeks afterwards. The reason of our being so long at sea was that, sailing with a convoy, we could none of us go faster than the slowest, being obliged every day to shorten sail or lay by till they came up.—Smyth 4:180. (1762.)

FRANKLIN (Benjamin), Falsely Accused of Extravagance.—It had been industriously reported that I had lived very extravagantly in England, and wasted a considerable sum of the public money, which I had received out of your treasury for the province; but the Assembly, when they came to examine my accounts and allow me for my services, found themselves £2,214 10s. d. sterling in my debt, to the utter confusion of the propagators of that falsehood, and the surprise of all they had made to believe it. The House accordingly ordered that sum to be paid me, and that the Speaker should, moreover, present me with their thanks for my fidelity, etc., in transacting their affairs.—Smyth 4:197. (1763.)

FRANKLIN (Benjamin), Another Bad Fall.—I am almost ashamed to tell you that I have had another fall and put my shoulder out. It is well reduced again, but is still affected with constant, though not very acute, pain. I am not yet able to travel rough roads, and must lie by awhile, as I can neither hold reins nor whip with my right hand till it grows stronger.—Smyth 4:207. (1763.)

FRANKLIN (Benjamin), Sustains

Established Authority Regardless of Personal Dislikes.—More wonders. You know that I don't love the proprietary and that he does not love me. Our totally different tempers forbid it. You might therefore expect that the late new appointments of one of his family would find me ready for opposition. And yet when his nephew arrived, our Governor, I considered government as government, and paid him all respect, gave him on all occasions my best advice, [and] promoted in the Assembly a ready compliance with everything he proposed or recommended. And when those daring rioters, encouraged by general approbation of the populace, treated his proclamation with contempt, I drew my pen in the cause, wrote a pamphlet (that I have sent you) to render the rioters unpopular, promoted an association to support the authority of the government and defend the Governor by taking arms, [and] signed it first myself and was followed by several hundreds, who took arms accordingly. The Governor offered me the command of them, but I chose to carry a musket and strengthen his authority by setting an example of obedience to his order. And would you think it, this proprietary Governor did me the honor, in an alarm, to run to my house at midnight, with his counsellors at his heels, for advice, and made it his headquarters for some time. And within four and twenty hours, your old friend was a common soldier, a counsellor, a kind of dictator, an ambassador to the country mob, and on his returning home, nobody again.—Smyth 4:222. (1764.)

FRANKLIN (Benjamin), Served as Agent of Pennsylvania Without Compensation.—I made no bargain for my future service when I was ordered to *England* by the Assembly; nor did they vote me any salary. I lived there near six years at my own expense, and I made no charge or demand when I came home.— Smyth 4:284. (1764.)

FRANKLIN (Benjamin), Departs for Second Mission to England.—I am now to take leave (perhaps a last leave) of the country I love, and in which I have spent the greatest part of my life. *Esto perpetua.* I wish every kind of prosperity to my friends; and I forgive my enemies.—Smyth 4:285. (1764.)

FRANKLIN (Benjamin), Pressure of Business in England.—I am excessively hurried, being, every hour that I am awake, either abroad to speak with members of Parliament, or taken up with people coming to me at home concerning our American affairs, so that I am much behindhand in answering my friends' letters.—Smyth 4:408. (1766.)

FRANKLIN (Benjamin), Frugality in Personal Affairs.—It seems now as if I should stay here another winter, and therefore I must leave it to your judgment to act in the affair of [our] daughter's match, as shall seem best. If you think it a suitable one, I suppose the sooner it is completed the better. In that case, I would only advise that you do not make an expensive feasting wedding, but conduct everything with frugality and economy, which our circumstances really now require to be observed in all our expenses. For since my partnership with Mr. Hall is expired, a great source of our income is cut off; and if I should lose the post office, which among the many changes here is far from being unlikely, we should be reduced to our rents and interest of money for a subsistence, which will by no means afford the chargeable housekeeping and entertainments we have been used to.

For my own part I live here as frugally as possible not to be destitute of the comforts of life, making no dinners for anybody, and contenting myself with a single dish when I dine at home; and yet such is the dearness of living here in every article, that my expenses amaze me. I see too, by the sums you have received in my absence, that yours are very great, and I am very sensible that your situation naturally brings you a great many visitors, which occasion an expense not easily to be avoided, especially when one has been long in the practice and habit of it. But when people's incomes are lessened, if they cannot proportionably lessen their outgoings, they must come to poverty.

If we were young enough to begin business again, it might be another matter; but ... we are past it, and business not well managed ruins one faster than no business. In short, with frugality and prudent care we may subsist decently on what we have, and leave it entire to our children; but without such care, we shall not be able to keep it together; it will melt away like butter in the sunshine; and we may live long enough to feel the miserable consequences of our indiscretion.—Smyth 5:31. (1767.)

FRANKLIN (Benjamin), Dress and Wig in Paris.—I had not been here six days before my tailor and perruquier had transformed me into a Frenchman. Only think what a figure I make in a little bag-wig and naked ears! They told me I was become 20 years younger, and looked very gallant.—Smyth 5:54. (1767.)

FRANKLIN (Benjamin), Zeal in Representing Colonies.—It gives me pleasure to hear that the people of the other colonies are not insensible of the zeal with which I occasionally espouse their respective interests, as well as the interests of the whole. I shall continue to do so as long as I reside here and am able.—Smyth 5:69. (1767.)

FRANKLIN (Benjamin), Too Much of an American.—I am told there has been a talk of getting me appointed under-secretary to Lord Hillsborough; but with little likelihood, as it is a settled point here that I am too much of an American.—Smyth 5:90. (1768.)

FRANKLIN (Benjamin), U.S. Postmaster.—As to the rumor you mention (which was, as Josiah tells me, that I had been deprived of my place in the post office on account of a letter I wrote to Philadelphia), it might have this foundation, that some of the ministry had been displeased on my writing such letters, and there were really some thoughts among them of showing that displeasure in that manner. But I had some friends, too, who, unrequired by me, advised the contrary. And my enemies were forced to content themselves with abusing me plentifully in the newspapers, and endeavoring to provoke me to resign. In this they are not likely to succeed, I being deficient in that Christian virtue of resignation. If they would have my office, they must take it....

Before my time, through bad management, it never produced the salary annexed to it; and, when I received it, no salary was to be allowed if the office did not produce it. During the first four years it was so far from defraying itself that it became nine hundred and fifty pounds sterling in debt to me and my colleague. I had been chiefly instrumental in bringing it to its present flourishing state, and therefore thought I had some kind of right to it. I had hitherto executed the duties of it faithfully, and to the perfect satisfaction of my superiors, which I thought was all that should be expected of me on that account. As to the letters complained of, it was true I did write them, and they were written in compliance with another duty, that to my country; a duty quite distinct from that of postmaster.—Smyth 5:289. (1770.)

FRANKLIN (Benjamin), How He Protected His Integrity.—My rule, in which I have always found satisfaction, is never to turn aside in public affairs through views of private interest, but to go straight forward in doing what appears to me right at the time, leaving the consequences with Providence. What in my younger days enabled me more easily to walk upright was that I had a trade, and that I knew I could live upon little; and thence (never having had views of making a fortune) I was free from avarice, and contented with the plentiful supplies my business afforded me. And now it is still more easy for me to preserve my freedom and integrity, when I consider that I am almost at the end of my journey, and therefore need less to complete the expense of it; and that what I now possess, through the blessing of God, may, with tolerable economy, be sufficient for me (great misfortunes excepted), though I should add nothing more to it by any office or employment whatsoever.—Smyth 5:290. (1770.)

FRANKLIN (Benjamin), English Ancestors.—I learned that the family had lived in the same village, Ecton, in Northamptonshire, for three hundred years, and how much longer he [my uncle] knew not (perhaps from the time when the name of Franklin, that before was the name of an order of people, was assumed by them as a surname when others took surnames all over the kingdom), on a freehold of about thirty acres, aided by the smith's business, which had continued in the family till his time, the eldest son being always bred to that business; a custom which he

and my father followed as to their eldest sons. When I searched the registers at Ecton, I found an account of their births, marriages and burials from the year 1555 only, there being no registers kept in that parish at any time preceding. By that register I perceived that I was the youngest son of the youngest son for five generations back.—Autobiography. Smyth 1:228. (1771.)

FRANKLIN (Benjamin), Discovers Book of His English Uncle.—Yesterday a very odd accident happened, which I must mention to you, as it relates to your grandfather. A person that deals in old books, of whom I sometimes buy, acquainted me that he had a curious collection of pamphlets bound in eight volumes folio, and twenty-four volumes quarto and octavo, which he thought, from the subjects, I might like to have, and that he would sell them cheap. I desired to see them, and he brought them to me. On examining, I found that they contained all the principal pamphlets and papers on public affairs that had been printed here from the Restoration down to 1715. In one of the blank leaves at the beginning of each volume the collector had written the titles of the pieces contained in it, and the price they cost him. Also notes in the margin of many of the pieces; and the collector, I find from the handwriting and various other circumstances, was your grandfather, my uncle Benjamin. Wherefore, I the more readily agreed to buy them. I suppose he parted with them when he left England and came to Boston, soon after your father, which was about the year 1716 or 1717, now more than fifty years since.—Smyth 5:333. (1771.)

FRANKLIN (Benjamin), Ignores Minor Expenses to Clients.—In yours of July 9th it is mentioned that the House desire I would annually send an account of the expense I am at in carrying on the affairs of the province. Having business to do for several colonies almost every time I go to the public offices, and to the ministers, I have found it troublesome to keep an account of small expenses, such as coach and chair hire, stationery, etc., and difficult to divide them justly. Therefore I have some time since omitted keeping any account or making any charge of them, but content myself with such salaries, grants, and allowances as have been made me. Where considerable sums have been disbursed, as in fees to counsel, payment of solicitors' bills, and the like, those I charge.— Smyth 5:351. (1772.)

FRANKLIN (Benjamin), Attitude Toward Assignment in England.— As to the agency, whether I am re-chosen or not, and whether the General Assembly is ever permitted to pay me or not, I shall nevertheless continue to exert myself in behalf of my country, as long as I see a probability of my being able to do it any service. I have nothing to ask or expect of ministers. I have, thanks to God, a competency (for the little time I may expect to live), and am grown too old for ambition of every other kind but that of leaving a good name behind me.—Smyth 5:357. (1772.)

FRANKLIN (Benjamin), Reputation and Influence.—A general respect paid me by the learned, a number of friends and acquaintance among them, with whom I have a pleasing intercourse; a character of so much weight that it has protected me when some in power would have done me injury, and continued me in an office they would have deprived me of; my company so much desired that I seldom dine at home in winter, and could spend the whole summer in the country-houses of inviting friends, if I chose it. Learned and ingenious foreigners that come to England almost all make a point of visiting me; for my reputation is still higher abroad than here. Several of the foreign ambassadors have assiduously cultivated my acquaintance, treating me as one of their *corps,* partly I believe from the desire they have, from time to time, of hearing something of American affairs, an object become of importance in foreign courts, who begin to hope Britain's alarming power will be diminished by the defection of her colonies; and partly that they may have an opportunity of introducing me to the gentlemen of their country who desire it. The King, too, has lately been heard to speak of me with great regard.— Smyth 5:414. (1772.)

FRANKLIN (Benjamin), Becomes Member of Royal Academy.—I received a letter from Paris...

Franklin in 1777 (age 71). Terra-cotta relief by Jean Baptiste Nini, after a drawing by Thomas Walpole.

acquainting me that I am chosen *Associe Etranger* (foreign member) of the Royal Academy there. There are but eight of the *Associes Etrangers* in all Europe, and those of the most distinguished names of science. The vacancy I have the honor of filling was made by the death of the late celebrated Van Swieten of Vienna. This mark of respect from the first academy in the world, which Abbe Nollet, one of its members, took so many pains to prejudice against my doctrines, I consider as a kind of victory without ink-shed, since I never answered him. I am told he has but one of his sect now remaining in the Academy. All the rest, who have in any degree acquainted themselves with electricity, are as he calls them *Franklinists.*—Smyth 5:415. (1772.)

FRANKLIN (Benjamin), Desires to Return from England.—In these circumstances, with an almost double expense of living by my family remaining in Philadelphia, the losses I am continually suffering in my affairs there through absence, together with my now advanced age, I feel renewed inclinations to return and spend the remainder of my days in private life, having had rather more than my share of public bustle.—Smyth 6:6. (1773.)

FRANKLIN (Benjamin), His Writings Published in French.—There is a new translation of my book at Paris and printed there, being the 3d edition in French. A fifth edition is now printing here. To the French edition they have prefixed a print of me, which, though a copy of that by Chamberlin, has got so French a countenance that you would take me for one of that lively nation.—Smyth 6:118. (1773.)

FRANKLIN (Benjamin), Recommends Nonviolent Protests.—They should carefully avoid all tumults and every violent measure, and content themselves with verbally keeping up their claims, and holding forth their rights whenever occasion requires; secure that, from the growing importance of America, those claims will ere long be attended to and acknowledged.—Smyth 6:144. (1773.)

FRANKLIN (Benjamin), Resigns as Agent for Massachusetts.—In mine of February 2nd, I informed you that, after the treatment I had received at the council board, it was not possible for me to act longer as your agent, apprehending I could as such be of no further use to the province. I have nevertheless given what assistance I could, as a private man, by speaking to members of both houses [of Parliament], and by joining in the petitions of the natives of America now happening to be in London.—Smyth 6:224. (1774.)

FRANKLIN (Benjamin), Fears Possible Arrest.—But I venture to stay, in compliance with the wish of others, till the result of the Congress arrives, since they suppose my being here might on that occasion be of use; and I confide in my innocence, that the worst which can happen to me will be an imprisonment on suspicion, though that is a thing I should much desire to avoid, as it may be expensive and vexatious, as well as dangerous to my health.—Smyth 6:254. (1774.)

FRANKLIN (Benjamin), Never Mixes Personal and Public Affairs.—It was a fixed rule with me not to mix my private affairs with those of the public; that I could join with my personal enemy in serving the public, or, when it was for its interest, with the public in serving that enemy.—Smyth 6:347. (1775.)

FRANKLIN (Benjamin), Willing to Sacrifice All His Possessions in the Cause of Freedom.—Since it was so easy for Britain to burn all our seaport towns, I grew warm [and] said that the chief part of my little property consisted of houses in those towns; that they might make bonfires of them whenever they pleased; that the fear of losing them would never alter my resolution to resist to the last that claim of Parliament; and that it behooved

this country to take care what mischief it did us; for that sooner or later it would certainly be obliged to make good all damages with interest!—Smyth 6:374. (1775.)

FRANKLIN (Benjamin), Describes Return Voyage from England.—I had a passage of six weeks, the weather constantly so moderate that a London wherry [rowboat] might have accompanied us all the way. I got home in the evening, and the next morning was unanimously chosen by the Assembly of Pennsylvania a delegate to the Congress now sitting.—Smyth 6:400. (1775.)

FRANKLIN (Benjamin), Eyesight Failing.—My eyes will now hardly serve me to write by night, and these short days have been all taken up by such a variety of business that I seldom can sit down ten minutes without interruption.—Smyth 6:439. (1776.)

FRANKLIN (Benjamin), Fears Mission to Canada May Cause Death.—I am here on my way to Canada, detained by the present state of the lakes, in which the unthawed ice obstructs navigation. I begin to apprehend that I have undertaken a fatigue that, at my time of life, may prove too much for me; so I sit down to write to a few friends by way of farewell.—Smyth 6:445. (1776.)

FRANKLIN (Benjamin), Nothing in His Private Affairs He Would Fear to Be Made Public.—I have long observed one rule which prevents any inconvenience from [being watched by spies]. It is simply this, to be concerned in no affairs that I should blush to have made public, and to do nothing but what spies may see and welcome. When a man's actions are just and honorable, the more they are known, the more his reputation is increased and established. If I were sure therefore that my valet de place was a spy, as probably he is, I think I should not discharge him for that, if in other respects I liked him.—Smyth 7:11. (1777.)

FRANKLIN (Benjamin), Physical Appearance in Paris.—I will describe myself to you. Figure me in your mind as jolly as formerly, and as strong and hearty, only a few years older; very plainly dressed, wearing my thin, gray, straight hair that peeps out under my only *coiffure,* a fine fur cap, which comes down my forehead almost to my spectacles. Think how this must appear among the powdered heads of Paris! I wish every gentleman and lady in France would only be so obliging as to follow my fashion, comb their own heads as I do mine, dismiss their *friseurs,* and pay me half the money they paid to them.—Smyth 7:26. (1777.)

FRANKLIN (Benjamin), Bold Initiative.—We are also ordered to build six ships of war. It is a pleasure to find the things ordered which we were doing without orders.—Smyth 7:33. (1777.)

FRANKLIN (Benjamin), Indifference Toward Personal Safety.—I thank you for your kind caution, but having nearly finished a long life, I set but little value on what remains of it. Like a draper, when one chaffers with him for remnant,

I am ready to say, "As it is only the fag end, I will not differ with you about it; take it for what you please." Perhaps the best use such an old fellow can be put to is to make a martyr of him.—Smyth 7:143. (1778.)

FRANKLIN (Benjamin), Incapacitated by Gout.—I don't complain much, even of the gout, which has harassed me ever since the arrival of the commission you so politely mention. There seems, however, some incongruity in a *plenipotentiary* who can neither stand nor go.—Smyth 7:260. (1779.)

My gout continues to disable me from walking longer than formerly. But on Tuesday the 23rd past I thought myself able to go through the ceremony, and accordingly went to court, had my audience of the King in the new character [i.e., as newly appointed American minister to France], presented my letter of credence, and was received very graciously. After which I went the rounds, with the other foreign ministers, in visiting all the royal family. The fatigue, however, was a little too much for my feet, and disabled me for near another week.—Smyth 7:278. (1779.)

FRANKLIN (Benjamin), Refuses to Screen Nephew If Guilty of Embezzling Public Funds.—I have no desire to screen Mr. Williams on account of his being my nephew; if he is guilty of what you charge him with I care not how soon he is deservedly punished and the family purged of him; for I take it that a rogue living in a family is a greater disgrace to it than one *hanged out of* it. If he is innocent, justice requires that his character should be speedily cleared from the heavy charge with which it has been loaded.—Smyth 7:273. (1779.)

FRANKLIN (Benjamin), "I-doll-ized" in France.—The clay medallion of me you say you gave to Mr. Hopkinson was the first of the kind made in France. A variety of others have been made since of different sizes; some to be set in the lids of snuffboxes, and some so small as to be worn in rings; and the numbers sold are incredible. These, with the pictures, busts, and prints (of which copies upon copies are spread everywhere), have made your father's face as well known as that of the moon, so that he durst not do anything that would oblige him to run away, as his phiz [face] would discover him wherever he should venture to show it. It is said by learned etymologists that the name *doll*, for the images children play with, is derived from the word *idol*. From the number of *dolls* now made of him, he may be truly said, *in that sense*, to be *i-doll-ized* in this country.—Smyth 7:347. (1779.)

FRANKLIN (Benjamin), Weary of Sitting for Portraits.—I have at the request of friends sat so much and so often to painters and statuaries, that I am perfectly sick of it. I know of nothing so tedious as sitting hours in one fixed posture. I would nevertheless do it once more to oblige you if it were necessary, but there are already so many good likenesses of the face that if the best of them is copied it will probably be better than a new one, and the body is only that of a lusty man which need not be drawn from the life; any artist can add such a body to the face.—Smyth 8:110. (1780.)

FRANKLIN (Benjamin), Worries over Finances.—But the little success that has attended your [John Jay's] late applications for money mortified me exceedingly; and the storm of bills, which I found coming upon us both, has terrified and vexed me to such a degree that I have been deprived of sleep, and so much indisposed by continual anxiety as to be rendered almost incapable of writing.—Smyth 8:142. (1780.)

FRANKLIN (Benjamin), Work Approved by Congress.—It gave me great satisfaction to find, by the unanimous choice you mention, that my services had not been unacceptable to Congress; and to hear also that they were favorably disposed towards my grandson. It was my desire to quit public business, fearing it might suffer in my hands through the infirmities incident to my time of life. But as they are pleased to think I may still be useful, I submit to their judgment, and shall do my best.—Smyth 8:303. (1781.)

FRANKLIN (Benjamin), Keeps Track of Relatives.—I have exact accounts of every person of my family since the year 1555, when it was established in England, and am certain that none of them but myself since that time were ever in Ireland. The name of Franklin is common among the English of the two nations, but there are a number of different families who bear it, and who have no relation to each other.—Smyth 8:329. (1781.)

FRANKLIN (Benjamin), Hopes to Retire.—I am now entering on my seventy-eighth year; public business has engrossed fifty of them; I wish now to be, for the little time I have left, my own master. If I live to see this peace concluded, I shall beg leave to remind the Congress of their promise then to dismiss me. I shall be happy to sing with old Simeon, *Now lettest thou thy servant depart in peace, for mine eyes have seen thy salvation.*—Smyth 8:636. (1782.)

FRANKLIN (Benjamin), Summary of Life at Age 78.—I ought to be satisfied with those [years] Providence has already been pleased to afford me, being now in my seventy-eighth; a long life to pass without any uncommon misfortune, the greater part of it in health and vigor of mind and body, near fifty years of it in continued possession of the confidence of my country, in public employments, and enjoying the esteem and affectionate, friendly regard of many wise and good men and women in every country where I have resided. For these mercies and blessings I desire to be thankful to God, whose protection I have hitherto had, and I hope for its continuance to the end, which now cannot be far distant.—Smyth 9:13. (1783.)

FRANKLIN (Benjamin), Fears He Will Feel Like a Stranger When He Returns to America.—I did intend returning this year; but the Congress, instead of giving me leave to do so, have sent me another commission, which will keep me here at least a year longer; and perhaps I may then be too old and feeble to bear the voyage. I am here among a people that love and respect me, a most amiable nation to live with; and perhaps I may conclude to die among them; for my friends in America are dying off, one after another, and I have been so long abroad that I should now be almost a stranger in my own country.—Smyth 9:253. (1784.)

FRANKLIN (Benjamin), Suffers from Bladder Stone.—I am grown very old, being now in my 80th year; I am engaged in much business that must not be neglected. Writing becomes more and more irksome to me; I grow more indolent; philosophic discussions, not being urgent like business, are postponed from time to time till they are forgotten. Besides, I have been these 20 months past afflicted with the stone, which is always giving me more or less uneasiness, unless when I am laid in bed; and, when I would write, it interrupts my train of thinking, so that I lay down my pen, and seek some light amusement.—Smyth 9:307. (1785.)

I thank you much for the postscript respecting my disorder, the stone. I have taken heretofore and am now again taking the remedy you mention, which is called *Blackrie's solvent.* It is the soap lye with lime water, and I believe it may have some effect in diminishing the symptoms, and preventing the growth of the stone, which is all

I expect from it. It does not hurt my appetite; I sleep well, and enjoy my friends in cheerful conversation as usual. But, as I cannot use much exercise, I eat more sparingly than formerly, and I drink no wine.—Smyth 9:318. (1785.)

As to my malady, concerning which you so kindly inquire, I have never had the least doubt of its being the stone. I am sensible that it is grown heavier; but on the whole it does not give me more pain than when at Passy, and except in standing, walking, or making water, I am very little incommoded by it. Sitting or lying in bed I am generally quite easy, God be thanked; and as I live temperately, drink no wine, and do daily the exercise of the dumbbell, I flatter myself that the stone is kept from augmenting so much as it might otherwise do, and that I may still continue to find it tolerable. People who live long, who will drink of the cup of life to the very bottom, must expect to meet with some of the usual dregs; and when I reflect on the number of terrible maladies human nature is subject to, I think myself favored in having to my share only the stone and the gout.—Smyth 9:560. (1787.)

As the roughness of the stone lacerates a little the neck of the bladder, I find that, when the urine happens to be sharp, I have much pain in making water and frequent urgencies. For relief under this circumstance, I take, going to bed, the bigness of a pigeon's egg of jelly of blackberries. The recipe for making it is enclosed. While I continue to do this every night, I am generally easy the day following, making water pretty freely, and with long intervals.—Smyth 9:622. (1787.)

The stone I have being a large one, as I find by the weight it falls with when I turn in bed, I have no hope of its being dissoluble by any medicine.—Smyth 10:1. (1789.)

I thank you much for your intimations of the virtues of hemlock, but I have tried so many things with so little effect that I am quite discouraged, and have no longer any faith in remedies for the stone. The palliating system is what I am now fixed in. Opium gives me ease when I am attacked by pain, and by the use of it I still make life at least tolerable. Not being able, however, to bear sitting to write, I now make use of the hand of one of my grandsons, dictating to him from my bed.—Smyth 10:49. (1789.)

FRANKLIN (Benjamin), Description of Final Journey from Europe.—When I was at Passy, I could not bear a wheel carriage; and, being discouraged in my project of descending the Seine in a boat, by the difficulties and tediousness of its navigation in so dry a season, I accepted the offer of one of the King's litters, carried by large mules, which brought me well, though in walking slowly to Havre. Thence I went over in a packet-boat to Southampton, where I stayed four days, till the ship came for me to Spithead. Several of my London friends came there to see me, particularly the good bishop of St. Asaph and family, who stayed with me to the last. In short, I am now so well as to think it possible that I may once more have the pleasure of seeing you both perhaps at New York.—Smyth 9:466. (1785.)

FRANKLIN (Benjamin), Elected to Office in His 80th Year.—I had on my return some right, as you observe, to expect repose; and it was my intention to avoid all public business. But I had not firmness enough to resist the unanimous desire of my country folks; and I find myself harnessed again in their service for another year. They engrossed the prime of my life. They have eaten my flesh and seem resolved now to pick my bones.—Smyth 9:476. (1785.)

FRANKLIN (Benjamin), Suffers from a Skin Disease for 14 Years.—You may remember the cutaneous malady I formerly complained of, and for which you and Dr. Pringle favored me with prescriptions and advice. It vexed me near fourteen years, and was, the beginning of this year, as bad as ever, covering almost my whole body, except my face and hands; when a fit of the gout came on, without very much pain, but a swelling in both feet, which at last appeared also in both knees, and then in my hands. As these swellings increased and extended, the other malady diminished, and at length disappeared entirely. Those swellings have some time since begun to fall, and are now almost gone; perhaps the cutaneous disease may return, or perhaps it is worn out. I may

hereafter let you know what happens. I am on the whole much weaker than when it began to leave me.—Smyth 9:670. (1788.)

FRANKLIN (Benjamin), Uses Opium to Endure Pain in His Last Year.—I have a long time been afflicted with almost constant and grievous pain, to combat which I have been obliged to have recourse to opium, which indeed has afforded me some ease from time to time, but then it has taken away my appetite and so impeded my digestion that I am become totally emaciated, and little remains of me but a skeleton covered with a skin.—Smyth 10:35. (1789.)

FRANKLIN (Mrs. Deborah), Commended for Punctual Correspondence.—I received your kind letters of March 12 and April 24. I think you are the most punctual of all my correspondents; and it is often a particular satisfaction to me to hear from you when I have no letter from anyone else.—Smyth 5:527. (1770.)

FRANKLIN (Mrs. Deborah), Franklin Advises His Wife Concerning Her Health.—I am glad to hear you continue so well, and that the pains in your side and head have left you. Eat light foods, such as fowls, mutton, etc., and but little beef or bacon, avoid strong tea, and use what exercise you can; by these means you will preserve your health better, and be less subject to lowness of spirits.—Smyth 5:620. (1772.)

FRANKLIN (Francis Folger), Died at Age 4.—All who have seen my grandson agree with you in their accounts of his being an uncommonly fine boy, which brings often afresh to my mind the idea of my son Franky, though now dead thirty-six years, whom I have seldom since seen equalled in everything, and whom to this day I cannot think of without a sigh.—Smyth 5:349. (1772.)

FRANKLIN (Josiah), Father of Benjamin.—Josiah, my father, married young, and carried his wife with three children into New England, about 1682. The conventicles [religious meetings] having been forbidden by law, and frequently disturbed, induced some considerable men of his acquaintance to remove to that country, and he was prevailed with to accompany them thither, where they expected to enjoy their mode of religion with freedom. By the same wife he had four children more born there, and by a second wife ten more, in all seventeen; of which I remember thirteen sitting at one time at his table, who all grew up to be men and women, and married; I was the youngest son, and the youngest child but two, and was born in Boston, New England.—Autobiography. Smyth 1:231. (1771.)

FRANKLIN (Temple), Criticism Following His Father's Arrest as a Tory.—I am surprised to hear that my grandson, Temple Franklin, being with me should be an objection against me, and that there is a cabal for removing him. Methinks it is rather some merit that I have rescued a valuable young man from the danger of

being a Tory, and fixed him in honest republican Whig principles; as I think, from the integrity of his disposition, his industry, his early sagacity, and uncommon abilities for business, he may in time become of great service to his country. It is enough that I have lost my *son;* would they add my *grandson?* An old man of seventy, I undertook a winter voyage at the command of the Congress, and for the public service, with no other attendant to take care of me. I am continued here in a foreign country, where, if I am sick, his filial attention comforts me, and, if I die, I have a child to close my eyes and take care of my remains. His dutiful behavior towards me, and his diligence and fidelity in business, are both pleasing and useful to me. His conduct, as my private secretary, has been unexceptionable, and I am confident the Congress will never think of separating us.—Smyth 7:345. (1779.)

FRANKLIN (William), Not to Expect a Large Inheritance.—Will is now nineteen years of age, a tall proper youth, and much of a beau. He acquired a habit of idleness on the expedition, but begins of late to apply himself to business, and I hope will become an industrious man. He imagined his father had got enough for him but I have assured him that I intend to spend what little I have myself, if it please God that I live long enough; and, as he by no means wants sense, he can see by my going on, that I am like to be as good as my word.—Smyth 3:4. (1750.)

FRANKLIN (William), Marriage and Appointment as Governor of New Jersey.—I thank you for your kind congratulations on my son's promotion and marriage. If he makes a good governor, and a good husband (as I hope he will, for I know he has good principles and good disposition), those events will both of them give me continual pleasure.—Smyth 4:183. (1762.)

FRANKLIN (William), Warmly Received as the New Governor of New Jersey.—I have received your favors of October 20th and November 1st by my son, who is safely arrived with my new daughter. I thank you for your friendly congratulations on his promotion. I am just returned from a journey I made through his government, and had the pleasure of seeing him received everywhere with the utmost respect and even affection of all ranks of people.—Smyth 4:196. (1763.)

FRANKLIN (William), Commended by Lord Dartmouth.—Lord Dartmouth came to town last week, and had his first levee on Wednesday, at which I attended. He received me very politely in his room, only Secretary Pownall present, expressing some regret that he happened to be from home when I was near him in the country, where he had hoped for the pleasure of seeing me, etc. I said I was happy to see his lordship in his present situation, in which for the good of both countries I hoped he would long continue; and I begged leave to recommend my son to his protection, who, says I, is one of

your governors in America. The secretary then put in, *And a very good governor he is.* Yes, says my lord, he has been a good governor, and has kept his province in good order during times of difficulty.—Smyth 5:444. (1772.)

FRANKLIN (William), Loyal to Crown.—From a long and thorough consideration of the subject, I am indeed of opinion that the Parliament has no right to make any law whatever, binding on the Colonies; that the King, and not the King, Lords, and Commons collectively, is their sovereign; and that the King, with their respective parliaments, is their only legislator. I know your sentiments differ from mine on these subjects. You are a thorough government man, which I do not wonder at, nor do I aim at converting you. I only wish you to act uprightly and steadily, avoiding that duplicity which...adds contempt to indignation.—Smyth 6:144. (1773.)

FRANKLIN (William), Advised by Father to Resign as Governor of New Jersey.—I don't understand it as any favor to me or to you, the being continued in an office by which, with all your prudence, you cannot avoid running behindhand if you live suitably to your station. While you are in it I know you will execute it with fidelity to your master, but I think independence more honorable than any service, and that in the state of American affairs which from the present arbitrary measures is likely soon to take place, you will find yourself in no comfortable situation, and perhaps wish you had soon disengaged yourself.—Smyth 6:399. (1775.)

FRANKLIN (William), Taken Prisoner as Tory Governor.—You inquire what is become of my son, the Governor of New Jersey. As he adhered to the party of the King, his people took him prisoner, and sent him under a guard into Connecticut, where he continues; but is allowed a district of some miles to ride about, upon his parole of honor not to quit that country. I have with me here his son, a youth of about 17, whom I brought with me partly to finish his education, having a great affection for him, and partly to have his assistance as a secretary, in which capacity he is very serviceable to me.—Smyth 7:51. (1777.)

FRANKLIN (William), Causes His Father Sorrow by Turning Tory.—I received your letter of the 22nd past, and am glad to find that you desire to revive the affectionate intercourse that formerly existed between us. It will be very agreeable to me; indeed, nothing has ever hurt me so much and affected me with such keen sensations as to find myself deserted in old age by my only son; and not only deserted, but to find him taking up arms against me in a cause wherein my good fame, fortune and life were all at stake. You conceived, you say, that your duty to your king and regard for your country required this. I ought not to blame you for differing in sentiment with me in public affairs. We are men, all subject to errors.

Our opinions are not in our own power; they are formed and governed much by circumstances that are often as inexplicable as they are irresistible. Your situation was such that few would have censured your remaining neuter, *though there are natural duties which precede political ones, and cannot be extinguished by them.* This is a disagreeable subject. I drop it.—Smyth 9:252. (1784.)

FREE TRADE, In the United States.—The general principle in America being for a free trade with all the world, and to leave every one of their merchants at liberty to prosecute it as he may judge most for his advantage, I do not think...companies can be established there with any exclusive rights or privileges.—Smyth 8:107. (1780.)

FREE TRADE, The Less Restrained, the Better.—In general I would only observe that commerce, consisting in a mutual exchange of the necessities and conveniences of life, the more free and unrestrained it is, the more it flourishes; and the happier are all the nations concerned in it. Most of the restraints put upon it in different countries seem to have been the projects of particulars for their private interest, under pretense of public good.—Smyth 9:19. (1783.)

FREE TRADE, Better for All Nations.—I have seen so much embarrassment and so little advantage in all the restraining and compulsive systems, that I feel myself strongly inclined to believe that a state which leaves all her ports open to all the world upon equal terms will, by that means, have foreign commodities cheaper, sell its own productions dearer, and be on the whole the most prosperous.—Smyth 9:63. (1783.)

FREEDOM, Motto Proposed by Franklin for National Seal.— Rebellion to tyrants is obedience to God.—Carl Van Doren, ed., *Benjamin Franklin's Autobiographical Writings* (New York: The Viking Press, 1945), p. 413. (1775.)

FREEMASONS, Beliefs Not Inconsistent with Religion.—As to the Freemasons, I know no way of giving my mother a better account of them than she seems to have at present, since it is not allowed that women should be admitted into that secret society. She has, I must confess, on that account some reason to be displeased with it; but for anything else, I must entreat her to suspend her judgment till she is better informed, unless she will believe me when I assure her that they are in general a very harmless sort of people, and have no principles or practices that are inconsistent with religion and good manners.—Smyth 2:215. (1738.)

FREEMEN, Advantages of.—I am of opinion that almost any profession a man has been educated in is preferable to an office held at pleasure, as rendering him more independent, more a freeman, and less subject to the caprices of superiors.—Smyth 5:376. (1772.)

FREEMEN, Franklin Describes a Basic Whig Concept Concerning.— *Every man* of the commonalty (excepting infants, insane persons, and criminals) is, of common right, and by the laws of God, *a freeman,* and entitled to the free enjoyment of *liberty.*—Smyth 10:130.

FREEMEN OF PENNSYLVANIA, Authorized to Organize a Militia. —With the advice and consent of the representatives of the freemen of the said province in General Assembly met, and by the authority of the same, . . . from and after the publication of this act, it shall and may be lawful for the freemen of this province to form themselves into companies, as heretofore they have used in time of war without law, and for each company, by majority of votes in the way of ballot, to choose its own officers.— Smyth 3:299. (1755.)

FRENCH AND INDIAN WAR, Colonies Paid Their Share.—Every year during the war, requisitions were made by the crown on the colonies for raising money and men; . . . accordingly they made more extraordinary efforts, in proportion to their abilities, than Britain did; . . . they raised, paid, and clothed, for five or six years, near twenty-five thousand men, besides providing for other services, as building forts, equipping guard ships, paying transports, etc. And that this was more than their fair proportion is not merely an opinion of mine, but was the judgment of government here [in England], in full knowledge of all the facts; for the then ministry, to make the burden more equal, recommended the case to Parliament and obtained a reimbursement to the Americans of about two hundred thousand pounds sterling every year, which amounted only to about two fifths of their expense; and [a] great part of the rest lies still a load of debt upon them, heavy taxes on all their estates, real and personal, being laid by acts of their assemblies to discharge it, and yet will not discharge it in many years.—Smyth 4:401. (1766.)

FRENCH REVOLUTION, Franklin's Anxiety Concerning.—The revolution in France is truly surprising. I sincerely wish it may end in establishing a good constitution for that country. The mischiefs and troubles it suffers in the operation, however, give me great concern.—Smyth 10:50. (1789.)

The convulsions in France are attended with some disagreeable circumstances; but if by the struggle she obtains and secures for the nation its future liberty, and a good constitution, a few years' enjoyment of those blessings will amply repair all the damages their acquisition may have occasioned. God grant that not only the love of liberty, but a thorough knowledge of the rights of man, may pervade all the nations of the earth, so that a philosopher may set his foot anywhere on its surface and say, "This is my country."—Smyth 10:72. (1789.)

FRENCH TROOPS, Did Not Plunder Civilians as Did the British.—In [the British army's 1755] march...from their landing till they got beyond the settlements, they had plundered and stripped the inhabitants, totally ruining some poor families, besides insulting, abusing, and confining the people if they remonstrated.... How different was the conduct of our French friends in 1781, who, during a march through the most inhabited part of our country 'from Rhode Island to Virginia, near seven hundred miles, occasioned not the smallest complaint for the loss of a pig, a chicken, or even an apple.—Autobiography. Smyth 1:403. (1788.)

FRIENDS, Business Dealings with.—I think it contributes to the duration of friendship to keep *its* accounts and those of business distinct and separate, and that as exact justice in pounds, shillings, and pence should be observed between friends as between strangers.—Smyth 6:37. (1773.)

FRIENDS, More Difficult to Forgive Than Enemies.—You have perfectly forgiven the royalists, and you seem to wonder that we should still retain any resentment against them for their joining with the savages to burn our houses, and murder and scalp our friends, our wives, and our children. I forget who it was that said, "We are commanded to forgive our enemies, but we are nowhere commanded to forgive our friends." Certain it is, however, that atrocious injuries done to us by our friends are naturally more deeply resented than the same done by enemies.—Smyth 10:65. (1789.)

FRIENDSHIP, How to Perpetuate from Generation to Generation.—But as the ancients who knew not how to write had a method of transmitting friendships to posterity—the guest who had been hospitably entertained in a strange country breaking a stick with every one who did him a kindness; and the producing such a tally at any time afterwards, by a descendant of the host, to a son or grandson of the guest, was understood as a good claim to special regard besides the common rights of hospitality—so if this letter should happen to be preserved, your son may produce it to mine as an evidence of the good will that once subsisted between their fathers, as an acknowledgement of the obligations you laid me under by your many civilities when I was in your country and a claim to all the returns due from me if I had been living.—Smyth 5:249. (1770.)

FRUGALITY, Makes Money.—When you incline to have new clothes, look first well over the old ones, and see if you cannot shift with them another year, either by scouring, mending, or even patching if necessary. Remember, a patch on your coat and money in your pocket is better and more creditable than a writ on your back and no money to take it off.—Smyth 3:294. (1755.)

FRUGALITY, Key to Success in Business.—So much for industry, my friends, and attention to one's own business; but to these we must add *frugality* if we would make our *industry* more certainly successful. A man may, if he knows not how to save as he gets, *keep his nose all his life to the grindstone,* and die not worth a *groat* at last. *A fat kitchen makes a lean will,* as *Poor Richard* says; and

Many estates are spent in the getting,
Since women for tea forsook spinning and
knitting,
And men for punch forsook hewing and
splitting.

If you would be wealthy, says he, in another almanack, *think of saving as well as of getting.* The Indies have not made Spain rich, because her outgoes are greater than her incomes.—Smyth 3:412. (1757.)

FRUGALITY, America and England Compared.—The manner of living in America is in general more simple and less expensive than in England. Plain tables, plain clothing, plain furniture in houses, few carriages of pleasure. In America an expensive appearance hurts credit, and is therefore avoided; in England it is often put on with a view of gaining credit, and continued to ruin. In *public* affairs, the difference is still greater. In England salaries of officers and emoluments of office are enormous.—Smyth 7:3. (1777.)

FRUGALITY, A Virtue of Great Worth.—Frugality is an enriching virtue; a virtue I never could acquire in myself; but I was once lucky enough to find it in a wife, who thereby became a fortune to me. Do you possess it? If you do, and I were 20 years younger, I would give your father 1,000 guineas for you.—Smyth 8:459. (1782.)

FUTURE LIFE, Justice in.—I cannot therefore part with the comfortable belief of a divine Providence; and the more I see the impossibility, from the number and extent of his crimes, of giving equivalent punishment to a wicked man in this life, the more I am convinced of a future state, in which all that here appears to be wrong shall be set right, all that is crooked made straight.—Smyth 8:562. (1782.)

FUTURE LIFE. See also IMMORTALITY.

G

GAGE (General Thomas), Colonial Reaction to His Attack on Concord.—The Congress met at a time when all minds were so exasperated by the perfidy of General Gage, and his attack on the country people, that propositions of attempting an accommodation were not much relished; and it has been with difficulty that we have carried another humble petition to the Crown, to give Britain one more chance, one opportunity more, of recovering the friendship of the colonies; which, however, I think she has not sense enough to embrace, and so I conclude she has lost them forever.—Smyth 6:408. (1775.)

GEOGRAPHY, Basic to a Good Education.—Geography, by reading with maps, and being required to point out the places *where* the greatest actions were done, to give their old and new names, with the bounds, situation, extent of the countries concerned, etc.—Smyth 2:392. (1749.)

GEOLOGY, Franklin's Theory of.—The present polar and equatorial diameters differing from each other near ten leagues, it is easy to conceive, in case some power should shift the axis gradually and place it in the present equator, and make the new equator pass through the present poles, what a sinking of the waters would happen in the present equatorial regions, and what a rising in the present polar regions; so that vast tracts would be discovered that now are under water, and others covered that are now dry, the water rising and sinking in the different extremes near five leagues. Such an operation as this, possibly, occasioned much of Europe, and among the rest this mountain of Passy, on which I live, and which is composed of limestone, rock and seashells, to be abandoned by the sea, and to change its ancient climate, which seems to have been a hot one.

The globe being now become a permanent magnet, we are perhaps safe from any future change of its axis. But we are still subject to the accidents on the surface which are occasioned by a wave in the internal ponderous fluid; and such a wave is producible by the sudden violent explosion you mention, happening from the junction of water and fire under the earth, which not only lifts the incumbent earth that is over the explosion, but impressing with the same force the fluid under it, creates a wave that may run a thousand leagues, lifting and thereby shaking successively all the countries under which it passes.—Smyth 8:600. (1782.)

GEORGE III, His Offenses Against Americans.—If, then, a king declares his people to be out of his protection;

If he violates and deprives them of their constitutional rights;

If he wages war against them;

If he plunders their merchants, ravages their coasts, burns their towns, and destroys their lives;

If he hires foreign mercenaries to help him in their destruction;

If he engages savages to murder their defenseless farmers, women, and children;

If he cruelly forces such of his subjects as fall into his hands to bear arms against their country, and become executioners of their friends and brethren;

If he sells others of them into bondage, in Africa and the East Indies;

If he excites domestic insurrections among their servants, and encourages servants to murder their masters—

Does not so atrocious a conduct towards his subjects dissolve their allegiance?—Smyth 8:445. (1782.)

GERMAN MERCENARIES, Forced into Service.—The conduct of those princes of Germany who have sold the blood of their people has subjected them to the contempt and odium of all Europe. The Prince of Anspach, whose recruits mutinied and refused to march, was obliged to disarm and fetter them, and drive them to the seaside by the help of his guards, himself attending in person. In his return he was publicly hooted by mobs through every town he passed in Holland, with all sorts of reproachful epithets.—Smyth 7:57. (1777.)

GERMANS, Early Immigrants to Pennsylvania.—As few of the English understand the German language, and so cannot address them either from the press or pulpit, it is almost impossible to remove any prejudices they may entertain. Their own clergy have very little influence over their people, who seem to take an uncommon pleasure in abusing and discharging the minister on every trivial occasion. Not being used to liberty, they know not how to make a modest use of it. And as Kolben in his history says of the young Hottentots, that they are not esteemed men until they have shown their manhood by *beating their mothers*, so these seem not to think themselves free till they can feel their liberty in abusing and insulting their teachers. Thus they are under no restraint from ecclesiastical government; they behave, however, submissively enough at present to the civil government, which I wish they may continue to do, for I remember when they modestly declined intermeddling in our elections, but now they come in droves and carry all before them, except in one or two counties.

Few of their children in the country learn English. They import many books from Germany; and of the six printing houses in the province, two are entirely German, two half-German [and] half-English, and but two entirely English. They have one German newspaper, and one half-German. Advertisements, intended to be general, are now printed in Dutch and English. The signs in our streets have inscriptions in both languages, and in some places only German.

They begin of late to make all their bonds and other legal instruments in their own language, which (though I think it ought not to be) are allowed good in our courts, where the German business so increases that there is continued need of interpreters; and I suppose in a few years they will also be necessary in the Assembly, to tell one half of our legislators what the other half say.

In short, unless the stream of their importation could be turned from this to other colonies, as you very judiciously propose, they will soon so outnumber us that all the advantages we have will not, in my opinion, be able to preserve our language, and even our government will become precarious. The French, who watch all advantages, are now themselves making a German settlement, back of us, in the Illinois country, and by means of these Germans they may in time come to an understanding with ours; and, indeed, in the last war, our Germans showed a general disposition that seemed to bode us no good. For when the English, who were not Quakers, alarmed by the danger arising from the defenseless state of our country, entered unanimously into an association, and within this government and the lower counties raised, armed, and disciplined near ten thousand men, the Germans, except a very few in proportion to their number, refused to engage in it, giving out, one amongst another, and even in print, that if they were quiet the French, should they take the country, would not molest them; at the same time abusing the Philadelphians for fitting out privateers against the enemy, and representing the trouble, hazard, and expense of defending the province as a greater inconvenience than any that might be expected from a change of government.

Yet I am not entirely for refusing to admit them into our colonies. All that seems to me necessary is to distribute them more equally, mix them with the English, establish English schools where they are now too thickly settled, and take some care to prevent the practice, lately fallen into by some of the ship owners, of sweeping the German jails to make up the number of their passengers. I say I am not against the admission of Germans in general, for they have their virtues. Their industry and frugality are exemplary. They are excellent husbandmen, and contribute greatly to the improvement of a country.—Smyth 3:139. (1753.)

GOD, Why He Should Be Worshiped.—I think it seems required of me, and my duty as a man, to pay divine regards to *something.*

I conceive, then, that the *infinite* has created many beings or Gods, vastly superior to man, who can better conceive his perfections than we, and return him a more rational and glorious praise....

It may be that these created Gods are immortal; or it may be that after many ages, they are changed, and others supply their places.

Howbeit, I conceive that each of these is exceeding wise and good, and very powerful; and that each has made for himself one glorious sun,

Franklin in 1777 (age 71). Engraving by Augustin de Saint Aubin, after a drawing by Charles Nicolas Cochin.

attended with a beautiful and admirable system of planets.

It is that particular wise and good God who is the author and owner of our system that I propose for the object of my praise and adoration.

For I conceive that he has in himself some of the passions he has planted in us, and that, since he has given us reason whereby we are capable of observing his wisdom in the creation, he is not above caring for us, being pleased with our praise, and offended when we slight him or neglect his glory.

I conceive for many reasons that he is a *good Being;* and as I should be happy to have so wise, good, and powerful a Being my friend, let me consider in what manner I shall make myself most acceptable to him.—Smyth 2:93. (1728.)

GOD, Created the World for Human Happiness.—And since he [God] has created many things which seem purely designed for the delight of man, I believe he is not offended when he sees his children solace themselves in any manner of pleasant exercises and innocent delights; and I think no pleasure innocent that is to man hurtful.

I *love* him therefore for his goodness, and I *adore* him for his wisdom.—Smyth 2:94. (1728.)

GOD, How to Worship.—Being mindful that before I address the Deity my soul ought to be calm and serene, free from passion and perturbation, or otherwise elevated with rational joy and pleasure, I ought to use a countenance that expresses a filial respect, with a kind of smiling, that signifies inward joy, and satisfaction, and admiration.—Smyth 2:94. (1728.)

GOD, Trust in.—Having taken care to do *what appears to be for the best,* we must submit to God's providence, which orders all things really for the best.—Smyth 3:103. (1752.)

GOD, Franklin's Confidence in Love and Kindness of.—That Being who gave me existence, and through almost threescore years has been continually showering his favors upon me, whose very chastisements have been blessings to me; can I doubt that he loves me? And, if he loves me, can I doubt that he will go on to take care of me, not only here but hereafter? This to some may seem presumption; to me it appears the best grounded hope: hope of the future, built on experience of the past.—Smyth 4:248. (1764.)

GOD, Has Favored America's Just Cause.—We have had a hard struggle, but the Almighty has favored the just cause; and I join most heartily with you in your prayers that he may perfect his work, and establish freedom in the new world as an asylum for those of the old, who deserve it.—Smyth 7:301. (1779.)

GOD. See also RELIGION.

GOD'S JUDGMENT, Not Feared by Franklin.—You conjure me in the name of the omniscient and just God before whom I must appear, and by my hopes of future fame, to consider if some expedient cannot be found to put a stop to the desolation of America and prevent the miseries of a general war. As I am conscious of having taken every step in my power to prevent the breach, and no one to widen it, I can appear cheerfully before that God, fearing nothing from his justice in this particular, though I have much occasion for his mercy in many others. As to my future fame, I am content to rest it on my past and present conduct, without seeking an addition to it in the crooked, dark paths you propose to me, where I should most certainly lose it. This your solemn address would therefore have been more properly made to your sovereign and his venal Parliament. He and they, who wickedly began and madly continue a war for the desolation of America, are alone accountable for the consequences.—Smyth 7:166. (1778.)

GOVERNMENT, Why So Economical in Early America.—The expense of our civil government we have always borne, and can easily bear, because it is small. A virtuous and laborious people may be cheaply governed. Determining, as we do, to have no offices of profit, nor any sinecures or useless appointments, so common in ancient or corrupted states, we can govern ourselves a year for the sum you [Englishmen] pay in a single department, or for what one jobbing contractor, by the favor of a minister, can cheat you out of in a single article.—Smyth 7:168. (1778.)

H

HANDWRITING, Essential to Teach Good.—All should be taught to write a *fair hand*, and swift, as that is useful to all.—Smyth 2:391. (1749.)

HAPPINESS, Attained Only Through Virtue.—Next to the praise resulting from and due to his [God's] wisdom, I believe he is pleased and delights in the happiness of those he has created; and since without virtue man can have no happiness in this world, I firmly believe he delights to see me virtuous, because he is pleased when he sees me happy.—Smyth 2:94. (1728.)

HAPPINESS, and Morality.—As the happiness or real good of men consists in right action, and right action cannot be produced without right opinion, it behoves us, above all things in this world, to take care that our opinions of things be according to the nature of things. The foundation of all virtue and happiness is thinking rightly. He who sees [that] an action is right, that is, naturally tending to good, and does it because of that tendency, he only is a moral man; and he alone is capable of that constant, durable, and invariable good.—Smyth 2:169. (1730.)

HAPPINESS, Internal Rather Than External.—Two of the former members of the Junto, you tell me, are departed this life, Potts and Parsons. Odd characters both of them. Parsons, a wise man that often acted foolishly; Potts, a wit that seldom acted wisely. If *enough* were the means to make a man happy, one had always the *means* of happiness without ever enjoying the *thing;* the other had always the *thing* without ever possessing the *means.* Parsons, even in his prosperity, always fretting; Potts, in the midst of his poverty, ever laughing. It seems, then, that happiness in this life rather depends on internals than externals; and that, besides the natural effects of wisdom and virtue, vice and folly, there is such a thing as a happy or an unhappy constitution.—Smyth 3:457. (1758.)

HAPPINESS, and Duty.—In fine, nothing can contribute to true happiness that is inconsistent with duty; nor can a course of action, conformable to it, be finally without an ample reward. For God governs; and he is *good.* I pray him to direct you; and, indeed, you will never be without his direction if you humbly ask it, and show yourself always ready to obey it.—Smyth 5:181. (1768.)

HAPPINESS, Rejoice in Success of Others.—Pray learn, if you have not already learned, like me, to be pleased with other people's pleasures, and happy with their happinesses, when none occur of your own.—Smyth 7:25. (1777.)

HARTLEY (David), Helps American Prisoners in England.—The subscription for the prisoners will have excellent effects in favor of Englishmen and of England. The Scotch subscription for raising troops to destroy us, though amounting to much greater sums, will not do their nation half so much good. If you have an opportunity, I wish you would express our respectful acknowledgments and thanks to your committee and contributors, whose benefactions will make our poor people as comfortable as possible.—Smyth 7:103. (1778.)

HEALTH, Rules for Good Health and Long Life.—Eat and drink such an exact quantity as the constitution of thy body allows of, in reference to the services of the mind.

They that study much ought not to eat so much as those that work hard, their digestion being not so good.

The exact quantity and quality, being found out, is to be kept to constantly.

Excess in all other things whatever, as well as in meat and drink, is also to be avoided.

Youth, age, and sick require a different quantity.

And so do those of contrary complexions; for that which is too much for a phlegmatic man is not sufficient for a choleric.

The measure of food ought to be (as much as possibly may be) exactly proportionable to the quality and condition of the stomach, because the stomach digests it.

That quantity that is sufficient, the stomach can perfectly concoct and digest, and it sufficeth the due nourishment of the body.

A greater quantity of some things may be eaten than of others, some being of lighter digestion than others.

The difficulty lies in finding out an exact measure; but eat for necessity, not pleasure, for lust knows not where necessity ends.

Would thou enjoy a long life, a healthy body, and a vigorous mind, and be acquainted also with the wonderful works of God, labor in the first place to bring thy appetite into subjection to reason.—Smyth 2:227. (1742.)

HILLSBOROUGH (Lord), Secretary to American Colonies.—His character is conceit, wrongheadedness, obstinacy, and passion. Those who would speak most favorably of him allow all this; they only add that he is an honest man, and means well. If that be true, as perhaps it may, I wish him a better place, where only honesty and well-meaning are required, and where his other qualities can do no harm. Had the war taken place, I have reason to believe he would have been removed.—Smyth 5:298. (1771.)

HILLSBOROUGH (Lord), Disliked by Colleagues.—One encouragement I have, the knowledge that he is not a whit better liked by his colleagues in the ministry than he is by me, that he cannot probably continue where he is much longer, and that he can scarce be succeeded by anybody who will not like me the better for his having been at variance with me.—Smyth 5:299. (1771.)

HILLSBOROUGH (Lord), Replaced by Lord Dartmouth.—At length we have got rid of Lord Hillsborough, and Lord Dartmouth takes his place, to the great satisfaction of all the friends of America.... You will hear it said among you, I suppose, that the interest of the Ohio planters has ousted him; but the truth is, what I wrote you long since, that all his brother ministers disliked him extremely, and wished for a fair occasion of tripping up his heels; so, seeing that he made a point of defeating our scheme, they made another of supporting it, on purpose to mortify him, which they knew his pride could not bear. I do not mean they would have done this if they had thought our proposal bad in itself, or his opposition well founded; but I believe, if he had been on good terms with them, they would not have differed with him for so small a matter. The King, too, was tired of him and of his administration, which had weakened the affection and respect of the colonies for a royal government, of which (I may say it to you) I used proper means from time to time that his Majesty should have due information and convincing proofs. More of this when I see you.—Smyth 5:410. (1772.)

Lord Hillsborough, mortified by the Committee of Council's approbation of our grant, in opposition to his report, has resigned. I believe when he offered to do so, he had such an opinion of his importance that he did not think it would be accepted; and that it would be thought prudent rather to set our grant aside than part with him. His colleagues in the ministry were all glad to get rid of him, and perhaps for this reason joined more readily in giving him that mortification. Lord Dartmouth succeeds him, who has much more favorable dispositions towards the colonies. He has heretofore expressed some personal regard for me, and I hope now to find our business with the Board more easy to transact.—Smyth 5:433. (1772.)

HILLSBOROUGH (Lord), Description of.—I know him to be as double and deceitful as any man I ever met with. But we have done with him, I hope, forever. His removal has, I believe, been meditated ever since the death of the Princess Dowager. For I recollect that on my complaining of him about that time to a friend at court, whom you may guess, he told me we Americans were represented by Hillsborough as an unquiet people, not easily satisfied with any ministry; that, however, it was thought too much occasion had been given us to dislike the present; and asked me whether, if he should be removed, I could name another likely to be more acceptable to us.—Smyth 5:413. (1772.)

HISTORY, Importance of Studying.—If the new *Universal History* were also read, it would give a *connected* idea of human affairs, so far as it goes, which should be followed by the best modern histories, particularly of our mother country; then of these colonies; which should be accompanied with observations on their rise, increase, use to *Great Britain*, encouragements, discouragements, etc., the means to make them flourish, secure their liberties, etc.—Smyth 2:394. (1749.)

Let them now begin to read *history*, after having got by heart a short table of the principal epochas in chronology. They may begin with Rollin's *Ancient and Roman Histories*, and proceed at proper hours as they go through the subsequent classes, with the best histories of our own nation and colonies. Let emulation be excited among the boys by giving, weekly, little prizes or other small encouragements to those who are able to give the best account of what they have read, as to times, places, names of persons, etc. This will make them read with attention, and imprint the history well in their memories.—Smyth 3:25. (1750.)

HOWE (Admiral Lord), Requests Franklin's Assistance.—The next morning I met Lord Howe, according to appointment.... He let me know that he was thought of to be sent commissioner for settling the differences in America; adding, with an excess of politeness, that sensible of his own unacquaintedness with the business, and of my knowledge and abilities, he could not think of undertaking it without me; but, with me, he should do it most readily; for he should found his expectations of success on my assistance. He therefore had desired this meeting to know my mind upon a proposition of my going with him in some shape or other, as a friend, an assistant, or secretary; that he was very sensible if he should be so happy as to effect anything valuable, it must be wholly owing to the advice and assistance I should afford him; that he should therefore make no scruple of giving me upon all occasions the full honor of it.—Smyth 6:384. (1775.)

HUMANE SOCIETY, Special Interest of Franklin.—I thank you for the pamphlet of the Humane Society. In return please to accept one of the same kind, which was published while I resided in France. If your Society have not hitherto seen it, it may possibly afford them useful hints.—Smyth 9:650. (1788.)

HUMILITY. See PRIDE.

HURRICANE, Miraculously Saved Americans from French Armada in 1746.—Your government [England] sent no fleet to protect us against the French under D'Anville. But they have been defeated by the hand of God.—Smyth 2:301. (1747.)

I

IDLENESS, Cause of Contention in Military.—This [Franklin's experience as a military commander on the Pennsylvania frontier in 1756] gave me occasion to observe that when men are employed, they are best contented; for on the days they worked they were good-natured and cheerful, and, with the consciousness of having done a good day's work, they spent the evening jollily; but on our idle days they were mutinous and quarrelsome, finding

fault with their pork, the bread, etc., and in continual ill humor. [This] put me in mind of a sea captain, whose rule it was to keep his men constantly at work; and, when his mate once told him that they had done everything, and there was nothing further to employ them about, "Oh," says he, "make them scour the anchor."—Autobiography. Smyth 1:410. (1788.)

IMMIGRANTS, Should Learn English.—The observation concerning the importation of *Germans* in too great numbers into *Pennsylvania* is, I believe, a very just one. This will in a few years become a *German* colony: instead of their learning our language, we must learn theirs, or live as in a foreign country.—Smyth 3:43. (1751.)

IMMORTALITY, Franklin's Religious Convictions Concerning.—We have lost a most dear and valuable relation. But it is the will of God and nature that these mortal bodies be laid aside when the soul is to enter into real life. This is rather an embryo state, a preparation for living. A man is not completely born until he be dead. Why then should we grieve that a new child is born among the immortals, a new member added to their happy society?

We are spirits. That bodies should be lent us, while they can afford us pleasure, assist us in acquiring knowledge, or in doing good to our fellow creatures, is a kind and benevolent act of God. When they become unfit for these purposes, and afford us pain instead of pleasure, instead of an aid become an encumbrance, and answer none of the intentions for which they were given, it is equally kind and benevolent that a way is provided by which we may get rid of them. Death is that way. We ourselves, in some cases, prudently choose a partial death. A mangled painful limb, which cannot be restored, we willingly cut off. He who plucks out a tooth parts with it freely, since the pain goes with it; and he who quits the whole body parts at once with all pains and possibilities of pains and diseases which it was liable to, or capable of making him suffer.

Our friend and we were invited abroad on a party of pleasure, which is to last forever. His chair was ready first, and he is gone before us. We could not all conveniently start together; and why should you and I be grieved at this, since we are soon to follow, and know where to find him?—Smyth 3:329. (1756.)

IMMORTALITY, Irrational to Deny Future Life.—I say that, when I see nothing annihilated, and not even a drop of water wasted, I cannot suspect the annihilation of souls, or believe that he [God] will suffer the daily waste of millions of minds ready made that now exist, and put himself to the continual trouble of making new ones. Thus finding myself to exist in the world, I believe I shall, in some shape or other, always exist; and, with all the inconveniences human life is liable to, I shall not object to a new edition of mine; hoping, however, that the *errata* of the last may be corrected.— Smyth 9:334. (1785.)

IMMORTALITY. See also FUTURE LIFE.

INDEPENDENCE, English Policies Provoking.—I think it likely that no thorough redress of grievances will be afforded to America this session. This may inflame matters still more in that country; farther rash measures there may create more resentment here, that may produce not merely ill-advised and useless dissolutions of their assemblies, as last year, but attempts to dissolve their constitutions; more troops may be sent over, which will create more uneasiness; to justify the measures of government, your writers will revile the Americans in your newspapers, as they have already begun to do, treating them as miscreants, rogues, dastards, rebels, etc., which will tend farther to alienate the minds of the people here from them, and diminish their affections to this country. Possibly, too, some of their warm patriots may be distracted enough to expose themselves by some mad action to be sent for hither; and government here be indiscreet enough to hang them, on the act of Henry the Eighth.

Mutual provocations will thus go on to complete the separation; and instead of that cordial affection that once and so long existed, and that harmony so suitable to the circumstances and so necessary to the happiness, strength, safety, and welfare of both countries; an implacable malice and mutual hatred, such as we now see subsisting between the Spaniards and Portuguese, the Genoese and Corsicans, from the same original misconduct in the superior governments, will take place; the sameness of nation, the similarity of religion, manners, and language not in the least preventing in our case, more than it did in theirs.—Smyth 5:244. (1769.)

INDEPENDENCE, Franklin Anticipates Sequence of Events Leading to.—I think one may clearly see, in the system of customs to be exacted in America by act of Parliament, the seeds sown of a total disunion of the two countries, though, as yet, that event may be at a considerable distance. The course and natural progress seems to be, first, the appointment of needy men as officers, for others do not care to leave England; then, their necessities make them rapacious, their office makes them proud and insolent, their insolence and rapacity make them odious, and, being conscious that they are hated, they become malicious; their malice urges them to a continual abuse of the inhabitants in their letters to administration, representing them as disaffected and rebellious, and (to encourage the use of severity) as weak, divided, timid, and cowardly. Government believes all [and] thinks it necessary to support and countenance its officers; their quarreling with the people is deemed a mark and consequence of their fidelity; they are therefore more highly rewarded, and this makes their conduct still more insolent and provoking.

The resentment of the people will, at times and on particular incidents, burst into outrages and violence upon such officers, and this naturally draws down severity and acts of further oppression from hence. The more the people are dissatisfied, the more vigor will be thought necessary; severe punishments will be inflicted to terrify; rights and privileges will be abolished; greater force will then be required to secure execution and submission; the expense will become enormous; it will then be thought proper, by fresh exactions, to make the people defray it; thence, the British nation and government will become odious, the subjection to it will be deemed no longer tolerable; war ensues, and the bloody struggle will end in absolute slavery to America, or ruin to Britain by the loss of her colonies; the latter most probable, from America's growing strength and magnitude.

But, as the whole empire must, in either case, be greatly weakened, I cannot but wish to see much patience and the utmost discretion in our general conduct, that the fatal period may be postponed, and that, whenever this catastrophe shall happen, it may appear to all mankind that the fault has not been ours.—Smyth 5:317. (1771.)

INDEPENDENCE, Foreshadowed.—That the possibility of [a] separation may always exist, [England takes] special care the provinces are never incorporated with the mother country; that they do not enjoy the same common rights, the same privileges in commerce; and that they are governed by *severer* laws, all of [*Britain's*] *enacting*, without allowing them any share in the choice of the legislators.—Smyth 6:127. (1773.)

INDEPENDENCE, No Safety Without.—We have no safety but in our independence; with that we shall be respected, and soon become great and happy. Without it, we shall be despised, lose all our friends, and then either be cruelly oppressed by the King, who hates and is incapable of forgiving us, or, having all that nation's enemies for ours, shall sink with it.—Smyth 8:558. (1782.)

INDIANS, French Policy More Effective Than British Bungling.— The *French* know the power and importance of the *Six Nations*, and spare no artifice, pains, or expense to gain them to their interest. By their priests they have converted many to their religion, and these have openly espoused their cause. The rest appear irresolute which part to take, no persuasions, though enforced with costly presents, having yet been able to engage them generally on our side, though we had numerous forces on their borders, ready to second and support them. What then may be expected now those forces are, by orders from the Crown, to be disbanded; when our boasted expedition is laid aside, through want (as it may appear to them) either of strength or courage; when they see that the *French* and their *Indians*, boldly and with impunity, ravage the frontiers of *New York* and scalp the inhabitants; when those few *Indians* that engaged with us

against the *French* are left exposed to their resentment; when they consider these things, is there no danger that, through disgust at our usage, joined with fear of the *French* power and greater confidence in their promises and protection than in ours, they may be wholly gained over by our enemies, and join in the war against us? If such should be the case, which God forbid, how soon may the mischief spread to our frontier counties? And what may we expect to be the consequence but deserting of plantations, ruin, bloodshed, and confusion!—Smyth 2:341. (1747.)

INDIANS, Importance of Securing Friendship.—Securing the friendship of the *Indians* is of the greatest consequence to these colonies; and...the surest means of doing it are to regulate the *Indian* trade so as to convince them, by experience, that they may have the best and cheapest goods, and the fairest dealing from the *English*, and to unite the several [colonial] governments so as to form a strength that the *Indians* may depend on for protection in case of a rupture with the *French*, or apprehend great danger from if they should break with us.—Smyth 3:40. (1751.)

INDIANS, Need to Provide Technical Aid to.—Everyone must approve the proposal of encouraging a number of sober discreet smiths to reside among the *Indians*. They would doubtless be of great service. The whole subsistence of *Indians* depends on keeping their guns in order; and if they are obliged to make a journey of two or three hundred miles to an English settlement to get a lock mended, it may, besides the trouble, occasion the loss of their hunting season. They are people that think much of their temporal, but little of their spiritual, interests; and therefore, as he would be a most useful and necessary man to them, a smith is more likely to influence them than a Jesuit.—Smyth 3:44. (1751.)

INDIANS, Human Incentives to Work Easily Lost.—The proneness of human nature to a life of ease, of freedom from care and labor, appears strongly in the little success that has hitherto attended every attempt to civilize our American Indians. In their present way of living, almost all their wants are supplied by the spontaneous productions of nature, with the addition of very little labor, if hunting and fishing may indeed be called labor, where game is so plenty. They visit us frequently, and see the advantages that arts, sciences, and compact societies procure us. They are not deficient in natural understanding; and yet they have never shown any inclination to change their manner of life for ours, or to learn any of our arts. When an Indian child has been brought up among us, taught our language, and habituated to our customs, yet, if he goes to see his relatives, and makes one Indian ramble with them, there is no persuading him ever to return. And that this is not natural to them merely as Indians, but as men, is plain from this, that when white persons, of either sex, have been taken prisoners by the Indians, and

lived awhile with them, though ransomed by their friends, and treated with all imaginable tenderness to prevail with them to stay among the English, yet in a short time they become disgusted with our manner of life, and the care and pains that are necessary to support it, and take the first opportunity of escaping again into the woods, from whence there is no redeeming them.—Smyth 3:136. (1753.)

INDIANS, Friendly Indians Massacred by Renegade Whites.— In December, we had two insurrections of the back inhabitants of our province, by whom twenty poor Indians were murdered that had, from the first settlement of the province, lived among us, under the protection of our government. This gave me a good deal of employment; for, as the rioters threatened farther mischief, and their actions seemed to be approved by an increasing party, I wrote a pamphlet entitled "A Narrative, etc." (which I think I sent you) to strengthen the hands of our weak government, by rendering the proceedings of the rioters unpopular and odious. * This had a good effect; and afterwards, when a great body of them with arms marched towards the capital, in defiance of the government, with an avowed resolution to put to death 140 Indian converts then under its protection, I formed an association at the Governor's request for his and their defense, we having no militia. Near 1000 of the citizens accordingly took arms; Governor Penn made my house for some time his headquarters, and did everything by my advice, so that, for about forty-eight hours, I was a very great man, as I had been once some years before in a time of public danger. But the fighting face we put on and the reasonings we used with the insurgents (for I went at the request of the Governor and council, with three others, to meet and discourse them) having turned them back and restored quiet to the city, I became a less man than ever; for I had, by these transactions, made myself many enemies among the populace; and the Governor (with whose family our public disputes had long placed me in an unfriendly light, and the services I had lately rendered him not being of the kind that make a man acceptable), thinking it a favorable opportunity, joined the whole weight of the proprietary interest to get me out of the Assembly; which was accordingly effected at the last election, by a majority of about 25 in 4000 voters.—Smyth 4:375. (1765.)

*For full text of the pamphlet, see Smyth 4:289–314.

INDIANS, Fictitious "Supplement to the Boston Independent Chronicle"* Written to Dramatize Atrocities.—(For full text, see Smyth 8:437–47. [1782.])

* Albert Henry Smyth wrote: "Upon his private press at Passy, Franklin printed a pretended 'Supplement to the *Boston Independent Chronicle*.' In typography, style, advertisements, and all things it simulated exactly the appearance of a Boston newspaper. The barbarities committed by the Indian allies of Great Britain suggested this savage piece of satire, which rises to the height of Swift. After a ghastly invoice of eight packages containing a thousand scalps, alleged to have been taken by the Seneca Indians in English pay, and 'cured, dried, hooped, and painted with all the Indian triumphal marks,' in order to be transmitted to England, the article quotes an imaginary letter from an Indian chief to Governor Haldimand. 'Father, we wish you to send these scalps over the water to the great King, that he may regard them and be refreshed; and that he may see our faithfulness in destroying his enemies, and be convinced that his presents have not been made to ungrateful people.' Franklin sent copies of the 'Supplement' to [Charles W.F.] Dumas in Holland, saying: 'Enclosed I send you a few copies of a paper that places in a striking light the English barbarities in America, particularly those committed by the savages at their instigation. The form may perhaps not be genuine but the substance is truth.... Make any use of them you may think proper to shame your Anglomanes, but do not let it be known through whose hand they came.'"—Smyth 1:174.

INDIANS, A Chief Replies to Offer of Virginia to Educate Indians.— Our ideas of this kind of education happen not to be the same with yours. We have had some experience of it. Several of our young people were formerly brought up at the colleges of the northern provinces; they were instructed in all your sciences; but, when they came back to us, they were bad runners, ignorant of every means of living in the woods, unable to bear either cold or hunger, knew neither how to build a cabin, take a deer, or kill an enemy, spoke our language imperfectly, were therefore neither fit for hunters, warriors, nor counsellors; they were totally good for nothing. We are, however, not the less obliged by your kind offer, though we decline accepting it; and, to show our grateful sense of it, if the gentlemen of Virginia will send us a dozen of their sons, we will take great care of their education, instruct them in all we know, and make *men* of them.—Smyth 10:98. (1784.)

INDIANS, Exemplary Conduct in Their Councils.—Having frequent occasions to hold public councils, they have acquired great order and decency in conducting them. The old men sit in the foremost ranks, the warriors in the next, and the women and children in the hindmost. The business of the women is to take exact notice of what passes, imprint it in their memories (for they have no writing), and communicate it to their children. They are the records of the council, and they preserve traditions of the stipulations in treaties 100 years back; which, when we compare with our writings, we always find exact. He that would speak rises. The rest observe a profound silence. When he has finished and sits down, they leave him five or six minutes to recollect, that if he has omitted anything he intended to say, or has anything to add, he may rise again and deliver it. To interrupt another, even in common conversation, is reckoned

highly indecent. How different this is from the conduct of a polite British House of Commons, where scarce a day passes without some confusion that makes the Speaker hoarse in calling *to order;* and how different from the mode of conversation in many polite companies of Europe, where, if you do not deliver your sentence with great rapidity, you are cut off in the middle of it by the impatient loquacity of those you converse with, and never suffered to finish it!—Smyth 10:99. (1784.)

INDIANS, Discord Often the Fault of Whites.—During the course of a long life in which I have made observations on public affairs, it has appeared to me that almost every war between the Indians and whites has been occasioned by some injustice of the latter towards the former. It is indeed extremely imprudent in us to quarrel with them for their lands, as they are generally willing to sell, and sell such good bargains; and a war with them is so mischievous to us, in unsettling frequently a great part of our frontier and reducing the inhabitants to poverty and distress, and is besides so expensive, that it is much cheaper, as well as more honest, to buy their lands than to take them by force.—Smyth 9:625. (1787.)

INDIANS, Peace Council.—The year following [i.e., in 1753], a treaty being to be held with the Indians at Carlisle, the Governor sent a message to the [Pennsylvania] House, proposing that they should nominate some of their members, to be joined with some members of [the Governor's] council, as commissioners for that purpose. The House named the speaker (Mr. Norris) and myself; and, being commissioned, we went to Carlisle, and met the Indians accordingly.

As those people are extremely apt to get drunk, and, when so, are very quarrelsome and disorderly, we strictly forbad the selling any liquor to them; and when they complained of this restriction, we told them that if they would continue sober during the treaty, we would give them plenty of rum when business was over. They promised this, and they kept their promise, because they could get no liquor, and the treaty was conducted very orderly, and concluded to mutual satisfaction. They then claimed and received the rum; this was in the afternoon; they were near one hundred men, women, and children, and were lodged in temporary cabins, built in the form of a square, just without the town. In the evening, hearing a great noise among them, the commissioners walked out to see what was the matter. We found they had made a great bonfire in the middle of the square; they were all drunk, men and women, quarreling and fighting. Their dark-colored bodies, half naked, seen only by the gloomy light of the bonfire, running after and beating one another with firebrands, accompanied by their horrid yelling, formed a scene the most resembling our ideas of hell that could well be imagined; there was no appeasing the tumult, and we retired to our lodging. At midnight a number of them came thundering at our door, demanding more rum, of which we took no notice.—Autobiography. Smyth 1:375. (1788.)

INDUSTRY, America and England Compared.—The same circumstances that give a private man credit ought to have, and will have, their weight with lenders of money to *public bodies* or to nations. . . . Every man in America is employed; the greatest number in cultivating their own lands, the rest in handicrafts, navigation, and commerce. An idle man there is a rarity; idleness and inutility is a character of disgrace. In England the quantity of that character is immense; fashion has spread it far and wide. Hence the embarrassment of private fortunes, and the daily bankruptcies, arising from the universal fondness for appearance and expensive pleasures; and hence, in some degree, the mismanagement of their public business; for habits of business, and ability in it, are acquired only by practice; and, where universal dissipation and the perpetual pursuit of amusement are the mode, the youths who are educated in it can rarely afterwards acquire that patient attention and close application to affairs which are so necessary to a statesman charged with the care of national welfare. Hence their frequent errors in policy, and hence the weariness at public councils, and the backwardness in going to them, the constant unwillingness to engage in any measure that requires thought and consideration, and the readiness for postponing every new proposition; which postponing is therefore the only part of business that they come to be expert in, an expertness produced necessarily by so much daily practice. Whereas, in America, men bred to close employment in their private affairs attend with habitual ease to those of the public when engaged in them, and nothing fails through negligence.—Smyth 7:2. (1777.)

INDUSTRY, Hard Worker Gains Rewards.—*Industry need not wish,* as *Poor Richard* says, *and he that lives upon hope will die fasting. There are no gains without pains; then help hands, for I have no lands,* or if I have, they are smartly taxed. And, as *Poor Richard* likewise observes, *He that hath a trade hath an estate; and he that hath a calling, hath an office of profit and honor;* but then the *trade* must be worked at, and the *calling* well followed, or neither the *estate* nor the *office* will enable us to pay our taxes. If we are industrious, we shall never starve; for, as *Poor Richard* says, *At the working man's house hunger looks in, but dares not enter.* Nor will the bailiff or the constable enter, for *Industry pays debts, while despair increaseth them,* says *Poor Richard.* What though you have found no treasure, nor has any rich relation left you a legacy, *Diligence is the mother of good luck,* as *Poor Richard* says, *and God gives all things to industry. Then plow deep, while sluggards sleep, and you shall have corn to sell and to keep,* says Poor Dick. Work while it is called today, for you know not how much you may be hindered tomorrow, which makes *Poor Richard* say, *One today is worth two tomorrows,* and farther, *have you somewhat to do tomorrow, do it today.* If you were a servant, would you not be ashamed that a good master should catch you

idle? Are you then your own master, *be ashamed to catch yourself idle.*—Smyth 3:410. (1757.)

INDUSTRY AND FRUGALITY, Franklin's Formula for Acquiring Wealth.—In short, the way to wealth, if you desire it, is as plain as the way to market. It depends chiefly on two words, *industry* and *frugality;* that is, waste neither *time* nor *money,* but make the best use of both. Without industry and frugality nothing will do, and with them everything. He that gets all he can honestly, and saves all he gets (necessary expenses excepted), will certainly become *rich,* if that Being who governs the world, to whom all should look for a blessing on their honest endeavors, doth not, in his wise providence, otherwise determine.—Smyth 2:372. (1749.)

INFALLIBILITY, Different Ways of Saying It.—Steele says that the difference between the Church of Rome and the Church of England on that point is only this: that the one pretends to be *infallible,* and the other to be *never in the wrong.* In this latter sense, we are Church of England men, though few of us confess it, and express it so naturally and frankly as a certain great lady here who said, "I don't know how it happens, but I meet with nobody, except myself, that is *always* in the right."—Smyth 9:180. (1784.)

INFLATION, A Tax.—They [Congress] hoped, notwithstanding its quantity, to have kept up the value of their paper [money]. In this they were mistaken. It depreciated gradually. But this depreciation, though in some circumstances inconvenient, has had the general good and great effect of operating as a tax, and perhaps the most equal of all taxes, since it depreciated in the hands of the holders of money, and thereby taxed them in proportion to the sums they held and the time they held it, which generally is in proportion to men's wealth. Thus, after having done its business, the paper is reduced to the sixtieth part of its original value.—Smyth 8:151. (1780.)

INHERITANCE, How Children Can Build Their Own.—Remember, for your encouragement in good economy, that whatever a child saves of its parents' money *will be its own another day.*—Smyth 6:32. (1773.)

INTERNATIONAL LAW, Should Protect Farmers and Fishermen in Wartime.—I even wish for the sake of humanity that the law of nations may be further improved by determining that, even in time of war, all those kinds of people who are employed in procuring subsistence for the species, or in exchanging the necessaries or conveniences of life which are for the common benefit of mankind, such as husbandmen on their lands, fishermen in their barks, and traders in unarmed vessels, shall be permitted to prosecute their several innocent and useful employments without interruption or molestation, and nothing taken from them, even when wanted by an enemy, but on paying a fair price for the same.—Smyth 8:82. (1780.)

INTERNATIONAL LAW, Proposed Rule to Protect Domestic Production.—All fishermen, all cultivators of the earth, and all artisans or manufacturers unarmed and inhabiting unfortified towns, villages, or places, who labor for the common subsistence and benefit of mankind, and peaceably follow their respective employments, shall be allowed to continue the same, and shall not be molested by the armed force of the enemy in whose power by the events of the war they may happen to fall; but, if anything is necessary to be taken from them, for the use of such armed force, the same shall be paid for at a reasonable price.—Smyth 9:7. (1783.)

INVENTIONS. See PROGRESS OF MAN.

INVENTORS, Initially Distrusted.—The treatment your friend has met with is so common that no man who knows what the world is, and ever has been, should expect to escape it. There are everywhere a number of people who, being totally destitute of any inventive faculty themselves, do not readily conceive that others may possess it. They think of inventions as of miracles; there might be such formerly, but they are ceased. With these, everyone who offers a new invention is deemed a pretender. He had it from some other country, or from some book. A man of *their own acquaintance,* one who has no more sense than themselves, could not possibly, in their opinion, have been the inventor of anything.—Smyth 3:258. (1755.)

INVENTORS, Victims of Envy and Jealousy.—Thus, through envy, jealousy, and the vanity of competitors for fame, the origin of many of the most extraordinary inventions, though produced within but a few centuries past, is involved in doubt and uncertainty. We scarce know to whom we are indebted for the *compass*, and for *spectacles*, nor have even *paper* and *printing*, that record everything else, been able to preserve with certainty the name and reputation of their inventors.—Smyth 3:259. (1755.)

IRELAND, Poverty in.—Ireland is itself a poor country; ... the appearances of general extreme poverty among the lower people are amazing. They live in wretched hovels of mud and straw, are clothed in rags, and subsist chiefly on potatoes.... In short, the chief exports of Ireland seem to be pinched off the backs and out of the bellies of the miserable inhabitants. But schemes are now under consideration among the humane gentry to provide some means of mending, if possible, their present wretched condition.—Smyth 5:368. (1772.)

IRISH, Desire to Migrate to America.—I received some time since a letter from a person at Belfast, informing me that a great number of people in those parts were desirous of going to settle in America, if passports could be obtained for them and their effects, and referring me to you for further information.—Smyth 7:331. (1779.)

IRISH, Deprived of Rights by English.—I admire the spirit with which I see the Irish are at length determined to claim some share of that freedom of commerce which is the right of all mankind, but which they have been so long deprived of by the abominable selfishness of

their fellow subjects. To enjoy all the advantages of the climate, soil, and situation in which God and nature have placed us is as clear a right as that of breathing, and can never be justly taken from men but as a punishment for some atrocious crime.

The English have long seemed to think it a right which none could have but themselves. Their injustice has already cost them dear, and, if persisted in, will be their ruin.—Smyth 7:332. (1779.)

IRISH, Political Influence Through Mass Migration.—It is a fact that the Irish emigrants and their children are now in possession of the government in Pennsylvania, by their majority in the Assembly as well as of a great part of the territory; and I remember well the first ship that brought any of them over.—Smyth 9:264. (1784.)

J

JACKSON (Captain William), Reprimanded by Franklin.—These superior airs you give yourself, young gentleman, of reproof to me, and reminding me of my duty, do not become you, whose special department and employ in public affairs, of which you are so vain, is but of yesterday, and would never have existed but by my concurrence, and would have ended in ... disgrace if I had not supported your enormous purchases by accepting your drafts.—Smyth 8:283. (1781.)

JOHNSON (The Reverend Samuel), Franklin Seeks to Induce Him to Come to Philadelphia.—I imagine you will receive something considerable yearly, arising from marriages and christenings in the best families, etc., not to mention presents that are not unfrequent from a wealthy people to a minister they like; and though the whole may not amount to more than a due support, yet I think it will be a comfortable one. And when you are well settled in a church of your own, your son may be qualified by years and experience to succeed you in the academy; or if you rather choose to continue in the academy, your son might probably be fixed in the church.—Smyth 3:14. (1750.)

JOHNSON (Dr. Samuel), Dictionary.—I must desire you to send us Johnson's dictionary, and one for the academy.—Smyth 3:263. (1755.)

JUDGES, Problem of Removal.—Judges should be free from all influence; and therefore whenever government here will grant commissions to able and honest judges during good behavior, the assemblies will settle permanent and ample salaries on them during their commissions. But at present they have no other means of getting rid of an ignorant or an unjust judge (and some of scandalous characters have, they say, been sometimes sent them) but by starving him out.—Smyth 5:84. (1768.)

JUNTO, Questions for Each Meeting.—(For full text, see Smyth 2:88-90. [1728.])

JUNTO, Franklin Encourages Its Continuance.—You tell me you sometimes visit the ancient Junto. I wish you would do it oftener. I know they all love and respect you, and regret your absenting yourself so much. People are apt to grow strange, and not understand one another so well, when they meet but seldom. Since we have held that club till we are grown grey together, let us hold it out to the end. For my own part, I find I love company, chat, a laugh, a glass, and even a song, as well as ever; and at the same time relish better than I used to do the grave observations and wise sentences of old men's conversation; so that I am sure the Junto will be still as agreeable to me as it ever has been. I therefore hope it will not be discontinued as long as we are able to crawl together.—Smyth 4:96. (1761.)

JUNTO, One of the First and Oldest Service Clubs in America.—I wish you would continue to meet the Junto, notwithstanding that some effects of our public political misunderstandings may sometimes appear there. 'Tis now perhaps one of the *oldest* clubs, as I think it was formerly one of the *best*, in the King's dominions. It wants but about two years of forty since it was established. We loved and still love one another; we are grown grey together, and yet it is too early to part. Let us sit till the evening of life is spent. The last hours are always the most joyous. When we can stay no longer, 'tis time enough then to bid each other good night, separate, and go quietly to bed.—Smyth 4:386. (1765.)

JUSTICE OF THE PEACE, Franklin's Experience as.—The office of justice of the peace I tried a little [in 1751 or 1752] by attending a few courts and sitting on the bench to hear causes; but finding that more knowledge of the common law than I possessed was necessary to act in that station with credit, I gradually withdrew from it, excusing myself by my being obliged to attend the higher duties of legislator in the Assembly.—Autobiography. Smyth 1:375. (1788.)

K

KINDNESS, A Debt to God and Humanity.—For my own part, when I am employed in serving others, I do not look upon myslf as conferring favors, but as paying debts. In my travels, and since my settlement, I have received much kindness from men, to whom I shall never have any opportunity of making the least direct return. And numberless mercies from God, who is infinitely above being benefited by our services. Those kindnesses from men I can therefore only return on their fellow men; and I can only show my gratitude for these mercies from God by a readiness to help his other children and my brethren.— Smyth 3:144. (1753.)

KINDNESS TO OTHERS, Merely Repayment to God.—It rejoices me to learn that you are freer than you used to be from the headache and that pain in your side. I am likewise in perfect health. God is very good to us both in many respects. Let us enjoy his favors with a thankful and cheerful heart; and, as we can make no direct return to him, show our sense of his goodness to us by continuing to do good to our fellow creatures, without regarding the returns they make us, whether good

Franklin in 1777 (age 71). Bust by Jean Jacques Caffieri.

or bad. For they are all his children, though they may sometimes be our enemies.—Smyth 4:383. (1765.)

L

LABOR, More Should Be Spent Producing Necessities.—It has been computed by some political arithmetician that, if every man and woman would work for four hours each day on something useful, that labor would produce sufficient to procure all the necessaries and comforts of life, want and misery would be banished out of the world, and the rest of the 24 hours might be leisure and pleasure. What occasions, then, so much want and misery? It is the employment of men and women in works that produce neither the necessaries nor conveniences of life, who, with those who do nothing, consume the necessaries raised by the laborious.—Smyth 9:246. (1784.)

LAFAYETTE (Marquis de), American Admiration for.—The Congress, sensible of your merit towards the United States, but unable adequately to reward it, determined to present you with a sword, as a small mark of their grateful acknowledgment. They directed it to be ornamented with suitable devices. Some of the principal actions of the war, in which you distinguished yourself by your bravery and conduct, are therefore represented upon it. These, with a few emblematic figures, all admirably well executed, make its principal value. By the help of the exquisite artists France affords, I find it easy to express everything but the sense we have of your worth and our obligations to you. For this, figures and even words are found insufficient.—Smyth 7:370. (1779.)

LAFAYETTE (Marquis de), and Benedict Arnold.—Your friends have heard of your being gone against the traitor Arnold, and are anxious to hear of your success, and that you have brought him to justice. Enclosed is a copy of a letter from his agent in England, by which the price of his treason may be guessed at. Judas sold only one man, Arnold three millions. Judas got for his one man 30 pieces of silver, Arnold not a halfpenny a head. A

miserable bargainer! Especially when one considers the quantity of infamy he has acquired to himself, and entailed on his family.—Smyth 8:250. (1781.) See also ARNOLD (Benedict).

LANGUAGES. See FOREIGN LANGUAGES.

LAWS, Same Law for All the People.—I say, when you are sure you have got a good principle, stick to it, and carry it through. I hear it is said, that though it was *necessary and right* for the ministry to advise a prohibition of the exportation of corn, yet it was *contrary to law;* and also, that though it was *contrary to law* for the mob to obstruct wagons, yet it was *necessary and right.* Just the same thing to a tittle. Now they tell me, an act of indemnity ought to pass in favor of the ministry, to secure them from the consequences of having acted illegally. If so, pass another in favor of the mob. Others say, some of the mob ought to be hanged, by the way of example. If so, —but I say no more than I have said before, *when you are sure that you have a good principle, go through with it.*—Smyth 5:537. (1772.)

LAWS, Should Be Uniformly Administered.—The ordaining of laws in favor of *one* part of the nation, to the prejudice and oppression of *another,* is certainly the most erroneous and mistaken policy.—Smyth 6:290. (1774.)

LAWSUITS, Avoided by Franklin. —It will be a pleasure to me to find it so, that I may have no occasion to have recourse to the law, which is so disagreeable a thing for me that through the whole course of my life

I have never entered an action against any man.—Smyth 4:152. (1762.)

LAZINESS, Great Waste.—Idleness taxes many of us much more [than ordinary taxes of the government], if we reckon all that is spent in absolute sloth, or doing of nothing, with that which is spent in idle employments or amusements that amount to nothing. *Sloth, like rust, consumes faster than labor wears; while the used key is always bright,* as Poor Richard says. *But dost thou love life, then do not squander time, for that's the stuff life is made of,* as Poor Richard says. How much more than is necessary do we spend in sleep, forgetting that *the sleeping fox catches no poultry,* and that *there will be sleeping enough in the grave,* as Poor Richard says.—Smyth 3:409. (1757.)

LEADERS, When Corrupt Endanger All.—Through the dissensions of our leaders, through *mistaken principles of religion,* joined with a love of worldly power, on the one hand; through *pride, envy,* and *implacable resentment* on the other; our lives, our families and little fortunes, dear to us as any great man's can be to him, are to remain continually exposed to destruction, from an enterprising, cruel, now well-informed, and by success encouraged, enemy. It seems as if Heaven, justly displeased at our growing wickedness, and determined to punish this once-favored land, had suffered our chiefs to engage in these foolish and mischievous contentions, for *little posts and paltry distinctions,* that our hands might be bound up, our understandings darkened and misled, and every means of our security neglected. It seems as if our greatest men, our *cives nobilissimi* of both parties, had *sworn the ruin of the country,* and *invited* the French, our *most inveterate enemy, to destroy it.*—Smyth 2:350. (1747.)

LEADERS, Should Set the Example.—I am glad to hear that you have frequent opportunities of preaching among the great. If you can gain them to a good and exemplary life, wonderful changes will follow in the manners of the lower ranks; for *ad exemplum regis,* etc. On this principle, Confucius, the famous Eastern reformer, proceeded. When he saw his country sunk in vice, and wickedness of all kinds triumphant, he applied himself first to the grandees; and having, by his doctrine, won *them* to the cause of virtue, the commons followed in multitudes.—Smyth 2:377. (1749.)

LEE (Arthur), Accused of Deceptive Tactics.—There is a style in some of your letters, I observe it particularly in the last, whereby superior merit is assumed to yourself in point of care and attention to business, and blame is insinuated on your colleagues, without making yourself accountable by a direct charge, of negligence or unfaithfulness, which has the appearance of being as artful as it is unkind. In the present case I think the insinuation groundless.—Smyth 7:129. (1778.)

LEE (Arthur), Rebuked by Franklin.—It is true I have omitted answering some of your letters. I do not like to answer angry letters. I hate disputes. I am old, cannot have long to live, have much to do and no time for altercation. If I have often received and borne your magisterial snubbings and rebukes without reply, ascribe it to the right causes my concern for the honor and success of our mission, which would be hurt by our quarreling, my love of peace, my respect for your good qualities, and my pity of your sick mind, which is forever tormenting itself with its jealousies, suspicions, and fancies that others mean you ill, wrong you, or fail in respect for you. If you do not cure yourself of this temper it will end in insanity, of which it is the symptomatic forerunner, as I have seen in several instances. God preserve you from so terrible an evil; and for his sake, pray suffer me to live in quiet.—Smyth 7:132. (1778.)

LEE (Arthur), Charges Against Franklin.—I am very easy about the efforts Messrs. Lee and Izard are using, as you tell me, to injure me on that side of the water. I trust in the justice of the Congress, that they will listen to no accusations against me that I have not first been acquainted with, and had an opportunity of answering. I know those gentlemen have plenty of ill will to me, though I have never done to either of them the smallest injury, or given the least just cause of offense. But my too great reputation, and the general good will this people have for me, and the respect they show me, and even the compliments they make me, all grieve those unhappy gentlemen; unhappy indeed in their tempers, and in the dark, uncomfortable passions of jealousy, anger,

suspicion, envy, and malice.—Smyth 7:344. (1779.)

I thank you for your intelligence of the state of affairs at home and for the extracts of Mr. Lee's philippics against me. Such they were intended, but when I consider him as the most malicious enemy I ever had (though without the smallest cause), that he shows so clear his abundant desire to accuse and defame me, and that all his charges are so frivolous, so ill founded, and amount to so little, I esteem them rather as panegyrics upon me and satires against himself.—Smyth 8:51. (1780.)

LEE (William), Disappointed Franklin.—No demand has been made on me by Mr. William Lee. I do not know where he is; and I think he did so little for the 3,000 guineas he received that he may wait without much inconvenience for the addition.—Smyth 8:402. (1782.)

LEISURE, Time for Doing Something Useful.—Methinks I hear some of you say, *Must a man afford himself no leisure?* I will tell thee, my friend, what *Poor Richard* says, *Employ thy time well, if thou meanest to gain leisure; and, since thou art not sure of a minute, throw not away an hour.* Leisure is time for doing something useful; this leisure the diligent man will obtain, but the lazy man never; so that, as *Poor Richard* says, *A life of leisure and a life of laziness are two things.* Do you imagine that sloth will afford you more comfort than labor? No, for as *Poor Richards* says, *Trouble springs from idleness, and grievous toil from needless ease. Many without labor would live by their wits only, but they break for want of stock.*

Whereas industry gives comfort, and plenty, and respect: *Fly pleasures, and they'll follow you. The diligent spinner has a large shift; and now I have a sheep and a cow, everybody bids me good morrow.*—Smyth 3:411. (1757.)

LIBERTY, Do Not Bargain Away for Security.—They who can give up essential liberty to obtain a little temporary safety deserve neither liberty nor safety.—Smyth 6:382. (1775.)

LIBERTY, In America, Inspires All Mankind.—Establishing the liberties of America will not only make that people happy, but will have some effect in diminishing the misery of those who in other parts of the world groan under despotism, by rendering it more circumspect and inducing it to govern with a lighter hand.—Smyth 8:416. (1782.)

LIBERTY, Franklin Hoped the Flame of Freedom in Europe Would Purify but Not Destroy.—I hope the fire of liberty, which you mention as spreading itself over Europe, will act upon the inestimable rights of man, as common fire does upon gold; purify without destroying them; so that a lover of liberty may find *a country* in any part of Christendom.—Smyth 10:63. (1789.)

LIBERTY. See also FREEDOM.

LIGHTNING, Drawn from the Clouds in Europe Before Franklin Did It in Philadelphia.—What gave my book the more sudden and general celebrity was the success of one of its proposed experiments, made [in 1752] by Messrs. Dalibard and de Lor at Marly, for drawing lightning from the clouds. This engaged the public attention everywhere. M. de Lor, who had an apparatus for experimental philosophy, and lectured in that branch of science, undertook to repeat what he called the *Philadelphia Experiments;* and, after they were performed before the king and court, all the curious of Paris flocked to see them. I will not swell this narrative with an account of that capital experiment, nor of the infinite pleasure I received in the success of a similar one I made soon after with a kite at Philadelphia, as both are to be found in the histories of electricity.—Autobiography. Smyth 1:420. (1788.)

LIGHTNING RODS, A Contribution of Franklin.—May not the knowledge of this power of points be of use to mankind, in preserving houses, churches, ships, etc., from the stroke of lightning, by directing us to fix, on the highest parts of those edifices, upright rods of iron made sharp as a needle, and gilt to prevent rusting, and from the foot of those rods a wire down the outside of the building into the ground, or down round one of the shrouds of a ship, and down her side till it reaches the water? Would not these pointed rods probably draw the electrical fire silently out of a cloud before it came nigh enough to strike, and thereby secure us from that most sudden and terrible mischief?—Smyth 2:437. (1749.)

LIGHTNING RODS, How to Construct and Install.—Prepare a steel rod five or six feet long, half an inch thick at its biggest end, and tapering to a sharp point; which point should be gilt to prevent its rusting. Let the big end of the rod have a strong eye or ring of half an inch diameter. Fix this rod upright to the chimney or highest part of the house, by means of staples, so as it may be kept steady. Let the pointed end be upwards, and rise three or four feet above the chimney or building that the rod is fixed to. Drive into the ground an iron rod of about an inch diameter, and ten or twelve feet long, that has also an eye or ring in its upper end. It is best that the rod should be at some distance from the foundation of the building, not nearer than ten feet if your ground will allow so much. Then take as much length of iron rod of about half an inch diameter as will reach from the eye in the rod above to that in the rod below; and fasten it securely to those rods, by passing its ends through the rings, and bending those ends till they likewise form rings.

This length of rod may either be in one or several pieces. If in several, let the ends of the pieces be also well hooked to each other. Then close and cover every joint with lead.— Smyth 4:127. (1762.)

LIGHTNING RODS, Not Considered Desirable in England.—You seem to think highly of the importance of this discovery, as do many others on our side of the water. Here it is very little regarded; so little, that though it is now seven or eight years since it was made public, I have not heard of a single house as yet attempted to be secured by it. It is true the mischiefs done by lightning are not so frequent here as with us, and those who calculate chances may perhaps find that not

one death (or the destruction of one house) in a hundred thousand happens from that cause, and that therefore it is scarce worthwhile to be at any expense to guard against it.—Smyth 4:147. (1762.)

LIGHTNING RODS, Effectiveness of.—A small quantity of metal is found able to conduct a great quantity of this [electrical] fluid. A wire no bigger than a goose quill has been known to conduct (with safety to the building as far as the wire was continued) a quantity of lightning that did prodigious damage both above and below it; and probably larger rods are not necessary, though it is common in America to make them of half an inch, some of three quarters, or an inch diameter.

The rod may be fastened to the wall, chimney, etc., with staples of iron. The lightning will not leave the rod (a good conductor) to pass into the wall (a bad conductor) through those staples. It would rather, if any were in the wall, pass out of it into the rod to get more readily by that conductor into the earth.—Smyth 5:58. (1767.)

LITERACY, Exceptionally High in America.—All the new books and pamphlets worth reading, that are published here [in England], in a few weeks are transmitted and found there, where there is not a man or woman born in the country but what can read; and it must, I think, be a pleasing reflection to those who write, either for the benefit of the present age or of posterity, to find their audience increasing with the increase of our colonies.—Smyth 5:209. (1769.)

LODGING, On the Frontier.—As to our lodging, it is on real featherbeds in warm blankets and much more comfortable than when we lodged at our inn the first night after we left home; for the woman being about to put very damp sheets on the bed, we desired her to air them first; half an hour afterwards, she told us the bed was ready, and the sheets *well aired*. I got into bed, but jumped out immediately, finding them as cold as death, and partly frozen. She had *aired* them indeed, but it was out upon the hedge. I was forced to wrap myself up in my great coat and woolen trousers. Everything else about the bed was shockingly dirty.—Smyth 3:324. (1756.)

LONDON, Life in.—Your kind advice about getting a chariot, I had taken some time before; for I found that every time I walked out I got fresh cold; and the hackney coaches at this end of the town, where most people keep their own, are the worst in the whole city, miserable, dirty, broken, shabby things, unfit to go into when dressed clean, and such as one would be ashamed to get out of at any gentleman's door. As to burning wood, it would answer no end, unless one would furnish all one's neighbors and whole city with the same. The whole town is one great smoky house, and every street a chimney, the air full of floating sea coal soot, and you never get a sweet breath of what is pure without riding some miles for it into the country.—Smyth 3:431. (1758.)

LOUDOUN (Lord), Franklin Pleased with Him at First.—Lord Loudoun arrived last week. I have had the honor of several conferences with him on our American affairs, and am extremely pleased with him. I think there cannot be a fitter person for the service he is engaged in.—Smyth 3:341. (1756.)

LOUDOUN (Lord), Declined to Pay Money Due Franklin.—There is a balance not very large due to me on my account of wagons and forage supplied to General Braddock. I presented the account to his Lordship, who had it examined and compared with the vouchers; and, on report made to him that it was right, ordered a warrant to be drawn for the payment. But before he signed it, he sent for me, told me that as the money became due before his time, he had rather not mix it in his accounts, if it would be the same thing to me to receive it in England. He believed it a fair and just account, and as such would represent it home, so that I should meet with no difficulty in getting it paid there. I agreed to his Lordship's proposal, and the warrant was laid aside.—Smyth 3:399. (1757.)

LOUDOUN (Lord), Doubts Franklin's Generosity in Helping Without a Commission.—On my observing [to Lord Loudoun in 1757] that it was not right I should be put to any further trouble or delay in obtaining the money I had advanced, as I charged no commission for my service, "O, Sir," says he, "you must not think of persuading us that you are no gainer; we understand better those affairs, and know that everyone concerned in supplying the army finds means, in the doing it, to fill his own pockets." I assured him that was not my case, and that I had not pocketed a farthing; but he appeared clearly not to believe me; and, indeed, I have since learned that immense fortunes are often made in such employments. As to my balance, I am not paid it to this day.—Autobiography. Smyth 1:430. (1788.)

LOUIS XVI, Generosity to America.—You will also see in the contract fresh marks of the King's goodness towards us, in giving so long a term for payment, and forgiving the first year's interest. I hope the ravings of a certain mischievous madman here against France and its ministers, which I hear of every day, will not be regarded in America, so as to diminish in the least the happy union that has hitherto subsisted between the two nations, and which is indeed the solid foundation of our present importance in Europe.—Smyth 9:17. (1783.)

LOUIS XVI, Franklin Prays a Blessing for the King and His Family.—May I beg the favor of you, Sir [the Comte de Vergennes], to express respectfully for me to his Majesty the deep sense I have of all the inestimable benefits his goodness has conferred on my country, a sentiment that it will be the business of the little remainder of life now left me to impress equally on the minds of all my countrymen. My sincere prayers are that God may shower down his blessings on the King, the Queen, their children, and all the royal family to the latest generations!—Smyth 9:321. (1785.)

LOUISBOURG, American Colonists' Capture of.—Is there no merit in the ardor with which all degrees and ranks of people quit their private affairs and ranged themselves under the banners of their king, for the honor, safety, and advantage of their country? Is there no merit in the profound secrecy guarded by a whole people, so that the enemy had not the least intelligence of the design, till they saw the fleet of transports cover the sea before their port? Is there none in the indefatigable labor the troops went through during the siege, performing the duty both of men and horses; the hardship they patiently suffered for want of tents and other necessaries; the readiness with which they learned to move, direct, and manage cannon, raise batteries, and form approaches; the bravery with which they sustained sallies; and finally, in their consenting to stay and garrison the place after it was taken, absent from their business and families, till troops could be brought from England for that purpose, though they undertook the service on a promise of being discharged as soon as it was over, were unprovided for so long an absence, and actually suffered ten times more loss by mortal sickness through want of necessaries than they suffered from the arms of the enemy? The nation, however, had a sense of this undertaking different from the unkind one of this gentleman. At the treaty of peace, the possession of Louisbourg was found of great advantage to our affairs in Europe; and if the brave men that made the acquisition for us were not rewarded, at least they were praised.—Smyth 5:213. (1769.)

LUXURIES, Profitable to Postpone.—When you incline to buy chinaware, chintzes, *India* silks, or any other of their flimsy, slight manufactures, I would not be so hard with you as to insist on your absolutely *resolving against it;* all I advise is to *put it off* (as you do your repentance) *till another year;* and this in some respects may prevent an occasion of repentance.—Smyth 3:294. (1756.)

M

MAIL, Opened by British Officers.
—Though a Secretary of the State has the power of ordering letters to be opened, I think it is seldom used but in times of war, rebellion, or on some great public occasion, and I have heard they have means of copying the seal so exactly . . . that it cannot be discovered that the letters have been looked into.—Smyth 5:462. (1772.)

MALICE, Franklin's Reaction to.—As to the abuses I meet with, . . . I number them among my honors. One cannot behave so as to obtain the esteem of the wise and good without drawing on oneself at the same time the envy and malice of the foolish and wicked, and the latter is a testimony of the former. The best men have always had their share of this treatment, and the more of it in proportion to their different and greater degrees of merit. A man has therefore some reason to be ashamed of himself when he meets with none of it. . . . And in the

meantime such enemies do a man some good, while they think they are doing him harm, by fortifying the character they would destroy; for when he sees how readily imaginary faults and crimes are laid to his charge, he must be more apprehensive of the danger of committing real ones.—Labaree & Willcox 14:72. (1767.)

MALICE. See also CRITICISM; ENEMIES.

MANIFEST DESTINY, Of America.
—Providence seems by every means intent on making us a great people. May our virtues public and private grow with us, and be durable, that liberty, civil and religious, may be secured to our posterity, and to all from every part of the Old World that take refuge among us.—Smyth 6:88. (1773.)

MANIFEST DESTINY, American Freedom Part of God's Plan.—It is with great sincerity I join you in acknowledging and admiring the dispensations of Providence in our favor. America has only to be thankful, and to persevere. God will finish his work, and establish their freedom; and the lovers of liberty will flock from all parts of Europe with their fortunes to participate with us of that freedom, as soon as peace is restored.—Smyth 7:289. (1779.)

MANIFEST DESTINY. See also AMERICA.

MARRIAGE, Encouraged by America's Conditions.—Land being thus plenty in *America,* and so cheap as that a laboring man, that understands husbandry, can in a short time save money enough to purchase a piece of new land sufficient for a plantation, whereon he may subsist a family, such are not afraid to marry; for, if they even look far enough forward to consider how their children, when grown up, are to be provided for, they see that more land is to be had at rates equally easy, all circumstances considered.—Smyth 3:65. (1751.)

MARRIAGE, Advantages of Youthful Wedlock.—The character you give me of your bride (as it includes every qualification that in the married state conduces to mutual happiness) is an addition to [my] pleasure. Had you consulted me, as a friend, on the occasion, youth on both sides I should not have thought any objection. Indeed, from the matches that have fallen under my observation, I am rather inclined to think that early ones stand the best chance for happiness. The tempers and habits of young people are not yet become so stiff and uncomplying, as when more advanced in life; they form more easily to each other, and hence many occasions of disgust are removed. And if youth has less of that prudence that is necessary to conduct a family, yet the parents and elder friends of young married persons are generally at hand to afford their advice, which amply supplies that defect; and, by early marriage, youth is sooner formed to regular and useful life; and possibly some of those accidents, habits, or connections that might have injured either the constitution or the reputation, or both, are thereby

happily prevented.—Smyth 5:157. (1768.)

MARRIAGE, Husbands Should Treat Wives Respectfully.—Treat your wife always with respect; it will procure respect to you, not from her only but from all that observe it. Never use a slighting expression to her, even in jest, for slights in jest, after frequent bandyings, are apt to end in angry earnest.—Smyth 5:158. (1768.)

MARRIAGE, The Happiest State.—The married state is, after all our jokes, the happiest, being conformable to our natures. Man and woman have each of them qualities and tempers in which the other is deficient, and which in union contribute to the common felicity. Single and separate, they are not the complete human being; they are like the odd halves of scissors; they cannot answer the end of their formation.—Smyth 9:14. (1783.)

MARRIAGE. See also BACHELORS; FAMILY.

MASONS. See FREEMASONS.

MATTER, Conservation of, Anticipated by Franklin.—The power of man relative to matter seems limited to the dividing it, or mixing the various kinds of it, or changing its form and appearance by different compositions of it, but does not extend to the making or creating of new matter or annihilating the old. Thus, if fire be an original element or kind of matter, its quantity is fixed and permanent in the universe. We cannot destroy any part of it, or make addition to it; we can only separate it from that which confines it, and so set it at liberty, as when we put wood in a situation to be burnt; or transfer it from one solid to another, as when we make lime by burning stone, a part of the fire dislodged from the wood being left in the stone.— Smyth 9:228. (1784.)

MILITARY OFFICERS, Leadership Style of.—It is a common maxim that, without severe discipline, 'tis impossible to govern the licentious rabble of soldiery. I own, indeed, that if a commander finds he has not those qualities in him that will make him beloved by his people, he ought, by all means, to make use of such methods as will make them fear him, since one or the other (or both) is absolutely necessary; but Alexander and Caesar, those renowned generals, received more faithful service, and performed greater actions, by means of the love their soldiers bore them, than they could possibly have done if, instead of being beloved and respected, they had been hated and feared by those they commanded.—Smyth 2:56. (1726.)

MILITIA, Military Spirit Important. —I was glad to see that attention in the general Court to the improvement of the militia. A war may happen in which Britain, like Rome of old, may find so much to do for her own defense as to be unable to spare troops or ships for the protection of her colonies. A minister may arise so little our friend as to neglect that protection, or to permit invasions of our country, in order to make us cry out for help, and thereby furnish stronger pretense for maintaining a standing army among us. If we once lose our military spirit and supinely depend on an army of mercenaries for our defense, we shall become contemptible; despised both by friends and enemies, as neither our friendship nor our enmity will be deemed of any importance. As our country is not wealthy so as to afford much ready plunder, the temptation to a foreign invasion of us is the less, and I am persuaded that the name of a numerous well-disciplined militia would alone be almost sufficient to prevent any thoughts of attempting it.—Smyth 5:326. (1771.)

MINISTERS, Should Preach Without Salaries.—If Christian preachers had continued to teach as Christ and his apostles did, without salaries, and as the Quakers now do, I imagine tests would never have existed; for I think they were invented, not so much to secure religion itself, as the emoluments of it. When a religion is good, I conceive that it will support itself; and when it cannot support itself, and God does not take care to support, so that its professors are obliged to call for the help of the civil power, it is a sign, I apprehend, of its being a bad one.—Smyth 8:154. (1780.)

MISSISSIPPI RIVER, Refusal to Sell Rights on.—Poor as we are, yet, as I know we shall be rich, I would rather agree with [Spain] to buy at a great price the whole of their right on the Mississippi than sell a drop of its waters. A neighbor might as well ask me to sell my street door.— Smyth 8:144. (1780.)

MISSISSIPPI RIVER, Necessary for Peace.—I will only mention that my conjecture of that [English] court's design to coop us up within the Allegheny Mountains is now manifested. I hope Congress will insist on the Mississippi as the boundary, and the free navigation of the river, from which they could entirely exclude us.—Smyth 8:580. (1782.)

MOBOCRACY, In Pennsylvania.— The outrages committed by the frontier people are really amazing! But impunity for former riots has emboldened them. Rising in arms to destroy property, public and private, and insulting the King's troops and fort, is going great lengths indeed. If, in Mr. Chief's opinion, our resolves might be called rebellion, what does the gentleman call this? I can truly say it gives me great concern. Such practices throw a disgrace over our whole country that can only be wiped off by exemplary punishment of the actors, which our *weak* government cannot or will not inflict. And the people I pity for their want of sense. Those who have inflamed and misled them have a deal to answer for.—Smyth 4:385. (1765.)

MOBOCRACY, Spirit of, Threatens England.—Even this capitol, the residence of the King, is now a daily scene of lawless riot and confusion. Mobs patrolling the streets at noonday, some knocking all down that will not roar for Wilkes and liberty; courts of justice afraid to give judgment against him; coal-heavers and porters pulling down the houses of coal merchants that refuse to give them more wages; sawyers destroying sawmills; sailors unrigging all the outward-bound ships, and suffering none to sail till merchants agree to raise their pay; watermen destroying private boats and threatening bridges; soldiers firing among the mobs and killing men, women, and children, which seems only to have produced a universal sullenness, that looks like a great black cloud coming on, ready to burst in a general tempest.

What the event will be, God only knows. But some punishment seems preparing for a people who are ungratefully abusing the best constitution and the best King any nation was ever blessed with, intent on nothing but luxury, licentiousness, power, places, pensions, and plunder; while the ministry, divided in their counsels, with little regard for each other, worried by perpetual oppositions, in continual apprehension of changes, intent on securing popularity in case they should lose favor, have for some years past had little time or inclination to attend to our [America's] small affairs, whose remoteness makes them appear still smaller.—Smyth 5:133. (1768.)

MOBOCRACY, Provoked by the Press.—While I am writing, a great mob of coal porters fills the street, carrying a wretch of their business upon poles to be ducked, and otherwise punished at their pleasure for working at the old wages. All respect to law and government seems to be lost among the common people, who are moreover continually inflamed by seditious scribblers to trample on authority and everything that used to keep them in order.—Smyth 5:134. (1768.)

MODESTY, Makes Women Lovely.
—Remember that modesty, as it makes the most homely virgin amiable and charming, so the want of it infallibly renders the most perfect beauty disagreeable and odious. But when that brightest of female virtues shines among other perfections of body and mind in the same person, it makes the woman more lovely than an angel.—Smyth 2:87. (1727.)

MONEY, Can Beget Money.—
Money can beget money, and its offspring can beget more, and so on. Five shillings turned is six, turned again it is seven and three-pence, and so on till it becomes an hundred pounds. The more there is of it, the more it produces every turning, so that the profits rise quicker and quicker. He that kills a breeding sow destroys all her offspring to the thousandth generation.—Smyth 2:371. (1748.)

MONEY, Paper Money Stimulated Commerce in Pennsylvania.—The balance of trade [in Pennsylvania] carried out the gold and siver as fast as it was brought in, the merchants raising the price of their goods in proportion to the increased denomination of the money. The difficulties for want of cash were accordingly very great, the chief part of the trade being carried on by the extremely inconvenient method of barter; when, in 1723, paper money was first made there, which gave new life to business, [and] promoted greatly the settlement of new lands, by lending small sums to beginners on easy interest, to be repaid by installments, whereby the province has so greatly increased in inhabitants, that the export from hence thither is now more than tenfold what it then was.—Smyth 5:3. (1767.)

MONEY, Issuing of, Must Be Regulated by Central Government.
—Particular circumstances in the *New England* colonies made paper money less necessary and less convenient to them. They have great and valuable fisheries of whale and cod, by which large remittances can be made. They are four distinct governments; but having much mutual intercourse of dealings with each other, the money of each used to pass current in all. But the whole of this common currency, not being under one common direction, was not so easily kept within due bounds, the prudent reserve of one colony in its emissions being rendered useless by excess in another.—Smyth 5:5. (1767.)

MONEY, Paper Currency Must Be Adequately Funded.—If government afterwards should have occasion for the credit of the bank, it must of necessity make its bills a legal tender, funding them, however, on taxes, by which they may in time be paid off, as has been the general practice in the colonies.—Smyth 5:8. (1767.)

MONEY, Advantages of Paper Currency over Gold and Silver Coins.—Paper money, well funded, has another great advantage over gold and silver: its lightness of carriage, and the little room that is occupied by a great sum, whereby it is capable of being more easily and more safely, because more privately, conveyed from place to place. Gold and silver are not *intrinsically* of equal value with iron, a metal in itself capable of many more beneficial uses to mankind. Their value rests chiefly in the estimation they happen to be in among the generality of nations, and the credit given to the opinion that that estimation will continue; otherwise a pound of gold would not be a real equivalent for even a bushel of wheat. Any other well-founded credit is as much an equivalent as gold and silver, and in some cases more so, or it would not be preferred by commercial people in different countries.—Smyth 5:9. (1767.)

MONEY, Fixed Value Important.— By its continually changing value, [the money in Maryland] appears a currency unfit for the purpose of money, which should be as fixed as possible in its own value, because it is to be the measure of the value of other things.—Smyth 5:12. (1767.)

MONEY, Paper Currency and Inflation.—(For full text of Franklin's treatise "Of the Paper Money of the United States of America" [1784], see Smyth 9:231–36.)

MONEY. See also PAPER MONEY.

MONROE DOCTRINE, Anticipated by Franklin.—Our *North American* colonies are to be considered as the frontier of the *British* empire on that side. The frontier of any dominion being attacked, it becomes not merely *"the cause"* of the people immediately affected (the inhabitants of that frontier), but properly *"the cause"* of the whole body. Where the frontier people owe and pay obedience, there they have a right to look for protection. No political proposition is better established than this. It is therefore invidious to represent the "blood and treasure" spent in this war as spent in "the cause of the colonies" only, and that they are "absurd and ungrateful" if they think we have done nothing unless we "make conquests for them," and reduce *Canada* to gratify their "vain ambition," etc.—Smyth 4:50. (1760.)

MORAVIANS, Marriage Customs of.—I inquired [in 1756] concerning the Moravian marriages, whether the report was true that they were by lot. I was told that lots were used only in particular cases; that generally, when a young man found himself disposed to marry, he informed the elders of his class, who consulted the elder ladies that governed the young women. As these elders of the different sexes were well acquainted with the tempers and dispositions of their respective pupils, they could best judge what matches were suitable, and their judgments were generally acquiesced in; but if, for example, it should happen that two or three young women were found to be equally proper for the young man, the lot was then recurred to. I objected, if the matches are not made by the mutual choice of the parties, some of them may chance to be very unhappy. "And so they may," answered my informer, "if you let the parties choose for themselves"; which, indeed, I could not deny.—Autobiography. Smyth 1:413. (1788.)

MOTTO, Proposed by Franklin for National Seal.—Rebellion to tyrants is obedience to God.—Carl Van Doren, ed., *Benjamin Franklin's Autobiographical Writings* (New York: The Viking Press, 1945), p. 413. (1775.)

MUSIC, Franklin Plays Duets with Daughter.—My daughter has been endeavoring to collect some of the music of this country production, to send Miss Dick, in return for her most acceptable present of Scotch songs. But music is a new art with us. She has only obtained a few airs adapted by a young gentleman of our acquaintance to some old songs, which she now desires me to enclose, and to repeat her thanks for the Scotch music with which we are all much delighted. She sings the songs to her harpsichord, and I play some of the softest tunes on my armonica, * with which entertainment our people here are quite charmed, and conceive the Scottish tunes to be the finest in the world.— Smyth 4:210. (1763.)

> *Regarding Franklin's love of music, Albert Henry Smyth noted: "He played the harp, the guitar, and the violin, and he invented the armonica, a now obsolete instrument, which he fancied was destined to supersede the piano and harpsichord."—Smyth 1:210.

MUSIC, Classical vs. Popular.—I only wished you had examined more fully the subject of music, and demonstrated that the pleasure which artists feel in hearing much of that composed in the modern taste is

Franklin in 1778 (age 72). Medallion by Jean Baptiste Nini, after a drawing by Thomas Walpole. Inscribed within the circular border is the Latin epigram which the French statesman Turgot devised for Franklin: "He snatched the lightning from the heavens and the scepter from tyrants."

not the natural pleasure arising from melody or harmony of sounds, but of the same kind with the pleasure we feel on seeing the surprising feats of tumblers and rope-dancers, who execute difficult things. For my part I take this to be really the case, and suppose it the reason why those who [are] unpracticed in music, and therefore unacquainted with those difficulties, have little or no pleasure in hearing this music. Many pieces of it are mere compositions of tricks. I have sometimes, at a concert attended by a common audience, placed myself so as to see all their faces, and observed no signs of pleasure in them during the performance of a great part that was admired by the performers themselves; while a plain old *Scottish tune*, which they [the musicians] disdained and could scarcely be prevailed on to play, gave manifest and general delight.— Smyth 4:377. (1765.)

MUSIC, Nature of Melody and Harmony.—An agreeable *succession* of sounds is called *melody*, and only the *co-existence* of agreeing sounds, *harmony*. But, since the memory is capable of retaining for some moments a perfect idea of the pitch of past sound, so as to compare with it the pitch of a succeeding sound, and judge truly of their agreement or disagreement, there may and does arise from thence a sense of harmony between the present and past sounds, equally pleasing with that between two present sounds.— Smyth 4:378. (1765.)

MUSIC, Social Influence on.—You, in the spirit of some ancient legislators, would influence the manners of your country by the united powers of poetry and music. By what I can learn of *their* songs, the music was simple, conformed itself to the usual pronunciation of words, as to measure, cadence or emphasis, etc., never disguised and confounded the language by making a long syllable short, or a short one long, when sung; their singing was only a more pleasing, because a melodious, manner of speaking; it was capable of all the graces of prose oratory, while it added the pleasure of harmony. A modern song, on the contrary, neglects all the proprieties and beauties of common speech, and in their place introduces its *defects and*

absurdities as so many graces.— Smyth 5:530. (1762?)

MUSIC, Opera Singers and Screaming.—As to the *screaming*, perhaps I cannot find a fair instance in this song; but whoever has frequented our operas will remember many. And yet here methinks the words *no* and *e'er*, when sung to these notes, have a little of the air of *screaming*, and would actually be screamed by some singers.—Smyth 5:533. (1762?)

MUTINY, Attempted on a Few American Ships.—There has been a conspiracy on board to seize and run away with the ship to England. Thirty-eight of the crew concerned in the plot were brought in under confinement, and the captain was much embarrassed with them, and suspicious of many more. We would not try them here for want of officers sufficient to make a court-martial. The French Admiralty could not take cognizance of their offense. The captain objected to carrying them back, as both troublesome and dangerous. In fine, we got leave to land and confine them in a French prison, where they continue till further orders.—Smyth 7:338. (1779.)

MUTINY, By Unpaid Sailors.—I received a letter signed by about 115 of the sailors of the *Alliance*, declaring that they would not raise the anchor, nor depart from L'Orient, till they had six months' wages paid them and the utmost farthing of their prize money, including the ships sent into Norway, and until their legal *Captain P. Landais* is restored to them; or to that effect, for I have not the letter before me. This mutiny has undoubtedly been excited by that captain, probably by making them believe that satisfaction has been received for those Norway prizes delivered up to the English, which God knows is not true.—Smyth 8:90. (1780.)

N

NEGROES, Heavier Perspiration an Advantage.—May there not be in Negroes a quicker evaporation of the persirable matter from their skins and lungs, which by cooling them more enables them to bear the sun's heat better than whites do? (If that is a fact, as it is said to be; for the alleged necessity of having Negroes rather than whites to work in the *West India* fields is founded upon it.) Though the color of their skins would otherwise make them more sensible of the sun's heat, since black cloth heats much sooner and more in the sun than white cloth.—Smyth 3:449. (1758.)

NEGROES, Not Deficient in Natural Understanding.—The Negroes who are free live among the white people, but are generally improvident and poor. I think they are not deficient in natural understanding, but they have not the advantage of education. They make good musicians.—Smyth 6:222. (1774.)

NEW ENGLAND, Best Example of Sound Community Life.—Your state would, I imagine, be much more secure from the mischiefs of Indian wars if you imitated the mode of settlement in the New England states, which was to grant their lands in townships of about six miles square to the families. These first chose a spot for their town, where they cleared a square of perhaps 20 acres, round which they fixed their houses 15 on a side all fronting inwards to the square; so that they were all in sight of each other. In the middle of the square they erected a house for public worship and a school, stockaded round as a fort for the reception and protection of their women and children in case of alarm. Behind each house was first a garden plot, then an orchard, and then a pasture for a cow or two, and behind all outwards their corn field. Thus situated, one house could not be attacked without its being seen and giving alarm to the rest, who were ready to run to its succor. This discouraged such attempts. Then they had the advantage of giving schooling to their children, securing their morals by the influence of religion, and improving each other by civil society and conversation. In our way of sparse and remote settlements, the people are without these advantages, and we are in danger of bringing up a set of savages of our own color.—Smyth 9:626. (1787.)

NEW ZEALAND, Proposed Voyage to Colonize.—Many voyages have been undertaken with views of profit or of plunder, or to gratify resentment; to procure some advantage to ourselves, or do some mischief to others. But a voyage is now proposed, to visit a distant people on the other side [of] the globe; not to cheat them, not to rob them, not to seize their lands, or enslave their persons; but merely to do them good, and make them, as far as in our power lies, to live as comfortably as ourselves.

It seems a laudable wish, that all the nations of the earth were connected by a knowledge of each other, and a mutual exchange of benefits; but a commercial nation particularly should wish for a general civilization of mankind, since trade is always carried on to much greater extent with people who have the arts and conveniences of life than it can be with naked savages. We may therefore hope, in this undertaking, to be of some service to our country as well as to those poor people who, however distant from us, are in truth related to us, and whose interests do, in some degree, concern every one who can say, *Homo sum, etc.*—Smyth 5:342. (1771.)

NON-CONSUMPTION AGREEMENT OF COLONIES, Proving Effective.—If the Non-Consumption Agreement should become general, and be firmly adhered to, this ministry must be ruined, and our friends succeed them, from whom we may hope a great constitutional charter to be confirmed by King, Lords, and Commons, whereby our liberties shall be recognized and established as the only sure foundation of that union so necessary for our common welfare.—Smyth 6:239. (1774.)

NON-CONSUMPTION AGREEMENT OF COLONIES, Could Cause Ministry to Fall.—In my opinion, all depends on the Americans themselves. If they make and keep firm resolutions not to consume British manufactures till their grievances are redressed and their rights acknowledged, this ministry must fall, and the aggrieving laws be repealed. This is the opinion of all wise men here.— Smyth 6:240. (1774.)

NON-IMPORTATION ACT BY COLONIES, Influencing British Merchants.—Now that it appears from late and authentic accounts that agreements continue in full force, that a ship is actually returned from Boston to Bristol with nails and glass (articles that were thought of the utmost necessity), and that the ships which were waiting here for the determination of Parliament are actually returning to North America in their ballast, the tone of the manufacturers begins to change, and there is no doubt that, if we are steady and persevere in our resolutions, these people will soon begin a clamor that many pains have hitherto been used to stifle.—Smyth 5:253. (1770.)

NOTE TAKING, While Reading.—I would advise you to read with a pen in your hand, and enter in a little book short hints of what you find that is curious, or that may be useful; for this will be the best method of imprinting such particulars in your memory, where they will be ready, either for practice on some future occasion, if they are matters of utility, or at least to adorn and improve your conversation, if they are rather points of curiosity.— Smyth 4:19. (1760.)

O

OBEDIENCE TO LAW, Essential to Good Government.—If any form of government is capable of making a nation happy, ours I think bids fair now for producing that effect. But, after all, much depends upon the people who are to be governed. We have been guarding against an evil that old states are most liable to, *excess of power* in the rulers; but our present danger seems to be *defect of obedience* in the subjects.—Smyth 10:7. (1789.)

OHIO VALLEY, Franklin's View Concerning Colony in.—I sometimes wish that you [the Reverend George Whitefield] and I were jointly employed by the Crown to settle a colony on the Ohio. I imagine we could do it effectually, and without putting the nation to much expense. But I fear we shall never be called upon for such a service. What a glorious thing it would be, to settle in that fine country a large, strong body of religious and industrious people! What a security to the other colonies; and advantage to Britain, by increasing her people, territory, strength and commerce. Might it not greatly facilitate the introduction of pure religion among the heathen if we could, by such a colony, show them a better sample of Christians than they commonly see in our Indian traders, the most vicious and abandoned wretches of our nation?—Smyth 3:339. (1756.)

OHIO VALLEY, Disadvantages If Occupied by French Colonists.—

1. Our [English] people, being confined to the country between the sea and the mountains, cannot much more increase in number; people increasing in proportion to their room and means of subsistence.

2. The French will increase much more, by that acquired room and plenty of subsistence, and become a great people behind us.

3. Many of our debtors and loose English people, our German servants, and slaves, will probably desert to them, and increase their numbers and strength, to the lessening and weakening of ours.

4. They will cut us off from all commerce and alliance with the western Indians, to the great prejudice of Britain, by preventing the sale and consumption of its manufactures.

5. They will both in time of peace and war (as they have always done against New England) set the Indians on to harass our frontiers, kill and scalp our people, and drive in the advanced settlers; and so, in preventing our obtaining more subsistence by cultivating of new lands, they discourage our marriages, and keep our people from increasing; thus (if the expression may be allowed) killing thousands of our children before they are born.—Smyth 3:359. (1756.)

OHIO VALLEY, Advantages If Occupied by English Colonists.—

1. They [English colonies on the Ohio] would be a great security to the frontiers of our other colonies, by preventing the incursions of the French and French Indians of Canada on the back parts of

Pennsylvania, Maryland, Virginia, and the Carolinas; and the frontiers of such new colonies would be much more easily defended than those of the colonies last mentioned now can be, as will appear hereafter.

2. The dreaded junction of the French settlements in Canada with those of Louisiana would be prevented.

3. In case of a war, it would be easy, from those new colonies, to annoy Louisiana, by going down the Ohio and Mississippi; and the southern part of Canada, by sailing over the lakes, and thereby confine the French within narrow limits.

4. We could secure the friendship and trade of the Miamis or Twigtwees (a numerous people consisting of many tribes, inhabiting the country between the west end of Lake Erie and the south end of Lake Huron and the Ohio), who are at present dissatisfied with the French, and fond of the English, and would gladly encourage and protect an infant English settlement in or near their country, as some of their chiefs have declared to the writer of this memoir. Further, by means of the lakes, the Ohio, and the Mississippi, our trade might be extended through a vast country, among many numerous and distant nations, greatly to the benefit of Britain.—Smyth 3:360. (1756.)

OLD AGE, Loss of Friends.—A few more such deaths will make me a stranger in my own country. The loss of friends is the tax a man pays for living long himself.—Smyth 7:407. (1779.)

OLD AGE, Last Years of Life the Most Productive.—You [Franklin's sister, Mrs. Jane Mecom] are now seventy-eight, and I am eighty-two; you tread fast upon my heels; but, though you have more strength and spirit, you cannot come up with me till I stop, which must now be soon; for I am grown so old as to have buried most of the friends of my youth, and I now often hear persons whom I knew when children, called *old* Mr. such-a-one, to distinguish them from their sons now men grown and in business; so that, by living twelve years beyond David's period, I seem to have intruded myself into the company of posterity, when I ought to have been abed and asleep. Yet, had I gone at seventy, it would have cut off twelve of the most active years of my life, employed too in matters of the greatest importance; but whether I have been doing good or mischief is for time to discover. I only know that I intended well, and I hope all will end well.—Smyth 9:588. (1787.)

OLD AGE, Best Time for Public Service.—When I informed your good friend Dr. Cooper that I was ordered to France, being then seventy years old, and observed that the public, having as it were eaten my flesh, seemed now resolved to pick my bones, he replied that he approved their taste, for that the nearer the bone the sweeter the meat.—Smyth 9:621. (1787.)

OLD PEOPLE, Kind Treatment of.—As *having their own way* is one the of the greatest comforts of life to old people, I think their friends should endeavor to accommodate them in that, as well as in anything else. When they have long lived in a house, it becomes natural to them; they are almost as closely connected with it, as the tortoise with his shell; they die, if you tear them out of it; old folks and old trees, if you remove them, it is ten to one that you kill them; so let our good old sister be no more importuned on that head. We are growing old fast ourselves, and shall expect the same kind of indulgences; if we give them, we shall have a right to receive them in our turn. . . . I hope you visit sister as often as your affairs will permit, and afford her what assistance and comfort you can in her present situation. *Old age, infirmities,* and *poverty,* joined, are afflictions enough. The *neglect* and *slights* of friends and near relations should never be added. People in her circumstances are apt to suspect this sometimes without cause; *appearances* should therefore be attended to, in our conduct towards them, as well as *realities.* —Smyth 3:391. (1757.)

OPINION, How to Express with the Least Offense.—I made it a rule to forbear all direct contradiction to the sentiments of others, and all positive assertion of my own. I even forbade myself, agreeably to the old laws of our Junto, the use of every word or expression in the language that imported a fixed opinion, such as *certainly, undoubtedly,* etc., and I adopted, instead of them, *I conceive, I apprehend,* or *I imagine* a thing to be so or so; or it *so appears to me at present.* When another asserted something that I thought an error, I denied myself the pleasure of contradicting

him abruptly, and of showing immediately some absurdity in his proposition; and in answering I began by observing that in certain cases or circumstances his opinion would be right, but in the present case there *appeared* or *seemed* to me some difference, etc. I soon found the advantage of this change in my manner: the conversations I engaged in went on more pleasantly; the modest way in which I proposed my opinions procured them a readier reception and less contradiction; I had less mortification when I was found to be in the wrong; and I more easily prevailed with others to give up their mistakes and join with me when I happened to be in the right. —Autobiography. Smyth 1:337. (1784.)

OPINIONS AND BELIEFS, Never Perfect.—Honored Father, I have your favors of the 21st of March, in which you both seem concerned lest I have imbibed some erroneous opinions. Doubtless I have my share; and when the natural weakness and imperfection of human understanding is considered, the unavoidable influence of education, custom, books, and company upon our ways of thinking, I imagine a man must have a good deal of vanity who believes, and a good deal of boldness who affirms, that all the doctrines he holds are true, and all he rejects are false. And perhaps the same may be justly said of every sect, church, and society of men, when they assume to themselves that infallibility which they deny to the Pope and councils.

I think opinions should be judged

of by their influences and effects; and, if a man holds none that tend to make him less virtuous or more vicious, it may be concluded he holds none that are dangerous; which I hope is the case with me.—Smyth 2:214. (1738.)

ORDER, Difficult for Franklin.—In truth, I found myself incorrigible with respect to order; and now I am grown old, and my memory bad, I feel very sensibly the want of it. But, on the whole, though I never arrived at the perfection I had been so ambitious of obtaining, but fell far short of it, yet I was, by the endeavor, a better and a happier man than I otherwise should have been if I had not attempted it.—Autobiography. Smyth 1:335. (1784.)

P

PAPER MONEY, Nature and Necessity.—(For full text of Franklin's tract, *A Modest Enquiry into the Nature and Necessity of a Paper Currency* [1729], see Smyth 2:133-55.)

PAPER MONEY, And Inflation.—This effect of paper currency is not understood on this side [of] the water [in France]. And indeed the whole is a mystery even to the politicians, how we have been able to continue a war four years without money, and how we could pay with paper that had no previously fixed fund appropriated specifically to redeem it. This currency, as we manage it, is a wonderful machine. It performs its office when we issue it; it pays and clothes troops, and provides victuals and ammunition;

and when we are obliged to issue a quantity excessive, it pays itself off by depreciation.—Smyth 7:294. (1779.)

PAPER MONEY, Depreciation Resulted from Rejecting Franklin's Plan.—I lament with you the many mischiefs, the injustices, the corruption of manners, etc., etc., that attended a depreciating currency. It is some consolation to me that I washed my hands of that evil by predicting it in Congress, and proposing means that would have been effectual to prevent it if they had been adopted. Subsequent operations that I have executed demonstrate that my plan was practicable. But it was unfortunately rejected.—Smyth 9:93. (1783.)

PAPER MONEY. See also MONEY.

PARENTS, Should Be Honored by Their Descendants.—Among the Chinese, the most ancient and, from long experience, the wisest of nations, honor does not *descend*, but *ascends*. If a man from his learning, his wisdom, or his valor is promoted by the Emperor to the rank of Mandarin, his parents are immediately entitled to all the same ceremonies of respect from the people that are established as due to the Mandarin himself on the supposition that it must have been owing to the education, instruction, and good example afforded him by his parents that he was rendered capable of serving the public.—Smyth 9:162. (1784.)

PARIS, Water and Streets Clean.—I must do Paris the justice to say that in two points of cleanliness they exceed us. The water they drink, though from the river, they render as pure as that of the best spring by filtering it through cisterns filled with sand; and the streets by constant sweeping are fit to walk in, though there is no paved footpath. Accordingly, many well-dressed people are constantly seen walking in them. —Smyth 5:52. (1767.)

PARLIAMENT, Colonies No Longer Wish to Send Representatives.—The measure ... of a union with the colonies is a wise one; but I [fear] it will hardly be thought so here [England], till it is too late to attempt it. The time has been, when the colonies would have esteemed it a great advantage as well as honor to be permitted to send members to Parliament, and would have asked for that privilege if they could have had the least hopes of obtaining it. The time is now come when they are indifferent about it, and will probably not ask it, though they might accept it if offered them; and the time will come, when they will certainly refuse it.—Smyth 4:400. (1766.)

PARLIAMENT, Historical Development.—[William Pitt] asserted that representation in Parliament was originally and properly of *landed property;* that every 40 shillings a year of landed property in England still is represented by the owners having a right to vote in county elections; but that though a man in America had 1000 pounds a year in land, it gave him no right to vote for a single member of Parliament. That the representation of the commons was not an original part of the constitution; the owners of lands

only were called to Parliament, and all the lands in England were divided between the King, the Church, and the barons. The Church, God bless it, had one third at least. The commons were mere tenants or copy holders. But now the case was greatly altered. The Church was stripped of most of its lands, and the nobles had sold so much of theirs that what remained in their hands was but like a drop of the bucket compared to what was now in the hands of the commons. It was therefore on account of their lands properly that the commons were represented in Parliament. As to the representatives of boroughs, it was wrong to suffer their sitting in Parliament. It was the rotten part of our constitution, and could not stand another century. How could we with any face maintain that a borough of half a dozen houses ought to have a representative in Parliament to take care of its interests, and yet three millions of people in America with many millions of landed property should not have a single vote in the election of any one member.—Smyth 4:406. (1766.)

PARLIAMENT, Colonial Representation in.—The Parliament here do at present think too highly of themselves to admit representatives from us, if we should ask it; and, when they will be desirous of granting it, we shall think too highly of ourselves to accept of it. It would certainly contribute to the strength of the whole if Ireland and all the dominions were united and consolidated under one common council for general purposes, each retaining its particular council or parliament for its domestic concerns. But this should have been more early provided for.—Smyth 4:456. (1766.)

I am fully persuaded...that a *consolidating union*, by a fair and equal representation of all the parts of this empire in Parliament, is the only firm basis on which its political grandeur and prosperity can be founded. Ireland once wished it, but now rejects it. The time has been when the colonies might have been pleased with it; they are now *indifferent* about it; and if it is much longer delayed, they too will *refuse* it.—Smyth 5:17. (1767.)

Every man in England seems to consider himself as a piece of a sovereign over America; seems to jostle himself into the throne with the King, and talks of *our subjects in the colonies.* The Parliament cannot well and wisely make laws suited to the colonies without being properly and truly informed of their circumstances, abilities, temper, etc. This it cannot be, without representatives from thence; and yet it is fond of this power, and averse to the only means of acquiring the necessary knowledge for exercising it; which is desiring to be *omnipotent,* without being *omniscient.*—Smyth 5:17. (1767.)

PARLIAMENT, No Right to Tax Colonies.—It is a common but mistaken notion here [Britain] that the colonies were planted at the expense of Parliament, and that therefore the Parliament has a right

to tax them, etc. The truth is, they were planted at the expense of private adventurers, who went over there to settle, with leave of the King, given by charter. On receiving this leave, and those charters, the adventurers voluntarily engaged to remain the King's subjects, though in a foreign country; a country which had not been conquered by either King or Parliament, but was possessed by a free people.

When our planters arrived, they purchased the lands of the natives, without putting King or Parliament to any expense. Parliament had no hand in their settlement, was never so much as consulted about their constitution, and took no kind of notice of them, till many years after they were established.... Thus all the colonies acknowledge the King as their sovereign; his Governors there represent his person; laws are made by their assemblies or little parliaments, with the Governor's assent, subject still to the King's pleasure to confirm or annul them; suits arising in the colonies, and differences between colony and colony, are determined by the King in Council. In this view, they seem so many separate little states, subject to the same Prince. The *sovereignty of the King* is therefore easily understood. But nothing is more common here than to talk of the *sovereignty of Parliament,* and the *sovereignty of this nation* over the colonies; a kind of sovereignty, the idea of which is not so clear, nor does it clearly appear on what foundation it is established.—Smyth 5:19. (1767.)

PARLIAMENT, Demands Loyalty Without Representation.—But a new kind of loyalty seems to be required of us, a loyalty to Parliament; a loyalty that is to extend, it is said, to a surrender of all our properties whenever a House of Commons (in which there is not a single member of our choosing) shall think fit to grant them away without our consent; and to a patient suffering [of] the loss of our privileges as Englishmen, if we cannot submit to make such surrender. We were separated too far from Britain by the ocean, but we were united to it by respect and love, so that we could at any time freely have spent our lives and little fortunes in its cause; but this unhappy new system of politics tends to dissolve those bands of union, and to sever us forever.—Smyth 5:88. (1768.)

PARLIAMENT, King Is Sovereign, Not Parliament.—I find myself confirmed in opinion that no middle doctrine can be well maintained, I mean not clearly with intelligible arguments. Something might be made of either of the extremes, that Parliament has a power to make *all laws* for us or that it has a power to make *no laws* for us; and I think the arguments for the latter more numerous and weighty than those for the former. Supposing that doctrine established, the colonies would then be so many separate states, only subject to the same king, as England and Scotland were before the union.—Smyth 5:115. (1768.)

PARLIAMENT, Errors Often Result of Pressures from Special Interest Groups.—I think...that the true principles of commerce are yet but little understood, and that most of the acts of Parliament, *arrets* and edicts of princes and states, relating to commerce, are political errors, solicited and obtained by particulars for private interest, under the pretext of public good.—Smyth 5:193. (1769.)

PARLIAMENT, Guilty of Usurpation.—To me those bodies seem to have been long encroaching on the rights of their and our sovereign, assuming too much of his authority, and betraying his interests. By our constitution he is, with his plantation parliaments, the sole legislator of his American subjects, and in that capacity is, and ought to be, free to exercise his own judgment, unrestrained and unlimited by his Parliament here. And our parliaments have right to grant him aids without the consent of this Parliament, a circumstance which, by the way, begins to give it some jealousy. Let us, therefore, hold fast our loyalty to our King, who has the best disposition towards us, and has a family interest in our prosperity; as that steady loyalty is the most probable means of securing us from the arbitrary power of a corrupt Parliament that does not like us, and conceives itself to have an interest in keeping us down and fleecing us.—Smyth 5:260. (1770.)

PARLIAMENT, Petitions to.—When I see that all petitions and complaints of grievances are so odious to government that even the mere pipe which conveys them becomes obnoxious, I am at a loss to know how peace and union are to be maintained or restored between the different parts of the empire. Grievances cannot be redressed unless they are known; and they cannot be known but through complaints and petitions. If these are deemed affronts, and the messengers punished as offenders, who will henceforth send petitions? And who will deliver them? It has been thought a dangerous thing in any state to stop up the vent of griefs. Wise governments have therefore generally received petitions with some indulgence, even when but slightly founded. Those who think themselves injured by their rulers are sometimes, by a mild and prudent answer, convinced of their error. But where complaining is a crime, hope becomes despair.—Smyth 6:190. (1774.)

PARLIAMENT, Bribery in.—But still if the temper of the Court continues, there will doubtless be a majority in the new Parliament for its measures, whatever they are; for as most of the members are bribing or purchasing to get in, there is little doubt of selling their votes to the minister for the time being, to reimburse themselves.—Smyth 6:251. (1774.)

PARLIAMENT, Some Strong Friends of Colonists in.—The Congress is in high esteem here [in England] among all the friends of liberty, and their papers much admired; perhaps nothing of the kind has been more thoroughly published, or more universally read. Lord Camden spoke highly of the Americans in general, and of the Congress particularly, in the House of Lords. Lord Chatham [William Pitt] said that, taking the whole together, and considering the members of the Congress as the unsolicited and unbiased choice of a great, free, and enlightened people, their unanimity, their moderation, and their wisdom, he thought it the most honorable assembly of men that had ever been known; that the histories of Greece and Rome gave us nothing equal to it.—Smyth 6:305. (1775.)

PARLIAMENT, Lord Chatham Proposes Conciliation.—I enclose Lord Chatham's [William Pitt's] proposed plan of conciliation, which was hastily and harshly rejected by the Lords. The friends of America generally wish it had been accepted.—Smyth 6:308. (1775.)

PARTNERSHIPS, Franklin's, Produce New Proprietors.—The partnership at Carolina having succeeded, I was encouraged to engage in others, and to promote several of my workmen who had behaved well by establishing them with printing houses in different colonies, on the same terms with that in Carolina. Most of them did well, being enabled at the end of our term, six years, to purchase the types of me and go on working for themselves, by which means several families were raised. Partnerships often finish in quarrels; but I was happy in this, that mine were all carried on and ended amicably, owing, I think, a good deal to the precaution of having very explicitly settled, in our articles, everything to be done by or expected from each partner, so that there was nothing to dispute, which precaution I would therefore recommend to all who enter into partnerships.—Autobiography. Smyth 1:360. (1788.)

PATENTS, Franklin Declines, on His Inventions.—I have no private interest in the reception of my inventions by the world, having never made, nor proposed to make, the least profit by any of them.—Smyth 7:65. (1777.)

PEACE, Efforts by David Hartley.—My dear friend, the true pains you are taking to restore peace, whatever may be the success, entitle you to the esteem of all good men. If your ministers really desire peace, methinks they would do well to *empower* some person to make propositions for that purpose. One or other of the parties at war must take the first step. To do this belongs properly to the wisest. America, being a novice in such affairs, has no pretense to that character; and, indeed, after the answer given by Lord Stormont).when we proposed to him something relative to the mutual treatment of prisoners with humanity), that *"the King's ministers receive no applications from rebels, unless when they come to implore his Majesty's clemency,"* it cannot be expected that we should hazard the exposing ourselves again to such insolence.—Smyth 8:383. (1782.)

PEACE, Half a Peace Not Enough.—Let us keep up, not only our courage, but our vigilance, and not be laid asleep by the pretended half peace the English make with us without asking our consent.—Smyth 8:406. (1782.)

PEACE, Need for Vigilance, Lest It Fail.—There are grounds for good hopes, however; but I think we should not therefore relax in our preparations for a vigorous campaign, as that nation [Britain] is subject to sudden fluctuations; and, though somewhat humiliated at present, a little success in the West Indies may dissipate their present fears, recall their natural insolence, and occasion the interruption of negotiation, and a continuance of the war. We have great stores purchased here for the use of your army, which will be sent as soon as transports can be procured for them to go under good convoy.—Smyth 8:412. (1782.)

PEACE, Need for a Perpetual.—God grant that there may be wisdom enough assembled to make, if possible, a peace that shall be perpetual, and that the idea of any nations being natural enemies to each other may be abolished, for the honor of human nature.—Smyth 8:414. (1782.)

PEACE NEGOTIATIONS, Must Be Wise and Honest.—With regard to those who may be commissioned from [the British] government, whatever personal preferences I may conceive in my own mind, it cannot become me to express them. I only wish for wise and honest men. With such, a peace may be speedily concluded. With contentious wranglers, the negotiation may be drawn into length, and finally frustrated.—Smyth 8:414. (1782.)

PEACE OVERTURES, Americans Refuse to Return to Former Status.—I was fond to a folly of our British connections, and it was with infinite regret that I saw the necessity you would force us into of breaking it. But the extreme cruelty with which we have been treated has now extinguished every thought of returning to it, and separated us for ever. You have thereby lost limbs that will never grow again.—Smyth 7:186. (1778.)

PEACE TREATIES, Bring Criticism to Negotiators.—I have never known a peace made, even the most advantageous, that was not censured as inadequate, and the makers condemned as injudicious or corrupt. *"Blessed are the peace-makers"* is, I suppose, to be understood in the other world; for in this they are frequently *cursed.* Being as yet rather too much attached to this world, I had therefore no ambition to be concerned in fabricating this peace, and know not how I came to be put into the commission. I esteem it, however, as an honor to be joined with you [John Adams] in so important a business; and, if the execution of it shall happen in my time, which I hardly expect, I shall endeavor to assist in discharging the duty according to the best of my judgment.—Smyth 8:316. (1781.)

PENN (Governor John), Complete Loss of Confidence in.—More wonders! The [Pennsylvania] Assembly received a Governor of the proprietary family with open arms, addressed him with sincere expressions of kindness and respect, opened their purses to them, and presented him with six hundred pounds; made a riot act and prepared a militia bill immediately, at his instance, granted supplies, and did everything that he requested, and promised themselves great happiness under his administration. But suddenly, his dropping all inquiries after the murderers [the "Paxton Boys," who had massacred a group of friendly Indians], and his answering the disputes of the rioters privately and refusing the presence of the Assembly, who were equally concerned in the matters contained in their remonstrance, brings him under suspicion; his insulting the Assembly without the least provocation by charging them with disloyalty and with making an infringement on the King's prerogatives, only because they had presumed to name in a bill offered for his assent a trifling officer) somewhat like one of your toll-gatherers on a turnpike) without consulting him, and his refusing several of their bills or proposing amendments needless disgusting.

These things bring him and his government into sudden contempt. All regard for him in the Assembly is lost. All hopes of happiness under a proprietary government are at an end.—Smyth 4:223. (1764.)

PENN FAMILY, Lost Pennsylvania When Declaration of Independence Proclaimed.—Lady Dowager Penn was here about the time of the treaty, and made application to me with great complaints, but I found she was not well informed of the state of her affairs, and could not clearly show that she had suffered any injury from the public of Pennsylvania, whatever she might from the agents of the family. Her husband's lands, I understand, were not confiscated as represented; but the proprietary government falling with that of the Crown, the Assembly took the opportunity of insisting upon justice in some points, which they could never obtain under that government.— Smyth 9:309. (1785.)

PENN FAMILY, Franklin's Complaints Against.—When I consider the meanness and cruel avarice of the late proprietor in refusing for several years of war to consent to any defense of the frontiers ravaged all the while by the enemy, unless his estate should be exempted from paying any part of the expense, not to mention other atrocities too long for this letter, I cannot but think the family well off, and that it will be prudent in them to take the money [voted by the Pennsylvania Assembly as a settlement after the war] and be quiet. William Penn, the first proprietor, father of Thomas, the husband of the present dowager, was a wise and good man, and as honest to the people as the extreme distress of his circumstances would permit him to be; but the said Thomas was a miserable churl, always intent upon griping and saving; and whatever good the father may have done for the province was amply undone by the mischief received from the son, who never did anything that had the appearance of generosity or public spirit but what was extorted from him by solicitation and the shame of

backwardness in benefits evidently incumbent on him to promote, and which was done at last in the most ungracious manner possible.— Smyth 9:310. (1785.)

PENNSYLVANIA, Franklin's Efforts to Promote Voluntary Militia in.—I first wrote and published [in 1747] a pamphlet entitled *Plain Truth*, in which I stated our defenseless situation in strong lights, with the necessity of union and discipline for our defense, and promised to propose in a few days an association, to be generally signed for that purpose. The pamphlet had a sudden and surprising effect. I was called upon for the instrument of association, and having settled the draft of it with a few friends, I appointed a meeting of the citizens in the large building before mentioned....

When the company separated and the papers were collected, we found above twelve hundred hands; and other copies being dispersed in the country, the subscribers amounted at length to upward of ten thousand. These all furnished themselves as soon as they could with arms, formed themselves into companies and regiments, chose their own officers, and met every week to be instructed in the manual exercise and other parts of military discipline. The women, by subscriptions among themselves, provided silk colors, which they presented to the companies, painted with different devices and mottos, which I supplied.—Autobiography. Smyth 1:361. (1788.)

Franklin in 1778 (age 72). Bust by Jean Antoine Houdon.

PENNSYLVANIA, Should Shift from Proprietary to Royal Government.—There seems to remain, then, but one remedy for our evils, a remedy approved by experience, and which has been tried with success by other provinces; I mean that of an immediate *royal government.*—Smyth 4:231. (1764.) See also PROPRIETARY GOVERNMENTS.

PEOPLE, Generally Right Unless Misled.—The people seldom continue long in the wrong, when it is nobody's interest to mislead them.—Smyth 5:461. (1772.)

PERSPIRATION, Discovered to Be a Cooling Agent.—During the hot Sunday at *Philadelphia,* in *June 1750,* when the thermometer was up at 100 in the shade, I sat in my chamber without exercise, only reading or writing, with no other clothes on than a shirt and a pair of long linen drawers, the windows all open, and a brisk wind blowing through the house; the sweat ran off the backs of my hands, and my shirt was often so wet as to induce me to call for dry ones to put on. In this situation, one might have expected that the natural heat of the body, 96, added to the heat of the air, 100, should jointly have created or produced a much greater degree of heat in the body; but the fact was that my body never grew so hot as the air that surrounded it, or the inanimate bodies immersed in the same air. For I remember well that the desk, when I laid my arm upon it; a chair, when I sat down in it; and a dry shirt out of the drawer, when I put it on, all felt exceeding warm to me, as if they had been warmed before a fire. And I suppose a dead body would have acquired the temperature of the air, though a living one, by continual sweating and by the evaporation of that sweat, was kept cold.—Smyth 3:448. (1758.) See also NEGROES.

PETITIONS, Loss of Confidence in Parliament.—I answered [Lord Dartmouth, Secretary of State for American affairs] that the slighting, evading, or refusing to receive petitions from the colonies, on some late occasions by the Parliament, had occasioned a total loss of the respect for and confidence in that body, formerly subsisting so strongly in America, and brought on a questioning of their authority; that his Lordship might observe petitions came no more from thence to Parliament, but to the King only. That the King appeared now to be the only connection between the two countries; and that as a continued union was essentially necessary to the well-being of the whole empire, I should be sorry to see that link weakened, as the other had been. That I thought it a dangerous thing for any government to refuse receiving petitions, and thereby prevent the subjects from giving vent to their griefs.—Smyth 5:449. (1772.)

PETITIONS, Ignored by Parliament.—To draw it [a petition for redress of grievances by the Continental Congress] into the attention of the House [of Commons], we petitioned to be heard upon it, but were not permitted; and, by the resolution of the committee of the whole House, which I enclose, you will see that it has made little impression; and, from the constant refusal, neglect, or discouragement of American petitions these many years past, our country will at last be convinced that petitions are odious here, and that petitioning is far from being a probable means of obtaining redress.—Smyth 6:304. (1775.)

PHILADELPHIA, Excessive Heat in Summer.—This town is a mere oven. How happily situated are our friends at Hempfield! I languish for the country, for air and shade and leisure, but fate has doomed me to be stifled and roasted and teased to death in a city.—Smyth 3:94. (1752.)

PHYSIOCRATS, Letter to Du Pont de Nemours.—I received your obliging letter of the 10th May, with the most acceptable present of your *Physiocratie,* which I have read with great pleasure, and received from it a great deal of instruction. There is such a freedom from local and national prejudices and partialities, so much benevolence to mankind in general, so much goodness mixed with the wisdom, in the principles of your new philosophy, that I am perfectly charmed with them, and wish I could have stayed in France for some time, to have studied in your school, that I might by conversing with its founders have made myself quite a master of that philosophy.—Smyth 5:155. (1768.)

PITT (William), Franklin Describes Pitt's Speech Against the Stamp Act.—(For full text, see Smyth 4:405–8. [1766.])

POLICE, Regular Force in Philadelphia First Proposed by Franklin.—The city watch was one of the first things that I conceived to want regulation. It was managed by the constables of the respective wards in turn; the constable warned a number of housekeepers to attend him for the night. Those who chose never to attend paid him six shillings a year to be excused, which was supposed to be for hiring substitutes, but was, in reality, much more than was necessary for that purpose, and made the constable-ship a place of profit; and the constable, for a little drink, often got such ragamuffins about him as a watch that respectable housekeepers did not choose to mix with.

Walking the rounds, too, was often neglected, and most of the nights spent in tippling....

[About 1736] I proposed, as a more effectual watch, the hiring of proper men to serve constantly in that business; and as a more equitable way of supporting the charge, the levying a tax that should be proportioned to the property.— Autobiography. Smyth 1:352. (1788.)

POLITICAL OFFICES, Franklin's Attitude Towards, at Age 42.—I shall never *ask*, never *refuse*, nor ever *resign* an office.—Autobiography. Smyth 1:364. (1788.)

POLITICAL OFFICES, Better to Stay in Business.—The proverb says, *He who has a trade has an office of profit and honor*, because he does not hold it during any other man's pleasure, and it affords him honest subsistence with independence.— Smyth 5:446. (1772.)

POLITICAL OFFICES, Efficiency of Men Working Without Pay.—My time was never more fully employed. In the morning at six, I am at the Committee of Safety, appointed by the Assembly to put the province in a state of defense; which committee holds till near nine, when I am at the Congress, and that sits till after four in the afternoon. Both these bodies proceed with the greatest unanimity, and their meetings are well attended. It will scarce be credited in Britain that men can be as diligent with us from zeal for the public good as with you for thousands per annum. Such is the difference between uncorrupted new states

and corrupted old ones.—Smyth 6:409. (1775.)

POLITICAL OFFICES, Salaries in America Compared to England.—In America, salaries, where indispensable, are extremely low; but much of public business is done gratis. The honor of serving the public ably and faithfully is deemed sufficient. *Public spirit* really exists there, and has great effects. In England it is universally deemed a non-entity, and whoever pretends to it is laughed at as a fool, or suspected as a knave.—Smyth 7:49. (1777.)

POLITICAL OFFICES, Small Compensation Recommended.— The 36th Article of the Constitution of Pennsylvania runs expressly in these words: "As every freeman, to preserve his independence (if he has not a sufficient estate), ought to have some profession, calling, trade, or farm, whereby he may honestly subsist, there can be no necessity for, nor use in, establishing offices of profit; the usual effects of which are dependence and servility, unbecoming freemen, in the possessors and expectants; faction, contention, corruption, and disorder among the people. Wherefore, whenever an office, through increase of fees or otherwise, becomes so profitable as to occasion many to apply for it, the profits ought to be lessened by the legislature."—Smyth 8:605. (1782.)

POLITICAL OFFICES, Should Be Filled Where Possible for the Honor Rather Than High Salaries.—You [William Strahan of England] do not "approve the annihilation of profitable places; for you do not see why a statesman who does his business well should not be paid for his labor as well as any other workman." Agreed. But why more than any other workman? The less the salary, the greater the honor. In so great a nation, there are many rich enough to afford giving their time to the public; and there are, I make no doubt, many wise and able men who would take as much pleasure in governing for nothing as they do in playing chess for nothing. It would be one of the noblest of amusements. That this opinion is not chimerical, the country I now live in affords a proof; its whole civil and criminal law administration being done for nothing, or in some sense for less than nothing.—Smyth 9:259. (1784.)

POLITICAL OFFICES, Should Not Become Attractive Because of High Salaries.—Sir, there are two passions which have a powerful influence in the affairs of men. These are *ambition* and *avarice;* the love of power and the love of money. Separately, each of these has great force in prompting men to action; but when united in view of the same object, they have in many minds the most violent effects. Place before the eyes of such men a post of *honor* that shall at the same time be a place of *profit,* and they will move heaven and earth to obtain it. The vast number of such places it is that renders the British government so tempestuous. The struggles for them are the true source of all those factions which are perpetually dividing the nation, distracting its

councils, hurrying it sometimes into fruitless and mischievous wars, and often compelling a submission to dishonorable terms of peace.

And of what kind are the men that will strive for this profitable preeminence, through all the bustle of cabal, the heat of contention, the infinite mutual abuse of parties, tearing to pieces the best of characters? It will not be the wise and moderate, the lovers of peace and good order, the men fittest for the trust. It will be the bold and the violent, the men of strong passions and indefatigable activity in their selfish pursuits. These will thrust themselves into your government and be your rulers. And these, too, will be mistaken in the expected happiness of their situation, for their vanquished competitors, of the same spirit, and from the same motives, will perpetually be endeavoring to distress their administration, thwart their measures, and render them odious to the people.

Besides these evils, Sir, though we may set out in the beginning with moderate salaries, we shall find that such will not be of long continuance. Reasons will never be wanting for proposed augmentations; and there will always be a party for giving more to the rulers, that the rulers may be able in return to give more to them. Hence, as all history informs us, there has been in every state and kingdom a constant kind of warfare between the governing and the governed, the one striving to obtain more for its support, and the other to pay less. And this has alone occasioned great convulsions, actual civil wars, ending either in dethroning of the princes or enslaving of the people.

Generally, indeed, the ruling power carries its point, and we see the revenues of princes constantly increasing, and we see that they are never satisfied, but always in want of more. The more the people are discontented with the oppression of taxes, the greater need the prince has of money to distribute among his partisans, and pay the troops that are to suppress all resistance, and enable him to plunder at pleasure. There is scarce a king in a hundred who would not, if he could, follow the example of Pharaoh—get first all the people's money, then all their lands, and then make them and their children servants forever.

It will be said that we do not propose to establish kings. I know it. But there is a natural inclination in mankind to kingly government. It sometimes relieves them from aristocratic domination. They had rather have one tyrant than 500. It gives more of the appearance of equality among citizens; and that they like. I am apprehensive, therefore—perhaps too apprehensive—that the government of these states may in future times end in a monarchy. But this catastrophe, I think, may be long delayed, if in our proposed system we do not sow the seeds of contention, faction, and tumult by making our posts of honor places of profit. If we do, I fear that, though we employ at first a number and not a single person, the number will in time be set aside; it

will only nourish the fetus of a king (as the honorable gentleman from Virginia very aptly expressed it), and a king will the sooner be set over us.

It may be imagined by some that this is an utopian idea, and that we can never find men to serve us in the executive department without paying them well for their services. I conceive this to be a mistake. Some existing facts present themselves to me, which incline me to a contrary opinion. The High Sheriff of a county in England is an honorable office, but it is not a profitable one. It is rather expensive, and therefore not sought for. But yet it is executed, and well executed, and usually by some of the principal gentlemen of the county.... I only bring the instance to show that the pleasure of doing good and serving their country, and the respect such conduct entitles them to, are sufficient motives with some minds to give up a great portion of their time to the public, without the mean inducement of pecuniary satisfaction....

To bring the matter nearer home, have we not seen the greatest and most important of our offices, that of General of our armies, executed for eight years together, without the smallest salary, by a patriot whom I will not now offend by any other praise; and this, through fatigues and distresses, in common with the other brave men, his military friends and companions, and the constant anxieties peculiar to his station? And shall we doubt finding three or four men in all the United States with public spirit enough to bear sitting in peaceful council, for perhaps an equal term, merely to preside over our civil concerns, and see that our laws are duly executed? Sir, I have a better opinion of our country. I think we shall never be without a sufficient number of wise and good men to undertake, and execute well and faithfully, the office in question.

Sir, the saving of the salaries, that may at first be proposed, is not an object with me. The subsequent mischiefs of proposing them are what I apprehend. And therefore it is that I move the amendment. If it is not seconded or accepted, I must be contented with the satisfaction of having delivered my opinion frankly, and done my duty.— Address at the Constitutional Convention. Smyth 9:591. (1787.)

POLITICAL REFORM, Usually Delayed Until Forced on Politicians by Necessity.—Those who govern, having much business on their hands, do not generally like to take the trouble of considering and carrying into execution new projects. The best public measures are therefore seldom *adopted from previous wisdom, but forced by the occasion.* —Autobiography. Smyth 1:389. (1788.)

POLITICAL SCIENCE, Basic Views of Franklin.—*Observations* on my reading history, in library, May 19th, 1731.

That the great affairs of the world, the wars, revolutions, etc., are carried on and affected by parties.

That the view of these parties is their present general interest, or what they take to be such.

That the different views of these different parties occasion all confusion.

That while a party is carrying on a general design, each man has his particular private interest in view.

That as soon as a party has gained its general point, each member becomes intent upon his particular interest; which, thwarting others, breaks that party into divisions, and occasions more confusion.

That few in public affairs act from a mere view of the good of their country, whatever they may pretend; and, though their actings bring real good to their country, yet men primarily considered that their own and their country's interest was united, and did not act from a principle of benevolence.

That fewer still, in public affairs, act with a view to the good of mankind.

There seems to me at present to be great occasion for raising a United Party for Virtue, by forming the virtuous and good men of all nations into a regular body, to be governed by suitable good and wise rules, which good and wise men may probably be more unanimous in their obedience to, than common people are to common laws.

I at present think that whoever attempts this aright, and is well qualified, cannot fail of pleasing God, and of meeting with success.— Autobiography. Smyth 1:339. (1788.)

POOR, Redistribution of Wealth Will Corrupt the.—I have often observed with wonder that temper of the poorer English laborers which you mention, and acknowledge it to be pretty general. When any of them happen to come here [to America], where labor is much better paid than in England, their industry seems to diminish in equal proportion. But it is not so with the German laborers; they retain the habitual industry and frugality they bring with them, and, receiving higher wages, an accumulation arises that makes them all rich. When I consider that the English are the offspring of Germans, that the climate they live in is much of the same temperature, and when I see nothing in nature that should create this difference, I am tempted to suspect it must arise from constitution; and I have sometimes doubted whether the laws peculiar to England, which *compel the rich to maintain the poor*, have not given the latter a dependence that very much lessens the care of providing against the wants of old age.—Smyth 3:133. (1753.)

POOR, Charity for the Idle and Lazy Contrary to God's Law.—To relieve the misfortunes of our fellow creatures is concurring with the Deity; it is godlike. But if we provide encouragement for laziness, and supports for folly, may we not be found fighting against the order of God and nature, which perhaps has appointed want and misery as the proper punishments for, and cautions against, as well as necessary consequences of, idleness and extravagance? Whenever we attempt to amend the scheme of Providence, and to interfere with the government of the world, we had need be very circumspect, lest we do more harm than good.—Smyth 3:135. (1753.)

POOR, Bare Survival Can Become Habitual with No Desire to Rise Above It.—We had here some years since a Transylvanian Tartar who had traveled much in the East, and came hither merely to see the West, intending to go home through the Spanish West Indies, China, etc. He asked me one day what I thought might be the reason that so many and such numerous nations as the Tartars in Europe and Asia, the Indians in America, and the Negroes in Africa continued a wandering, careless life, and refused to live in cities and cultivate the arts they saw practiced by the civilized parts of mankind. While I was considering what answer to make him, he said in his broken English, "God make man for Paradise. He make him for live lazy. Man make God angry. God turn him out of Paradise, and bid workee. Man no love workee; he want to go to Paradise again; he want to live lazy. So all mankind love lazy."

However this may be, it seems certain that the hope of becoming at some time of life free from the necessity of care and labor, together with fear of penury, are the mainsprings of most people's industry. To those, indeed, who have been educated in elegant plenty, even the provision [of charity] made for the poor may appear misery; but to those who have scarce ever been better provided for, such provision may seem quite good and sufficient. These latter, then, have nothing to fear worse than their present condition, and scarce hope for anything better than a parish maintenance. So that there is only the difficulty of getting that maintenance allowed while they are able to work, or a little shame they suppose attending it, that can induce them to work at all; and what they do will only be from hand to mouth.—Smyth 3:135. (1753.)

POOR, Human Incentives to Work Easily Lost.—The proneness of human nature to a life of ease, of freedom from care and labor, appears strongly in the little success that has hitherto attended every attempt to civilize our American Indians. In their present way of living, almost all their wants are supplied by the spontaneous productions of nature, with the addition of very little labor, if hunting and fishing may indeed be called labor, where game is so plenty. They visit us frequently, and see the advantages that arts, sciences, and compact societies procure us. They are not deficient in natural understanding; and yet they have never shown any inclination to change their manner of life for ours, or to learn any of our arts. When an Indian child has been brought up among us, taught our language, and habituated to our customs, yet, if he goes to see his relatives, and makes one Indian ramble with them, there is no persuading him ever to return.

And that this is not natural to them merely as Indians, but as men, is plain from this, that when white persons of either sex have been taken prisoners by the Indians, and lived awhile with them, though ransomed by their friends and treated with all imaginable tenderness to prevail with them to stay among the English, yet in a short time they become disgusted with our manner of life, and the care and pains that are necessary to support it, and take the first opportunity of escaping again into the woods, from whence there is no redeeming them. One instance I remember to have heard, where the person was brought home to possess a good estate; but, finding some care necessary to keep it together, he relinquished it to a younger brother, reserving to himself nothing but a gun and a match-coat with which he took his way again into the wilderness.—Smyth 3:136. (1753.)

POOR, Essential to Develop Work as Part of Either Charity or Welfare Program.—I am apt to imagine that close societies, subsisting by labor and art, arose first not from choice but from necessity, when numbers, being driven by war from their hunting grounds, were crowded together into some narrow territories, which without labor could not afford them food. However, as matters now stand with us, care and industry seem absolutely necessary to our well-being. They should therefore have every encouragement we can invent, and not one motive to diligence be subtracted; and the support of the poor should not be by maintaining them in idleness, but by employing them in some kind of labor suited to their abilities of body, as I am informed begins to be of late the practice in many parts of England, where workhouses are erected for that purpose. If these were general, I should think the poor would be more careful, and work voluntarily to lay up something for themselves against a rainy day, rather than run the risk of being obliged to work at the pleasure of others for a bare subsistence, and that too under confinement.— Smyth 3:137. (1753.)

POOR, Political Agitators Provoke to Violence.—I have met with much invective in the papers for these two years past against the hard-heartedness of the rich, and much complaint of the great oppressions suffered in this country by the laboring poor. Will you admit a word or two on the other side of the question? I do not propose to be an advocate for oppression or oppressors. But when I see that the poor are, by such writings, exasperated against the rich, and excited to insurrections, by which much mischief is done, and some forfeit their lives, I could wish the true state of things were better understood, the poor not made by these busy writers more uneasy and unhappy than their situation subjects them to be, and the nation not brought into disrepute among foreigners, by public groundless accusations of ourselves, as if the rich in England had no compassion for the poor, and Englishmen wanted common humanity.—Smyth 5:122. (1768.)

POOR, The Rich Pass Laws in England to Help the.—In justice, then, to this country, give me leave to remark that the condition of the poor here [in England] is by far the best in Europe, for that, except in England and her American colonies, there is not in any country of the known world, not even in Scotland or Ireland, a provision by law to enforce a support of the poor. Everywhere else necessity reduces to beggary. This law was not made by the poor. The legislators were men of fortune. By that act they voluntarily subjected their own estates, and the estates of all others, to the payment of a tax for the maintenance of the poor, encumbering those estates with a kind of rent-charge for that purpose, whereby the poor are vested with an inheritance, as it were, in all the estates of the rich.—Smyth 5:123. (1768.)

POOR, Charity to Poor Far Less Beneficial than Expected.—I wish they were benefited by this generous provision in any degree equal to the good intention with which it was made, and is continued; but I fear the giving mankind a dependence on anything for support, in age or sickness, besides industry and frugality during youth and health, tends to flatter our natural indolence, to encourage idleness and prodigality, and thereby to promote and increase poverty, the very evil it was intended to cure; thus multiplying beggars instead of diminishing them.

Besides this tax which the rich in England have subjected themselves to in behalf of the poor, amounting in some places to five or six shillings in the pound of the annual income, they have, by donations and subscriptions, erected numerous schools in various parts of the kingdom for educating gratis the children of the poor in reading and writing, and in many of those schools the children are also fed and clothed. They have erected hospitals at immense expense for the reception and cure of the sick, the lame, the wounded, and the insane poor, for lying-in women and deserted children. They are also continually contributing towards making up losses occasioned by fire, by storms, or by floods, and to relieve the poor in severe seasons of frost, in times of scarcity, etc., in which benevolent and charitable contributions no nation exceeds us. Surely, there is some gratitude due for so many instances of goodness.—Smyth 5:123. (1768.)

POOR, Best Means of Helping.—I am for doing good to the poor, but I differ in opinion about the means. I think the best way of doing good to the poor is not making them easy *in* poverty, but leading or driving them *out* of it.—Smyth 5:537. (1772.)

POOR, Corrupted by Welfare Aid.—In my youth I traveled much, and I observed in different countries that the more public provisions were made for the poor, the less they provided for themselves, and of course became poorer. And, on the contrary, the less was done for them, the more they did for

themselves, and became richer. There is no country in the world where so many provisions are established for them [as in England]; so many hospitals to receive them when they are sick or lame, founded and maintained by voluntary charities; so many almshouses for the aged of both sexes, together with a solemn general law made by the rich to subject their estates to a heavy tax for the support of the poor. Under all these obligations, are our poor modest, humble, and thankful? And do they use their best endeavors to maintain themselves, and lighten our shoulders of this burden? On the contrary, I affirm that there is no country in the world in which the poor are more idle, dissolute, drunken, and insolent. The day you passed that act, you took away from before their eyes the greatest of all inducements to industry, frugality, and sobriety, by giving them a dependence on somewhat else than a careful accumulation during youth and health, for support in age or sickness.

In short, you offered a premium for the encouragement of idleness, and you should not now wonder that it has had its effect in the increase of poverty. Repeal that law, and you will soon see a change in their manners. *Saint Monday* and *Saint Tuesday* will soon cease to be holidays. *Six days shalt thou labor,* though one of the old commandments long treated as out of date, will again be looked upon as a respectable precept; industry will increase, and with it plenty among the lower people; their circumstances will mend, and more will be done for their happiness by inuring them to provide for themselves than could be done by dividing all your estates among them.—Smyth 5:538. (1772.)

POOR, English System of Caring for Poor a Mistake.—I have long been of . . . opinion that your [England's] legal provision for the poor is a very great evil, operating as it does to the encouragement of idleness. We have followed your example, and begin now to see our error, and, I hope, shall reform it.— Smyth 10:64. (1789.)

POPULARITY, Virtue the Best Means of Achieving.—Almost every man has a strong natural desire of being valued and esteemed by the rest of his species, but I am concerned and grieved to see how few fall into the right and only infallible method of becoming so. That laudable ambition is too commonly misapplied and often ill employed. Some to make themselves considerable pursue learning, others grasp at wealth; some aim at being thought witty; and others are only careful to make the most of an handsome person; but what is wit, or wealth, or form, or learning, when compared with virtue? 'Tis true, we love the handsome, we applaud the learned, and we fear the rich and powerful; but we even worship and adore the virtuous. Nor is it strange; since men of virtue are so rare, so very rare to be found. If we were as industrious to become good as to make ourselves great, we should become really great by being

good, and the number of valuable men would be much increased; but it is a grand mistake to think of being great without goodness; and I pronounce it as certain, that there was never yet a truly great man that was not at the same time truly virtuous.—Smyth 2:108. (1729.)

POPULATION, of America, Should Double About Every Twenty Years.—Hence marriages in *America* are more general, and more generally early, than in *Europe*. And if it is reckoned there that there is but one marriage per annum among 100 persons, perhaps we may here reckon two; and if in *Europe* they have but four births to a marriage (many of their marriages being late), we may here reckon eight, of which if one half grow up, and our marriages are made, reckoning one with another at 20 years of age, our people must at least be doubled every 20 years.—Smyth 3:65. (1751.)

POPULATION, Eventually to Cover North America.—But notwithstanding this increase, so vast is the territory of *North America* that it will require many ages to settle it fully; and, till it is fully settled, labor will never be cheap here.—Smyth 3:65. (1751.)

POPULATION, of America, to Exceed That of England.—This million [now in America] doubling, suppose but once in 25 years, will, in another century, be more than the people of *England,* and the greatest number of *Englishmen* will be on this side [of] the water.—Smyth 3:71. (1751.)

POST OFFICE, Headquarters in Philadelphia.—I need not tell you that Philadelphia, being the center of the ... colonies and having constant communication with the West India Islands, is by much a fitter place for the situation of a general post office than Virginia, and that it would be some reputation to our province to have it established here.—Smyth 3:50. (1751.)

POST OFFICE, Mails Transported Day and Night.—I will now only just mention that we hope in the spring to expedite the communication between Boston and New York, as we have already that between New York and Philadelphia, by making the mails travel by night as well as by day, which has never heretofore been done in America. It passes now between Philadelphia and New York so quick that a letter can be sent from one place to another and an answer received the day following, which before took a week, and when our plan is executed between Boston and New York, letters may be sent and answers received in four days, which before took a fortnight; and between Philadelphia and Boston in six days, which before required three weeks.—Smyth 4:215. (1764.)

PRAISE, All Desire to Hear It.—What you mention concerning the love of praise is indeed very true; it reigns more or less in every heart; though we are generally hypocrites, in that respect, and pretend to disregard praise, and our nice, modest ears are offended, forsooth, with what one of the ancients calls *the sweetest kind of music.*—Smyth 3:54. (1751.)

PRAYER, For Daily Use, Written by Franklin at Age 27.—And conceiving God to be the fountain of wisdom, I thought it right and necessary to solicit his assistance for obtaining it; to this end I formed the following little prayer ... for daily use.

"O powerful Goodness! bountiful Father! merciful Guide! Increase in me that wisdom which discovers my truest interest. Strengthen my resolutions to perform what that wisdom dictates. Accept my kind offices to thy other children as the only return in my power for thy continual favors to me."—Autobiography. Smyth 1:332. (1784.)

PRAYER, For Peace and Protection During Wartime.—May the God of wisdom, strength, and power, the Lord of the armies of Israel, inspire us with prudence in this time of danger; take away from us all the seeds of contention and division, and unite the hearts and counsels of all of us, of whatever sect or nation, in one bond of peace, brotherly love, and generous public spirit; may He give us strength and resolution to amend our lives, and remove from among us everything that is displeasing to Him; afford us His most gracious protection, confound the designs of our enemies, and give peace in all our borders.—Smyth 2:353. (1747.)

PRAYER, Franklin's Plea for, at the Constitutional Convention.—The small progress we have made, after four or five weeks' close attendance and continual reasonings with each other, our different sentiments on almost every question, several of the last producing as many *noes* as *ayes*, is, methinks, a melancholy proof of the imperfection of the human understanding. We indeed seem to *feel* our own want of political wisdom, since we have been running all about in search of it. We have gone back to ancient history for models of government, and examined the different forms of those republics which, having been originally formed with the seeds of their own dissolution, now no longer exist; and we have viewed modern states all round Europe, but find none of their constitutions suitable to our circumstances.

In this situation of this assembly, groping, as it were, in the dark to find political truth, and scarce able to distinguish it when presented to us, how has it happened, Sir, that we have not hitherto once thought of humbly applying to the Father of Lights to illuminate our understandings? In the beginning of the contest with Britain, when we were sensible of danger, we had daily prayers in this room for the divine protection. Our prayers, Sir, were heard—and they were graciously answered. All of us who were engaged in the struggle must have observed frequent instances of a superintending Providence in our favor. To that kind providence we owe this happy opportunity of consulting in peace on the means of establishing our future national felicity. And have we now forgotten that powerful Friend? Or do we imagine we no longer need [His] assistance?

I have lived, Sir, a long time; and the longer I live, the more convincing proofs I see of this truth, *that God governs in the affairs of men.* And if a sparrow cannot fall to the ground without His notice, is it probable that an empire can rise without His aid? We have been assured, Sir, in the sacred writings, that "except the Lord build the house, they labor in vain that build it." I firmly believe this; and I also believe that, without His concurring aid, we shall succeed in this political building no better than the builders of Babel; we shall be divided by our little, partial, local interests, our projects will be confounded, and we ourselves shall become a reproach and a byword down to future ages. And, what is worse, mankind may hereafter, from this unfortunate instance, despair of establishing government by human wisdom and leave it to chance, war, and conquest.

I therefore beg leave to move,

That henceforth prayers, imploring the assistance of Heaven and its blessing on our deliberations, be held in this Assembly every morning before we proceed to business; and that one or more of the clergy of this city be requested to officiate in that service. *—Smyth 9:600. (1787.)

*See page 259 of the biography for an explanation of the convention's response to this motion.—Ed.

PRAYER OF PRAISE, Written by Franklin at Age 22.—O wise God, my good Father! Thou beholdest the sincerity of my heart and of my devotion; grant me a continuance of thy favor!

O Creator, O Father! I believe that thou art good, and that thou art *pleased with the pleasure* of thy children.—Praised be thy name forever!

By thy power hast thou made the glorious sun, with his attending worlds; from the energy of thy mighty will they first received their prodigious motion, and by thy wisdom hast thou prescribed the wondrous laws by which they move.—Praised be thy name forever!

By thy wisdom hast thou formed all things. Thou hast created man, bestowing life and reason, and placed him in dignity superior to thy other earthly creatures.—Praised be thy name forever!

Thy wisdom, thy power, and thy goodness are everywhere clearly seen; in the air and in the water, in the heaven and on the earth; thou providest for the various winged fowl, and the innumerable inhabitants of the water; thou givest cold and heat, rain and sunshine, in their season, and to the fruits of the earth increase.—Praised be thy name forever!

Thou abhorrest in thy creatures treachery and deceit, malice, revenge, *intemperance,* and every other hurtful vice; but thou art a lover of justice and sincerity, of friendship and benevolence, and every virtue. Thou art my Friend, my Father, and my Benefactor.— Praised be thy name, O God, forever! Amen!—Smyth 2:94. (1728.)

PRAYER OF PETITION, Written by Franklin at Age 22.—That I may be preserved from atheism and infidelity, impiety and profaneness, and, in my addresses to thee, carefully avoid irreverence and ostentation, formality and odious hypocrisy—Help me, O Father!

That I may be loyal to my Prince, and faithful to my country, careful for its good, valiant in its defense, and obedient to its laws, abhorring treason as much as tyranny—Help me, O Father!

That I may to those above me be dutiful, humble, and submissive; avoiding pride, disrespect, and contumacy—Help me, O Father!

That I may to those below me be gracious, condescending, and forgiving, using clemency, protecting *innocent distress,* avoiding cruelty, harshness, and oppression, insolence, and unreasonable severity— Help me, O Father!

That I may refrain from censure, calumny and detraction; that I may avoid and abhor deceit and envy, fraud, flattery, and hatred, malice, lying, and ingratitude—Help me, O Father!

That I may be sincere in friendship, faithful in trust, and impartial in judgment, watchful against pride, and against anger (that momentary madness)—Help me, O Father!

That I may be just in all my dealings, temperate in my pleasures, full of candor and ingenuity, humanity and benevolence—Help me, O Father !

That I may be grateful to my benefactors, and generous to my friends, exercising charity and liberality to the poor, and pity to the miserable—Help me, O Father!

That I may avoid avarice and ambition, jealousy and intemperance, falsehood, luxury, and lasciviousness—Help me, O Father!

That I may possess integrity and evenness of mind, resolution in difficulties, and fortitude under affliction; that I may be punctual in performing my promises, peaceable and prudent in my behavior—Help me, O Father!

That I may have tenderness for the weak, and reverent respect for the ancient; that I may be kind to my neighbors, good-natured to my companions, and hospitable to strangers—Help me, O Father!

That I may be averse to talebearing, backbiting, detraction, slander, and craft, and overreaching, abhor extortion, perjury, and every kind of wickedness—Help me, O Father!

That I may be honest and open-hearted, gentle, merciful, and good, cheerful in spirit, rejoicing in the good of others—Help me, O Father!

That I may have a constant regard to honor and probity, that I may possess a perfect innocence and a good conscience, and at length become truly virtuous and magnanimous—Help me, good God; help me, O Father!

And, forasmuch as ingratitude is one of the most odious of vices, let me not be unmindful gratefully to acknowledge the favors I receive from Heaven.—Smyth 2:98. (1728.)

PRAYER OF THANKSGIVING, Written by Franklin at Age 22.—For peace and liberty, for food and raiment, for corn, and wine, and milk, and every kind of healthful nourishment—Good God, I thank thee!

For the common benefits of air and light; for useful fire and delicious water—Good God, I thank thee!

For knowledge, and literature, and every useful art, for my friends and their prosperity, and for the fewness of my enemies—Good God, I thank thee!

For all thy innumerable benefits; for life, and reason, and the use of speech; for health, and joy, and every pleasant hour—My good God, I thank thee!—Smyth 2:99. (1728.)

PRAYER SERVICE, Lack of Attendance Remedied.—We had for our chaplain [on the Pennsylvania frontier in 1756] a zealous Presbyterian minister, Mr. Beatty, who complained to me that the men did not generally attend his prayers and exhortations. When they enlisted, they were promised, besides pay and provisions, a gill of rum a day, which was punctually served out to them, half in the morning, and the other half in the evening; and I observed they were as punctual in attending to receive it; upon which I said to Mr. Beatty, "It is, perhaps, below the dignity of your profession to act as steward of the rum, but if you were to deal it out and only just after prayers, you would have them all about you." He liked the thought, undertook the office, and, with the help of a few hands to measure out the liquor, executed it to satisfaction, and never were prayers more generally and more punctually attended; so that I thought this method preferable to the punishment inflicted by some military laws for non-attendance on divine service.—Autobiography. Smyth 1:411. (1788.)

PRAYERS, For Battle of Cape Breton.—Our people are extremely impatient to hear of your success at Cape Breton.... You have a fast and prayer day for that purpose; in which I compute five hundred thousand petitions were offered up to the same effect in New England, which, added to the petitions of every family morning and evening, multiplied by the number of days since January 25th, make forty-five millions of prayers; which, set against the prayers of a few priests in the garrison, to the Virgin Mary, give a vast balance in your favor.

If you do not succeed, I fear I shall have but an indifferent opinion of Presbyterian prayers in such cases, as long as I live.—Smyth 2:283. (1745.)

PRESS, Qualities of a Good Reporter.—There are many who have long desired to see a good newspaper in Pennsylvania; and we hope those gentlemen who are able will contribute towards the making this [the *Pennsylvania Gazette*] such. We ask assistance because we are fully sensible that to publish a good newspaper is not so easy an undertaking as many people imagine it to be. The author of a gazette (in the opinion of the learned) ought to be qualified with an extensive acquaintance with languages, a great easiness and command of writing and relating things clearly and intelligibly, and in few words; he should be able to speak of war both

Franklin in 1783 (age 77). Portrait by Joseph Siffred Duplessis.

by land and sea; be well acquainted with geography, with the history of the time, with the several interests of princes and states, the secrets of courts, and the manners and customs of all nations. Men thus accomplished are very rare in this remote part of the world; and it would be well if the writer of these papers could make up among his friends what is wanting in himself.—Smyth 2:156. (1729.)

PRESS, Always Offending Somebody.—The business of printing has chiefly to do with men's opinions; most things that are printed tending to promote some, or oppose others....

Hence arises the peculiar unhappiness of that business which other callings are no way liable to; they who follow printing being scarce able to do anything in their way of getting a living which shall not probably give offense to some, and perhaps to many.—Smyth 2:173. (1731.)

PRESS, Should Present Both Sides of an Issue.—Printers are educated in the belief that when men differ in opinion, both sides ought equally to have the advantage of being heard by the public; and that when truth and error have fair play, the former is always an overmatch for the latter. Hence they cheerfully serve all contending writers that pay them well, without regarding on which side they are of the question in dispute.—Smyth 2:174. (1731.)

PRESS, Views Reported May Not Be Those of the Publisher.—It is unreasonable to imagine printers approve of everything they print, and to censure them on any particular thing accordingly; since in the way of their business they print such great variety of things opposite and contradictory. It is likewise as unreasonable what some assert, "That printers ought not to print anything but what they approve," since if all of that business should make such a resolution, and abide by it, an end would thereby be put to free writing, and the world would afterwards have nothing to read but what happened to be the opinions of printers.—Smyth 2:174. (1731.)

PRESS, Publishes What People Demand.—If they sometimes print vicious or silly things not worth reading, it may not be because they approve such things themselves, but because the people are so viciously and corruptly educated that good

things are not encouraged. I have known a very numerous impression of Robin Hood's songs go off in this province at 2 shillings per book, in less than a twelvemonth, when a small quantity of David's psalms (an excellent version) have lain upon my hands above twice the time.—Smyth 2:175. (1731.)

PRESS, Freedom of, Carries Social Responsibilities.—Printers do continually discourage the printing of great numbers of bad things, and stifle them in the birth. I myself have constantly refused to print anything that might countenance vice, or promote immorality; though by complying in such cases with the corrupt taste of the majority I might have got much money. I have also always refused to print such things as might do real injury to any person, how much soever I have been solicited, and tempted with offers of great pay; and how much soever I have by refusing got the ill will of those who would have employed me. I have hitherto fallen under the resentment of large bodies of men for refusing absolutely to print any of their party or personal reflections. In this manner I have made myself many enemies, and the constant fatigue of denying is almost insupportable.—Smyth 2:175. (1731.)

In the conduct of my newspaper, I carefully excluded all libeling and personal abuse, which is of late years become so disgraceful to our country.... Now, many of our printers make no scruple of gratifying the malice of individuals by false accusations of the fairest characters among ourselves, augmenting animosity even to the producing of duels; and are, moreover, so indiscreet as to print scurrilous reflections on the government of neighboring states, and even on the conduct of our best national allies, which may be attended with the most pernicious consequences. These things I mention as a caution to young printers, and that they may be encouraged not to pollute their presses and disgrace their profession by such infamous practices, but refuse steadily, as they may see by my example that such a course of conduct will not, on the whole, be injurious to their interests.— Autobiography. Smyth 1:343. (1788.)

PRESS, Laden with Irresponsible Allegations.—But the inconsistency that strikes me the most is that between the name of your city, Philadelphia (*Brotherly Love*), and the spirit of rancor, malice, and *hatred* that breathes in its newspapers. For I learn from those papers that your state is divided into parties, that each party ascribes all the public operations of the other to vicious motives; that they do not even suspect one another of the smallest degree of honesty; that the Anti-Federalists are such, merely from the fear of losing power, places, or emoluments, which they have in possession or in expectation; that the Federalists are a set of *conspirators,* who aim at establishing a tyranny over the persons and property of their countrymen, and

to live in splendor on the plunder of the people.—Smyth 9:640. (1788.)
PRESS, Obituaries Turn Devils into Angels.—There is, however, one of your *inconsistencies* that consoles me a little, which is that, though *living* you give one another the characters of devils, *dead,* you are all angels! It is delightful, when any of you die, to read what good husbands, good fathers, good friends, good citizens, and good Christians you were, concluding with a scrap of poetry that places you, with certainty, every one in Heaven. So that I think Pennsylvania a good country *to die in,* though a very bad one to *live in.*—Smyth 9:642. (1788.)
PRESS, Performs Disservice to America by Giving Wrong Impressions Abroad.—There is, indeed, a good deal of manifest *inconsistency* in all this, and yet a stranger, seeing it in your own prints, though he does not believe it all, may probably believe enough of it to conclude that Pennsylvania is peopled by a set of the most unprincipled, wicked, rascally, and quarrelsome scoundrels upon the face of the globe. I have sometimes, indeed, suspected that those papers are the manufacture of foreign enemies among you, who write with a view of disgracing your country, and making you appear contemptible and detestable all the world over; but then I wonder at the indiscretion of your printers in publishing such writings.— Smyth 9:642. (1788.)
PRESS, Franklin's Indictment of Irresponsibility Among Reporters. —(For full text of Franklin's

"Account of the Supremest Court of Judicature in Pennsylvania, Viz. the Court of the Press" [1789], see Smyth 10:36–40.)

PRIDE, Costly.—*Poor Dick* farther advises, and says,

> Fond pride of dress is sure a very curse;
> E'er fancy you consult, consult your purse.

And again, *Pride is as loud a beggar as want, and a great deal more saucy.* When you have bought one fine thing, you must buy ten more, that your appearance may be all of a piece; but *Poor Dick* says, *'Tis easier to suppress the first desire, than to satisfy all that follow it.* And 'tis as truly folly for the poor to ape the rich, as for the frog to swell in order to equal the ox.

> Great estates may venture more,
> But little boats should keep near shore.

'Tis, however, a folly soon punished; for *Pride that dines on vanity sups on contempt,* as *Poor Richard* says. And in another place, *Pride breakfasted with plenty, dined with poverty, and supped with infamy.*—Smyth 3:415. (1757.)

PRIDE, Hard to Subdue.—There is perhaps no one of our natural passions so hard to subdue as *pride.* Disguise it, struggle with it, beat it down, stifle it, mortify it as much as one pleases, it is still alive and will every now and then peep out and show itself.... Even if I could conceive that I had completely overcome it, I should probably be proud of my humility.—Autobiography. Smyth 1:339. (1784.)

PRISONERS, British Treatment of American.—It has been said that among the civilized nations of Europe the ancient horrors of that state [war] are much diminished. But the compelling men by chains,

stripes, and famine to fight against their friends and relations is a new mode of barbarity which your nation [England] alone has the honor of inventing. And the sending American prisoners of war to Africa and Asia, remote from all probability of exchange, and where they can scarce hope ever to hear from their families even if the unwholesomeness of the climate does not put a speedy end to their lives, is a manner of treating captives that you can justify by no precedent or custom except that of the black savages of Guinea.—Smyth 7:37. (1777.)

You in England, if you wish for peace, have at present the opportunity of trying this means, with regard to the prisoners now in your jails. They complain of very severe treatment. They are far from their friends and families, and winter is coming on, in which they must suffer extremely, if continued in their present situation; fed scantily on bad provisions, without warm lodging, clothes, or fire, and not suffered to invite or receive visits from their friends, or even from the humane and charitable of their enemies.—Smyth 7:70. (1777.)

PRISONERS, British, Receive Kind Treatment from Americans.—I can assure you, from my own certain knowledge, that your people, prisoners in America, have been treated with great kindness; they have been served with the same rations of wholesome provisions with our own troops, comfortable lodgings have been provided for them, and they have been allowed large bounds of villages in a healthy air, to walk and amuse themselves with on their parole.—Smyth 7:70. (1777.)

Our captains have set at liberty above 200 of your people, made prisoners by our armed vessels and brought into France, besides a great number dismissed at sea on your coasts, to whom vessels were given to carry them in; but you have not returned us a man in exchange. If we had sold your people to the Moors at Sallee, as you have many of ours to the African and East India Companies, could you have complained?—Smyth 7:72. (1777.)

PRISONERS, Americans Sent to Africa.—We have received late and authentic information that numbers of such prisoners, some of them fathers of families in America, having been sent to Africa, are now in the fort of Senegal, condemned in that unwholesome climate to the hardest labor and most inhuman treatment.—Smyth 7:165. (1778.)

PRISONERS, England Reneges on Exchange.—I a long time believed that your government [officials] were in earnest in agreeing to an exchange of prisoners. I begin now to think I was mistaken. It seems they cannot give up the pleasing idea of having at the end of the war one thousand Americans to hang for high treason. You were also long of opinion that the animosity against America was not national or general; but having seen the exterminating proclamation of the commissioners approved by King, Lords, and Commons, and that not attended by any marks of popular disapprobation, perhaps you too

begin to think you are mistaken.—Smyth 7:219. (1779.)

PRISONERS, Americans Threatened and Deceived.—And it is now evident that the delays have been of design, to give more opportunity of seducing the men by promises and hardships to seek their liberty in engaging against their country. For we learn from those who have escaped that there are persons continually employed in cajoling and menacing them, representing to them that we neglect them, that your government is willing to exchange them; and that it is our fault it is not done; that all the news from America is bad on their side; we shall be conquered and they will be hanged, if they do not accept the gracious offer of being pardoned, on condition of serving the King, etc.—Smyth 7:267. (1779.)

PRISONERS, Exchange of.—The prisoners in England are increasing by the late practice of sending our people from New York, and the refusal of the English admiralty to exchange any Americans for Englishmen not taken by American armed vessels. I would mention it for the consideration of Congress, whether it may not be well to set apart 500 or 600 English prisoners, and refuse them all exchange in America, but for our countrymen now confined in England.—Smyth 8:254. (1781.)

PRISONERS, Privateers Bring None to Exchange.—Our privateers, when in the European seas, will rarely bring in their [British] prisoners when they can get rid of them at sea. Some of our poor brave countrymen have been in that cruel captivity now near four years. I hope the Congress will take this matter into immediate consideration and find some means for their deliverance, and to prevent the sending more from America. By my last accounts, the number now in the several prisons amounts to upwards of 800.—Smyth 8:323. (1781.)

There are now near a thousand of our brave fellows prisoners in England, many of whom have patiently endured the hardships of that confinement several years, resisting every temptation to serve our enemies. Will not your [Congress'] late great advantages put it in your power to do something for their relief? The slender supply I have been able to afford, of a shilling a week to each, for their greater comfort during the winter, amounts weekly to fifty pounds sterling. An exchange would make so many of our countrymen happy, add to our strength, and diminish our expense. But our privateers, who cruise in Europe, will not be at the trouble of bringing in their prisoners, and I have none to exchange for them.— Smyth 8:392. (1782.)

PRISONERS, Many Die Daily.—I just hear from Ireland that there are 200 of our people prisoners there, who are destitute of every necessary, and die daily in numbers. You are about to have a new ministry, I hear. If a sincere reconciliation is desired, kindness to the captives on both sides may promote it greatly.—Smyth 8:409. (1782.)

PRISONERS, Release Could Facilitate Reconciliation.—When you consider the injustice of your war with us and the barbarous manner in which it has been carried on, the many suffering families among us from your burning of towns, scalping by savages, etc., etc., will it not appear to you that, though a cessation of the war may be a peace, it may not be a reconciliation? Will not some volunatry acts of justice, and even of kindness on your part, have excellent effects towards producing such a *reconciliation*? Can you not find means of repairing in some degree those injuries? You have in England and Ireland twelve hundred of our people prisoners, who have for years bravely suffered all the hardships of that confinement, rather than enter into your service to fight against their country. Methinks you ought to glory in descendants of such virtue. What if you were to begin your measures of *reconciliation* by setting them at liberty? I know it would procure for you the liberty of an equal number of your people, even without a previous stipulation; and the confidence in our equity, with the apparent good will in the action, would give very good impressions of your change of disposition towards us.—Smyth 8:414. (1782.)

PRISONERS, Exchange of Americans for General Burgoyne and Lord Cornwallis.—The Congress having, by a resolution of the 14th of June last, empowered me to offer an exchange of General Burgoyne for the Honorable Henry Laurens, then a prisoner in the Tower of London, and whose liberty they much desire to obtain, which exchange, though proposed by me, according to the said resolution, had not been accepted or executed, when advice was received that General Burgoyne was exchanged in virtue of another agreement; and Mr. Laurens thereupon having proposed another lieutenant-general, viz. Lord Cornwallis, as an exchange for himself, promising that, if set at liberty, he would do his utmost to obtain a confirmation of that proposal.—Smyth 8:537. (1782.)

PRISONERS, American, Befriended by a Presbyterian Minister in England.—Our people who were prisoners in England are now all discharged. During the whole war, those who were in Forton prison, near Portsmouth, were much befriended by the constant charitable care of Mr. [Thomas] Wren, a Presbyterian minister there, who spared no pains to assist them in their sickness and distress, by procuring and distributing among them the contributions of good Christians, and prudently dispensing the allowance I made them, which gave him a great deal of trouble, but he went through it cheerfully. I think some public notice should be taken of this good man. I wish the Congress would enable me to make him a present, and that some of our universities would confer upon him the degree of Doctor.—Smyth 9:72. (1783.)

PRISONERS. See also TREASON.

PRIVATE AFFAIRS, Managed Far Better than Public Affairs.—Naturally one would imagine that the interest of a few individuals should give way to general interest, but individuals manage their affairs with so much more application, industry, and address than the public do theirs that general interest most commonly gives way to particular. We assemble parliaments and councils, to have the benefit of their collected wisdom; but we necessarily have, at the same time, the inconvenience of their collected passions, prejudices, and private interests. By the help of these, artful men overpower their wisdom, and dupe its possessors; and if we may judge by the acts, *arrets*, and edicts, all the world over, for regulating commerce, an assembly of great men is the greatest fool upon earth.—Smyth 9:241. (1784.)

PRIVATEERING, Generally Unprofitable.—The practice of robbing merchants on the high seas, a remnant of the ancient piracy, though it may be accidentally beneficial to particular persons, is far from being profitable to all engaged in it, or to the nation that authorizes it. In the beginning of a war, some rich ships, not upon their guard, are surprised and taken. This encourages the first adventurers to fit out more armed vessels, and many others to do the same. But the enemy at the same time become more careful, arm their merchant ships better, and render them not so easy to be taken; they go also more under protection of convoys; thus, while the privateers to take them are multiplied, the vessels subject to be taken, and the chances of profit, are diminished, so that many cruises are made wherein the expenses overgo the gains; and, as is the case in other lotteries, though particulars have got prizes, the mass of adventurers are losers, the whole expense of fitting out all the privateers, during a war, being much greater than the whole amount of goods taken.— Smyth 9:4. (1783.)

PRIVATEERING, Used by England During Revolutionary War.— Privateering is the universal bent of the English nation, at home and abroad, wherever settled. No less than 700 privateers were, it is said, commissioned in the last war! These were fitted out by merchants to prey upon other merchants, who had never done them any injury. Is there probably any one of those privateering merchants of London, who were so ready to rob the merchants of Amsterdam, that would not readily plunder another London merchant of the next street, if he could do it with impunity?— Smyth 9:296. (1785.)

PRIVATEERING, U.S. Seeks to Outlaw.—The United States of America, though better situated than any European nation to make profit by privateering (most of the trade of Europe, with the West Indies, passing before their doors), are, as far as in them lies, endeavoring to abolish the practice, by offering in all their treaties with other powers an article, engagingly solemn, that in case of future war, no privateer shall be commissioned

on either side; and that unarmed merchant ships, on both sides, shall pursue their voyages unmolested. This will be a happy improvement of the law of nations.—Smyth 9:299. (1785.)

PROGRESS OF MAN, Recent Trends Make Franklin Wish He Had Been Born at a Later Time.—I have been long impressed with...the growing felicity of mankind, from the improvements in philosophy, morals, politics, and even the conveniences of common living, by the invention and acquisition of new and useful utensils and instruments, that I have sometimes almost wished it had been my destiny to be born two or three centuries hence. For invention and improvement are prolific, and beget more of their kind. The present progress is rapid. Many of great importance, now unthought of, will before that period be produced; and then I might not only enjoy their advantages, but have my curiosity gratified in knowing what they are to be.— Smyth 9:651. (1788.)

PROPERTY, Subject to Regulation by the State.—All the property that is necessary to a man for the conservation of the individual and the propagation of the species is his natural right, which none can justly deprive him of. But all property superfluous to such purposes is the property of the public, who, by their laws, have created it, and who may therefore by other laws dispose of it, whenever the welfare of the public shall demand such disposition. He that does not like civil society on these terms, let him retire and live among savages. He can have no right to the benefit of society who will not pay his club towards the support of it.—Smyth 9:138. (1783.)

PROPRIETARY GOVERNMENTS, All Troublesome Until Becoming Colonies of the Crown.—It is very remarkable that disputes of the same kind have arisen in *all* proprietary governments, and subsisted till their dissolution. All were made unhappy by them, and found no relief but in recurring finally to the immediate government of the Crown.—Smyth 4:227. (1764.)

PROPRIETARY GOVERNMENTS, Inherently Defective.—I see no reason to suppose that all proprietary rulers are worse men than other rulers, nor that all people in proprietary governments are worse people than those in other governments. I suspect, therefore, that the cause is radical, interwoven in the constitution, and so become of the very nature, of proprietary governments; and will therefore produce its effects as long as such governments continue.—Smyth 4:228. (1764.)

PUNCTUALITY, A Prime Virtue in Business.—After industry and frugality, nothing contributes more to the raising of a young man in the world than punctuality and justice in all his dealings; therefore never keep borrowed money an hour beyond the time you promised, lest a disappointment shut up your friend's purse forever.—Smyth 2:371. (1748.)

Q

QUAKERS, Vote for Arms Even If They Will Not Bear Arms.—I know the Quakers now think it their duty, when chosen, to consider themselves as representatives of the *whole people*, and not of their own sect only; they consider the public money as raised from and belonging to the *whole public*, and not for their own sect only; and therefore, though they can neither bear arms themselves nor compel others to do it, yet very lately when our frontier inhabitants, who are chiefly Presbyterians or Churchmen [Anglicans], thought themselves in danger, and the poor among them were unable to provide arms, and petitioned the [Pennsylvania] House, a sum was voted for these purposes, and put into the hands of a committee to procure and supply them.—Smyth 3:277. (1755.)

QUAKERS, Decline Seats in the Assembly.—The Quakers have now pretty generally declined their seats in Assembly, very few remaining. We shall soon see if matters will be better managed by a majority of different religious persuasions.—Smyth 3:345. (1756.)

QUAKERS, Accused of War Mongering.—You tell me the Quakers are charged on your side of the water [in England] with being, by their aggressions, the cause of the war. Would you believe it that they are charged here, not with offending the Indians and thereby provoking the war, but with gaining their friendship by presents, supplying them privately with arms and ammunition, and engaging them to fall upon and murder the poor white people on the frontiers? Would you think it possible that thousands even here should be made to believe this, and many hundreds of them be raised in arms, not only to kill some converted Indians, supposed to be under the Quakers' protection, but to punish the Quakers who were supposed to give that protection? Would you think these people audacious enough to avow such designs in a public declaration, sent to the Governor? Would you imagine that innocent Quakers, men of fortune and character, should think it necessary to fly for safety out of Philadelphia into the Jerseys, fearing the violence of such armed mobs and confiding little in the power or inclination of the government to protect them?—Smyth 4:222. (1764.)

QUAKERS, Should Not Pay Tax for Other Clergy.—I would only mention at present one article, that of maintenance for the clergy. It seems to me that by the [Massachusetts] Constitution, the Quakers may be obliged to pay the tax for that purpose. But as the great end in imposing it is professedly the promotion of piety, religion, and morality, and those people have found means of securing that end among themselves without a regular clergy, and their teachers are not allowed to receive money, I should think it not right to tax them, and give the money to the teacher of the parish.—Smyth 8:256. (1781.)

QUARTERING OF ENGLISH TROOPS, In Colonial Homes.—There was a bill brought in with a clause to empower the military officers to quarter soldiers on private houses. This, if it had passed, we apprehended might be used to awe us, and as an instrument of oppression upon occasion, and therefore we opposed it vigorously. I think I may value myself on having a considerable place in getting this clause struck out, and another put in that may occasionally save our province a great deal of money.—Smyth 4:388. (1765.)

R

READING, Observations on Proper Oral Training.—Reading should also be taught, and pronouncing, properly, distinctly, emphatically; not with an even tone, which *under-does*, nor a theatrical, which *over-does* nature.—Smyth 2:391. (1749.)

READING, By Phonetic Syllabication.—It is expected that every scholar to be admitted into this school [an English school which Franklin proposed to the Philadelphia Academy] be at least able to pronounce and divide the syllables in reading, and to write a legible hand.—Smyth 3:21. (1750.)

READING, Selection of Material Important.—Let the lessons for reading be varied, that the youth may be made acquainted with good styles of all kinds in prose and verse, and the proper manner of reading each kind. Sometimes a well-told story, a piece of a sermon, a general's speech to his soldiers, a speech in a tragedy, some part of a comedy, an ode, a satire, a letter, blank verse,

Hudibrastic, heroic, etc. But let such lessons for reading be chosen as contain some useful instruction, whereby the understandings or morals of the youth may at the same time be improved.—Smyth 3:23. (1750.)

READING, Importance of Understanding Content.—When our boys read *English* to us, we are apt to imagine *they* understand what *they* read, because *we* do, and because it is their mother tongue. But they often read as parrots speak, knowing little or nothing of the meaning. And it is impossible a reader should give the due modulation to his voice, and pronounce properly, unless his understanding goes before his tongue and makes him master of the sentiment. Accustoming boys to read aloud what they do not first understand is the cause of those even, set tones so common among readers, which, when they have once got a habit of using, they find so difficult to correct; by which means, among fifty readers, we scarcely find a good one.—Smyth 3:24. (1750.)

REASON, Seldom Used.—They [some Englishmen with whom Franklin was disputing] added other reasons, that were no reasons at all, and made me, as upon a hundred other occasions, almost wish that mankind had never been endowed with a reasoning faculty, since they know so little how to make use of it, and so often mislead themselves by it, and that they had been furnished with a good sensible instinct instead of it.—Smyth 5:48. (1767.)

REBELLION, Not Justified in Minor Matters.—As between friends every affront is not worth a duel, between nations every injury not worth a war, so between the governed and the governing, every mistake in government, every encroachment on rights, is not worth a rebellion. 'Tis, in my opinion, sufficient for the present that we hold them [our rights] forth on all occasions, not giving up any of them; using at the same time every means to make them generally understood and valued by the people; cultivating a harmony among the colonies, that their union in the same sentiments may give them greater weight; remembering withal that this Protestant country (our Mother, though of late an unkind one) is worth preserving.—Smyth 6:273. (1774.)

RECOMMENDATION, Model Letter of.—Sir: The bearer of this, who is going to America, presses me to give him a letter of recommendation, though I know nothing of him, not even his name. This may seem extraordinary, but I assure you it is not uncommon here. Sometimes, indeed one unknown person brings another equally unknown, to recommend him; and sometimes they recommend one another! As to this gentleman, I must refer you to himself for his character and merits, with which he is certainly better acquainted than I can possibly be. I recommend him, however, to those civilities which every stranger, of whom one knows no harm, has a right to; and I request you will do him all the good offices, and show him all the favor, that on further acquaintance you shall find him to deserve. I have the honor to be, etc.—Smyth 7:36. (1777.)

RELATIVES, Take Financial Advantage of Franklin.—I have been hurt too much by endeavoring to help cousin Ben Mecom. I have no opinion of the punctuality of cousins. They are apt to take liberties with relations they would not take with others, from a confidence that a relation will not sue them.—Smyth 6:18. (1773.)

RELIGION, Basic Beliefs of Franklin.—I had been religiously educated as a Presbyterian; and though some of the dogmas of that persuasion, such as *the eternal decrees of God, election, reprobation, etc.*, appeared to me unintelligible, others doubtful, and I early absented myself from the public assemblies of the sect, Sunday being my studying day, I never was without some religious principles. I never doubted, for instance, the existence of the Deity; that he made the world, and governed it by his providence; that the most acceptable service of God was the doing good to man; that our souls are immortal; and that all crime will be punished, and virtue rewarded, either here or hereafter. These I esteemed the essentials of every religion; and, being to be found in all the religions we had in our country, I respected them all, though with different degrees of respect, as I found them more or less mixed with other articles which, without any tendency to inspire, promote, or confirm morality,

served principally to divide us, and make us unfriendly to one another. This respect to all, with an opinion that the worst had some good effects, induced me to avoid all discourse that might tend to lessen the good opinion another might have of his own religion; and as our province increased in people, and new places of worship were continually wanted, and generally erected by voluntary contribution, my mite for such purpose, whatever might be the sect, was never refused.

Though I seldom attended any public worship, I had still an opinion of its propriety, and of its utility when rightly conducted, and I regularly paid my annual subscription for the support of the only Presbyterian minister or meeting we had in Philadelphia.—Autobiography. Smyth 1:324. (1784.)

RELIGION, Franklin's Ideas for a "United Party for Virtue."—Revolving this project in my mind [in 1731], as to be undertaken hereafter when my circumstances should afford me the necessary leisure, I put down from time to time, on pieces of paper, such thoughts as occurred to me respecting it. Most of these are lost; but I find one purporting to be the substance of an intended creed, containing, as I thought, the essentials of every known religion, and being free of everything that might shock the professors of any religion. It is expressed in these words, viz.:

"That there is one God, who made all things.

"That he governs the world by his providence.

"That he ought to be worshiped by adoration, prayer, and thanksgiving.

"But that the most acceptable service of God is doing good to man.

"That the soul is immortal.

"And that God will certainly reward virtue and punish vice, either here or hereafter."

My ideas at that time were that the sect should be begun and spread at first among young and single men only; that each person to be initiated should not only declare his assent to such creed, but should have exercised himself with the thirteen weeks' examination and practice of the virtues, as in the before-mentioned model [see VIRTUES]; that the existence of such a society should be kept a secret till it was become considerable, to prevent solicitations for the admission of improper persons, but that the members should each of them search among his acquaintance for ingenuous, well-disposed youths to whom, with prudent caution, the scheme should be gradually communicated; that the members should engage to afford their advice, assistance, and support to each other in promoting one another's interests, business, and advancement in life; that, for distinction, we should be called *The Society of the Free and Easy;* free, as being, by the general practice and habit of the virtues, free from the dominion of vice; and particularly, by the practice of industry and frugality, free from debt, which exposes a man to

confinement, and a species of slavery to his creditors.—Autobiography. Smyth 1:340. (1788.)

RELIGION, Best Judged by Its Fruits.—I think vital religion has always suffered when orthodoxy is more regarded than virtue; and the scriptures assure me that at the last day we shall not be examined [by] what we *thought,* but what we *did;* and our recommendation will not be that we said, *Lord! Lord!* but that we did good to our fellow creatures. See Matt. xxv.—Smyth 2:215. (1738.)

RELIGION, Essential to Good Government.—*History* will also afford frequent opportunities of showing the necessity of a *public religion,* from its usefulness to the public; the advantage of a religious character among private persons; the mischiefs of superstition, etc., and the excellency of the *Christian religion* above all others ancient or modern.—Smyth 2:393. (1749.)

RELIGION, A Basic Part of American Culture, Atheism Unknown.—Serious religion, under its various denominations, is not only tolerated, but respected and practiced. Atheism is unknown there [in the United States]; infidelity rare and secret; so that persons may live to a great age in that country without having their piety shocked by meeting with either an atheist or an infidel. And the Divine Being seems to have manifested his approbation of the mutual forbearance and kindness with which the different sects treat each other, by the remarkable prosperity with which he has been pleased to favor the whole country.—Smyth 8:613. (1782.)

RELIGION, Franklin's Answer to an Attack on.—I have read your [an unidentified writer's] manuscript with some attention. By the argument it contains against the doctrines of a particular Providence, though you allow a general providence, you strike at the foundation of all religion. For without the belief of a Providence that takes cognizance of, guards, and guides, and may favor particular persons, there is no motive to worship Deity, to fear [his] displeasure, or to pray for [his] protection. I will not enter into any discussion of your principles, though you seem to desire it. At present I shall only give you my opinion, that, though your reasonings are subtile, and may prevail with some readers, you will not succeed so as to change the general sentiments of mankind on that subject, and the consequence of printing this piece will be a great deal of odium drawn upon yourself, mischief to you, and no benefit to others. He that spits against the wind spits in his own face.

But, were you to succeed, do you imagine any good would be done by it? You yourself may find it easy to live a virtuous life without the assistance afforded by religion; you having a clear perception of the advantages of virtue, and the disadvantages of vice, and possessing a strength of resolution sufficient to enable you to resist common temptations. But think how great a proportion of mankind consists of weak and ignorant men and women, and of inexperienced and inconsiderate youth of both sexes, who have need of the motives of religion to restrain them from vice, to support their virtue, and retain them in the practice of it till it becomes *habitual*, which is the great point for its security. And perhaps you are indebted to her originally, that is, to your religious education, for the habits of virtue upon which you now justly value yourself. You might easily display your excellent talents of reasoning upon a less hazardous subject, and thereby obtain a rank with our most distinguished authors. For among us it is not necessary, as among the Hottentots, that a youth, to be received into the company of men, should prove his manhood by beating his mother.

I would advise you, therefore, not to attempt unchaining the tiger, but to burn this piece before it is seen by any other person; whereby you will save yourself a great deal of mortification from the enemies it may raise against you, and perhaps a good deal of regret and repentance. If men are as wicked as we now see them *with religion*, what would they be *if without it*.—Smyth 9:520. (1786.)

RELIGION, Franklin Responds to an Inquiry from Ezra Stiles, President of Yale University.—You desire to know something of my religion. It is the first time I have been questioned upon it. But I cannot take your curiosity amiss, and shall endeavor in a few words to gratify it. Here is my creed. I believe in one God, creator of the universe.

That he governs it by his providence. That he ought to be worshipped. That the most acceptable service we render to him is doing good to his other children. That the soul of man is immortal, and will be treated with justice in another life respecting its conduct in this. These I take to be the fundamental principles of all sound religion, and I regard them as you do in whatever sect I meet with them.

As to Jesus of Nazareth, my opinion of whom you particularly desire, I think the system of morals and his religion, as he left them to us, the best the world ever saw or is likely to see; but I apprehend it has received various corrupting changes, and I have, with most of the present dissenters in England, some doubts as to his divinity; though it is a question I do not dogmatize upon, having never studied it, and think it needless to busy myself with it now, when I expect soon an opportunity of knowing the truth with less trouble. I see no harm, however, in its being believed, if that belief has the good consequence, as probably it has, of making his doctrines more respected and better observed; especially as I do not perceive that the Supreme [Being] takes it amiss, by distinguishing the unbelievers in his government of the world with any peculiar marks of his displeasure.

I shall only add, respecting myself, that, having experienced the goodness of that Being in conducting me prosperously through a long life, I have no doubt of its continuance in the next, though without the smallest conceit of meriting such goodness.—Smyth 10:84. (1790.)

RELIGION. See also GOD; IMMORTALITY.

REPARATION, Justice by.—An injury done can only give the party injured a right to full reparation; or in case that be refused, a right to return an equal injury.—Smyth 6:397. (1775.)

REPARATION, God's Law Preferable to English Code of Criminal Justice.—The English author is for hanging *all* thieves. The Frenchman is for proportioning punishments to offenses.

If we really believe, as we profess to believe, that the law of Moses was the law of God, the dictate of divine wisdom infinitely superior to human; on what principles do we ordain death as the punishment of an offense which, according to that law, was only to be punished by a restitution fourfold? To put a man to death for an offense which does not deserve death, is it not murder?—Smyth 9:292. (1785.)

REPARATION, Is God's Form of Justice.—I see in the last newspaper from London that a woman is capitally convicted at the Old Bailey, for privately stealing out of a shop some gauze, value 14 shillings and threepence; is there any proportion between the injury done by a theft, value 14/3, and the punishment of a human creature by death on a gibbet? Might not that woman, by her labor, have made the reparation ordained by God, in paying fourfold? Is not all punishment

Franklin in 1785 (age 79). Portrait by
Charles Willson Peale.

inflicted beyond the merit of the
offense so much punishment of
innocence? In this light, how vast is
the annual quantity of not only
injured, but *suffering* innocence, in
almost all the civilized states of
Europe!—Smyth 9:294. (1785.)

**REPRESENTATION, Should Be
Proportioned to Population.**—I
must own that I was originally of
opinion it would be better if every
member of Congress, or our
national council, were to consider
himself rather as a representative of
the whole than as an agent for the
interests of a particular state; in
which case the proportion of
members for each state would be of
less consequence, and it would not
be very material whether they voted
by states or individually. But as I find
this is not to be expected, I now

think the number of representatives
should bear some proportion to the
number of the represented, and that
the decisions should be by the
majority of members, not by the
majority of states. This is objected to
from an apprehension that the
greater states would then swallow
up the smaller.... But, Sir, in the
present mode of voting by states, it
is equally in the power of the lesser
states to swallow up the greater.—
Smyth 9:596. (1787.)

**REVELATION, Only Way to Know
Some Things.**—But our reasoning
powers, when employed about what
may have been before our existence
here, or shall be after it, cannot go
far, for want of history and facts.
Revelation only can give us the
necessary information, and that, in
the first of these points especially,
has been very sparingly afforded
us.—Smyth 5:292. (1771.)

**REVOLUTIONARY WAR, Report
in December 1775.**—We inform you
[Charles W.F. Dumas] that the
whole continent is very firmly
united, the party for the measures of
the British ministry being very
small, and much dispersed; that we
have had on foot, the last campaign,
an army of near twenty-five
thousand men, wherewith we have
been able, not only to block up the
King's army in Boston, but to spare
considerable detachments for the
invasion of Canada, where we have
met with great success, as the
printed papers sent herewith will
inform you, and have now reason to
expect that whole province may be
soon in our possession; that we
purpose greatly to increase our force

for the ensuing year, and thereby we hope, with the assistance of a well-disciplined militia, to be able to defend our coast, notwithstanding its great extent; that we have already a small squadron of armed vessels to protect our coasting trade, which have had some success in taking several of the enemy's cruisers, and some of their transport vessels and store ships.—Smyth 6:434. (1775.)

REVOLUTIONARY WAR, Why Bows and Arrows Should Be Included in the Armory.—We have got a large quantity of saltpeter, one hundred and twenty tons, and thirty more expected. Powder-mills are now wanting. I believe we must set to work and make it by hand. But I still wish, with you, that pikes could be introduced, and I would add bows and arrows. These were good weapons, not wisely laid aside;

1st. Because a man may shoot as truly with a bow as with a common musket.

2dly. He can discharge four arrows in the time of charging and discharging one bullet.

3dly. His object is not taken from his view by the smoke of his own side.

4thly. A flight of arrows, seen coming upon them, terrifies and disturbs the enemies' attention to their business.

5thly. An arrow striking in any part of a man puts him *hors du combat* till it is extracted.

6thly. Bows and arrows are more easily provided everywhere than muskets and ammunition.—Smyth 6:438. (1776.)

REVOLUTIONARY WAR, Why Colonists Rejected Amnesty in 1776.—It is impossible we should think of submission to a government that has, with the most wanton barbarity and cruelty, burnt our defenseless towns in the midst of winter, excited the savages to massacre our peaceful farmers, and our slaves to murder their masters, and is even now bringing foreign mercenaries to deluge our settlements with blood. These atrocious injuries have extinguished every remaining spark of affection for that parent country we once held so dear; but, were it possible for *us* to forget and forgive them, it is not possible for *you* (I mean the British nation) to forgive the people you have so heavily injured.—Smyth 6:459. (1776.)

REVOLUTIONARY WAR, Situation in 1777.—I suppose you would like to know something of the state of affairs in America. In all probability we shall be much stronger the next campaign than we were in the last; better armed, better disciplined, and with more ammunition. When I was at the camp before Boston, the army had not five rounds of powder a man. This was kept a secret even from our people. The world wondered that we so seldom fired a cannon; we could not afford it; but we now make powder in plenty.—Smyth 7:19. (1777.)

REVOLUTIONARY WAR, Franklin's Prophecy of Eventual Victory.—To me it seems, as it has always done, that this war must end in our favor, and in the ruin of Britain, if she does not speedily put an end to it. An English gentleman here the other day, in company with some French, remarked that it was folly in France not to make war immediately; *and in England,* replied one of them, *not to make peace.*—Smyth 7:19. (1777.)

REVOLUTIONARY WAR, British Threaten Triple-Thrust Assault.— They threaten, however, and give out that Lord Howe is to bombard Boston this summer, and Burgoyne, with the troops from Canada, to destroy Providence, and lay waste Connecticut; while Howe marches against Philadelphia. They will do us undoubtedly as much mischief as they can; but the virtue and bravery of our countrymen will, with the blessing of God, prevent part of what they intend, and nobly bear the rest.—Smyth 7:54. (1777.)

REVOLUTIONARY WAR, Considered "the Cause of All Mankind." —All Europe is on our side of the question, as far as applause and good wishes can carry them. Those who live under arbitrary power do nevertheless approve of liberty, and wish for it; they almost despair of recovering it in Europe; they read the translations of our separate colony constitutions with rapture; and there are such numbers everywhere who talk of removing to America with their families and fortunes, as soon as peace and our independence shall be established, that 'tis generally believed we shall have a prodigious addition of strength, wealth, and arts from the emigrations of Europe; and 'tis thought that, to lessen or prevent such emigrations, the tyrannies established there must relax, and

allow more liberty to their people. Hence 'tis a common observation here that our cause is *the cause of all mankind,* and that we are fighting for their liberty in defending our own.—Smyth 7:56. (1777.)

REVOLUTIONARY WAR, Winning Freedom a Task Assigned by Providence.—'Tis a glorious task assigned us by Providence; which has, I trust, given us spirit and virtue equal to it, and will at last crown it with success.—Smyth 7:56. (1777.)

REVOLUTIONARY WAR, Franklin Opposes Recruiting Foreign Officers.—I was very sensible before I left America of the inconveniencies attending the employment of foreign officers, and therefore immediately on my arrival here I gave all the discouragement in my power to their going over; but numbers had been previously engaged by Mr. Deane, who could not refuse the applications made to him. . . . I wish we had an absolute order to give no letter of recommendation or even introduction [in] the future to any foreign officer whatever.—Smyth 7:66. (1777.)

REVOLUTIONARY WAR, French and British Fleets Sail at the Same Time.—The English and French fleets, of nearly equal force, are now both at sea. It is not doubted but that if they meet there will be a battle; for, though England through fear affects to understand it to be still peace, and would excuse the depredations she has made on the commerce of France by pretenses of illicit trade, etc., yet France considers the war begun, from the time of the King's message to Parliament complaining of the insult France had given by treating with us, and demanding aids to resist it, and the answer of both Houses offering their lives and fortunes.—Smyth 7:180. (1778.)

REVOLUTIONARY WAR, Pillaging English Cruisers Fly American Flag.—I imagine that all the injuries complained of are not justly chargeable to us, some of the smaller English cruisers having pillaged Spanish vessels under American colors, of which we have proof upon oath.—Smyth 7:390. (1779.)

REVOLUTIONARY WAR, British Defeat Should Be Conclusive.—I remember that when I was a boxing boy, it was allowed, even after an adversary said he had enough, to give him a rising blow. Let ours be a douser.—Smyth 8:397. (1782.)

REVOLUTIONARY WAR, Losses.—During these six years past, he [King George III] has destroyed not less than forty thousand of those [American] subjects, by battles on land or sea, or by starving them, or poisoning them to death, in the unwholesome air, with the unwholesome food of his prisons. And he has wasted the lives of at least an equal number of his own soldiers and sailors; many of whom have been *forced* into this odious service, and *dragged* from their families and friends, by the outrageous violence of his illegal pressgangs. You are a gentleman of letters, and have read history. Do you recollect any instance of any tyrant, since the beginning of the world, who in the course of so few years had done so much mischief, by murdering so many of his own people?—Smyth 8:445. (1782.)

REVOLUTIONARY WAR, Franklin Sends His Peace Treaty Message.—This is to inform you, and to request you to inform the Congress, that the preliminaries of peace between France, Spain, and England were yesterday signed, and a cessation of arms agreed to by the ministers of those powers, and by us in behalf of the United States, of which act, so far as relates to us, I enclose a copy.—Smyth 9:9. (1783.)

REVOLUTIONARY WAR, Won by the Blessings of God.—But after all, my dear friend, do not imagine that I am vain enough to ascribe our success to any superiority in any of those points. I am too well acquainted with all the springs and levers of our machine not to see that our human means were unequal to our undertaking, and that, if it had not been for the justice of our cause, and the consequent interposition of Providence, in which we had faith, we must have been ruined. If I had ever before been an atheist, I should now have been convinced of the being and government of a Deity! It is he who abases the proud and favors the humble. May we never forget his goodness to us, and may our future conduct manifest our gratitude.—Smyth 9:262. (1784.)

REVOLUTIONARY WAR. See also PRISONERS.

RICHES, Wisely Preserved or Foolishly Spent.—In our commercial towns upon the seacoast, fortunes will occasionally be made.

Some of those who grow rich will be prudent, live within bounds, and preserve what they have gained for their posterity; others, fond of showing their wealth, will be extravagant and ruin themselves. Laws cannot prevent this; and perhaps it is not always evil to the public. A shilling spent idly by a fool may be picked up by a wiser person, who knows better what to do with it. It is therefore not lost. A vain, silly fellow builds a fine house, furnishes it richly, lives in it expensively, and in four years ruins himself; but the masons, carpenters, smiths, and other honest tradesmen have been by his employ assisted in maintaining and raising their families; the farmer has been paid for his labor, and encouraged, and the estate is now in better hands. In some cases, indeed, certain modes of luxury may be a public evil, in the same manner as it is a private one. If there be a nation, for instance, that exports its beef and linen to pay for its importation of claret and porter, while a great part of its people live upon potatoes and wear no shirts, wherein does it differ from the sot who lets his family starve and sells his clothes to buy drink?—Smyth 9:244. (1784.)

RIGHTS, Should Be Frequently Asserted.—I hope the colony assemblies will show, by frequently repeated resolves, that they know their rights and do not lose sight of them. Our growing importance will ere long compel an acknowledgment of them, and establish and secure them to our posterity.—Smyth 5:293. (1771.)

RIGHTS, Negative Form of.—Have you then forgotten the incontestable principle which was the foundation of Hampden's glorious lawsuit with Charles the First, that "what an English king has no right to demand, an English subject has a right to refuse"?—Smyth 8:444. (1782.)

ROADS, In England.—You wonder how I did to travel 72 miles in a short winter day on my landing in England, and think I must have practiced flying. But the roads here are so good, with post chaises and fresh horses every ten or twelve miles, that it is no difficult matter. A lady that I know has come from Edinburgh to London, being 400 miles, in three days and a half.—Smyth 4:382. (1765.)

S

SARATOGA, English Reaction to Battle of.—The pride of England was never so humbled by anything as by your [Horatio Gates's] capitulation of Saratoga. They have not yet got over it.—Smyth 7:333. (1779.)

SAVINGS, Source of Wealth.—*Get what you can, and what you get hold; 'Tis the stone that will turn all your lead into gold,* as *Poor Richard* says.—Smyth 3:417. (1757.)

SCIENCE, Advances Resisted by Scientists.—We see how long even philosophers, men of extensive science and great ingenuity, can hold out against the evidence of new knowledge that does not square with their preconceptions; and how long men can retain a practice that is conformable to their prejudices, and expect a benefit from such practice, though constant experience shows its inutility.—Smyth 5:138. (1768.)

SCIENCE, Jealousy of Peers.—One would think that a man . . . laboring disinterestedly for the good of his fellow creatures could not possibly by such means make himself enemies; but there are minds who cannot bear that another should distinguish himself even by greater usefulness; and though he demands no profit, nor anything in return but the good will of those he is serving, they will endeavor to deprive him of that, first by disputing the truth of his experiments, then their utility; and, being defeated there, they finally dispute his right to them, and would give the credit of them to a man that lived 3000 years ago, or at 3000 leagues distance, rather than to a neighbor or even a friend. Go on, however, and never be discouraged. Others have met with the same treatment before you, and will after you. And whatever some may think and say, it is worthwhile to do men good for the self-satisfaction one has in the reflection.—Smyth 8:310. (1781.)

SEASICKNESS, Advice Concerning.—Doubtless they thought that when they had paid for their breakfast, they had a right to it, and that when they had swallowed it they were sure of it. But they had scarce been out half an hour before the sea laid claim to it, and they were obliged to deliver it up. So it seems there are uncertainties even beyond those between the cup and the lip. If ever you go to sea, take my advice and live sparingly a day or two

beforehand. The sickness, if any, will be lighter and sooner over.—Smyth 5:49. (1767.)

SEEDS, Rhubarb and Lucerne (Alfalfa).—I am glad the rhubarb seed got safe to hand. I make no doubt of its thriving well in our country, where the climate is the same with that of the Chinese wall, just outside which it grows in plenty and of the best quality. I shall be glad to know how you find the juniper. I asked Solander about the lucerne seed you wrote for. He could give me no account of it, nor can I learn anything of it from others. You may rely upon my friendship in recommending your seeds. I send all that inquire of me about American seeds to Mr. Freeman.—Smyth 5:432. (1772.)

SILK, Best Italian.—He [a friend in England] gave me a skein of what is called the best Italian silk imported here, and advised me to send it over as a pattern for our people to endeavor to imitate, with regard to its evenness, cleanness from nibs, and lustre; and, that they might better see the difference and understand his remarks, he wished the skeins sent over hither might be returned with it. I send them all together accordingly.

He says the silk reeled from twelve cocoons fetches nearly as good a price as that from six, because it winds well and there is less *fine waste;* the dropping accidentally, or through inattention, three or four of the cocoons out of twelve not weakening the thread so much in proportion, as when the same number are dropped out of six; nor is the thread so apt to break in winding. I observe that the Italian silk has a sweet smell, as if perfumed. He thinks it is the natural smell of the silk, when prepared in perfection. He understands that the Piedmontese reel is esteemed preferable to Mr. Pullein's. He says we may carry that produce to what length we please. It is impossible to overstock the market, as the demand is continually increasing, silk being more and more worn, and daily entering into the composition of more and a greater variety of manufactures.—Smyth 5:331. (1771.)

SILK, Franklin's Notes on.—The European silk I understand is all yellow, and most of the India silk. What comes from China is white. In Ogilby's account of that country, I find that, in the province of Chekiang, "they prune their mulberry trees once a year, as we do our vines in Europe, and suffer them not to grow up to high trees, because through long experience they have learned that the leaves of the smallest and youngest trees make the best silk, and know thereby how to distinguish the first spinning of the threads from the second, viz. the first is that which comes from the young leaves, that are gathered in March, with which they feed their silkworms; and the second is of the old summer leaves. And it is only the change of food, as to the young and old leaves, which makes the difference in the silk. The prices of the first and second spinning differ among the Chinese. The best silk is

that of March, the coarsest of June, yet both in one year."

I have copied this passage to show that in Chekiang they keep the mulberry trees low; but I suppose the reason to be the greater facility of gathering the leaves. It appears, too, by this passage that they raise two crops a year in that province, which may account for the great plenty of silk there. But perhaps this would not answer with us, since it is not practiced in Italy, though it might be tried. Chekiang is from twenty-seven to thirty-one degrees of north latitude. Duhalde has a good deal on the Chinese management of the silk business.—Smyth 5:336. (1771.)

SILK INDUSTRY, Advantages of, for Colonies.—If some provision were made by the Assembly for promoting the growth of mulberry trees in all parts of the province, the culture of silk might afterwards follow easily. For the great discouragement to breeding worms at first is the difficulty of getting leaves and the being obliged to go far for them.

There is no doubt with me but that it might succeed in our country. It is the happiest of all inventions for clothing. Wool uses a good deal of land to produce it, which, if employed in raising corn, would afford much more subsistence for man than the mutton amounts to. Flax and hemp require good land, impoverish it, and at the same time permit it to produce no food at all. But mulberry trees may be planted in hedge rows on walks or avenues, or for shade near a house, where nothing else is wanted to grow. The food for the worms which produce the silk is in the air, and the ground under the trees may still produce grass, or some other vegetable good for man or beast. Then the wear of silken garments continues so much longer, from the strength of the materials, as to give it greatly the preference. Hence it is that the most populous of all countries, China, clothes its inhabitants with silk, while it feeds them plentifully, and has besides a vast quantity both raw and manufactured to spare for exportation.

Raw silk here, in skeins well wound, sells from twenty to twenty-five shillings per pound; but, if badly wound, is not worth five shillings. Well wound is when the threads are made to cross each other every way in the skein, and only touch where they cross. Badly wound is when they are laid parallel to each other; for so they are glued together, break in unwinding them, and take a vast deal of time more than the other, by losing the end every time the thread breaks. When once you can raise plenty of silk, you may have manufactures enough from hence.—Smyth 5:228. (1769.)

SLAVERY, Economic Liability of.— The labor of slaves can never be so cheap here as the labor of working men is in *Britain*. Anyone may compute it. Interest of money is in the colonies from 6 to 10 percent. Slaves one with another cost 30 pounds sterling per head. Reckon then the interest of the first purchase of a slave, the insurance or risk on his life, his clothing and diet, expenses in his sickness and loss of time, loss by his neglect of business (neglect is natural to the man who is not to be benefited by his own care or diligence), expense of a driver to keep him at work, and his pilfering from time to time, almost every slave being *by nature* a thief, and compare the whole amount with the wages of a manufacturer of iron or wool in *England*, [and] you will see that labor is much cheaper there than it ever can be by Negroes here. Why then will *Americans* purchase slaves? Because slaves may be kept as long as a man pleases, or has occasion for their labor; while hired men are continually leaving their masters (often in the midst of his business) and setting up for themselves.—Smyth 3:66. (1751.)

SLAVERY, Cultural Liability of.— The whites who have slaves, not laboring, are enfeebled, and therefore not so generally prolific; the slaves being worked too hard, and ill fed, their constitutions are broken, and the deaths among them are more than the births; so that a continual supply is needed from *Africa*. The northern colonies, having few slaves, increase in whites. Slaves also pejorate the families that use them; the white children become proud, disgusted with labor, and, being educated in idleness, are rendered unfit to get a living by industry.—Smyth 3:68. (1751.)

SLAVERY, British Trade in.—I made a little extract from yours [abolitionist Anthony Benezet] of April 27, of the number of slaves imported and perishing, with some close remarks on the hypocrisy of this country [England], which encourages such a detestable commerce by laws for promoting the Guinea trade, while it piqued itself on its virtue, love of liberty, and the equity of its courts in setting free a single Negro. This was inserted in the *London Chronicle* of the 20th of June last.

I thank you for the Virginia address, which I shall also publish with some remarks. I am glad to hear that the disposition against keeping Negroes grows more general in North America. Several pieces have been lately printed here against the practice, and I hope in time it will be taken into consideration and suppressed by the legislature.— Smyth 5:431. (1772.)

SLAVERY, Franklin's "Address to the Public."—(For full text, see Smyth 10:66–68. [1789.])

SLAVERY, Need to Educate Emancipated Slaves and Facilitate Their Adaptation to Freedom.—To instruct, to advise, to qualify those who have been restored to freedom for the exercise and enjoyment of civil liberty, to promote in them habits of industry, to furnish them with employments suited to their age, sex, talents, and other circumstances, and to procure their children an education calculated for their future situation in life; these are the great outlines of the . . . plan which we [the Pennsylvania Abolition Society] have adopted, and which we conceive will essentially promote the public good, and the happiness of these our hitherto too-much-neglected fellow creatures.— Smyth 10:67. (1789.)

SLAVERY, Why It Debilitates the Capacity of a Human Being to Survive in Freedom.—Slavery is such an atrocious debasement of human nature that its very extirpation, if not performed with solicitous care, may sometimes open a source of serious evils.

The unhappy man who has long been treated as a brute animal too frequently sinks beneath the common standard of the human species. The galling chains that bind his body do also fetter his intellectual faculties, and impair the social affections of his heart. Accustomed to move like a mere machine, by the will of a master, reflection is suspended; he has not the power of choice; and reason and conscience have but little influence over his conduct, because he is chiefly governed by the passion of fear. He is poor and friendless; perhaps worn out by extreme labor, age, and disease.

Under such circumstances, freedom may often prove a misfortune to himself, and prejudicial to society.—Smyth 10:67. (1789.)

SLAVERY, Franklin's Parody Against Those Seeking to Justify It.—(For full text of this article, written less than a month before Franklin's death [1790], see Smyth 10:87–91.)*

*Concerning this piece, Albert Henry Smyth wrote the following: "In the *Federal Gazette* of March 25th, 1790, there appeared an essay signed *Historicus,* written by Dr.

Franklin, in which he communicated a speech said to have been delivered in the Divan of Algiers, in 1687, in opposition to the prayer of the petition of a sect called *Erika*, or Purists, for the abolition of piracy and slavery. This pretended African speech was an excellent parody of one delivered by Mr. Jackson, [a Congressman] of Georgia. All the arguments urged in favor of Negro slavery are applied with equal force to justify the plundering and enslaving of Europeans. It affords, at the same time, a demonstration of the futility of the arguments in defense of the slave trade, and of the strength of mind and ingenuity of the author at his advanced period of life."—Smyth 10:87.

SLAVERY, Franklin's Plan for Emancipated Slaves.—(For full text of his "Plan for Improving the Condition of the Free Blacks" [1788?], see Smyth 10:127-29.)

SMALLPOX, Inoculations to Prevent, in Philadelphia.—The smallpox spreads apace, and is now in all quarters; yet as we have only children to have it, and the doctors inoculate apace, I believe they will soon drive it through [from] the town; so that you may possibly visit us with safety in the spring.—Smyth 3:19. (1750.)

SMALLPOX, Used by British as a Form of Biological Warfare.—Virginia suffered great loss in this kind of property by another ingenious and humane British invention. Having the smallpox in their army while in that country, they inoculated some of the Negroes they took as prisoners belonging to a number of plantations, and then let them escape, or sent them, covered with the pock, to mix with and spread the distemper among the others of their color, as well as among the white country people; which occasioned a great mortality of both.—Smyth 10:111. (1786?)

SMITH (Adam), Friendship with Franklin.—(Albert Henry Smyth noted that "Adam Smith communicated with him [Franklin] on some particulars of *The Wealth of Nations* several years before that epoch-making work was published."—Smyth 1:136.)

SMUGGLING, Considered an Act of Patriotism.—A coast 1500 miles in length could not in all parts be guarded even by the whole navy of England, especially where the restraining authority was by all the inhabitants deemed unconstitutional, and smuggling of course considered as patriotism. The needy wretches, too, who with small salaries were trusted to watch the ports day and night, in all weathers, found it easier and more profitable, not only to *wink*, but to sleep in their beds, the merchant's pay being more generous than the King's. Other India goods also, which by themselves would not have made a smuggling voyage sufficiently profitable, accompanied tea to advantage; and it is feared the cheap French silks, formerly rejected, as not to the taste of the colonies, may have found their way with the wares of India, and now established themselves in the popular use and opinion.—Smyth 5:455. (1772.)

SOAP, American Reputed to Be Best.—I'll put in a few cakes of

484 The Real Benjamin Franklin

American soap made of myrtle wax, said to be the best soap in the world for shaving or washing fine linens, etc. Mrs. Franklin requests your daughter would be so good as to accept three or four cakes of it, to wash your grandson's finest things with.—Smyth 3:263. (1755.)

SPAIN, No Basis for Friendship.— Since Spain does not think our friendship worth cultivating, I wish you would inform me of the whole sum we owe her, that we may think of some means of paying it off speedily.—Smyth 8:399. (1782.)

SPAIN, American Relations with.— Spain has taken four years to consider whether she should treat with us or not. Give her forty, and let us in the meantime mind our own business.—Smyth 8:434. (1782.)

SPEECH, Freedom of.—Without freedom of thought there can be no such thing as wisdom, and no such thing as public liberty without freedom of speech, which is the right of every man as far as by it he does not hurt or control the right of another; and this is the only check it ought to suffer, and the only bounds it ought to know. This sacred privilege is so essential to free governments that the security of property and the freedom of speech always go together; and in those wretched countries where a man cannot call his tongue his own, he can scarce call anything else his own. Whoever would overthrow the liberty of a nation must begin by subduing the freeness of speech....

The administration of government is nothing else but the attendance of the *trustees of the people* upon the interest and affairs of the people; and as it is the part and business of the people, for whose sake alone all public matters are or ought to be transacted, to see whether they be well or ill transacted, so it is the interest and ought to be the ambition of all honest magistrates to have their deeds openly examined and publicly scanned. Only the wicked governors of men dread what is said of them.— Smyth 2:25. (1722.)

SPELLING, Emphasis on.—Let the first class learn the *English grammar* rules, and at the same time let particular care be taken to improve them in *orthography*. Perhaps the latter is best done by *pairing* the scholars, two of those nearest equal in their spelling to be put together; let these strive for victory, each propounding ten words every day to the other to be spelled. He that spells truly most of the other's words is victor for that day; he that is victor most days in a month, to obtain a prize, a pretty, neat book of some kind useful in their future studies. This method fixes the attention of children extremely to the orthography of words, and makes them good spellers very early. 'Tis a shame for a man to be so ignorant of this little art, in his own language, as to be perpetually confounding words of like sound and different significations; the consciousness of which defect makes some men, otherwise of good learning and understanding, averse to writing even a common letter.—Smyth 3:22. (1750.)

SPITE, Leads Some to Their Own Destruction.—*Conscience* enjoins it as a duty on you [Pennsylvania citizens] (and indeed I think it such on every man) to defend your country, your friends, your aged parents, your wives, and helpless children; and yet you resolve not to perform this duty, but act *contrary to your own* consciences, because the Quakers act *according to theirs.* Till of late, I could scarce believe the story of him who refused to pump in a sinking ship, because one on board, whom he hated, would be saved by it as well as himself.—Smyth 2:349. (1747.)

SQUIRREL, Gift to Bishop Shipley Killed.—The fine large grey squirrel you sent, who was a great favorite in the Bishop's family, is dead. He had got out of his cage in the country, rambled, and was rambling over a common three miles from home, when he met a man with a dog. The dog pursuing him, he fled to the man for protection; running up to his shoulder, who shook him off, and set the dog on him, thinking him to be, as he said afterward, *some varmint or other.* So poor *Mungo,* as his mistress called him, died. To amuse you a little, and nobody out of your own house, I enclose you the little correspondence between her and me on the melancholy occasion. Skugg, you must know, is a common name by which all squirrels are called here, as all cats are called *Puss.* Miss Georgiana is the Bishop's youngest daughter but one. There are five in all. Mungo was buried in the garden, and the enclosed epitaph put upon his monument. So much for squirrels.—Smyth 6:16. (1773.)

SQUIRREL, Franklin's Epitaph to Pet.—*Alas! poor Mungo!*
Happy wert thou, hadst thou known
Thy own felicity.
Remote from the fierce bald eagle,
Tyrant of thy native woods,
Thou hadst nought to fear from his piercing talons,
Nor from the murdering gun
Of the thoughtless sportsman.
Safe in thy wired castle,
Grimalkin never could annoy thee.
Daily wert thou fed with the choicest viands,
By the fair hand of an indulgent mistress;
But, discontented,
Thou wouldst have more freedom.
Too soon, alas! didst thou obtain it;
And wandering,
Thou art fallen by the fangs of wanton, cruel Ranger!
Learn hence,
Ye who blindly seek more liberty,
Whether subjects, sons, squirrels or daughters,
That apparent restraint may be a real protection;
Yielding peace and plenty
With security.—Smyth 5:439. (1772.)

STAMP ACT, Franklin's Efforts to Prevent Passage of.—I took every step in my power to prevent the passing of the Stamp Act. Nobody could be more concerned in interest than myself to oppose it sincerely and heartily. But the tide was too strong against us. The nation was provoked by American claims of independence, and all parties joined in resolving by this act to settle the point. We might as well have hindered the sun's setting.—Smyth 4:390. (1765.)

STAMP ACT, Ameliorating Policy of Franklin.—As to the Stamp Act, though we purpose doing our endeavor to get it repealed, in which I am sure you would concur with us, yet the success is uncertain. If it continues, your undertaking to execute it may make you unpopular for a time, but your acting with coolness and steadiness, and with every circumstance in your power of favor to the people, will by degrees reconcile them. In the meantime, a firm loyalty to the Crown and faithful adherence to the government of this nation, which it is the safety as well as honor of the colonies to be connected with, will always be the wisest course for you and I to take, whatever may be the madness of the populace or their blind leaders, who can only bring themselves and country into trouble and draw on greater burdens by acts of rebellious tendency.—Smyth 4:392. (1765.)

STAMP ACT, Repeal of.—The ministry are fixed for us, and we have obtained a majority in the House of Commons for repealing the Stamp Act, and giving us ease in every commercial grievance. God grant that no bad news of further excesses in America may arrive to strengthen our adversaries, and weaken the hands of our friends, before this good work is quite completed.

The partisans of the late ministry have been strongly crying out *rebellion,* and calling for force to be sent against America. The consequence might have been terrible; but milder measures have prevailed. I hope, nay, I am confident, America will show itself grateful to Britain on this occasion, and behave prudently and decently.—Smyth 4:410. (1766.)

STAMP ACT, "The Examination of Doctor Benjamin Franklin in the British House of Commons."—(For full text, see Smyth 4:412–48. [1766.])*

*Albert Henry Smyth wrote: "No previous event in the life of Dr. Franklin gave him so much celebrity as his examination before the House of Commons, while the repeal of the Stamp Act was under discussion in Parliament. The promptness and pertinency with which he replied to every question, the perfect knowledge of the subject manifested in his answers, his enlarged and sound views of political and commercial affairs, and the boldness and candor with which he expressed his sentiments, excited the surprise of his auditors, and were received with admiration by the public when the results of the examination appeared in print."—Smyth 4:412.

STAMP ACT, Franklin's Reasons for Seeking Its Repeal.—As agent for the colonies, I opposed the Stamp Act and endeavored to obtain its repeal, as an infringement of the rights of the colonists, of no real advantage to Britain, since she might ever be sure of greater aids from our voluntary grants than she could expect from arbitrary taxes, as by losing our respect and affection, on which much of her commerce with us depended, she would lose more in that commerce than she could possibly gain by such taxes, and as it was detrimental to the harmony which had till then so happily subsisted, and which was so essential to the welfare of the whole.—Smyth 6:261. (1774.)

STAMP ACT, Used Compulsion Instead of Persuasion.—I am sure he [George Grenville, the British minister] would have obtained more money from the colonies by their voluntary grants than he himself expected from the stamps. But he chose compulsion rather than persuasion, and would not receive from their good-will what he thought he could obtain without it.—Smyth 7:120. (1778.)

STEUBEN (Baron von), Franklin Recommends to Washington.—Sir: The gentleman who will have the honor of waiting upon you with this letter is the Baron de Steuben, lately a lieutenant-general in the king of Prussia's service, whom he attended in all his campaigns, being his aide-de-camp, quartermaster general, etc. He goes to America with a true zeal for our cause, and a view of engaging in it and rendering it all the service in his power. He is recommended to us by two of the best judges of military merit in this country, M. de Vergennes and M. de St. Germain, who have long been personally acquainted with him, and interest themselves in promoting his voyage, from a full persuasion that the knowledge and experience he has acquired by 20 years' study and practice in the Prussian school may be of great use in our armies. I therefore cannot but wish that our service may be made agreeable to him. I have the honor to be, etc. B.F.—Smyth 7:63. (1777.)

STOVE, Invented by Franklin.—Having, in 1742, invented an open stove for the better warming of rooms, and at the same time saving fuel, as the fresh air admitted was warmed in entering, I made a present of the model to Mr. Robert Grace, one of my early friends, who, having an iron-furnace, found the casting of the plates for these stoves a profitable thing, as they were growing in demand. To promote that demand, I wrote and published a pamphlet, entitled *"An account of the new-invented Pennsylvania Fireplaces; wherein their construction and manner of operation is particularly explained; their advantages above every other method of warming rooms demonstrated; and all objections that have been raised against the use of them answered and obviated,"* etc. This pamphlet had a good effect. Governor Thomas was so pleased with the construction of this stove, as described in it, that he offered to give me a patent for the sole vending of them for a term of years; but I declined it from a principle which has ever weighed with me on such occasions, viz., *That, as we enjoy great advantages from the inventions of others, we should be glad of an opportunity to serve others by any invention of ours; and this we should do freely and generously.*— Autobiography. Smyth 1:370. (1788.)

STREET CLEANING, Initiated in the 1750s by Franklin.—After some inquiry, I found a poor, industrious man who was willing to undertake keeping the pavement clean by sweeping it twice a week, carrying off the dirt from before all the neighbors' doors for the sum of sixpence per month, to be paid by each house. I then wrote and printed a paper setting forth the advantages to the neighborhood that might be obtained by this small expense; the greater ease in keeping our houses clean, so much dirt not being brought in by people's feet; the benefit to the shops by more customers, etc., etc., as buyers could more easily get at them; and by not having, in windy weather, the dust blown in upon their goods, etc.— Autobiography. Smyth 1:380. (1788.)

STREET PAVING, Initiated by Franklin.—After some time I drew a bill for paving the city, and brought it into the Assembly. It was just before I went to England, in 1757, and did not pass till I was gone.— Autobiography. Smyth 1:381. (1788.)

SURGEONS, Should Never Be Detained as Prisoners. In my opinion, surgeons should never be detained as prisoners, as it is their duty and their practice to help the sick and wounded of either side when they happen to have an opportunity. They should therefore be considered, not as parties in any war, but as friends to humanity.— Smyth 7:374. (1779.)

SWIMMING, Aids for.—When I was a boy, I made two oval palettes, each about ten inches long and six broad, with a hole for the thumb in order to retain it fast in the palm of my hand. They much resembled a painter's palettes. In swimming I pushed the edges of these forward, and I struck the water with their flat surfaces as I drew them back. I

remember I swam faster by means of these pallets, but they fatigued my wrists. I also fitted to the soles of my feet a kind of sandals; but I was not satisfied with them, because I observed that the stroke is partly given by the inside of the feet and the ankles, and not entirely with the soles of the feet.—Smyth 5:543. (1773.)

SWIMMING, How to Cure a Cramp.—When [a swimmer] is seized with the cramp in the leg, the method of driving it away is to give to the parts affected a sudden, vigorous, and violent shock, which he may do in the air as he swims on his back.—Smyth 5:543. (1773.)

SWIMMING, For Health.—The exercise of swimming is one of the most healthy and agreeable in the world. After having swum for an hour or two in the evening, one sleeps cooly the whole night, even during the most ardent heat of summer. Perhaps, the pores being cleansed, the insensible perspiration increases and occasions this coolness. It is certain that much swimming is the means of stopping a diarrhea, and even of producing a constipation. With respect to those who do not know how to swim, or who are affected with a diarrhea at a season which does not permit them to use that exercise, a warm bath, by cleansing and purifying the skin, is found very salutary, and often effects a radical cure. I speak from my own experience, frequently repeated, and that of others, to whom I have recommended this.— Smyth 5:544. (1773.)

SWIMMING, With a Kite.—There is a method in which a swimmer may pass to great distances with much facility, by means of a sail. This discovery I fortunately made by accident, and in the following manner.

When I was a boy, I amused myself one day with flying a paper kite; and approaching the bank of a pond, which was near a mile broad, I tied the string to a stake, and the kite ascended to a very considerable height above the pond while I was swimming. In a little time, being desirous of amusing myself with my kite and enjoying at the same time the pleasure of swimming, I returned; and, loosing from the stake the string with the little stick which was fastened to it, went again into the water, where I found that, lying on my back and holding the stick in my hands, I was drawn along the surface of the water in a very agreeable manner. Having then engaged another boy to carry my clothes round the pond to a place which I pointed out to him on the other side, I began to cross the pond with my kite, which carried me quite over without the least fatigue, and with the greatest pleasure imaginable. I was only obliged occasionally to halt a little in my course, and resist its progress, when it appeared that, by following too quick, I lowered the kite too much; by doing which occasionally I made it rise again. I have never since that time practiced this singular mode of swimming, though I think it not impossible to cross in this manner from Dover to Calais. The packet

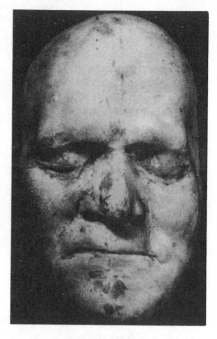

Death mask of Franklin, 1790 (age 84).

boat, however, is still preferable.— Smyth 5:545. (1773.)

T

TAXATION, Without Representation.—[The colonists] will say, and perhaps with justice, that...it is supposed an undoubted right of Englishmen not to be taxed but by their own consent, given through their representatives.

That the colonies have no representatives in Parliament.

That to propose taxing them by Parliament, and refuse them the liberty of choosing a representative council to meet in the colonies and consider and judge of the necessity of any general tax, and the quantum, shows suspicion of their loyalty to the Crown, or of their regard for their country, or of their common sense and understanding, which they have not deserved.

That compelling the colonies to pay money without their consent would be rather like raising contributions in an enemy's country than taxing of Englishmen for their own public benefit.

That it would be treating them as a conquered people and not as true British subjects.*—Smyth 3:233. (1754.)

*Albert Henry Smyth noted: "Respecting this letter [to Governor William Shirley of Massachusetts], John Adams said in his 'History of the Dispute with America,' first published in 1774: 'Dr. Franklin, who was known to be an active and very able man, and to have great influence in the province of Pennsylvania, was in Boston in the year 1754, and Mr. Shirley communicated to him the profound secret—the great design of taxing the colonies by an act of Parliament. This sagacious gentleman and distinguished patriot, to his lasting honor, sent the governor an answer in writing, with the following remarks on his scheme.' Mr. Adams then quotes the principal parts of the above letter."—Smyth 3:237.

It equally militated against the American principle above mentioned, *that money is not to be raised on English subjects without their consent.*—Smyth 5:81. (1768.)

We of the colonies have never insisted that we ought to be exempt from contributing to the common expenses necessary to support the prosperity of the empire. We only assert that, having parliaments of our own, and not having representatives in that of Great Britain, our parliaments are the only judges of what we can and what we ought to contribute in this case; and that the English Parliament has no right to take our money without our consent. In fact, the British empire is not a single state; it comprehends many; and though the Parliament of Great Britain has arrogated to itself the power of taxing the colonies, it has no more right to do so than it has to tax Hanover. We have the same King, but not the same legislatures. —Smyth 5:280. (1770.)

TAXATION, Unpopular in Colonies, But Parliament Reluctant to Capitulate.—The doctrine of the right of Parliament to lay taxes on America is now almost generally given up here [in England], and one seldom meets in conversation with any who continue to assert it. But there are still many who think that the dignity and honor of Parliament, and of the nation, are so much engaged as that no formal renunciation of the claim is ever to be expected. We ought to be contented, they say, with a forbearance of any attempt hereafter to exercise such right; and this they would have us rely on as a certainty.—Smyth 5:292. (1771.)

TAXATION, Compulsion Justified to Pay the People's Debts.—The remissness of our people in paying taxes is highly blameable; the unwillingness to pay them is still more so. I see, in some resolutions of town meetings, a remonstrance against giving Congress a power to take, as they call it, the people's money out of their pockets, though only to pay the interest and principal of debts duly contracted. They seem to mistake the point. Money justly due from the people is their creditors' money, and no longer the money of the people, who, if they withhold it, should be compelled to pay by some law.—Smyth 9:138. (1783.)

TAXES, Heavy, But Not the Only "Lost Revenue."—Taxes are indeed very heavy, and if those laid on by the government were the only ones we had to pay, we might more easily discharge them; but we have many others, and much more grievous to some of us. We are taxed twice as much by our *Idleness,* three times as much by our *Pride,* and four times as much by our *Folly;* and from these taxes the commissioners cannot ease or deliver us by allowing an abatement.—Smyth 3:408. (1757.)

TAXES, Colonies' Attitude Toward.—The colonies are not supposed to be within the realm; they have assemblies of their own, which are their parliaments, and they are, in that respect, in the same situation with Ireland. When money is to be raised for the Crown upon the subject in Ireland, or in the colonies, the consent is given in the Parliament of Ireland, or in the assemblies of the colonies. They think the Parliament of Great Britain cannot properly give that consent, till it has representatives from America; for the Petition of

Right expressly says it is to be by common consent in Parliament; and the people of America have no representatives in Parliament to make a part of that common consent.—Smyth 4:441. (1766.)

TAXES, Duty to Pay.—When the government finds it necessary for the common benefit, advantage, and safety of the nation, for the security of our liberties, property, religion, and everything that is dear to us, that certain sums shall be yearly raised by taxes, duties, etc., and paid into the public treasury, thence to be dispensed by government for those purposes, ought not every *honest man* freely and willingly to pay his just proportion of this necessary expense? Can he possibly preserve a right to that character if, by any fraud, stratagem, or contrivance, he avoids that payment in whole or in part?—Smyth 5:61. (1767.)

TAXES, Direct, Difficult to Collect, and Source of More Complaints than Indirect Taxes.—We shall, as you suppose, have imposts on trade, and custom-houses, not because other nations have them, but because we cannot at present do without them. We want to discharge our public debt occasioned by the late war. Direct taxes are not so easily levied on the scantily settled inhabitants of our wide extended country; and what is paid in the price of merchandise is less felt by the consumer, and less the cause of complaint. When we are out of debt we may leave our trade free, for our ordinary charges of government will not be great.—Smyth 9:638. (1788.)

TEA ACT, Destroying British Commerce.

—It is supposed that at least a million of Americans drink tea twice a day, which, at the first cost here, can scarce be reckoned at less than half a guinea a head *per annum*. This market, that in the five years which have run on since the act passed would have paid 1,500,000 guineas *for tea alone* into the coffers of the company, we have wantonly lost to foreigners.... Hence the tea and other India goods, which might have been sold in America, remain rotting in the company's warehouses; while those of foreign ports are known to be cleared by the American demand. Hence, in some degree, the [India] Company's inability to pay their bills; the sinking of their stock, by which millions of property have been annihilated; the lowering of their dividend, whereby so many must be distressed; the loss to government of the stipulated 400,000 pounds a year, which must make a proportionable reduction in our savings towards the discharge of our enormous debt; and hence, in part, the severe blow suffered by credit in general, to the ruin of many families; the stagnation of business in Spitalfield and at Manchester, through want of vent for their goods; with other future evils, which, as they cannot, from the numerous and secret connections in general commerce, easily be foreseen, can hardly be avoided.—Smyth 5:456. (1772.)

TEA ACT, Bankrupting India Company.

—[A circumstance which has] diverted me lately...is the present difficulties of the India Company, and of government on their account. The company have accepted bills which they find themselves unable to pay, though they have the value of two millions in tea and other India goods in their stores, perishing under a want of demand; their credit thus suffering, and their stock falling 120 percent. The bank will not advance for them, and no remedy is thought of but lowering their dividend from 12½ to 6¼ percent, whereby government will lose the 400,000 pounds per annum, it having been stipulated that it should no longer be paid if the dividend fell to that mark. And although it is known that the American market is lost by continuing the duty on tea, and that we are supplied by the Dutch, who doubtless take the opportunity of smuggling other India goods among us with the tea, so that for the five years past we might probably have otherwise taken off the greatest part of what the company have on hand, and so have prevented their present embarrassment, yet the honor of government is supposed to forbid the repeal of the American tea duty; while the amount of all the duties goes on decreasing, so that the balance of this year does not (as I have it from good authority) exceed 80 pounds after paying the collection; not reckoning the immense expense of *Guarda-Costas*, etc. Can an American forbear smiling at these blunders? Though, in a national light, they are truly deplorable.—Smyth 5:459. (1772.)

The ministry are more embarrassed with the India affairs. The continued refusal of North America to take tea from hence has brought infinite distress on the company. They imported great quantities in the faith that that agreement could not hold; and now they can neither pay their debts nor dividends; their stock has sunk to the annihilating near three millions of their property, and government will lose its 400,000 pounds a year; while their teas lie upon hand. The bankruptcies, brought on partly by this means, have given such a shock to credit as has not been experienced here [in Britain] since the South Sea year. And this has affected the great manufacturers so much as to oblige them to discharge their hands, and thousands of Spitalfield and Manchester weavers are now starving, or subsisting on charity. Blessed effects of pride, pique, and passion in government, which should have no passions.— Smyth 6:12. (1773.)

TEA ACT, British Miscalculate American Temperament.—It was thought at the beginning of the session [of Parliament] that the American duty on tea would be taken off. But now the wise scheme is to take off so much duty here [in England] as will make tea cheaper in America than foreigners can supply us, and to confine the duty there to keep up the exercise of the right. They have no idea that any people can act from any other principle but that of interest; and they believe,

that 3d in a lb. of tea, of which one does not perhaps drink 10 in a year, is sufficient to overcome all the patriotism of an American.—Smyth 6:57. (1773.)

TEA ACT, Colonial Embargo Having Its Effect.—Our steady refusal to take tea from hence for several years past has made its impressions.—Smyth 6:151. (1773.)

TEACHING TALENT, A Gift of God.—I think, moreover, that talents for the education of youth are the gift of God; and that he on whom they are bestowed, whenever a way is opened for the use of them, is as strongly *called* as if he heard a voice from heaven, nothing more surely pointing out duty in a public service than *ability* and *opportunity* of performing it.— Smyth 3:17. (1750.)

TIME, Is Money.—Remember that *time* is money. He that can earn ten shillings a day by his labor, and goes abroad or sits idle one half of that day, though he spends but sixpence during his diversion or idleness, ought not to reckon *that* the only expense; he has really spent, or rather thrown away, five shillings besides.—Smyth 2:370. (1748.)

TIME, Don't Waste It.—*If time be of all things the most precious, wasting time must be*, as *Poor Richard* says, *the greatest prodigality;* since, as he elsewhere tells us, *Lost time is never found again; and what we call time enough, always proves little enough.* Let us then up and be doing, and doing to the purpose; so by diligence shall we do more with less perplexity. *Sloth makes all things difficult, but industry all easy,* as *Poor Richard* says; and *He that riseth late* *must trot all day, and shall scarce overtake his business at night;* while *Laziness travels so slowly, that poverty soon overtakes him,* as we read in *Poor Richard,* who adds, *Drive thy business, let not that drive thee;* and *Early to bed, and early to rise, makes a man healthy, wealthy, and wise.*—Smyth 3:409. (1757.)

TORNADO, Close-up Observation by Franklin.—The rest of the company stood looking after it, but my curiosity being stronger, I followed it, riding close by its side, and observed its licking up, in its progress, all the dust that was under its smaller part. As it is a common opinion that a shot, fired through a water-spout, will break it, I tried to break this little whirlwind by striking my whip frequently through it, but without any effect. Soon after, it quitted the road and took into the woods, growing every moment larger and stronger, raising, instead of dust, the old dry leaves with which the ground was thick covered, and making a great noise with them and the branches of the trees, bending some tall trees round in a circle swiftly and very surprisingly, though the progressive motion of the whirl was not so swift but that a man on foot might have kept pace with it; but the circular motion was amazingly rapid. By the leaves it was now filled with, I could plainly perceive that the current of air they were driven by moved upwards in a spiral line; and when I saw the trunks and bodies of large trees enveloped in the passing whirl, which continued entire after it had

left them, I no longer wondered that my whip had no effect on it in its smaller state. I accompanied it about three quarters of a mile, till some limbs of dead trees, broken off by the whirl, flying about and falling near me, made me more apprehensive of danger; and then I stopped, looking at the top of it as it went on, which was visible, by means of the leaves contained in it, for a very great height above the trees.—Smyth 3:274. (1755.)

TORNADOES, Or Whirlwinds.—Whirlwinds and spouts are not always, though most commonly, in the daytime. The terrible whirlwind which damaged a great part of Rome, June 11, 1749, happened in the night of that day. The same was supposed to have been first a spout [hurricane], for it is said to be beyond doubt that it gathered in the neighboring sea, as it could be tracked from Ostia to Rome.—Smyth 3:111. (1753.)

TRADE. See FREE TRADE.

TREASON, American Prisoners Not to Be Tried for Treason Against England.—The last act of Parliament for exchanging American prisoners as *prisoners of war* according to the laws of nations, *anything in their commitments notwithstanding,* seems to me a renunciation of the British pretensions to try our people as subjects guilty of high treason, and to be a kind of tacit acknowledgment of our independence.—Smyth 8:431. (1782.)

TREATIES, Must Be Mutually Beneficial.—I believe, with you, that if our plenipotentiary is desirous of concluding a treaty of commerce, he may need patience. If I were in his place, and not otherwise instructed, I should be apt to say, "Take your own time, gentlemen. If the treaty cannot be made as much to your advantage as to ours, don't make it. I am sure the want of it is not more to our disadvantage than to yours. Let the merchants on both sides treat with one another. *Laissez-les faire.*"— Smyth 9:588. (1787.)

TURKEY, Better American Symbol Than a Bald Eagle.—I am ... not displeased that the figure [on the new United States seal] is not known [recognized] as a bald eagle, but looks more like a turkey. For in truth, the turkey is in comparison a much more respectable bird, and withal a true original native of America. Eagles have been found in all countries, but the turkey was peculiar to ours; the first of the species seen in Europe being brought to France by the Jesuits from Canada, and served up at the wedding table of Charles the Ninth. He is (though a little vain and silly, it is true, but not the worse emblem for that) a bird of courage, and would not hesitate to attack a grenadier of the British guards who should presume to invade his farmyard with a *red* coat on.— Smyth 9:167. (1784.)

TURKEY. See also EAGLE.

U

UNITED STATES. See AMERICA; COLONIES.

UNITY, Indispensable.—At present we are like the separate filaments of flax before the thread is formed, without strength, because without connection; but *Union* would make us strong, and even formidable.— Smyth 2:351. (1747.)

UNIVERSITY OF PENNSYLVANIA, Initiated by Franklin.—I turned my thoughts again [in 1749] to the affair of establishing an academy. The first step I took was to associate in the design a number of active friends, of whom the Junto furnished a good part; the next was to write and publish a pamphlet, entitled *Proposals Relating to the Education of Youth in Pennsylvania.* This I distributed among the principal inhabitants gratis; and as soon as I could suppose their minds a little prepared by the perusal of it, I set on foot a subscription for opening and supporting an academy. It was to be paid in quotas yearly for five years; by so dividing it, I judged the subscription might be larger, and I believe it was so, amounting to no less, if I remember right, than five thousand pounds.—Autobiography. Smyth 1:371. (1788.)

V

VERSAILLES, Mixture of Grandeur and Neglect.—Versailles has had infinite sums laid out in building it and supplying it with water. Some say the expenses exceeded 80 millions sterling. The range of building is immense; the garden front most magnificent, all of hewn stone; the number of statues, figures, urns, etc., in marble and bronze of exquisite workmanship, is beyond conception. But the waterworks are out of repair, and so is a great part of the front next [to] the town, looking, with its shabby half-brick walls and broken windows, not much better than the houses in Durham Yard. There is, in short, both at Versailles and Paris, a prodigious mixture of magnificence and negligence, with every kind of elegance except that of cleanliness, or what we call tidiness.—Smyth 5:52. (1767.)

VICES, Why Fewer in America.—The almost general mediocrity of fortune that prevails in America obliging its people to follow some business for subsistence, those vices that arise usually from idleness are in a great measure prevented. Industry and constant employment are great preservatives of the morals and virtue of a nation.—Smyth 8:613. (1782.)

VIRTUE, Required for Happiness.—Without virtue, man can have no happiness in this world.—Smyth 2:94. (1728.)

VIRTUE, Should Be Taught in Public Schools.—It is said that the Persians, in their ancient constitution, had public schools in which virtue was taught as a liberal art or science; and it is certainly of more consequence to a man, that he has learned to govern his passions; in spite of temptation to be just in his dealings, to be temperate in his pleasures, to support himself with fortitude under his misfortunes, to behave with prudence in all affairs, and in every circumstance of life; I say, it is of much more real

advantage to him to be thus qualified, than to be a master of all the arts and sciences in the world beside.—Smyth 2:106. (1729.)

VIRTUE, Is Reflected in the Countenance.—I believe long habits of virtue have a sensible effect on the countenance. There was something in the air of his [Cato's] face that manifested the true greatness of his mind, which likewise appeared in all he said, and in every part of his behavior, obliging us to regard him with a kind of veneration. His aspect is sweetened with humanity and benevolence, and at the same time emboldened with resolution, equally free from a diffident bashfulness and an unbecoming assurance. The consciousness of his own innate worth and unshaken integrity renders him calm and undaunted in the presence of the most great and powerful, and upon the most extraordinary occasions. His strict justice and known impartiality make him the arbitrator and decider of all differences that arise for many miles around him, without putting his neighbors to the charge, perplexity, and uncertainty of lawsuits.—Smyth 2:107. (1729.)

VIRTUE, Important Field of Study.—The general natural tendency of reading good history must be to fix in the minds of youth deep impressions of the beauty and usefulness of virtue of all kinds, public spirit, fortitude, etc.—Smyth 2:392. (1749.)

VIRTUE, Required for Preservation of Freedom.—Let me add that only a virtuous people are capable of freedom. As nations become corrupt and vicious, they have more need of masters.—Smyth 9:569. (1787.)

VIRTUE. See also POPULARITY.

VIRTUES, Franklin's Goals of Moral Perfection at Age 27.—I included under thirteen names of virtues all that at that time occurred to me as necessary or desirable, and annexed to each a short precept which fully expressed the extent I gave to its meaning. These names of virtues, with their precepts, were:

1. *Temperance.* Eat not to dullness; drink not to elevation.

2. *Silence.* Speak not but what may benefit others or yourself; avoid trifling conversation.

3. *Order.* Let all your things have their places; let each part of your business have its time.

4. *Resolution.* Resolve to perform what you ought; perform without fail what you resolve.

5. *Frugality.* Make no expense but to do good to others or yourself; i.e., waste nothing.

6. *Industry.* Lose no time; be always employed in something useful; cut off all unnecessary actions.

7. *Sincerity.* Use no hurtful deceit; think innocently and justly, and, if you speak, speak accordingly.

8. *Justice.* Wrong none by doing injuries, or omitting the benefits that are your duty.

9. *Moderation.* Avoid extremes; forbear resenting injuries so much as you think they deserve.

10. *Cleanliness.* Tolerate no uncleanliness in body, clothes, or habitation.

11. *Tranquility.* Be not disturbed at trifles, or at accidents common or unavoidable.

12. *Chastity.* Rarely use venery but for health or offspring, never to dullness, weakness, or the injury of your own or another's peace or reputation.

13. *Humility.* Imitate Jesus and Socrates.—Autobiography. Smyth 1:327. (1784.)

W

WAGES, Increased Wages Not for More Drink and Less Work.—These are so many laws for the support of our laboring poor, made by the rich and continued at their expense; all the difference of price, between our own and foreign commodities, being so much given by our rich to our poor; who would indeed be enabled by it to get by degrees above poverty if they did not, as too generally they do, consider every increase of wages only as something that enables them to drink more and work less; so that their distress in sickness, age, or times of scarcity continues to be the same as if such laws had never been made in their favor.—Smyth 5:124. (1768.)

WAGES, Must Not Price Goods Out of the Market.—A law might be made to raise...wages; but if our manufactures are too dear, they will not vend abroad, and all that part of employment will fail, unless by fighting and conquering we compel other nations to buy our goods, whether they will or no, which some have been mad enough at times to propose.—Smyth 5:126. (1768.)

WAGES, Increase Must Depend on Productivity.—I have said a law might be made to raise . . . wages; but I doubt much whether it could be executed to any purpose, unless another law, now indeed almost obsolete, could at the same time be revived and enforced; a law, I mean, that many have often heard and repeated, but few have ever duly considered. *Six days shalt thou labor.* This is as positive a part of the commandment as that which says, *The Seventh day thou shalt rest.* But we remember well to observe the indulgent part, and never think of the other. *Saint Monday* is generally as duly kept by our working people as *Sunday;* the only difference is that, instead of employing their time cheaply at church, they are wasting it expensively at the alehouse.—Smyth 5:127. (1768.)

WAR, To Be Avoided If Possible.—I would try anything, and bear anything that can be borne with safety to our just liberties, rather than engage in a war with such near relations [as the British], unless compelled to it by dire necessity in our own defense.—Smyth 6:312. (1775.)

WAR, Caused by Wicked Men.—I believe in my conscience that mankind are wicked enough to continue slaughtering one another as long as they can find money to pay the butchers. But of all the wars in my time, this on the part of England appears to me the wickedest, having no cause but malice against liberty, and the jealousy of commerce. And I think the crime seems likely to meet with its proper punishment; a total loss of her own liberty, and the destruction of her own commerce.—Smyth 7:18. (1777.)

WAR, Alleviate Calamity Where Possible.—Since the foolish part of mankind will make wars from time to time with each other, not having sense enough otherwise to settle their differences, it certainly becomes the wiser part, who cannot prevent those wars, to alleviate as much as possible the calamities attending them.—Smyth 8:319. (1781.)

WAR, Futility of Most.—At length we are in peace, God be praised, and long, very long, may it continue. All wars are follies, very expensive and very mischievous ones. When will mankind be convinced of this, and agree to settle their differences by arbitration? Were they to do it, even by the cast of a die, it would be better than by fighting and destroying each other.—Smyth 9:12. (1783.)

WAR, A Terrible Waste.—In my opinion, *there never was a good war, or a bad peace.* What vast additions to the conveniences and comforts of living might mankind have acquired if the money spent in wars had been employed in works of public utility! What an extension of agriculture, even to the tops of our mountains; what rivers rendered navigable, or joined by canals; what bridges, aqueducts, new roads, and other public works, edifices, and improvements, rendering England a complete paradise, might have been obtained by spending those millions in doing good which in the last war have been spent in doing mischief; in bringing misery into thousands of families, and destroying the lives of so many thousands of working people, who might have performed the useful labor!—Smyth 9:74. (1783.)

WAR, Evils of.—Abstracted from the inhumanity of it, I think it wrong in point of human prudence; for whatever advantage one nation would obtain from another, whether it be part of their territory, the liberty of commerce with them, free passage on their rivers, etc., etc., it would be much cheaper to purchase such advantage with ready money than to pay the expense of acquiring it by war. An army is a devouring monster, and when you have raised it you have, in order to subsist it, not only the fair charges of pay, clothing, provisions, arms, and ammunition, with numberless other contingent and just charges to answer and satisfy, but you have all the additional knavish charges of the numerous tribe of contractors to defray, with those of every other dealer who furnishes the articles wanted for your army, and takes advantage of that want to demand exorbitant prices. It seems to me that if statesmen had a little more arithmetic, or were more accustomed to calculation, wars would be much less frequent.—Smyth 9:612. (1787.)

WASHINGTON (George), Acclaimed in Europe.—You [Washington] would, on this side of the sea, enjoy the great reputation you have acquired, pure and free from those little shades that the jealousy and envy of a man's countrymen and contemporaries are ever endeavoring to cast over living merit. Here [in France] you would know, and enjoy, what posterity will say of Washington. For 1000 leagues have nearly the same effect with 1000 years. The feeble voice of those grovelling passions cannot extend so far either in time or distance. At present I enjoy that pleasure for you, as I frequently hear the old generals of this martial country (who study the maps of America, and mark upon them all your operations) speak with sincere approbation and great applause of your conduct, and join in giving you the character of one of the greatest captains of the age.—Smyth 8:28. (1780.)

WASHINGTON (George), Franklin Praises His Achievements to the English.—An American planter who had never seen Europe was chosen by us to command our troops, and continued during the whole war. This man sent home to you, one after another, five of your best generals baffled, their heads bare of laurels, disgraced even in the opinion of their employers.—Smyth 9:261. (1784.)

WASHINGTON (George), Franklin and Jefferson Arrange for Houdon to Make Statue.—I am just arrived from a country [France] where the reputation of General Washington runs very high, and where everybody wishes to see him in person; but, being told that it is not likely he will ever favor them with a visit, they hope at least for a sight of his perfect resemblance by means of their principal statuary, M. Houdon, whom Mr. Jefferson and myself agreed with to come over for the purpose of taking a bust in order to make the intended statue for the State of Virginia. He is here, but the materials and instruments he sent down the Seine from Paris not being arrived at Havre when we sailed, he was obliged to leave them, and is now busied in supplying himself here. As soon as that is done, he proposes to wait on you [Washington] in Virginia, as he understands there is no prospect of your coming hither [Philadelphia], which would indeed make me very happy, as it would give me an opportunity of congratulating with you personally on the final success of your long and painful labors in the service of our country, which have laid us all under eternal obligations.—Smyth 9:464. (1785.)

WASHINGTON (George), Franklin Supported Him for President.— General Washington is the man that all our eyes are fixed on for *President,* and what little influence I may have is devoted to him.—Smyth 9:658. (1788.)

WASHINGTON (George), Franklin's Last Letter to Him.—My malady renders my sitting up to write rather painful to me; but I cannot let my son-in-law Mr. Bache part for New York without congratulating you by him on the recovery of your health, so precious to us all, and on the growing strength of our new government under your administration. For my own personal ease, I should have died two years ago; but, though those years have been spent in excruciating pain, I am pleased that I have lived them, since they have

brought me to see our present situation. I am now finishing my 84th [year], and probably with it my career in this life; but in whatever state of existence I am placed hereafter, if I retain any memory of what has passed here, I shall with it retain the esteem, respect, and affection with which I have long been, my dear friend, yours most sincerely, B. Franklin.—Smyth 10:41. (1789.)

WATERSPOUTS, Vacuum in the Center.—I agree with you [John Perkins], that by means of a vacuum in a whirlwind, water cannot be supposed to rise in large masses to the region of the clouds; for the pressure of the surrounding atmosphere could not force it up in a continued body or column to a much greater height than thirty feet. But if there really is a vacuum in the center, or near the axis of whirlwinds, then I think water may rise in such a vacuum to that height, or to less height, as the vacuum may be less perfect.—Smyth 3:108. (1753.)

WEALTH, Honest Acquisition of, Through Agriculture.—Finally, there seem to be but three ways for a nation to acquire wealth. The first is by *war,* as the Romans did, in plundering their conquered neighbors. This is *robbery.* The second by *commerce,* which is generally *cheating.* The third by *agriculture,* the only *honest way,* wherein man receives a real increase of the seed thrown into the ground, in a kind of continual miracle, wrought by the hand of God in his favor, as a reward for his innocent life and his virtuous industry.—Smyth 5:202. (1769.)

WELFARE. See POOR.

WEST INDIES, Cheaper for Europe If They Were Liberated.—I sincerely believe that if France and England were to decide, by throwing dice, which should have the whole of their sugar islands, the loser in the throw would be the gainer. The future expense of defending them would be saved; the sugars would be bought cheaper by all Europe, if the inhabitants might make it without interruption, and, whoever imported the sugar, the same revenue might be raised by duties at the customhouses of the nation that consumed it. And, on the whole, I conceive it would be better for the nations now possessing sugar colonies to give up their claim to them, let them govern themselves, and put them under the protection of all the powers of Europe as neutral countries, open to the commerce of all, the profits of the present monopolies being by no means equivalent to the expense of maintaining them.—Smyth 9:6. (1783.)

WHEELS, New Type of Wooden.—I know of nothing new here [England] worth communicating to you [William Deane], unless perhaps the new art of making carriage wheels, the fellies of one piece bent into a circle and surrounded by a hoop of iron, the whole very light and strong, there being no crossed grain in the wood, which is also a great saving of timber. The wood is first steamed in the vapor from boiling water, and then bent by a forcible machine. I have seen pieces so bent of six inches wide, and three-and-a-half thick, into a circle of four feet diameter. These, for duration, can only be exceeded by your iron wheels.—Smyth 6:40. (1773.)

WHIGS, Commit "Unpardonable Sin."—Other provinces have done as offensive things, but *Whiggism* is thought to be more thoroughly the principle in New England, and that is now an *unpardonable* sin. The rest, however, are to have their punishment in their turn, though perhaps less severe. That is, if this Tory ministry continues in power; but, though they have by the late deceptive motion amused many people here, so as to give an appearance as if they intended pacific measures, on which the stocks, which were falling apace, have risen again; yet, when this deceit is understood, and time proves the intended offer to America futile and ineffectual, the redoubled clamor of the trading, manufacturing, and Whig interests here [in England] will infallibly overthrow all the enemies of America, and produce an acknowledgment of her rights and satisfaction for her injuries.—Smyth 6:309. (1775.)

WHIGS, What English Commonwealth Should Provide If Whig Principles Were Adopted.—Declaration of those rights of the Commonalty [Commonwealth] of Great Britain, *without which they cannot be free.*

It is declared,

First, That the government of this realm, and the making of laws for the same, ought to be lodged in the hands of King, Lords of Parliament, and representatives of *the whole body* of the freemen of this realm.

Secondly, That *every man* of the commonalty (excepting infants, insane persons, and criminals) is, of common right, and by the laws of God, *a freeman*, and entitled to the free enjoyment of *liberty*.

Thirdly, That liberty, or freedom, consists in having *an actual share* in the appointment of those who frame the laws, and who are to be the guardians of every man's life, property, and peace; for the *all* of one man is as dear to him as the *all* of another; and the poor man has an *equal* right, but *more* need, to have representatives in the legislature than the rich one.

Fourthly, That they who have *no* voice nor vote in the electing of representatives *do not enjoy* liberty, but are absolutely *enslaved* to those who *have* votes, and to their representatives; for to be enslaved is to have governors whom *other men have set over us*, and be subject to laws *made by the representatives of others*, without having had representatives of our own to give consent in *our* behalf.

Fifthly, That *a very great majority* of the commonalty of this realm are denied the privilege of voting for representatives in Parliament; and, consequently, they are enslaved to a *small number*, who do now enjoy the privilege exclusively to themselves; but who, it may be presumed, are far from wishing to continue in the exclusive possession of a privilege by which their fellow-subjects are

deprived of *common right, of justice, of liberty;* and which, if not communicated to all, must speedily cause *the certain overthrow of our happy constitution,* and enslave us *all*.

And, sixthly and lastly, We also say and do assert, that it is *the right* of the commonalty of this realm to elect a *new* House of Commons once in *every year*, according to the ancient and sacred laws of the land; because whenever a Parliament continues in being for a longer term, very great numbers of the commonalty, who have arrived at years of manhood since the last election, and *therefore* have a right to be actually represented in the House of Commons, are then *unjustly deprived* of that right.—Smyth 10:130.

WHITEFIELD (The Reverend George), Arrives in America.—In 1739 arrived among us from Ireland the Reverend Mr. Whitefield, who had made himself remarkable there as an itinerant preacher. He was at first permitted to preach in some of our churches; but the clergy, taking a dislike to him, soon refused him their pulpits, and he was obliged to preach in the fields. The multitudes of all sects and denominations that attended his sermons were enormous, and it was a matter of speculation to me, who was one of the number, to observe the extraordinary influence of his oratory on his hearers, and how much they admired and respected him, notwithstanding his common abuse of them, by assuring them they were naturally *half beasts and half devils*. It was wonderful to see the change soon made in the manners of our inhabitants. From being thoughtless or indifferent about religion, it seemed as if all the world were growing religious, so that one could not walk through the town in an evening without hearing psalms sung in different families of every street.—Autobiography. Smyth 1:354. (1788.)

WOMEN, As Peacemakers.—You [Mrs. Deborah Franklin] are very prudent not to engage in party disputes. Women never should meddle with them except in endeavors to reconcile their husbands, brothers, and friends who happen to be of contrary sides. If your sex can keep cool, you may be a means of cooling ours the sooner, and restoring more speedily that social harmony among fellow citizens that is so desirable after long and bitter dissensions.—Smyth 3:439. (1758.)

WOMEN, Power of Intuition.—As long as I was fortunate enough to have a wife, I had adopted the habit of letting myself be guided by her opinion on difficult matters, for women, I believe, have a certain feel, which is more reliable than our reasonings.—Claude-Anne Lopez and Eugenia W. Herbert, *The Private Franklin* (New York: W.W. Norton & Company, Inc., 1975), p. 36. (1780.)

WOMEN, Practical Education for.—I mention this affair chiefly for the sake of recommending that branch of education [business and accounting] for our young females, as likely to be of more use to them and their children, in case of widowhood, than either music or dancing, by preserving them from

losses by imposition of crafty men, and enabling them to continue, perhaps, a' profitable mercantile house, with established correspondence, till a son is grown up fit to undertake and go on with it, to the lasting advantage and enriching of the family.—Autobiography. Smyth 1:345. (1788.)

WOOD, Becoming Less Available for Fuel.—Wood, our common fuel, which within these 100 years might be had at every man's door, must now be fetched near 100 miles to some towns, and makes a very considerable article in the expense of families.—Smyth 2:247. (1744.)

WORKS, Better than Words.—You may remember an ancient poet, whose works we have all studied and copied at school long ago.

"A man of words and not of deeds
Is like a garden full of weeds."

'Tis a pity that good works, among some sorts of people, are so little valued, and good words admired in their stead.—Smyth 3:460. (1758.)

Y

YELLOW FEVER.—Besides the measles and flux, which have carried off many children, we have lost some grown persons by what we call the *yellow fever;* though that is almost, if not quite, over, thanks to God, who has preserved all our family in perfect health.—Smyth 2:379. (1749.)

YORKTOWN, Reaction of Franklin from France.—Most heartily do I congratulate you [John Adams] on the glorious news! The infant Hercules in his cradle has now strangled his second serpent, and gives hopes that his future history will be answerable.

I enclose a packet which I have just received from General Washington, and which I suppose contains the articles of capitulation. It is a rare circumstance, and scarce to be met with in history, that in one war two armies should be taken prisoners completely, not a man in either escaping. It is another singular circumstance that an expedition so complex, formed of armies of different nations, and of land and sea forces, should with such perfect concord be assembled from different places by land and water, form their junction punctually, without the least regard by cross accidents of wind or weather, or interruption from the enemy; and that the army

which was their object should in the meantime have the goodness to quit a situation from whence it might have escaped, and place itself in another from whence an escape was impossible.—Smyth 8:333. (1781.)

YORKTOWN, Washington Commended for Victory at.—I received duly the honor of your letter, accompanying the capitulation of General Cornwallis. All the world agrees that no expedition was ever better planned or better executed; it has made a great addition to the military reputation you had already acquired, and brightens the glory that surrounds your name, and that must accompany it to our latest posterity. No news could possibly make me more happy.—Smyth 8:411. (1782.)